Brief Contents

Real
Skills

with Readings

Fourth Edition

Real
Skills

with Readings

**Sentences and Paragraphs for
College, Work, and Everyday Life**

Susan Anker

with **Miriam Moore**

Bedford/St.Martin's
A Macmillan Education Imprint
Boston   •   New York

For Bedford/St. Martin's

Vice President, Editorial, Macmillan Higher Education Humanities: Edwin Hill
Editorial Director, English and Music: Karen S. Henry
Senior Publisher for Composition, Business and Technical Writing, Developmental Writing: Leasa Burton
Executive Editor: Vivian Garcia
Senior Developmental Editor: Caroline Thompson
Media Producer: Sarah O'Connor
Production Editor: Louis C. Bruno, Jr.
Publishing Services Manager: Andrea Cava
Senior Production Supervisor: Jennifer Wetzel
Editorial Assistant: Cara Kaufman
Project Management: Graphic World, Inc.
Director of Rights and Permissions: Hilary Newman
Senior Art Director: Anna Palchik
Text Design: Claire Seng-Niemoeller
Cover Design: John Callahan
Cover Art: Kali Nine LLC/Getty Images
Composition: Graphic World, Inc.
Printing and Binding: C.O.S. Printers Pte Ltd - Singapore

Printed in Singapore.
0   9   8   7   6
f   e   d   c   b

For information, write: Bedford/St. Martin's, 75 Arlington Street, Boston, MA 02116 (617-399-4000)

ISBN 978-1-4576-9818-7 (Student Edition)
ISBN 978-1-319-04227-1 (Loose-leaf Edition)

Acknowledgments

Text acknowledgments and copyrights appear at the back of the book on page 534, which constitutes an extension of the copyright page. Art acknowledgments and copyrights appear on the same page as the art selections they cover. It is a violation of the law to reproduce these selections by any means whatsoever without the written permission of the copyright holder.

A note to students from Susan Anker

Courtesy James D. Anker.

For the past twenty years or so, I have traveled the country talking to students about their goals and, more important, about the challenges they face on the way to achieving those goals. Students always tell me that they want good jobs and that they need a college degree to get those jobs. I designed *Real Skills* with those goals in mind—strengthening the writing, reading, and editing skills needed for success in college, at work, and in everyday life.

Here is something else: Good jobs require not only a college degree but also a college education: knowing not only how to read and write but how to think critically and learn effectively. So that is what I stress here, too. It is worth facing the challenges. All my best wishes to you in this course and in all your future endeavors.

A note to students from Miriam Moore

Since 1991, I have taught writing, grammar, reading, and ESL in a variety of places, including a university, an Intensive English program, two community colleges, and even a chicken processing plant! In each place, I have tried to share my love of words with students, and I have learned by listening to their words, their rhythms of speech, their questions, and their frustrations.

Words, and the ways we put them together, help us accomplish ordinary tasks and (as our skills improve) some incredible feats: getting a date, making a sale, convincing the boss to try a new idea, changing a law, or solving a long-standing problem. The words we use to read and write can also help us to think more creatively, more deeply, and more effectively. In *Real Skills*, I wanted to help you see the value of language skills like reading and writing, and the power of practicing them together. Sure, it takes time and attention to learn new words, understand them when you read, and master rules for combining and punctuating them accurately. But in the end, after working for these skills, you will begin to see them working for you. It will be worth the effort.

I applaud your decision to take this course, and I wish you every success.

Contents

Thematic Table of Contents

Preface

Real Skills has always had a twofold goal: to show students that writing is essential to success in the real world and to help them develop the skills they need to achieve that success. When students believe that good writing skills are both *essential* and *attainable*, they can start fresh, reframing the writing course for themselves not as an irrelevant hoop to jump through, but as a central gateway—a potentially life-changing opportunity, worthy of their best efforts. In large and small ways, this book is designed to help students prepare for their futures. It connects the writing class to their other courses, to their real lives, and to the expectations of the larger world.

Real Skills underscores this powerful message in its initial chapter, "Reading and Critical Thinking"; in its practical advice on writing different kinds of paragraphs; and in its diverse collection of readings written by students and professionals. In addition, step-by-step grammar sections build confidence and proficiency by focusing first on the four most serious errors students commonly make. *Real Skills* presents all material in manageable increments, with many opportunities for writing, interaction, practice, and assessment.

Real Skills shares this practical, real-world approach with its companion texts—*Real Writing*, *Real Essays*, and *Real Reading and Writing*, an integrated reading and writing text. All four books put writing in a real-world context and link writing skills to students' own goals in and beyond college.

Core Features

Successful and popular features of earlier editions of *Real Skills* have been carried over to this edition, with revisions based on suggestions from many insightful instructors and students.

USE A VISUAL TO WRITE A DESCRIPTION
Look at the photo below. Write a paragraph describing this food stand.

A food stand at the Florida State Fair.

- **A Comprehensive Teaching and Learning Package:** *Real Skills* combines carefully curated readings, writing samples, writing assignments, grammar instruction, critical thinking and reading coverage, and online practice in one convenient volume, allowing instructors to focus on their students.

- **Abundant Writing Practice:** Not only does *Real Skills* feature a number of student model paragraphs and short essays, workplace writing, and professional readings, it asks students to write their own sentences and paragraphs in multiple assignments throughout the book. These assignments aid students in translating their writing skills to the real world, asking them to practice concepts through the lens of tasks such as identifying successful study strategies, choosing roommates, and dressing for a

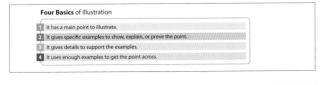

Four Basics of Illustration

1 It has a main point to illustrate.
2 It gives specific examples to show, explain, or prove the point.
3 It gives details to support the examples.
4 It uses enough examples to get the point across.

1 Although people starting out in the nursing field may feel that they do not have any relevant work experience, they may actually have gained valuable and transferrable skills in other jobs, which they may possibly have held earlier. 2 For example, working in a restaurant does not sound as though it would be a job that would particularly help a person prepare for a career in nursing, but, in fact, it can. 3 Like nursing, restaurant work requires good listening skills, a sharp memory, and constant attention to detail. It builds experience in dealing with demanding customers who might not always be at their best. And working in a restaurant can also help a person develop the important skills of prioritizing and multitasking. 2 Caring for young children is another job that can provide some relevant background experience to a person who is entering the nursing profession. 3 Child-care workers as well as parents develop important communication skills, patience, and compassion that can be helpful if they enter a career in nursing. The steady and capable caregiving skills gained from work with children can help prepare nursing students for caring for others, of any age. 2 A third type of background, customer service, can also establish a groundwork of relevant experience for beginning nursing students. 3 A demanding job as a retail salesclerk, receptionist, cashier, or landscape worker requires the ability to do hard jobs, keep focused, and interact with many different kinds of people. 1 All of these skills—multitasking, caregiving, listening and communicating well, relating to people—are essential to being a good nurse, and they can all be learned in a variety of jobs.

4 Enough examples to make the writer's point

career. Each rhetorical mode section (see Chapters 6–8) also features a step-by-step writing guide, a guided outline, suggested topics, a visual writing prompt, and a checklist that students can refer to when completing their writing assignments.

- **The Four Basics and the Four Most Serious Errors:** *Real Skills* breaks the writing process down into logical steps, focusing on the four basics of each rhetorical mode as well as the four most serious errors in grammar. This approach lets students digest information at their own pace, helping them really understand each concept before starting a new one.

- **Basic Grammar Coverage Up Front:** Part 2, Grammar Basics, provides students with a concise guide to the fundamentals of grammar in three chapters. Using clear explanations and brief practice exercises, these chapters help students recognize and understand the parts of speech as well as basic sentence elements and sentence types. This foundation boosts students' confidence for later chapters on finding and fixing errors.

- **2PR Critical Reading Process:** Introduced in Chapter 1, this process helps students tackle readings using critical thinking skills, asking them to preview, read, pause, review, and respond to each reading. Students can use this process not only with the readings in this course but also in all of their college courses.

READING ROADMAP

Learning Objectives

Chapter Goal: Identify characteristics that make writing successful.

Tools to Achieve the Goal

- Four Basics of Good Writing (p. 17)
- Four Basics of a Good Paragraph (p. 19)
- Steps in the Writing Process (p. 20)

Key Terms

Skim Chapter 2 before you begin reading. Can you find each of these words in **bold** type? Put a check mark next to each word once you have located it in the chapter.

___ purpose	___ paragraph
___ audience	___ topic sentence
___ informal English	___ body sentences
___ formal English	___ concluding
___ main point	sentence
___ support	___ writing process

Highlight or circle any of these words that you already know.

Before You Read

Before you begin reading this chapter, fill out the following chart. For each skill, think of a time when you have used this skill and what you would like to know on completing the chapter. At the end of the chapter, you will be asked to share what you learned about this skill.

Skill	When I have used this skill	What I want to know about this skill
Identify a specific audience and purpose for writing		
Provide support for a main idea		
Use a process to write a paragraph or essay		

New to This Edition

This edition of *Real Skills* includes carefully developed new features to help students become better readers and writers.

- **Guided Reading Support:** Starting with Chapter 2, every chapter in the book now begins with a Reading Roadmap consisting of Learning Objectives, Key Terms, and a Before You Read activity that helps students zero in on the skills they should be learning in each chapter. At the end of these chapters, Reflecting on the Journey allows students to track their own progress on those skills. Together, these new features help students become stronger readers by pointing them precisely where they need to focus.

> ### REFLECTING ON THE JOURNEY
>
> **Skills Learned**
>
> Now that you've completed the chapter, share what you've learned about each skill by completing the following chart.
>
> | Skill | What I learned about this skill |
> | --- | --- |
> | Identify a specific audience and purpose for writing | |
> | Provide support for a main idea | |
> | Use a process to write a paragraph or an essay | |

- **A Wealth of New Readings, Integrated with Writing Instruction:** Thirty-six readings—including twenty-five new to this edition—are now integrated with the modes-based instruction on developing paragraphs, helping students make immediate connections between what they learn and what they read. Readings for each mode focus on a relatable theme such as life-changing moments, family ties, or skills for success.

- **More Examples of Student Writing:** Fully half of the readings in this edition are by student writers, showing students that they, too, can succeed at writing. Each mode of paragraph development is now illustrated with paragraph-length and essay-length readings by students as well as an equal number of examples by professional writers.

- **A New Design and a Streamlined Text:** The visually appealing, redesigned interior allows students to focus on the most important elements of the text. Careful edits guided by instructor feedback have sharpened the instructional content, removing less frequently used features and making important concepts easier for students to absorb—and simpler for instructors to teach.

Acknowledgments

This edition of *Real Skills* is the product of many people's voices, suggestions, and hard work. The brevity of my thanks belies the gratitude I feel.

I would like to thank the following instructors who reviewed the third edition and provided invaluable ideas and suggestions for revision: Geoffrey Bellah, Orange Coast College; Judy Covington, Trident Technical College; Anthony Gargano, Long Beach City College; Vivian Hoskins, Phillips Community College; Ryan Kerr, Elgin Community College; Tonya Kram, Horry Georgetown Technical College; Stephanie Landon, College of the Desert; Jennifer McCann, Bay College; Brent Mix, City Colleges of Chicago; Steve Moore, Arizona Western College; Clarence Nero, Baton Rouge Community College; Jessica Rabin, Anne Arundel Community College; Harvey Rubinstein, Hudson Community College; Mary Snow, Horry Georgetown Technical College; and Tad Wakefield, Santa Rosa Junior College. I also want to acknowledge the invaluable help provided by reviewers of previous editions. The book, and the series, would not be what they are without their help and advice.

I am grateful to those students whose writing appears in this edition: Mary Adams, Alieh Alfakeeh, Rashad Brown, Andrew Dillon Bustin, Delia Cleveland,

Tony Felts, Kristy Fouch, Sheena Ivey, Christina Mevs, Sabina Pajazetovic, Faye Phelps, Kendal Rippel, Spencer Rock, James Sellars, Jonathan Simon-Valdez, Sydney Tasey, Yolanda Castaneda Vasquez, and Lauren Woodrell.

I have been extremely fortunate to work with the incredibly talented staff of Bedford/St. Martin's, whose perceptiveness, hard work, and dedication to everything they do are without parallel. Thanks to Edwin Hill, Vice President of Humanities for Macmillan Education; Leasa Burton, Senior Publisher for Composition; and Vivian Garcia, Executive Editor for Developmental English. Editorial assistant Cara Kaufman helped with manuscript and art preparation, Julie Tesser with photo research, and Kathleen Karcher with text permissions. We were very fortunate to have production editor Louis Bruno shepherding *Real Skills* through production. Overseeing and thoughtfully contributing to all aspects of the design was Anna Palchik, senior art director. Thanks to John Callahan for his work on the cover design. I must also extend tremendous gratitude to the sales and marketing team. Christina Shea, senior marketing manager, has been a great advocate for all my books and has helped me to forge greater connections with the developmental market and to stay up to date on its needs. And I continue to be deeply thankful for the hard work and smarts of all the sales managers and representatives. This book would not have reached its fullest potential without the input and attention it received, from the earliest stages of development, from executives and long-time friends in the Boston office. Thanks also to Karrin Varucene for her contributions to the plan for this edition and to senior editor Caroline Thompson for seeing it through to publication.

As he has in the past, to my great good fortune, my husband, Jim Anker, provides assurance, confidence, steadiness, and the best companionship throughout the projects and the years. His surname is supremely fitting.

— *Susan Anker*

I would like to echo Susan's gratitude to everyone at Bedford/St. Martin's who worked on this edition. Karrin Varucene and Caroline Thompson walked me through the revision process, providing clear direction while still allowing me to experiment with different approaches to new content.

I would also like to thank the many students with whom I have worked over the past twenty years; their insights and their tenacity have challenged me and inspired me. Thanks also to the incredibly dedicated developmental English instructors at Lord Fairfax Community College and across the Virginia Community College System. They make textbooks come to life in the classroom.

Finally, I would like to thank my husband, Michael, and my children, Mandy, Mallory, and Murray. Their constant love—and laughter—encourage me daily.

— *Miriam Moore*

Get the Most out of Your Course with Real Skills, *Fourth Edition*

Bedford/St. Martin's offers resources and format choices that help you and your students get even more out of your book and your course. To learn more about or to order any of the following products, contact your Bedford/St. Martin's sales representative, email sales support (**sales_support@bfwpub.com**), or visit the Web site at **macmillanhighered.com/realskills/catalog**.

CHOOSE FROM ALTERNATIVE FORMATS OF *REAL SKILLS*

Bedford/St. Martin's offers a range of affordable formats, allowing students to choose the one that works best for them. For details, visit **macmillanhighered.com /realskills/catalog**.

- *Paperback* To order the paperback edition use ISBN 978-1-4576-9818-7.

- *Loose-leaf edition* The loose-leaf edition does not have a traditional binding; its pages are loose and hole-punched to provide flexibility and a low price to students. To order the loose-leaf edition, use ISBN 978-1-319-04227-1.

- *Popular e-book formats Real Skills* is available as a value-priced e-book in a variety of formats for use with computers, tablets, and e-readers. For details, visit **macmillanhighered.com/ebookpartners.**

SELECT VALUE PACKAGES

Add value to your text by packaging one of the following resources with *Real Skills*. To learn more about package options for any of the following products, contact your Bedford/St. Martin's sales representative or visit **macmillanhighered.com /realskills/catalog**.

- **LaunchPad Solo for Readers and Writers** includes multimedia content and assessments, including diagnostics on grammar and reading and LearningCurve adaptive quizzing, organized into pre-built, curated units for easy assigning and monitoring of student progress. For critical reading practice, twenty-five reading selections with quizzes are also provided. Get all our great resources and activities in one fully customizable space online; then assign and mix our resources with yours. To order *LaunchPad Solo for Readers and Writers* packaged with the print book, contact your sales representative for a package ISBN. For details, visit **macmillanhighered.com/launchpadsolo/readwrite.**

- **LearningCurve for Readers and Writers,** Bedford/St. Martin's adaptive quizzing program, quickly learns what students already know and helps them practice what they don't yet understand. Game-like quizzing motivates students to engage with their course, and reporting tools help teachers discern their students' needs. *LearningCurve for Readers and Writers* can be packaged with *Real Skills* at a significant discount. An activation code is required. To order LearningCurve packaged with the print book, contact your sales representative for a package ISBN. For details, visit **learningcurveworks.com**.

- **Writer's Help 2.0** is a powerful online handbook that includes the instruction that free online resources lack. Its tools, built around a smart search that recognizes nonexpert terminology, are as simple as they are innovative. To package *Writer's Help* with *Real Skills*, contact your sales representative for a package ISBN. Instructors may request free access by registering as an instructor at **macmillanhighered.com/writershelp2.**

- **The Bedford/St. Martin's ESL Workbook** includes a broad range of exercises covering grammar issues for multilingual students of varying language skills and backgrounds. Answers are at the back. To order the *ESL Workbook* packaged with the print book, contact your sales representative for a package ISBN.

- **Bedford/St. Martin's Planner** includes everything that students need to plan and use their time effectively, with advice on preparing schedules and to-do lists plus blank schedules and calendars (monthly and weekly). The *Planner* fits easily into a backpack or purse, so students can take it anywhere. To order the *Planner* packaged with the print book, contact your sales representative for a package ISBN.

MAKE LEARNING FUN WITH *RE:WRITING 3*

Bedford's free and open online resource includes videos and interactive elements to engage students in new ways of writing. You'll find tutorials about using common digital writing tools, an interactive peer review game, Extreme Paragraph Makeover, and more. Visit **bedfordstmartins.com/rewriting**.

INSTRUCTOR RESOURCES

You have a lot to do in your course. Bedford/St. Martin's wants to make it easy for you to find the support you need—and to get to it quickly. For information on the following resources, visit **macmillanhighered.com/realskills/catalog**.

- *Instructor's Annotated Edition of Real Skills*, **Fourth Edition,** gives answers to exercises and practical page-by-page advice on teaching with *Real Skills,* Fourth Edition. Teaching Tips in the margins include discussion prompts, strategies for teaching ESL students, ideas for additional classroom activities, and cross-references useful to teachers at all levels of experience. To order the *Instructor's Annotated Edition,* contact your Macmillan sales representative or use ISBN 978-1-4576-9833-0.

- *Instructor's Manual for Real Skills*, **Fourth Edition,** is available as a PDF that can be downloaded from the Bedford/St. Martin's online catalog at the URL above. It provides helpful information and advice on teaching developmental writing, including sample syllabi, tips on building students' critical-thinking skills, resources for teaching nonnative speakers, ideas for using journal writing and collaborative assignments, and suggestions for assessing students' writing and progress. The instructor's manual also includes a robust collection of handouts, activities, supplemental exercises, and assessments to supplement the text.

- **Lecture Slides for *Real Skills*** can be downloaded from the Bedford/St. Martin's online catalog at the URL above. The slide presentations complement the book's instruction with a review of main concepts and additional examples for many of the chapters, and they're easy to customize to suit your course.

- **TeachingCentral** offers the entire list of Bedford/St. Martin's print and online professional resources in one place. You will find landmark reference works, sourcebooks on pedagogical issues, award-winning collections, and practical advice for the classroom—all free for instructors. Recent titles include *The Bedford Bibliography for Teachers of Basic Writing,* Fourth Edition, by Chitralekha Duttagupta and Robert Miller; *Teaching Developmental Reading: Historical, Theoretical, and Practical Background Readings,* Second Edition, by Sonya Armstrong, Norman A. Stahl, and Hunter Boylan; and *The Bedford Bibliography for Teachers of Adult Learners* by Barbara Gleason and Kimme Nuckles. Visit **macmillanhighered.com/teachingcentral**.

Real
Skills

with Readings

Part 1
Writing Paragraphs

Reading and Critical Thinking

Keys to Successful Writing

Recognize What You Already Know

The keys to succeeding in a college writing course will not come as a surprise to you. Anytime you take on a challenge, you need to keep at it, stay on schedule, and work hard to achieve your goal. Writing is no different.

Visit **LaunchPad Solo for Readers and Writers > Reading** for more practice with reading and building vocabulary.

What might surprise you, however, is that you already have many skills to succeed in college writing. You practice some form of **reading**, **critical thinking**, and **writing** every day without even realizing it. Consider the billboard shown here, for example. How effective do you think it is?

You most likely read ads, signs, e-mails, Facebook posts, and bumper stickers on a regular basis. Even when you read brief items like these, you often think critically about what is being presented. You question how persuasive or effective a point is. You consider how the new point fits or conflicts with what you know already (from your own experience and from other things you have read or heard). This questioning attitude and the ability to look at new material from fresh and skeptical perspectives are important building blocks for successful academic writing.

WALTER BIBIKOW/GETTY IMAGES

As you read, question, respond, and write in college, keep in mind that you have done these activities before—and often. You have reflected on topics and supported your views with facts. You have tested and revised your ideas as you look at topics more closely. Trust that, in college, you can jump into the ongoing conversation that goes on about ideas, and you can add something thoughtful and valuable to that conversation.

PRACTICE 1

Look at the following advertisement directed at veterans.

First *read* the ad. Next, *think* about the main point the ad is making. Finally, *write* in your own words what you think the ad is trying to say.

_____

_____

_____

_____

_____

In addition to thinking critically and questioning new material, you also make decisions all the time. You think about whatever information is available to you, and you decide what to do. The more thoughtful you are about your choices, the better decisions you will make. For example, you may be considering driving yourself to school or work rather than taking public transportation. At first, it may seem like an easy choice to have your own car with you, but answer these questions:

- How much will driving cost, when you total up parking fees, gas, and additional mileage on your car?
- Are the parking-lot locations just as convenient as the transportation stations?
- If you drive, will you be giving up time you could use for reading or studying on the bus or train?

As these questions indicate—and you can probably think of more questions on this topic—making decisions often involves weighing several factors.

PRACTICE 2

Think of a decision you made recently when you had a choice about something. Maybe you started making coffee at home instead of buying it at a coffee shop to save money. Maybe you decided to work less so you could attend school. Maybe you bought a new computer or became a vegetarian.

What decision did you make? _____

_____

What options did you have? _____

_____

What points did you consider to arrive at your choice?

- _____

- _____

- _____

- _____

- _____

Do you think you made the right decision? Why or why not?

_____

_____

_____

_____

Careful thinking and reading lead not only to better decision making but also to better writing, both in college and at work. The next two sections talk about ways to become a better writer by improving your reading and thinking skills.

Improve Your Reading Skills

When you read for college, get in the habit of taking the following four steps, no matter what you are reading. In this section of the book, the four steps of the critical reading process are identified with the letters **2PR**.

2PR   The Critical Reading Process

Preview the reading.

Read the piece, finding the main point and support.

Pause to think during reading. Ask yourself questions about what you are reading. Talk to the author.

Review the reading, your notes, and your questions. Build your vocabulary by looking up any unfamiliar words.

Critical Reading

- **Preview**
- Read
- Pause
- Review

2PR   *Preview the Reading*

Before you begin to read, look ahead. Go quickly through whatever you are reading (essay, chapter, article, and so on) to get an idea of what it contains. Many books, especially textbooks, help you figure out what is important by using headings (separate lines in larger type, like "Preview the Reading" above). They may also have words in **boldface**. In textbooks, magazines, and journals, important words may be defined in the margin, or quotations may be pulled out in larger type. When you are reading a textbook or an essay or article in a college course, look through the chapter or piece for headings, boldface type, definitions in the margin, and quotations.

In this textbook, Chapter 2 and all the following chapters in Parts 1–6 include a feature that will help you preview the chapter: the **Reading Roadmap**. Each Reading Roadmap helps you identify a purpose for reading and guides you to think about the vocabulary and the skills you will learn in the chapter. Spending just a few minutes previewing each chapter will help you read, remember, and apply what you are learning.

In Chapters 6, 7, and 8 of this textbook, you will find paragraph and essay examples from both students and professional writers. These examples illustrate different ways of organizing writing. To preview these readings, look at the title, the information about the author and the situation for which the author was writing, and the vocabulary notes in the margins. In addition, each essay includes a **guiding question**. A guiding question helps you focus your reading by giving you a specific question to answer.

2PR *Read the Piece, Finding the Main Point and Support*

Critical Reading

Preview
Read
Pause
Review

Identifying the main point and support in a reading is necessary to understand the author's message.

MAIN POINT

The **main point** of a reading is the major message that the writer wants you to understand. In an advertisement or a tweet, the main point is usually easy to determine. In a longer reading, you might have to think deeply about what the main point is. It may not be lying on the surface, stated clearly and easy to spot. But in most readings, the main point is introduced early, so read the first few sentences (of a short reading) or paragraphs (of a longer reading) with special care. If the writer has stated the main point in a single sentence or a couple of sentences, highlight or double-underline those. You will remember the main point better if you write it in your own words, in either your notes or the margin of the reading.

The particular combination of skill and luck necessary to succeed at poker (especially the no-limit "Texas hold 'em" variation that's now dominant[1]) helps explain why it, rather than some other game, has become such a seminal[2] feature of the online-gambling scene. Hold 'em requires more skill than most casino games, such as blackjack and slots. The more time you put into the game, the better you get, and because skilled players do, in fact, win more money than unskilled players, there's a motivation to keep playing and learning. But poker also involves enough chance, unlike a pure-skill game like chess, so that if you play reasonably well, you can get lucky enough to win a big tournament. Unlike slots, for instance, poker is an inherently[3] social and competitive game, with players up against one another rather than against the house.

1. **dominant:** most common

2. **seminal:** important

3. **inherently:** basically; by nature

Main Point: *Online poker has become so popular because it requires experience and skill but also relies on luck.*

PRACTICE 3

Read the paragraph that follows and double-underline or highlight the main point. In the space after the paragraph, write the main point in your own words.

Your career as a health-care professional will give you much more than a steady job. You will have the satisfaction of using technical skills to help people. Whether your work involves helping children or adults, you will enjoy the respect and confidence that your training bestows.[1] Allied professionals will be very much in demand through this year and the next several years. Careers such as dental assistants, medical assistants, pharmacy technicians, medical secretaries, phlebotomy[2] technicians, and professional coders are

1. **bestows:** grants

2. **phlebotomy:** the process of drawing blood from a vein

open to you. You might perform tests, handle records and materials for dental and medical tests, assist in procedures, and learn how to use the medical or dental technical equipment. Every day can be challenging and different for you because no two patients are alike and neither are their treatments.

Main Point: _____

_____

SUPPORT

The **support** in a reading is the information that shows, explains, or proves the main point. To understand the main point fully, you need to be able to identify the support. If you highlighted the main point, use a different-colored marker to highlight the support. If you double-underlined the main point, underline the support, perhaps using a different-colored pencil. Using different colors will help you when you review the material for class, a writing assignment, or a test.

In the example below, the main point is double-underlined and the support is single-underlined.

Information technology (IT) is not just about computer science and engineering anymore. It can be applied as a tool in just about any pursuit from biology to fashion design. New applications in every field imaginable are being invented daily. Did you know, for example, that Sun Microsystems does a lot of its recruiting and marketing on Second Life,[1] and even holds virtual meetings there? IT has become mainstream, interwoven into the fabric of our lives.

1. **Second Life:** an online virtual world for gaming and socializing

PRACTICE 4

Reread the paragraph in Practice 3, and underline or highlight three sentences that directly support the main point. Then, briefly state the support in your own words.

Support: _____

_____

PRACTICE 5

Find a piece of writing to share with the class. It can be an advertisement, an e-mail from a friend, a magazine or newspaper story, or anything you like. Underline or highlight the main point and support in different colors.

Critical
Reading

Preview
Read
Pause
Review

2PR   *Pause to Think*

Critical reading requires you to actively think as you read, and taking notes and asking questions is a part of this process. As you pause to think about what you are reading, use check marks and other symbols and jot notes to yourself, so you can understand what you have read when you finish it (rather than having just looked at the words without thinking about their meaning and purpose). Here are some ways to take notes as you read.

- Note the main idea by highlighting it or writing it in the margin.
- Note the major support points by underlining them.
- Note ideas you do not understand with a question mark (?).
- Note ideas you agree with by placing a check mark next to them (✓).
- Note ideas that you do not agree with or that surprise you with an **X** or **!**.
- Note examples of an author's or expert's bias and how they seem biased.
- Pause to consider your reactions to parts of the reading and how a part or sentence relates to the main point.

2PR   *Review*

Often, your instructor will ask you to answer questions about a reading or to write about it. To respond thoughtfully, review the reading, look at your notes, and use your critical thinking skills. In addition, look up any words from the reading that you are unfamiliar with.

REVIEW THE READING

When you have finished reading an assignment, review the parts you highlighted or underlined and answer two questions:

1. What point does the author want me to "get"?
2. What does he or she say to back up that point?

If you cannot answer these two questions, review the reading again. You need to know the answers to be able to participate in class discussion, do a writing assignment, take a test, or relate the reading to other ideas you are studying.

In this textbook, Chapter 2 and all the following chapters in Parts 1–6 end with a section called **Reflecting on the Journey**. The charts in this section help you to review and think about what you have learned. Like many textbooks, this book also includes **Chapter Review** questions at the end of each chapter. Use these questions to test yourself and review the material from the chapter.

Critical Reading

> Preview
> Read
> Pause
> Review

Tip You may find that reading aloud improves your understanding.

PRACTICE 6

Read the paragraphs that follow, highlighting or underlining the main point and the five sentences that most directly support the main point.

Consolidated Machinery offers excellent employee benefits, such as generous family leave programs and a menu of insurance plans. The family leave program offers paid two-week leaves to new parents, both mothers and fathers. These leaves are automatic, meaning that employees don't have to apply for them. Leave for new parents may be extended, without pay, for an additional four weeks. Employees may also apply for a one-week paid leave for a family emergency or a death in the immediate family. These leaves are part of what makes the company family-friendly.

1. **HMOs:** Health Maintenance Organizations; health-care plans that restrict patients to certain doctors to reduce costs

The company also offers several insurance plans: two different HMOs[1] and several options of Blue Cross/Blue Shield. The company pays half of the insurance premiums for general health insurance. It also pays the entire cost of dental insurance for employees and their dependents. If employees would rather have child-care benefits than dental benefits, they can put the money that would have gone to dental care toward day care. These programs are expensive, but Consolidated Machinery has found that the additional costs are more than covered by employee loyalty and productivity.

BUILD YOUR VOCABULARY

Building a good vocabulary helps you to understand everything you read and to write better papers and essay tests in college. It also helps you to communicate better with coworkers, bosses, and customers at work. Students who are able to speak, write, and read more effectively are more successful in both their college and work careers, and even in their personal lives.

One of the best ways to improve your vocabulary is to look up new words from your reading in a dictionary. Sometimes, as in many of the readings in this textbook, words that may be unfamiliar to some readers are highlighted and their meanings given at the end of the piece or in the margins.

Here are some tips for learning and remembering these new words:

- Keep a journal with new words, definitions, and sample sentences. Also note where you found the word.

- Challenge yourself to use at least one word from your journal in each new writing assignment.

- If a word occurs in a reading and on the Academic Word List on page 11, focus on that word. Make flash cards with the word and its definition and practice these three or four times a week.

- In your journal or on your flash cards, note whether the word is a noun, a verb, an adjective, or an adverb. For more information about these terms, see Chapter 10.

- Make a note of synonyms (words with similar meanings) and antonyms (words with opposite meanings).

- Make a note of any hints that can help you remember what a word means or how it is used.

Sample Vocabulary Journal Entry

Inherently: adverb. "basically; by nature"

Source: *Real Skills*, Chapter 1, p. 7

Example: "Unlike slots, for instance, poker is an inherently social and competitive game."

My sentence: Going back to school as an older adult is inherently frightening and even risky.

Hint: Inherently—something is IN me, so it is a part of my nature.

Synonym: basically, essentially

PRACTICE 7

Choose three words that are defined in the margins of this chapter. Write a vocabulary journal entry for each one.

In addition to keeping track of words as you go, your reading and writing will be much improved if you become familiar with commonly used academic words. The following list of words, taken from the Academic Word List, occur frequently in college-level work.

analyze	define	indicate	proceed
approach	derive	individual	process
area	distribute	interpret	require
assess	economy	involve	research
assume	environment	issue	respond
authority	establish	labor	role
available	estimate	legal	section
benefit	evident	legislate	sector
concept	export	major	significant
consist	factor	method	similar
constitute	finance	occur	source
context	formula	percent	specific
contract	function	period	structure
create	identify	policy	theory
data	income	principle	vary

Source: Averil Coxhead, "A New Academic Word List," *TESOL Quarterly* 34 (2000): 213–38, app. A, sublist 1. The entire Academic Word List is available at www.victoria.ac.nz/lals/resources/academicwordlist.

PRACTICE 8

Review the Academic Word List above. Look up any words you are unfamiliar with in a dictionary or on an online dictionary site.

Think Critically

In all college courses, instructors expect you to think about the content and question it rather than just remember and repeat it. This ability to think carefully and ask questions is called **critical thinking**. Asking questions is the mark of an intelligent, responsible person. In college and other situations, asking the right questions will help you learn more about any subject—and about yourself.

When reading about a subject in college or about an important matter at work or in your everyday life, ask questions as you read and as you think about what you have read. What does it mean—to the writer, to you, and to your experience? Be an active reader, not just a passive viewer.

Four Basic Critical Thinking Questions

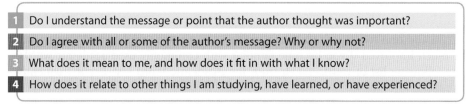

1 Do I understand the message or point that the author thought was important?

2 Do I agree with all or some of the author's message? Why or why not?

3 What does it mean to me, and how does it fit in with what I know?

4 How does it relate to other things I am studying, have learned, or have experienced?

The following diagram summarizes what you and other critical thinkers do.

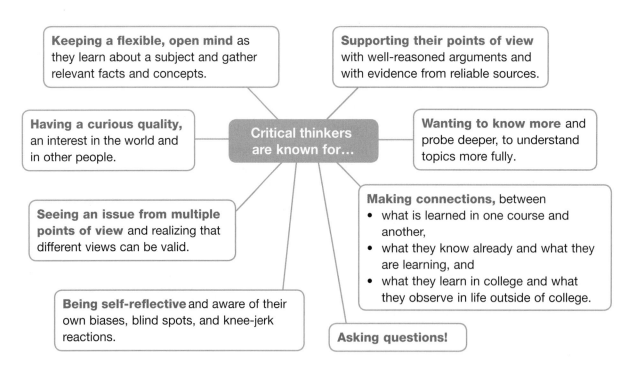

Keeping a flexible, open mind as they learn about a subject and gather relevant facts and concepts.

Supporting their points of view with well-reasoned arguments and with evidence from reliable sources.

Having a curious quality, an interest in the world and in other people.

Critical thinkers are known for...

Wanting to know more and probe deeper, to understand topics more fully.

Seeing an issue from multiple points of view and realizing that different views can be valid.

Making connections, between
- what is learned in one course and another,
- what they know already and what they are learning, and
- what they learn in college and what they observe in life outside of college.

Being self-reflective and aware of their own biases, blind spots, and knee-jerk reactions.

Asking questions!

The following text appeared on the Web site for SoBe Lifewater Strawberry Apricot B-Energy drink and has been marked up with comments and questions that show critical thinking about the content and the message.

Why is the word "energy" in the drink's name?

Strawberry Apricot B-Energy

With other natural flavors

Launch your day with an ultra-efficient mix: sweet strawberry and delectable apricot flavors loaded with guarana, ginseng, and B-vitamins. You'll never believe 10 calories tasted this good.

What are guarana and ginseng?

What do B-vitamins do?

Only 10 calories— how is it sweetened?

PRACTICE 9

Examine the advertisement below. Read it and think about the main points it is trying to make. Note any questions or comments you have in the margins, and then answer the questions that follow.

COURTESY OF THE CORPORATION FOR NATIONAL AND COMMUNITY SERVICE

What organization is sponsoring the ad? _____

What does the organization want you (the reader) to do?

_____

Was the ad successful in capturing your interest? Why or why not?

_____

_____

_____

_____

Write and Edit Your Own Work

Read the paragraphs below, which appeared in a college newspaper. Double-underline the main point sentences, and single-underline the support. Note any comments or questions you may have in the margin. Then write a paragraph in your own words using the following structure:

- Explain the main point in your first sentence.
- Explain the support in the next two or three sentences.
- Provide your own reaction and thoughts about the main point in the final two or three sentences.

More than 98 brands of bottled water are sold in the United States, a country that has some of the most reliable, sanitary, and clean tap water in the world. Do we really need to be purchasing these bottles? A growing movement on college campuses nationwide claims we do not, arguing against the bottled water industry and calling on universities across the country to ban the product's sale on campuses. By replacing bottled water with public reusable-water-bottle filling stations, colleges are making it easier for students to quit their habit. We believe that [our school] should join the movement.

Those promoting the ban are correct to label disposable bottles as detrimental[1] to the environment. They produce large quantities of unnecessary waste, and reports suggest that over 68 percent of recyclable bottles are not recycled properly. Despite appearances, bottled water is often merely normal tap water that has been filtered through a process called reverse osmosis, which can require almost 10 gallons of water to purify one gallon. Such waste is simply unnecessary.

Additionally, packaging and transportation produce carbon emissions that could easily be avoided. Considering that the tap water available in our faucets is already filtered and of high quality, buying a bottle provides negligible[2] benefits

1. **detrimental:** harmful

2. **negligible:** barely noticeable

while contributing to the accumulation[3] of greenhouse gases in the atmosphere. By banning the sale of bottled water on campus, [our school] could do its part to decrease these harmful emissions.

3. **accumulation:** buildup

Chapter Review

1. What skills do you already have to help you succeed in college?

   _____

2. What do careful thinking and reading lead to? _____

   _____

3. What are the four steps in the 2PR Critical Reading Process? _____

   _____

   _____

4. What is the main point of a reading? _____

   _____

5. What is the support in a reading? _____

   _____

6. What is critical thinking? _____

   _____

7. What are the Four Basic Critical Thinking Questions? _____

   _____

   _____

   _____

2

Understanding the Basics of Good Writing

How to Write in College and Other Formal Settings

READING ROADMAP

Learning Objectives

Chapter Goal: Identify characteristics that make writing successful.

Tools to Achieve the Goal

- Four Basics of Good Writing (p. 17)
- Four Basics of a Good Paragraph (p. 19)
- Steps in the Writing Process (p. 20)

Key Terms

Skim Chapter 2 before you begin reading. Can you find each of these words in **bold** type? Put a check mark next to each word once you have located it in the chapter.

_____ purpose	_____ paragraph
_____ audience	_____ topic sentence
_____ informal English	_____ body sentences
_____ formal English	_____ concluding sentence
_____ main point	
_____ support	_____ writing process

Highlight or circle any of these words that you already know.

Before You Read

Before you begin reading this chapter, fill out the following chart. For each skill, think of a time when you have used this skill and what you would like to know on completing the chapter. At the end of the chapter, you will be asked to share what you learned about this skill.

Skill	When I have used this skill	What I want to know about this skill
Identify a specific audience and purpose for writing		
Provide support for a main idea		
Use a process to write a paragraph or essay		

Understand the Basics of Good Writing

Good writing has four basic features.

Four Basics of Good Writing

1	It achieves the writer's purpose.
2	It considers the readers (the audience).
3	It includes a main point.
4	It has details that support the main point.

Purpose and Audience: Considering Your Writing Situation

Your **purpose** is your reason for writing. Your writing purpose depends on the situation. For many college writing assignments, the purpose is included within the instructions. You may be asked to show something, to explain something, or to convince someone of something. At work, your purpose in writing may be to propose something, to request something, or to summarize something. In your everyday life, your writing purpose may be to entertain or to express your feelings about something.

Closely linked to your purpose in writing is your audience. Your **audience** is the person or people who will read what you write. When you write, always have a real person in mind as a reader. In college, that person is usually your instructor, who represents the general reader. Think about what that person knows and what he or she needs to know to understand the point that you want to make.

Tip Each chapter begins with a goal and a list of the tools you can use to achieve this goal. Before you begin reading the chapter, think about the goal and locate the tools provided for you.

PRACTICE 1

Consider these three different writing situations, and fill in the purpose and audience for each.

1. On Facebook, a friend posts a link to an article about bullying, and you want to write your own comment about the article and about bullying.

   Purpose: _____

   Audience: _____

2. At school, your instructor has you write a paragraph, based on some articles you have been reading and your own observations, about how bullying can affect teenagers.

   Purpose: _____

   Audience: _____

3. At work for a school district, your boss asks you to write a memo proposing a new, stronger policy against any kind of bullying on school grounds.

    Purpose: _____

    Audience: _____

What you say and how you say it will vary depending on your audience and purpose. We communicate with our friends differently than we do with people in authority, like employers or instructors. When you post a Facebook comment, you might use **informal English** because Facebook is a space for casual writing. If a friend sends you a link to a disturbing article about a bullying incident at your school, you might respond with a brief comment like this:

> tx for that, hadnt seen. . . . ugh, so 2 bad u know???

In contrast, when writing a paragraph on bullying for your instructor, you would use **formal English** (with a serious tone and correct grammar and spelling) because the relationship is more formal. Also, the purpose is serious—to improve your writing skills and to achieve a good grade. You might write a passage like this:

> Bullying can have long-lasting negative effects on teenagers. When a bully picks on another student, it can hurt that person's self-esteem, in some cases permanently. If the situation is not dealt with right away, the person being bullied can spiral down into depression or even consider suicide. In some cases, bullies can cause physical harm that the person may never recover from. Some people think it is fine to look the other way when bullies pick on weaker kids, but many schools are now taking a stronger stand against bullying. New policies against bullying may save some self-esteem or even some lives.

Tip For practice with writing for a formal audience, see the Editing Paragraphs exercises in Chapters 13–16.

In college, at work, and in everyday life, when you are speaking or writing to someone in authority for a serious purpose, use formal English. Otherwise, you will not achieve your purpose, whether that is to pass a course, to get and keep a good job, or to solve a personal problem (like being billed on your credit card for a purchase you did not make or reporting a landlord who does not turn on your heat). Formal English gives you power in these situations, so it is important to know how to use it. This book will give you practice in writing and speaking formal English and also in hearing it so that it sounds right to you.

Main Point and Support

Tip For more on main point and support, see Chapters 1 and 4.

Your **main point** is what you want to get across to your readers about a topic or situation. In college, instructors usually expect you to state your main point in a sentence. You may also include main-point statements in writing you do at work. Here is the main-point statement from the sample student paragraph about bullying:

> Bullying can have negative effects on teenagers.

You back up such statements by providing **support**—details that show, explain, or prove your main point. In the sample student paragraph, the support consisted of examples of the negative effects of bullying: low self-esteem, depression and suicide, physical harm. Providing enough support for your main point helps you get your ideas across and ensures that you are taken seriously.

Visit **LaunchPad Solo for Readers and Writers > Topics and Main Ideas** and **Topic Sentences and Supporting Details** for practice identifying main points and support.

Understand What a Paragraph Is

A **paragraph** is a short piece of writing that presents a main point and supports it. A paragraph has three parts:

1. A **topic sentence** states your main point.

2. **Body sentences** support (show, explain, or prove) your main point.

3. A **concluding sentence** reminds readers of your main point and makes an observation.

Here is an example of a paragraph:

Indentation marks start of paragraph

   Blogs (short for *Web logs*) are now an important part of many people's lives. Thousands of people write thousands of blogs on as many topics as you can think of. The topics range from cars to entertainment to medicine to important national and international events. Many people use blogs as diaries to record their opinions, feelings, and observations. Others use blogs as a source of news instead of reading newspapers or watching television news. People visit blogs before buying things to learn what others think about certain products, features, and prices. Want to find out what others think about a movie? You can probably find any number of blogs on the subject. Blogs are a common part of our current culture, and new ones appear every minute. If you have not visited a blog, give it a try, but be careful: You might get completely hooked and become someone who writes and reads blogs every day.

Topic sentence with main point

Body sentences with support

Concluding sentence

Paragraphs can be short or long, but for this course, your instructor will probably want you to have at least three to five body sentences in addition to your topic and concluding sentences. When you write a paragraph, make sure that it includes the following basic features.

Four Basics of a Good Paragraph

1 It has a topic sentence that includes the main point the writer wants to make.

2 It has detailed examples (support) that show, explain, or prove the main point.

3 It is organized logically, and the ideas are joined together so that readers can move smoothly from one idea to the next. (See Chapter 5 for more details.)

4 It has a concluding sentence that reminds readers of the main point and makes a statement about it.

Understand the Writing Process

The following chart shows the basic steps of the **writing process**—the stages that you will move through to produce a good piece of writing. It also shows the parts of this book where you can get more information on each step.

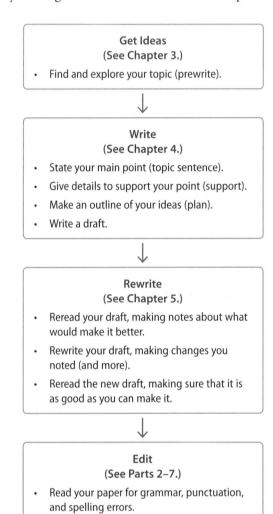

Get Ideas
(See Chapter 3.)

• Find and explore your topic (prewrite).

↓

Write
(See Chapter 4.)

• State your main point (topic sentence).
• Give details to support your point (support).
• Make an outline of your ideas (plan).
• Write a draft.

↓

Rewrite
(See Chapter 5.)

• Reread your draft, making notes about what would make it better.
• Rewrite your draft, making changes you noted (and more).
• Reread the new draft, making sure that it is as good as you can make it.

↓

Edit
(See Parts 2–7.)

• Read your paper for grammar, punctuation, and spelling errors.

While you may not always go in a straight line through the four stages (you might sometimes go back to an earlier stage), it helps as a writer to have these steps in mind.

Write and Edit Your Own Work

Write a paragraph that describes an unsuccessful communication between you and someone in authority, such as a teacher, religious leader, returns manager at a store, or boss. You might use the following structure:

• Identify the communication situation and the participants.
• Give a few details about what each person said.

- State the outcome.
- Comment on what you might have done differently.

Chapter Review

1. What is *purpose* in writing? _____

2. What is the word for the person or people who read your writing? _____

3. In your own words, explain what formal English is and why it is important.

   _____

   _____

4. In the most recent piece of writing that you did (in college or not), who was your
   audience and what was your purpose? _____

   _____

5. Label the topic sentence, body sentences, and concluding sentence in the
   following paragraph about a career as a personal trainer.

© RICK GOMEZ/COPYRIGHT RICK GOMEZ 2004/CORBIS

A career in the field of personal training requires knowledge of human anatomy and physiology, experience with exercise equipment and training methods, and strong communication skills. First, trainers need to understand how the human body works. They should know not only how muscles can be strengthened or how fat can be burned but also how clients can exercise safely and avoid injury. In addition, trainers ought to have experience using gym machines such as treadmills, stationary bicycles, and elliptical devices so that they can demonstrate these for their clients. If the trainer follows a specific toning method such as Pilates, he or she must have experience with tools and accessories needed for that exercise program. Finally, the trainer should have strong communication skills, in both speaking and writing. Trainers need to be able to give clients clear instructions during an exercise session to avoid injuries and to motivate clients to continue when the exercises become difficult. Also, many trainers write exercise plans for clients to use when they are not working with the trainer face-to-face. If the trainer does not explain the plan clearly and effectively, a client might not be successful, or, in the worst cases, sustain injuries through accidents. Personal training offers a rewarding career for people with the knowledge, experience, and communication skills to succeed.

REFLECTING ON THE JOURNEY

Skills Learned

Now that you've completed the chapter, share what you've learned about each skill by completing the following chart.

Skill	What I learned about this skill
Identify a specific audience and purpose for writing	
Provide support for a main idea	
Use a process to write a paragraph or an essay	

3

Narrowing and Exploring Your Topic

How to Decide What to Write About

READING ROADMAP

Learning Objectives

Chapter Goal: Learn strategies to select and develop a writing topic.

Tools to Achieve the Goal

- Asking questions (p. 24)
- Freewriting (p. 25)
- Brainstorming (p. 26)
- Mapping or clustering (p. 26)
- Keeping a journal (p. 26)
- Using the Internet (p. 27)

Key Terms

Skim Chapter 3 before you begin reading. Can you find each of these words in **bold** type? Put a check mark next to each word once you have located it in the chapter.

_____ topic   _____ journal

_____ narrow   _____ plagiarism

_____ prewriting
       technique

Highlight or circle any of these words that you already know.

Before You Read

Before you begin reading this chapter, fill out the following chart. For each skill, think of a time when you have used this skill and what you would like to know on completing the chapter. At the end of the chapter, you will be asked to share what you learned about this skill.

Skill	When I have used this skill	What I want to know about this skill
Asking questions to narrow a topic		
Freewriting		
Brainstorming		
Mapping or Clustering		
Keeping a journal to explore a topic		
Using the Internet to explore a topic		

Narrow Your Topic

Ⓜ LaunchPadSolo

Visit **LaunchPad Solo for Readers and Writers > Prewriting** for practice with narrowing and exploring topics.

Your **topic** is what you are going to write about. Often, instructors assign a general topic that you need to make more specific so that you can write about it in a paragraph or short essay. To **narrow** a topic, break it into smaller parts that might interest you.

Patti Terwiller, a community college student in a writing class, was given an assignment to write on the general topic "A lesson that you learned." Her mind went blank. Her first thought was "I can't think of any ideas. I don't have anything to write about on that topic." Encouraged by her teacher, she tried to narrow the general topic to a small, manageable topic (see diagram on p. 25). She also wanted to see if the narrowing process sparked any interesting ideas. First, she asked herself a question that would slightly narrow the topic. After she answered that question, she asked herself a series of questions that helped her focus on her recent experiences. Note how she keeps asking herself questions.

> **PRACTICE 1**
>
> Choose one of the following general topics, and, on a separate sheet of paper, write three narrower topics for it. Use Patti's method as a model, asking yourself a narrowing question and then a series of focusing questions. Then, select the narrowed topic that interests you most, and write it in the space provided.
>
> | | |
> |---|---|
> | A lesson that you learned | Someone that you admire |
> | A campus problem | Something that you do well |
> | Being a single parent | Something that you enjoy |
> | Something that annoys you | Something that you fear |
> | A family tradition | Stresses on students |
> | A favorite time of day | Worries about college |
> | A personal goal | Your best subject in school |
>
> Narrowed topic that interests you most: _____

Explore Your Topic

To get ideas to write about, use the **prewriting techniques** described in the following sections. Writers rarely use all the techniques shown here, so choose the ones that work best for you after you have tried them out. Use a prewriting technique to get ideas at any time during your writing—to narrow or explore your topic or to add details and explanations after you have begun writing a paragraph or an essay.

The examples in the rest of this chapter show Patti Terwiller, the writing student who shared her narrowing diagram, using different prewriting techniques to get ideas about the topic "A lesson that you learned." She narrowed her topic to "How I learned self-respect."

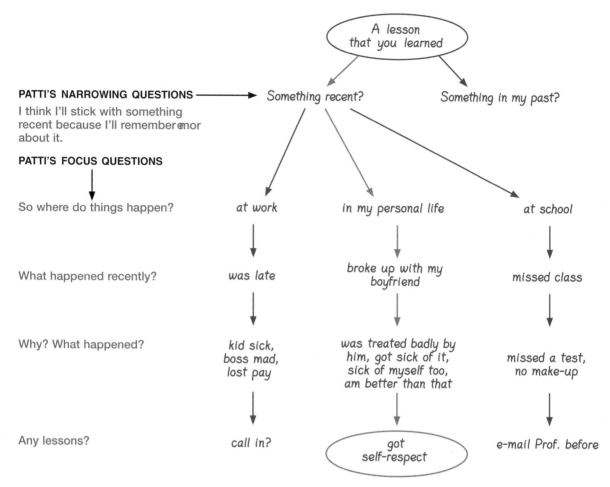

PATTI'S NARROWING QUESTIONS ———→ Something recent?   Something in my past?

I think I'll stick with something recent because I'll remember more about it.

PATTI'S FOCUS QUESTIONS

So where do things happen?   at work   in my personal life   at school

What happened recently?   was late   broke up with my boyfriend   missed class

Why? What happened?   kid sick, boss mad, lost pay   was treated badly by him, got sick of it, sick of myself too, am better than that   missed a test, no make-up

Any lessons?   call in?   got self-respect   e-mail Prof. before

Any of these topics I want to write about?   *The only one I'm interested in and might have something to write about is my boyfriend and getting respect.*

PATTI'S NARROWED TOPIC: *How I learned self-respect.*

Freewrite

Freewriting is like having a conversation with yourself on paper. Just start writing about your topic, and continue nonstop for five minutes. Do not worry about how you write or whether your ideas are good. Just write.

> *Got tired of my boyfriend pushing me around, making all the decisions, not caring what I thought. Just let it happen because I wanted to keep him. Mean to me, rude to friends, late or didn't show up. Borrowed money. At a party he started hitting on[1] someone else. Told him I had to go home. Before that, let him get away with stuff like that. He said no just wait baby. Something snapped and I got home on my own. He's history[2] and I'm kind of sad but it's okay.*

1. **hitting on:** approaching another person with romantic intentions (slang)

2. **history:** part of the past (slang)

PRACTICE 2

Freewrite about your narrowed topic from Practice 1.

Brainstorm

Brainstorming is listing all the ideas that you can think of without worrying about how good they are. You can brainstorm by yourself or by talking to others. Again, here is Patti Terwiller on her narrowed topic, "How I learned self-respect."

> Always tried to please everyone, especially my boyfriends
> Thought everything was fine
> Thought love was about keeping guys happy, not myself
> Always got dumped anyway, couldn't figure it out
> Finally I just blew up, I don't really know what happened
> Glad it did
> My boyfriend was surprised, so was I
> He had no respect for me at all, I didn't respect myself
> My friends all told me but I never listened
> That party everything changed
> Never again

Map or Cluster

To map, or cluster, write your narrowed topic at the top or in the center of a page. Then, write ideas about the topic that occur to you around or under your narrowed topic—anything you can think of. As details about those ideas come to you, write those around or under the ideas. Patti Terwiller's cluster diagram is shown on page 27.

PRACTICE 3

Using a blank sheet of paper, create a map or cluster to explore your narrowed topic from Practice 1.

Keep a Journal

Set aside a regular time to write in a **journal**. You can keep your journal on a computer or in a notebook or other small book. Write about:

- your personal thoughts and feelings,
- things that happen to you or to others, and
- things you care about but do not really understand.

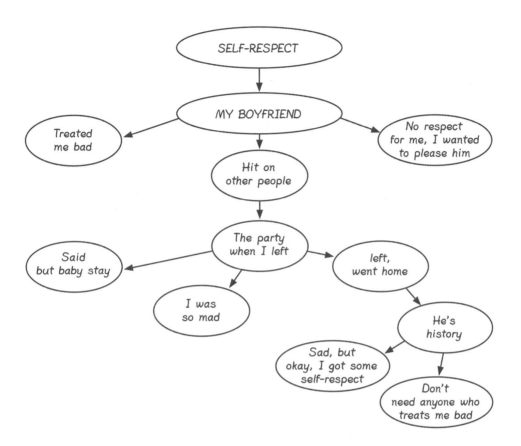

Journals are useful for keeping track of ideas that you might turn into papers later.

PRACTICE 4

Over the next week, write in a journal every day. Each day, write at least ten lines about your narrowed topic. At the end of the week, reread what you have written and write a few sentences about it.

Use the Internet

The Internet can be a great source of ideas. Type your narrowed topic into Google or another search engine. Visit some of the sites that come up, and write down any new ideas that you get about your topic. Visit a blog (meaning *Web log*, a kind of Web journal) that is related to your topic, and write down ideas. For links to different types of blogs, try Blogcatalog.com. Go to its home page and click on the Browse tab to find a list of categories. Or go to YouTube (www.youtube.com), and see what the top topics are.

   Important Note about the Internet and Writing: The Internet is a resource for all kinds of things, including papers that you can download and turn in as your own. Doing so is called **plagiarism** and is one of the worst errors that you can make in college. Students who plagiarize may be given a failing grade automatically or may even be suspended or dismissed from college. Also, keep in mind that most instructors are expert in detecting plagiarism, and many use the Internet and software tools to check student work for originality. Do not take the risk.

PRACTICE 5

Use the Internet to get ideas for your topic. Save sites that interest you by using the Bookmark or Favorites feature in the browser that you use to view the Internet.

By now, you should have some good ideas about your narrowed topic. You will use them in the next chapters as you write your own paragraph.

Write and Edit Your Own Work

Write a first-try paragraph about your narrowed topic, using the ideas that you wrote down in the practices in this chapter. You will not be graded on this; it is a first practice. You might use the following structure:

- State your narrowed topic.
- Give the background information that the reader needs to know about the situation (who? what? when? where? why?).
- State what you learned or what is important to you about your topic, and why it is important.

Chapter Review

1. How can you narrow a topic? _____

   _____

   _____

   _____

2. Which prewriting technique worked best for you? Why? _____

   _____

   _____

   _____

REFLECTING ON THE JOURNEY

Skills Learned

Now that you've completed the chapter, share what you've learned about each skill by completing the following chart.

Skill	What I learned about this skill
Asking questions to narrow a topic	
Freewriting	
Brainstorming	
Mapping or Clustering	
Keeping a journal to explore a topic	
Using the Internet to explore a topic	

4

Writing Your Paragraph

How to Put Your Ideas Together

Learning Objectives

Chapter Goal: Put ideas together in a paragraph.

Tools to Achieve the Goal
- Four basics of a good topic sentence (p. 32)
- Four basics of good support (p. 35)
- Four basics of a good draft (p. 39)

Key Terms

Skim Chapter 4 before you begin reading. Can you find each of these words in **bold** type? Put a check mark next to each word once you have located it in the chapter.

____ topic sentence   ____ details
____ support   ____ concluding
____ primary support   sentence

Highlight or circle any of these words that you already know.

Before You Read

Before you begin reading this chapter, fill out the following chart. For each skill, think of a time when you have used this skill and what you would like to know on completing the chapter. At the end of the chapter, you will be asked to share what you learned about this skill.

Skill	When I have used this skill	What I want to know about this skill
Write a strong topic sentence		
Provide good support		
Make a plan or outline		
Write a draft		

Make a Point

Every piece of writing should have some point. Your **topic sentence** presents that point and is usually the first or the last sentence of the paragraph. In this book, the examples will have the topic sentence first. Many people find that putting the topic sentence first helps them set up the rest of the paragraph. In the following paragraph, the topic sentence (main point) is underlined.

Tip The main point of an essay is the thesis statement. For more information, see Chapter 9.

<u>Caring for my first accident victim as a student nurse was the toughest job I ever had</u>. A young mother, Serena, had been admitted to the intensive care unit after her car collided head-on with a truck. She had suffered a head injury, a collapsed lung, and a broken arm. I knew that my supervisor, a kind and highly skilled nurse, would be with me the whole time, but I was afraid. I had never assisted with a patient who was so severely injured. After Serena was wheeled into the ICU, the medical team began working on her immediately. While the doctor and senior nurses gave Serena blood and administered other care, I managed the medical pumps and kept a detailed record of everything that was being done to help her. In the end, we stabilized Serena, and my supervisor complimented me for being so calm and responsible. I will never forget how hard that time was, but it gave me confidence that I carry into every new day at work.

One way to write a topic sentence is to use the following basic formula:

| Narrowed topic | + | Main point / position | = | Topic sentence |

Caring for my first accident victim as a student nurse was the toughest job I ever had.

If you have trouble coming up with a main point about your topic, look back over your prewriting. For example, to write her topic sentence, Patti Terwiller, the student introduced in Chapter 3, reviewed her narrowing and prewriting about how she learned self-respect (see pp. 24–28). She realized that the lesson that she learned through a painful experience with her boyfriend could be applied to all her relationships. Here is her topic sentence:

> I finally learned self-respect in relationships.

PRACTICE 1

Reread the prewriting that you did in Chapter 3. What is the point that you want to make about your narrowed topic? Think about why the topic interests you or is important to you.

Point you want to make about your narrowed topic: _____

_____

A good topic sentence has four necessary features.

Four Basics of a Good Topic Sentence

> **1** It has a single main point stated in a sentence.
>
> **2** It is something that you can write about in a paragraph; it is not too broad.
>
> **3** It is something that you can say something about; it is not a simple fact.
>
> **4** It is a confident statement; it is not weak and it does not start with *I think, I hope,* or *In this paper I will try to.*

Two main points	Daily exercise can keep the mind alert, and eating right aids weight loss.

[How could the writer cover these two large topics in only one paragraph?]

Revised	Daily exercise keeps the mind alert.

Too broad	Sports are popular in every culture.

[How could the writer cover this large topic in only one paragraph?]

Revised	Baseball evolved from the British game of rounders.

Simple fact	Basketball is popular at my gym.

[What else is there to say?]

Revised	Playing basketball has taught me the value of teamwork.

Weak	Until students get real benefits for the activity fees they pay, I think that the college should lower these fees.

[*I think* weakens the statement.]

Revised	Until students get real benefits for the activity fees they pay, the college should lower these fees.

PRACTICE 2

Review the Four Basics of a Good Topic Sentence above. Then, read the following topic sentences and, to the left of each, write the number of the basic that is missing. Be ready to say why you chose a certain number. (More than one number may apply.)

Example: __4__ I think that video games help people in some ways.

1. ____ Video games take mental skill, and they are coming down in price.

2. _____ The census[1] is taken every ten years.

3. _____ There are many religions in this world.

4. _____ Fashion changes every year.

5. _____ In this paper, I hope to show that Wal-Mart hurts small businesses.

1. **census:** a regular population count

PRACTICE 3

Decide whether each of the following sentences is too broad or okay, and write **B** (broad) or **OK** in the space to the left of the sentence. Think about whether you could write a good paragraph about the sentence. Rewrite any that are too broad.

Example: _B_ **I like programs on Comedy Central.**

Rewritten: *On Trevor Noah's The Daily Show, news is entertaining.*

1. _____ People love their pets.

    Rewritten: _____

2. _____ Colleges offer many different kinds of degree programs.

    Rewritten: _____

3. _____ My grandmother saved things that most people would have thrown out.

    Rewritten: _____

4. _____ I love all kinds of food.

    Rewritten: _____

5. _____ Standardized tests are not a good measure of my abilities.

    Rewritten: _____

PRACTICE 4

Narrow each of the following topics. Then, circle the one that interests you most, and write a possible topic sentence for it.

Example:

Topic: Favorite pastimes

   Narrowed: _____ movies   walking   cooking _____

   Topic sentence: *I enjoy seeing movies because they take me out of my everyday life.*

1. Topic: Things that you are good at

   Narrowed: _____

   Topic sentence: _____

   _____

   _____

2. Topic: Benefits of an education

   Narrowed: _____

   Topic sentence: _____

   _____

   _____

3. Topic: Difficulties that you have overcome

   Narrowed: _____

   Topic sentence: _____

   _____

   _____

Here, again, is student Patti Terwiller's topic sentence:

> **Topic sentence:** I finally learned self-respect in relationships.

After rereading her topic sentence and prewriting, Patti thought of a way to make the sentence more specific.

> **Revised:** One evening in May, I finally learned to practice self-respect in my relationships.

PRACTICE 5

Using your narrowed topic from Chapter 3 (Practice 1, p. 24) and the point that you want to make about it (Practice 1 of this chapter, p. 31), write a topic sentence. Your first try may not be perfect, so review the Four Basics of a Good Topic Sentence (p. 32), and rewrite the topic sentence to make it clearer, more specific, or more confident.

   Narrowed topic: _____

   Topic sentence: _____

   Rewritten: _____

Support Your Point

A good topic sentence is important for making a main point, but it cannot stand on its own. To make sure that your writing is powerful and convincing, provide good **support**—detailed examples that show what you mean.

In the paragraph on page 31, for example, the support consists of the events that happened on the day that the student nurse cared for her first accident victim. The events show how important the day was for the writer's growth as a nurse.

Four Basics of Good Support

1 It relates to your topic sentence.

2 It tells your readers what they need to know to understand your point.

3 It uses details that show, explain, or prove your main point.

4 The details do not just repeat your main point; they explain it.

Read the following two paragraphs, which start with the same topic sentence. They were addressed to a financial aid officer by a student seeking tuition assistance.

> Financial aid is key to my goal of getting a college degree. I will not have enough money to pay for tuition without financial aid. If I can get financial aid, I know that I will succeed in college. Going to college is important to me, but I will not be able to afford it unless I can get financial aid.

> Financial aid is key to my goal of getting a college degree. I am the oldest of six children, and although my mother works two jobs to support us, she cannot help me with tuition. My mother did not graduate from high school, but she has always made us work hard in school so that we could go to college and have a better life. Like my mother, I have worked two jobs through high school to save for college, but they both pay the minimum wage, and my savings will not cover tuition. If I can get financial assistance, I know that I will succeed in college. Even with two jobs, I have maintained good grades. It has not been easy, but I am very motivated. I will continue to work hard, and I know from experience that hard work pays off. Financial aid will not be wasted on me.

PRACTICE 6

1. Why is the second paragraph more convincing than the first? _____

   _____

2. What details does the second paragraph give that the first does not?

   _____

   _____

   _____

3. What impression of the writer do you have from the first paragraph?

_____

From the second paragraph? _____

4. Why is the second paragraph more likely than the first to result in a

financial aid offer? _____

_____

The first paragraph does not provide support. After the topic sentence, the student simply repeats the main point using different words. The first paragraph does not contain any details explaining why financial aid is important to the student.

The second paragraph provides details that help the financial aid officer understand the writer's situation. If you put yourself in the role of the reader, you can provide support that will appeal to him or her.

The main support for a topic sentence is known as **primary support**. Good writers also provide **details** about the primary support to help readers understand the main point.

Patti Terwiller reread her prewriting and did more prewriting to get additional details about her story. Then, after rereading her topic sentence, she chose the support points that most clearly explained her main point, numbering them according to when they happened. After each point, she wrote down additional details.

Tip Try prewriting to get detailed examples that support your point. See Chapter 3 for details.

2. **put up with:** to tolerate

Topic sentence: One evening in May, I finally learned to practice self-respect in my relationships.
Primary support point 1: Used to put up with[2] anything to keep my boyfriend happy.
 Details: He could be late, drunk, or rude, and I'd put up with it. Could call me names around his friends or ignore me, and that was okay. I just wanted to keep him.
Primary support point 2: One night at a party, he was ignoring me as usual, but then something happened.
 Details: He started making out with another girl. Something inside me snapped—knew I didn't need this.
Primary support point 3: I confronted him, said it was over, and walked out.
 Details: He was screaming, but I didn't look back, and I didn't answer his calls.

PRACTICE 7

First, fill in the blank in each of the following topic sentences. Then, write three primary support points for each sentence. Finally, pick one of the topics, and write two supporting details for each primary support point. You may want to use a separate sheet of paper.

1. _____ is an important role model for me.

   Topic sentence: _____

   Primary support point 1: _____

   Primary support point 2: _____

   Primary support point 3: _____

2. There are _____ advantages (or disadvantages) to studying with a group. (See photo below.)

   Topic sentence: _____

   Primary support point 1: _____

   Primary support point 2: _____

   Primary support point 3: _____

3. _____ is the most important thing in the world to me.

   Topic sentence: _____

   Primary support point 1: _____

   Primary support point 2: _____

   Primary support point 3: _____

On a separate sheet of paper, write your topic sentence from Practice 5 and three or four primary support points. Then, add at least two supporting details for each primary support point. Try prewriting to get ideas, and choose the ideas that show or explain your main point most effectively.

Make a Plan

Once you have your topic sentence and support points, you are ready to write, but it is easier to write if you have a plan or an outline. As you make an outline, try to shape your support into sentences.

In the following outline, Patti turned her primary support and supporting details into complete, separate sentences. Notice also how Patti changed some of her support as she made her outline. As you write, you can change what you want to say if you come up with better ideas or words.

I.   **Topic sentence:** One evening in May, I finally learned to practice self-respect in my relationships.

   A. **Support sentence 1:** I always put up with anything my boyfriend did because I was afraid he might leave me.

      1. **Details:** He was always late and drunk. I never said anything.

      2. **Details:** He never had any money, and around his friends he ignored me or was totally rude.

   B. **Support sentence 2:** At a party, he was ignoring me, as usual, but then something happened.

      1. **Details:** Right in front of me, he was coming on to[3] another girl.

      2. **Details:** I could feel something inside me snap.

   C. **Support sentence 3:** I knew I did not need this.

      1. **Details:** I told him it was over.

      2. **Details:** Then, I walked out. He was screaming, but I did not look back. I have not answered his calls.

3. **coming on to:** showing romantic interest in (slang)

Tip For more advice on organizing your ideas, see Chapter 5.

Sometimes, it is useful to outline writing that you have already done. This gives you a quick, visual way to see if you have too many details for one support sentence but not enough for another.

Write an outline of your paragraph using Patti's outline (above) as an example.

Write a Draft

Working with your outline, you are ready to write a first draft of your paragraph. Write it in complete sentences, using the details that you have developed to support your topic sentence. Include your topic sentence and a concluding sentence.

You will have as many chances as you want to make changes in your draft. The important thing now is to express your ideas in full sentences, in paragraph form.

LaunchPadSolo

Visit **LaunchPad Solo for Readers and Writers > Drafting** for more help with writing a draft.

Four Basics of a Good Draft

1 It has a topic sentence and a concluding sentence.

2 The first sentence, often the topic sentence, is indented.

3 The paragraph has complete sentences that start with capital letters.

4 It has details that show, explain, or prove the main point.

A **concluding sentence** is the last sentence in the paragraph. It reminds readers of the main point and makes a comment based on what is in the paragraph. Do not just repeat your main point.

Notice how the topic sentence and concluding sentence from the paragraph on page 31 are connected:

Topic sentence: Caring for my first accident victim as a student nurse was the toughest job I ever had.

Concluding sentence: I will never forget how hard that time was, but it gave me confidence that I carry into every new day at work.

In her concluding sentence, the writer reminds readers that the job was difficult but makes a new point about the experience: It gave her confidence.

> **PRACTICE 10**
>
> Read the following two paragraphs, and write a concluding sentence for each.
>
> 1.   A good mentor can mean the difference between success and failure. Fortunately for me, I found a good one in Professor Robinson. He was my English teacher during my first year in college, and without him, I would not have lasted. After four weeks of classes, I was ready to drop out. I was not doing well in my course work, and I was exhausted from working, going to class, and trying to do homework. Because he seemed to care about his students, I went up to him after class and told him that I was leaving school. I said I would try again later. Professor Robinson asked me to come to his

office, where we talked for over an hour. He said that he would help me in his class and that he would arrange a meeting with my other teachers, too. He also said that I should go to the tutoring center for free extra help. He urged me to stay until the end of the semester and then decide whether to leave. I got lots of extra help from some of my teachers, and I was surprised that they were willing to spend time with me. I also made friends at the tutoring center, and we began to help each other out. I am proud to say that I stayed and passed all of my courses.

Concluding sentence: _____

_____

_____

2.   A career in welding offers more opportunities than you might think. Even in today's world, where so much seems to have "gone digital," many metal parts need to be put together in the physical world. Welders can work in a wide range of fields such as manufacturing, plumbing, automotive assembly and repair, construction, salvage, and mining. After some years of on-the-job experience, a welder can move up to a position as supervisor or inspector. Some experienced welders might choose to work as sales and marketing representatives, promoting and selling specialized welding tools and equipment. In the realm of art, some metal sculptors hire welders as apprentices and studio assistants to help make their artistic visions and creations a reality, and some welders are metal sculptors themselves. Other job options in the welding field include machine technicians, metal engineers, and welding instructors.

Concluding sentence: _____

_____

_____

Read Patti's draft paragraph below. Notice how Patti made changes from her outline, including the addition of a concluding sentence.

> One evening in May, I finally learned to practice self-respect in my relationships. I had always put up with anything my boyfriend did because I was afraid that he might leave me. He was always late and drunk, but I never said anything. He never had any money, and around his friends he either ignored me or was totally rude. At a party, he was ignoring me, as usual, but then something happened. Right in front of me, he was hitting on another girl. Something inside me snapped, and I knew I did not need this. I went up to him, told him our relationship was over, and walked out. He was screaming, but I did not look back. I have not answered his calls; he is history. I have learned about self-respect.

PRACTICE 11

On a separate piece of paper, write a draft paragraph. Use your outline as a guide. Feel free to make any changes that you think will improve your draft, including adding more details and changing your topic sentence or concluding sentence.

Write and Edit Your Own Work

Using some of the steps in this chapter, rewrite the first-try paragraph that you wrote at the end of Chapter 3. Once again, you will not be graded on this draft. As you reread your first-try paragraph, try to identify your main point and its primary support. Then, find places where you could add details about the support.

You might use the following format:

- Start with a topic sentence that includes the Four Basics of a Good Topic Sentence (see p. 32). You might try using this diagram:

Narrowed topic	+	Main point
_____		_____

- Make sure that you have at least three primary supports for your topic sentence. List them here:

_____

_____

_____

- Add details to each primary support.
- Add one or two concluding sentences. These sentences are the last ideas of yours that your reader will read. Give your concluding sentences some extra time and thought so that they are meaningful and memorable.

Chapter Review

1. Using the headings in this chapter, list the steps in writing a paragraph. _____

_____

_____

2. What is a topic sentence? Highlight the answer in this chapter.

3. What are some words that can weaken your topic sentence? _____
   _____

4. What is support in writing? Highlight the answer in this chapter.

5. What is the point of making a plan? _____
   _____

6. What is a concluding sentence, and what should it do? Highlight the answers in this chapter.

REFLECTING ON THE JOURNEY

Skills Learned

Now that you've completed the chapter, share what you've learned about each skill by completing the following chart.

Skill	What I learned about this skill
Write a strong topic sentence	
Provide good support	
Make a plan or outline	
Write a draft	

5

Improving Your Paragraph

How to Make It the Best It Can Be

READING ROADMAP

Learning Objectives

Chapter Goal: Revise your paragraph to make it better.

Tools to Achieve the Goal

- Four basics of revision (p. 44)
- Checklist for peer reviewers (p. 44)
- Transitions (pp. 48, 50, 52)
- Four basics of a good paragraph (p. 54)
- Checklist for revision (p. 56)

Key Terms

Skim chapter 5 before you begin reading. Can you find each of these words in **bold** type? Put a check mark next to each word once you have located it in the chapter.

_____ revision	_____ time order
_____ peer review	_____ space order
_____ coherence	_____ order of importance
_____ transitions	

Highlight or circle any of these words that you already know.

Before You Read

Before you begin reading this chapter, fill out the following chart. For each skill, think of a time when you have used this skill and what you would like to know on completing the chapter. At the end of the chapter, you will be asked to share what you learned about this skill.

Skill	When I have used this skill	What I want to know about this skill
Get feedback from peers		
Give feedback to peers		
Improve support by adding or deleting details		
Use time order, space order, or order of importance to arrange ideas		

Understand What Revision Is

LaunchPadSolo

Visit **LaunchPad Solo for Readers and Writers > Revising** for more advice about revising your writing.

Revision means "reseeing." When you revise, you read your writing with fresh eyes and think about how to improve it. You also try to order and connect your ideas in a way that makes your meaning clear to readers.

Four Basics of Revision

> 1 Take a break from your draft (at least a few hours).
>
> 2 Get feedback (comments and suggestions) from someone else.
>
> 3 Improve your support, deciding what to add or drop.
>
> 4 Make sure that your ideas are ordered and connected in a way that readers will understand.

The rest of this chapter focuses on steps 2–4.

Get Feedback

Getting feedback from a reader will help you improve your first draft. Also, giving other people feedback on their writing will build your own understanding of what good writing is. Use the following questions to get and give feedback.

CHECKLIST

Questions for a Peer Reviewer

☐ Is the writing style appropriate for the audience and purpose? (Most college assignments should be written in formal English.)

☐ What is the main point (topic sentence)?

☐ Is the topic sentence focused on a single topic, narrow enough for a paragraph, more than just a simple fact, and confident (without *I think* or *I hope*)?

☐ Is there enough support for the main point? Where could there be more support?

☐ Do any parts seem unrelated to the main point?

☐ Are there places where you have to stop and reread something to understand it? If so, where?

☐ Could the concluding sentence be more forceful?

☐ What do you like best about the paper?

☐ Where could the paper be better? What improvements would you make if it were your paper?

☐ If you were getting a grade on this paper, would you turn it in as is?

☐ What other comments or suggestions do you have?

Exchanging papers with another student to comment on each other's writing is called **peer review**. Although it may feel awkward at first, that feeling will wear off as you give and get more peer review.

Peer review may be done in writing, but it is best to work face-to-face with your partner so that you can discuss each other's comments and ask questions.

Improve Your Support

Peer comments will help you see how you might improve your support. Also, highlight the examples you use to support your point, and ask: Are there any examples that do not really help make the point? What explanations or examples could I add to make my writing clearer or more convincing?

To practice answering these questions, read what a seller posted on craigslist.com about her iPod:

> The silver iPod Mini I am selling is great. I need an iPod with more memory, but this one has nothing wrong with it. I got it for Christmas, and it was a great gift. It is lightweight and in good condition because it is fairly new. It holds a charge for a long time and can hold a lot of iTunes. It comes with the original case. The price is negotiable. You will want to pursue this great deal! Contact me for more details.

PRACTICE 1

Working with another student or students, answer the following questions.

1. What is the seller's main point? _____

2. Underline the one sentence that has nothing to do with the main point.

3. Circle any words that do not provide enough information. List three of these terms, and say what details would be useful.

   _____

   _____

   _____

   _____

4. What vague word does the author repeat too often? _____

5. Rewrite the seller's main point/topic sentence to make it more

   convincing. _____

Tip The following are two good online writing labs: **owl .english.purdue.edu** and **grammar.ccc.commnet .edu/grammar**.

PRACTICE 2

Read the two paragraphs that follow, and underline the sentence that does not relate to the main point.

1.   Service learning[1] provides excellent opportunities for college students. While students are helping others, they are learning themselves. For example, a student in the medical field who works at a local free clinic provides much-needed assistance, but he is also learning practical skills that relate to his major. He learns about dealing with people who are afraid, who do not know the language, or who are in pain. He might meet someone he likes. When he has to write about his experience for class, he has something real and important to write about. And for many students, working for an organization provides a strong sense of community and purpose. Students have as much to gain from service learning as the organizations they work for do.

2.   Before choosing roommates, think about your own habits so that you find people whom you can stand living with. For example, if you regularly stay up until 1:00 a.m., you probably should not get a roommate who wants quiet at 10:00 p.m. If you are sloppy and like it that way, do not live with people who demand that you wash every dish every day or clean up after yourself every morning. Cleaning is one of those chores that most people hate. If you want to share all expenses, think about how you will handle discussions on how money should be spent. How much do you want to spend every month, and on what kinds of things do you want to spend it? Roommates can be a blessing for many reasons but only if you can live with them.

PRACTICE 3

To each of the five sentences, add two sentences that give more details.

Example: Modern life is full of distractions.

E-mails and text messages demand our attention.

Even bathrooms and grocery carts have advertising.

1.   _____ (your favorite music group) creates music that has an important message.

_____

_____

2. _____ (your favorite sport) is the most exciting sport.

_____

_____

3. Every family has unique traditions that they carry on from one generation
to the next.

_____

_____

4. Fast-food restaurants are not completely unhealthy. (See photo.)

IMAGE SOURCE VIA AP IMAGES

_____

_____

Check the Arrangement of Your Ideas

After you have improved your support by cutting sentences that do not relate to your main idea and adding more details and examples, check that you have ordered and linked your ideas in a way that readers will understand. This process is called improving your writing's **coherence**.

There are three common ways to organize ideas—by time order, space order, and order of importance. Each of these arrangements uses words that help readers move smoothly from one idea to the next. These words are called **transitions**.

Time Order

Use **time order** to present events according to when they happened, as in the following paragraph. Time order is useful for telling stories.

Read the following paragraph, paying attention to the order of ideas and words that link one idea to the next.

A few months ago, when I was waiting for a train in a subway station, I witnessed a flash mob demonstration. First, I noticed that the station was filling up with more people than usual for a Sunday afternoon. As people kept coming down the stairs, I began to get nervous. Then, someone yelled, "Huh!" and about twenty people yelled back, "Hah!" The yelling was so loud that it echoed down the subway tunnel. During this time, I was just wishing that my train would arrive. But what happened next surprised me. After one person turned on a portable CD player, a bunch of people started dancing as if they were on a stage. Before I knew it, I was part of a large audience that encircled the dancers. As I watched the performance, I was amazed at how well rehearsed it seemed. When it ended, someone went around with a hat, collecting money. I gave a dollar, and I later decided that it was the best entertainment I had ever gotten for such a low price.

The paragraph describes the order of events in the flash mob, moving from the writer's sense of confusion to the performance to the writer's later reflection about the event. Time transitions move the reader from one event to the next.

Time Transitions

after	finally	next	soon
as	first	now	then
before	last	second	when
during	later	since	while

PRACTICE 4

In each item in this practice, the first sentence begins a paragraph. Put the rest of the sentences in the paragraph in time order, using **1** for the first event, **2** for the second event, and so on.

Example: **The annual sale of designer bridal gowns at the bridal warehouse was about to start, and the atmosphere was tense.**

___5___ The women ran to their favorite designers' items and threw as many dresses as they could hold into one another's arms.

___2___ Clusters of friends planned their strategy for when the doors opened.

___3___ As the guard approached to open the doors, the crowd pushed forward to get inside.

__1__ **Hundreds of women lined up outside the door two hours before opening time.**

__4__ **When the doors opened, the women flooded in, holding on to others in their group so that they would not become separated.**

1. Edward VIII, King of Britain, gave up his throne in 1936 after what was considered scandalous behavior.

   _____ Their relationship was a problem because the British constitution did not allow royals to marry divorced individuals.

   _____ After he gave up the throne, Edward became Duke of Windsor, and he and Wallis were free to marry.

   _____ Edward fell madly in love with Wallis Simpson, a commoner and an American divorcée.

   _____ After the marriage, the couple lived most of their lives in France.

   _____ Edward and Wallis were so in love that Edward gave up his throne in order to marry her.

2. Born in 1951, Sally Ride, one of the first American woman astronauts, had many successes and achieved many accomplishments in her life.

   _____ In 1978, she was accepted into the astronaut training program, one of only thirty-five trainees selected from the eight thousand applicants.

   _____ Later, at Stanford University, she earned four degrees.

   _____ To become an astronaut, she successfully completed a regimen of difficult physical training.

   _____ In her youth, she was a star junior tennis player.

   _____ In 1983, she became the first American woman to orbit Earth.

Space Order

Use **space order** to present details in a description of a person, place, or thing.

Read the following paragraph, paying attention to the order of ideas and words that link one idea to the next.

Thirteenth Lake in the Adirondacks of New York is an unspoiled place of beauty. Because the law protects the lake, there are no homes on it, and only nonmotorized boats like canoes and kayaks are allowed. I often just sit at the end of the lake and look out. In front of me, the water is calm and smooth, quietly lapping against the shore. Near the shore, wild brown ducks, a mother leading a line of six or seven ducklings, paddle silently, gliding. Farther out, the water is choppy, forming whitecaps as the wind blows over it. On each side are trees of all sorts, especially huge white birches hanging out over the water. From across the water, loons call to each other, a clear and hauntingly beautiful sound. Beyond the lake are mountains as far as the eye can see, becoming hazier in the distance until they fade out into the horizon. I find peace at Thirteenth Lake, always.

JEFF FARBANIEC

The paragraph describes what the writer sees, starting near and moving farther away. Other ways of using space order are far to near, top to bottom, and side to side. To move readers' attention from one part of the lake to another, the writer uses space transitions.

Space Transitions

above	beyond	next to
across	farther	on the side
at the bottom/top	in front of	over
behind	in the distance	to the left/right/side
below	inside	under
beside	near	

PRACTICE 5

The first sentence of each item below begins a description. Put the phrases that follow it in space order, using **1** for the first detail, **2** for the second detail, and so on. There can be more than one right order for each item. Be ready to explain why you used the order you did.

Example: **The apartment building I looked at was run-down.**

_1_ **trash scattered all over the front steps**

_3_ **boarded-up and broken windows**

_4_ **tattered plastic bags waving from the roof**

_2_ **front door swinging open with no lock**

1. For once, my blind date was actually good-looking.

   ____ muscular arms

   ____ flat stomach

   ____ long brown hair

   ____ dark brown eyes and a nice smile

   ____ great legs in tight jeans

2. As the police officer drove toward the accident site, she made note of the scene.

   ____ Another police car stopped on the right in the breakdown lane.

   ____ Another car was in the middle of the road, its smashed hood smoking.

   ____ Two cars spun off to the left, between the northbound and southbound lanes.

   ____ Witnesses stood to the right of the police car, speaking to an officer.

Order of Importance

Order of importance builds up to the most important point, putting it last. When you are writing or speaking to convince or persuade someone, order of importance is effective.

Read the following paragraph, paying attention to the order of ideas and words that link one idea to the next.

> The Toyota Prius is definitely the next car that I will buy because it is affordable, safe, and environmentally friendly. I cannot afford a new Prius, but I can buy a used one for somewhere between $6,000 and $7,000. I will need to get a car loan, but it will be a good investment. Using less gas will save me a lot of money in the long run. More important than the price and savings is the safety record of the Prius, which is good. _Consumer Reports_ rates the car as safe. Most important to me, however, is that it is a "green" car, making it better for the environment than a regular car. It runs on a combination of electric power and gasoline, which means that it gets higher gas mileage than cars with standard gasoline engines. On the highway, the 2010 Prius gets fifty-one miles per gallon, and in the city the mileage is about forty-eight miles per gallon. Because I believe that overuse of gasoline is harmful to the environment, I want to drive a car that does the least harm.

The paragraph states the writer's reasons for wanting to buy a Prius. He ordered the reasons according to how important they are to him, starting with the least important and ending with the most important. Transitions signal the importance of his ideas.

Importance Transitions

above all	more important	most
best	most important	one reason/another reason
especially	another important	worst

PRACTICE 6

The first sentence of each item below begins a paragraph. Put the sentences that follow it in order of importance, using **1** for the first detail, **2** for the second detail, and so on. There can be more than one right order for each item, although the most important detail should be last. Be ready to explain why you used the order you did.

Example: **Making friends at college is important for several reasons.**

_2_ **Having a friend in class can help if you have to miss class, by updating you on lessons and assignments.**

_4_ **Beyond practical concerns, a friend can make you feel a part of the college community and enrich your life.**

_3_ **With a friend, you can study together and quiz each other.**

_1_ **A friend gives you someone to sit with and talk to.**

1. I have always wanted to be a police officer.

   _____ I understand the risk involved with being a police officer, but at least the job is never boring.

   _____ My father was a police officer until he retired four years ago.

   _____ I will be able to earn extra money by working overtime on construction projects, security details, and other jobs.

   _____ The benefits and job security are good.

2. Laughter is one of life's greatest pleasures.

   _____ People who laugh regularly are able to cope better with life's inevitable rough patches.

   _____ We tend to be close to people who share a similar sense of humor, so laughter can help us bond with and stay in close touch with friends and family.

_____ Laughter reduces built-up mental stress and gives us a chance to relax.

_____ Laughter helps us to not take ourselves so seriously and "not sweat the small stuff."

Even if you are not using time, space, or importance orders, use transitions to link your ideas. The following are some other ways to use transitions:

Purpose	Transitions
To give an example	for example, for instance, for one thing/for another, one reason/another reason
To add information	also; and; another; in addition; second, third, and so on
To show contrast	although, but, however, in contrast, instead, yet
To indicate a result	as a result, because, so, therefore

Title Your Paragraph

Choose a title for your paragraph that tells the reader what the topic is. Here are some guidelines for choosing a good title:

- It gives the reader an idea of the topic of the paragraph.
- It is usually not a complete sentence.
- It is short and related to your main point.

PRACTICE 7

Look at the following photos. Write a title (or caption) for each one.

AP PHOTO/ERIC ANDERSON

AP PHOTO/NATACHA PISARENKO

PRACTICE 8

Either by yourself or with a partner, reread student Patti Terwiller's revised draft on page 55. Then, write two possible titles for it.

_____

_____

PRACTICE 9

Write two possible titles for your draft paragraph.

_____

_____

Check for the Four Basics of a Good Paragraph

When you revise your draft, check that it has these basic features.

Four Basics of a Good Paragraph

> **1** It has a topic sentence that includes the main point you want to make.
>
> **2** It has detailed examples (support) that show, explain, or prove your main point.
>
> **3** It is organized logically, and the ideas are joined together with transitions so that readers can move smoothly from one idea to the next.
>
> **4** It has a concluding sentence that reminds readers of your main point and makes a statement about it.

Read student Patti Terwiller's draft paragraph below, which you first saw in Chapter 4. Then, read the revised draft with her changes. The colors in the revised paragraph, matched to the Four Basics of a Good Paragraph, show how Patti used the basics to revise. Notice that most of Patti's changes involved adding detailed examples (the words highlighted in red). She also added transitions (highlighted in yellow), especially time transitions, since her paragraph is organized by time order. She also crossed out words or phrases she did not like.

Patti's first draft

> One evening in May, I finally learned to practice self-respect in my relationships. I had always put up with anything my boyfriend did because I was afraid that he might leave me. He was always late and drunk, but I never said anything. He never had any money, and around his friends he either ignored me or was totally rude. At a party, he was ignoring me, as ▸

usual, but then something happened. Right in front of me, he was hitting on another girl. Something inside me snapped, and I knew I did not need this. I went up to him, told him our relationship was over, and walked out. He was screaming, but I did not look back. I have not answered his calls; he is history. I have learned about self-respect.

Patti's revised draft

1 One 2 hot, steamy 1 evening in May, I 3 finally learned to practice self-respect in my relationships. 2 I had always put up with anything my boyfriend did because I was afraid that he might leave me. He was always late and drunk, and he was often abusive, but I never said anything. He never had any money, and around his friends he either ignored me or was totally rude, calling me disrespectful names and cursing at me. At a party 3 in May, he was ignoring me, as usual, but then something happened. 3 Then, right in front of me, he was hitting on started kissing another girl. 3 Next, they were all over each other. 3 And then, my boyfriend smirked right at me. Something inside me snapped, and I knew I did not need this. I felt my blood rush to my face. I gritted my teeth for a moment, thinking and gathering my resolve. 3 Then, I narrowed my eyes, went walked up to him, and hissed, "It's over." As I walked stormed out, he was screaming to me, but I did not look back. 3 Since that night, I have not answered his calls or believed his sweet-talking messages, he is history. I have learned about self-respect that I do not need him or anyone like him who does not treat me right. 4 What I do need is self-respect, and 3 now I have it.

PRACTICE 10

With a partner, read the first and revised drafts aloud. Talk about why the revised draft is better, and be specific. For example, do not just say, "It has more examples." Discuss why the examples make Patti's experience come alive. Then, answer the following questions.

1. What emotions was Patti feeling? _____

   What words showing those emotions are in the revised draft but not in the

   first draft? _____

2. What sentence describes what her boyfriend did to anger her the most?

   _____

3. What two sentences do you think have the most emotion? _____

   _____

PRACTICE 11

Revise your own draft, thinking about how Patti made her paragraph stronger. Take a close look at your topic and concluding sentences, revising them at least once more. Use the following checklist as a guide.

CHECKLIST

Revising Your Writing

☐ My paragraph fulfills the assignment, and it is written in the appropriate style for the audience and purpose. (Most college assignments should be written in formal English.)

☐ My paragraph includes the Four Basics of a Good Paragraph, p. 54.

- My topic sentence is focused on a single topic, is narrow enough for a paragraph, is more than just a simple fact, and is confident (without *I think* or *I hope*).

- The body sentences have detailed examples that show, explain, or prove my main point.

- The sentences are organized logically, and transitions link my ideas.

- My concluding sentence reminds readers of my main point and ends the paragraph on a strong note.

☐ This paragraph is the best I can do, and I am ready to turn it in for a grade.

Edit Your Paragraph

After you revise your paragraph, you are ready to edit it. When you edit, you read your writing not for ideas (as you do when revising) but for correctness of grammar, punctuation, spelling, and word choice.

Parts 2 through 7 contain information that will help you edit your writing. As you work through the chapters in these parts, you will learn what errors are most noticeable to people and practice how to edit your writing for correct grammar, punctuation, spelling, and word choice. When you learn to edit, you are learning how to use formal English, the English that you need to succeed in college, at work, and in parts of your everyday life.

Write and Edit Your Own Work

Write a letter to your instructor about the paper that you have just revised. You might use the following format:

- Start with the title of your paragraph, and tell your instructor what your main point is.

- Explain why you chose this topic.
- Say what step of the writing process was most difficult and, if you can, explain why.
- State what you think are two strengths of the paragraph (such as a particular detail, sentence, or point), and explain why.
- Tell your instructor what you learned in writing this paragraph and how what you learned might help you write other papers.

Chapter Review

1. What does *revision* mean? _____ Reread and highlight the paragraph in this chapter where it is defined.

2. Getting _____ from a reader will help you improve your first draft.

3. What are three ways to organize your writing? Highlight them where they appear in the chapter. _____

4. What purpose do transitions serve? _____

   _____

   _____

5. How is editing different from revising? _____

   _____

   _____

REFLECTING ON THE JOURNEY

Skills Learned

Now that you've completed the chapter, share what you've learned about each skill by completing the following chart.

Skill	What I learned about this skill
Get feedback from peers	
Give feedback to peers	
Improve support by adding or deleting details	
Use time order, space order, or order of importance to arrange ideas	

6

Developing Narration, Illustration, and Description Paragraphs

Different Ways to Present Your Ideas

Learning Objectives

Chapter Goal: Write paragraphs using different patterns of development: narration, illustration, and description.

Tools to Achieve the Goal

- Four Basics of Narration (p. 60)
- Sample narration paragraphs and essays (p. 63)
- Four Basics of Illustration (p. 71)
- Sample illustration paragraphs and essays (p. 74)
- Four Basics of Description (p. 80)
- Sample description paragraphs and essays (p. 83)

READING ROADMAP

Key Terms

Skim Chapter 6 before you begin reading. Can you find each of these words in **bold** type? Put a check mark next to each word once you have located it in the chapter.

_____ narration   _____ illustration
_____ topic sentence   _____ description
_____ transitions

Highlight or circle any of these words that you already know.

Before You Read

Before you begin reading this chapter, complete the following chart. For each skill, think of a time when you have used this skill and what you would like to know on completing the chapter. At the end of the chapter, you will be asked to share what you learned about this skill.

Skill	When I have used this skill	What I want to know about this skill
Write a narration paragraph (tell a story to make a point)		
Write an illustration paragraph (use examples to make a point)		
Write a description paragraph (describe a topic to make an impression)		

In this course and other college classes, instructors will expect you to express your ideas in logical patterns so that what you say or write is clear. There are nine common patterns: narration, illustration, description, process analysis, classification, definition, comparison and contrast, cause and effect, and argument. Understanding how to use these patterns will be helpful in many areas of your life.

College	Tests and papers require you to understand and use these patterns.
Work	E-mails, reports, memos, and oral and written communication with coworkers and bosses often follow these patterns.
Everyday life	Whenever it is important that someone understand your point in speech or writing, these patterns will serve you well.

Chapters 6, 7, and 8 contain the following elements related to each of the nine common patterns of development:

- **The Four Basics of the pattern:** A summary of the essential characteristics of the pattern.
- **An example for analysis:** A paragraph written using the pattern, color-coded to show the Four Basics. Following the paragraph are some questions about its structure and content.
- **A Guided Outline:** An outline for a paragraph that you fill in. You are given a topic sentence, and you provide the support and a concluding sentence.
- **A writing assignment.**
- **A checklist:** A set of statements to help you evaluate the paragraph you wrote for the assignment.
- **Sample student and professional paragraphs.**
- **Sample student and professional essays.**

In this chapter, you will learn about the first three patterns: narration, illustration, and description.

Narration

Narration is telling a story of an event or experience and showing why it is important through details about the experience.

Four Basics of Narration

1	It reveals something of importance (your main point).
2	It includes all the major events of the story (support).
3	It gives details about the major events, bringing the event or experience to life for your readers.
4	It presents the events using time order (according to when things happened).

The numbers and colors in the following paragraph correspond to the Four Basics of Narration.

1 In 1848, Ellen and William Craft planned and carried out what I think was a daring escape from the plantation in Georgia where they lived. **2** Ellen and William were both born into slavery before the Civil War. **3** They knew they would never be free while living on their master's plantation. A slave with dark skin, like William, would easily be caught if he tried to go to a northern state. A woman, even if she had light skin like Ellen did, would raise suspicion if she dared to travel on her own. **2** Several years after they got married, Ellen and William came up with an escape plan. **3** They agreed it was risky, but they could no longer face their lives as slaves. **2** First, they would need to save up some money. **3** When he was not working for the master on the plantation, William worked odd jobs in town to earn the cash they required. **2** Next, they used the money to buy a disguise for Ellen. **3** Ellen cut her hair short and wore a suit, glasses, and a top hat. She looked like a white gentleman, and William posed as her servant. **2** Now the Crafts were ready to begin their journey north. **3** Rather than traveling at night and staying hidden, the couple traveled openly by train and steamship. Nobody questioned the right of a white man to travel with his black slave. **2** Ellen and William Craft finally arrived in Philadelphia on Christmas Day in 1848 and lived the rest of their lives in freedom.

1. Underline the **topic sentence**.

2. What is important about this event? _____

_____

3. What detail made the biggest impression on you? Why? _____

_____

_____

4. Circle the **transitions**.

5. Name one way that the paragraph could be better. _____

_____

_____

_____

Guided Outline: Narration

Fill in the outline on the next page with events and details that support the topic sentence. Try prewriting to get ideas, and arrange the events according to time order.

Tip To complete this chapter, you will need to know about prewriting (Chapter 3); writing the main point (topic sentence), supporting that point, and planning/outlining (Chapter 4); and using transitions and revising (Chapter 5).

Topic sentence: The _____ (funniest /saddest / most emotional / most embarrassing /scariest) thing that I ever _____ (saw /experienced) was _____.

First event: _____

_____

    Details: _____

_____

Second event: _____

_____

    Details: _____

_____

Third event: _____

_____

    Details: _____

_____

Concluding sentence: Whenever I remember that time, I think _____

_____.

Write a Narration Paragraph

Write a narration paragraph using the outline that you developed, one of the following topics, or a topic of your own. Then, complete the narration checklist on page 63.

- An experience or event that you witnessed
- An experience or event that you will remember for a long time
- A funny story about yourself or another person
- Something important that is happening in your town / city
- The plot of a movie that you liked
- A time that you helped a friend or family member in trouble
- An unusual news story
- A rumor that is going around
- A story that is told in the lyrics of a song you like

USE A VISUAL TO WRITE NARRATION

Look at the photo on the next page. Write a paragraph to tell the story of a time when you felt you were in the right (or wrong) place at the right (or wrong) time.

ANDREW BUSTIN

A sidewalk in a college campus.

CHECKLIST

Evaluating Your Narration Paragraph

☐ My writing style is appropriate for the audience and purpose. (Most college assignments should be written in formal English.)

☐ The paragraph has the Four Basics of Narration (p. 60).

- My topic sentence states what is important about the event or experience.

- I have included all the important events with details so that readers can understand what happened.

- I have included time-order transitions to move readers smoothly from one event to the next.

☐ I have reread the paragraph, making improvements and checking for grammar and spelling errors.

Explore Narration Further: Life-Changing Moments

As you read the sample paragraphs and essays below, look for the Four Basics of Narration (p. 60). Also, remember to use the 2PR strategy: preview, read, pause, and review (see pages 6-10).

Student Narration Paragraph

Alieh Alfakeeh

What Girls Are For

In the following paragraph, student writer Alieh Alfakeeh, who grew up in Saudi Arabia, tells the story of how she learned to stand up for herself and earn the respect of her brothers.

When my father turned 78, he had three different strokes, which made him lose part of his memory. During his illness, my brothers understood that my father wanted me to get married as soon as possible, so my brothers arranged a marriage for me without my father's and my permission. At that time, the groom had 3 wives, and I was 20 years old. The groom sent women to bribe me, saying that if I married him, I could be wealthy, and my family would have better chances for renting the groom's lands, but I refused. When the groom came to my house and talked to my father to ask for my hand, my father asked me if I wanted him or not; that was a big surprise for me because my father was breaking one of the major rules of marriage. Again, I refused the groom's request. After that, my family had business problems because the groom was the owner of the lands which my family rented for their business. In my culture, only older men can discuss those kinds of business problems. While my brothers were debating what to do about the problems, my father interrupted my brothers and asked me quietly, "What do you think, Alieh, about this problem?" I answered, "Change the business to farming." My brothers felt offended that my father would take a girl's opinion rather than grown men's opinions. However, my father showed that girls are not only for marriage; girls are for more important decisions, too. Since that time, my brothers have respected me.

Professional Narration Paragraph

Womenshealth.gov

A 911 Call Saved My Life

The following paragraph, by an anonymous stroke sufferer, is adapted from part of a stroke fact sheet published on **www.womenshealth.gov**, the Web site of the U.S. Department of Health and Human Services' Office on Women's Health. The writer tells the story of how, with the help of a friend, she was able to get help quickly when her life was on the line.

One day at work, a 911 call saved my life. When I walked into the locker room, I realized something was wrong. I couldn't speak. I tried to pick up my lock, but my right hand couldn't grab it. One of my coworkers noticed something was wrong and asked if I could write. With my left hand, I scribbled 911 on a piece of paper. Luckily, my friend knew the signs of stroke and got help. She called an ambulance, and I was rushed to the emergency room. The doctors ran some tests and put a drug into my

IV. Within ten minutes I could speak again. I didn't know a thing about stroke before I had one. Now, I make sure that all my family knows the signs of stroke so they can get help if they need it.

UNDERSTANDING NARRATION

After you have read the two narrative paragraphs, "What Girls Are For" and "A 911 Call Saved My Life," complete the following.

1. Underline the **topic sentence** of each paragraph.

2. Double-underline a **major event** from each story.

3. Circle **two details** in each paragraph that bring the event to life for readers.

4. List two transition words or phrases used in each paragraph that help tell the story in time order. _____

_____

_____

Student Narration Essay

Christina Mevs

How My Community College Experience Has Changed My Life

Student writer Christina Mevs wrote the following essay for a scholarship competition. She tells the story of how a head injury affected her academic career and how her community college gave her the support she needed to succeed.

Guiding question　How did community college help the writer get her life back on track?

1　　Lone Star College-CyFair has saved my life, and changed it for the better. The absolute compassion of this community college and its entire staff has encouraged an insecure teenager who didn't know her place in this world to believe in herself again. Lone Star College-CyFair has intelligent and caring professors, challenging and relevant course selections, and a staff who truly cares about their students' success. All of these factors contributed to my substantial growth and continued academic success at my community college.

2　　To be honest, I never pictured myself attending a community college growing up. My grades throughout high school put me in the top fifteen percent of my class, which would allow me to attend almost any university of my choice. My teachers loved me, and I loved going to school. I was headed directly towards greatness, and then my dreams were slightly derailed.[1]

Tip　A guiding question can help you focus when you are reading. Make sure you can answer the guiding question when you have finished. For more information on reading and guiding questions, see Chapter 1.

1. **derailed:** caused to fail or be delayed

2. **concussion:** a head injury
3. **debilitating:** making weak or unable to function

3   During my senior year of high school, I suffered a concussion[2] during one of my athletic events, starting a cycle of debilitating[3] conditions that would force me to postpone my academic career for a number of years. I was diagnosed with post-concussive syndrome, which includes symptoms such as constant headaches, severe loss of short term memory, and personality changes. It is also an illness that many people, even doctors, do not understand. As a result of the concussion, I started to lose interest in school and sports, causing my grades, and my reputation, to suffer. Depression was settling in and I was losing who I really was. I was always very vibrant,[4] patient, and outgoing, and now I was pessimistic[5] and defensive, especially to anyone who had authority over me.

4. **vibrant:** full of energy
5. **pessimistic:** expecting the worst

4   Immediately after graduating from high school, I enrolled in a four year university. To put it mildly, it was a nightmare. It was the first time I had been away from home in my entire life, and I honestly was not ready to lead a life on my own. I didn't feel like anyone on campus really knew me or wanted to know me, so in turn, I isolated myself. I was alone, in constant pain, and my professors were not supportive of my condition, so I packed my belongings and headed home. I spent an entire year of my life recuperating,[6] and I know now how much that year helped me get my life back. I needed some time for me to realize what was important for my life and my future, and it finally became clear to me that school was the answer.

6. **recuperating:** recovering, regaining health and strength

5   I wanted to start over, and the first place I thought of was Lone Star College-CyFair. It had become very well-known and well-perceived since its establishment in 2004, and I was willing to give it a try. Everyone there was helpful, and I felt they went out of their way to make me feel at home. The staff looked happy to be there, and so did I. I started slowly, first only taking two classes, and then worked my way up to four classes a semester. At first it was a struggle, but both the professors and the students offered their help as soon as they found out about my condition.

7. **preconceived:** formed before experience, without evidence

6   During my first semester here at Lone Star College-CyFair, I knew that my preconceived[7] notions about community colleges were wrong. I felt so relatable to my professors, and I always felt comfortable coming to them if I had a problem. For example, during this past semester, I informed my biology teacher that I was having trouble taking the tests due to my memory lapses. She noticed I was participating in discussions and was reading the material, and she offered to help me as much as she could. Both of us noticed the same thing was still happening, so we came up with a plan to take the same course next semester so she could help me ahead of time.

7   Lone Star College-CyFair is my second home. I love being involved on campus and feel like I can make an impact on campus. This school has saved my life. I know I still have limitations, but I see a future again. A future where I can do what was almost lost to me three years ago.

CHECK YOUR COMPREHENSION

1. Which of the following best expresses the main idea of this essay?
   a. Concussions are dangerous to student athletes.
   b. Faculty members at four-year universities do not care about student difficulties.
   c. A caring college campus helped turn the writer's life around.
   d. It's important to start slowly in education.

2. What event caused the struggles that Mevs faced?
   a. isolation at the four-year university
   b. a severe concussion
   c. a helpful biology professor
   d. a problem with people in authority

3. What example does Mevs use to show how her experience at the community college was different from her experience at the four-year university?

4. Does this essay include the Four Basics of Narration? Be prepared to say why or why not.

5. Write sentences using the following vocabulary words: *debilitating* (para. 3), *vibrant* (3), *recuperating* (4), *preconceived* (6).

READ CRITICALLY

1. In paragraph 6, Mevs says her "preconceived ideas about community colleges were wrong." How did Mevs imagine community colleges before she attended Lone Star College–CyFair? (Hint: Use her description of herself in paragraph 2 to help you determine your answer.)

2. What are the symptoms associated with post-concussive syndrome? How does Mevs illustrate those symptoms in her story?

3. What were the first impressions that Mevs had of her community college (para. 5)? Do you think Mevs was surprised by her experience? Explain.

4. Does Mevs provide enough detail about her experiences to convince her readers that community college changed her life? If you could ask for additional information, what would you like to know?

5. The final sentence of the essay is a fragment (see Chapter 13 for more on fragments). What effect does this fragment have on the reader?

WRITE

1. Mevs describes her first impressions of Lone Star College-CyFair and how the staff made her feel. Write a narrative paragraph or essay about your first day on campus. What happened during that day, and how did that make you feel? Describe the events that occurred that day, and include vivid details about what you saw and heard.

2. Mevs's beliefs about community colleges changed after she attended one. Write a narrative paragraph or essay about an experience that changed your beliefs or expectations. Be sure to describe your beliefs before the experience, and include the major events of your experience in time order. Explain how your belief changed after the experience.

Professional Narration Essay

Sandra Cisneros

Only Daughter

Sandra Cisneros is an acclaimed Mexican American writer whose works include novels, short stories, and poetry that explore, among many themes, Chicana culture and identity. This selection, describing her experience of being an only daughter in a family of seven children, appeared in a compilation of thirty stories written by Hispanic American women. She currently lives in Central Mexico.

Guiding question How did Cisneros's relationship with her father change?

1. **anthology:** a collection of stories, essays, or poems

1   Once several years ago, when I was just starting out my writing career, I was asked to write my own contributor's note for an anthology[1] I was part of, I wrote: "I am the only daughter in a family of six sons. *That* explains everything."

2   Well, I've thought about that ever since, and yes, it explains a lot to me, but for the reader's sake I should have written: "I am the only daughter in a *Mexican* family of six sons." Or even: "I am the only daughter of a Mexican father and a Mexican-American mother." Or: "I am the only daughter of a working-class family of nine." All of these had everything to do with who I am today.

3   I was/am the only daughter and *only* a daughter. Being an only daughter in a family of six sons forced me by circumstance to spend a lot of time by myself because my brothers felt it beneath them to play with a *girl* in public. But that aloneness, that loneliness, was good for a would-be writer—it allowed me time to think, to imagine, to read and prepare myself.

4   Being only a daughter for my father meant my destiny would lead me to become someone's wife. That's what he believed. But when I was in fifth grade and shared my plans for college with him, I was sure he understood. I remember my father saying, "*Que bueno, mi'ja*, that's good." That meant a lot to me, especially since my brothers thought the idea hilarious. What I didn't realize was that my father thought college was good for girls—good for finding a husband. After four years in college and two more in graduate school, and still no husband, my father shakes his head even now and says I wasted all that education.

5   In retrospect,[2] I'm lucky my father believed daughters were meant for husbands. It meant it didn't matter if I majored in something silly like English. After all, I'd find a nice profession eventually, right? This allowed me the liberty to putter about[3] embroidering my little poems and stories without my father interrupting with so much as a "What's that you're writing?"

6   But the truth is, I wanted him to interrupt. I wanted my father to understand what it was I was scribbling, to introduce me as "My only daughter, the writer." Not as "This is only my daughter. She teaches." *Es maestra*—teacher. Not even *profesora*.

7   In a sense, everything I have ever written has been for him, to win his approval even though I know my father can't read English words, even though my father's only reading includes the brown-ink *Esto* sports magazines from Mexico City and the bloody *¡Alarma!* magazines that feature yet another sighting of *La Virgen de Guadalupe* on a tortilla or a wife's revenge on her philandering[4] husband by bashing his skull in with a *molcajete* (a kitchen mortar[5] made of volcanic rock). Or the *foto-novelas*, the little picture paperbacks with tragedy and trauma erupting from the characters' mouths in bubbles.

8   My father represents, then, the public majority. A public who is disinterested in reading, and yet one whom I am writing about and for, and privately trying to woo[6].

9   When we were growing up in Chicago, we moved a lot because of my father. He suffered periodic bouts[7] of nostalgia.[8] Then we'd have to let go our flat, store the furniture with mother's relatives, load the station wagon with baggage and bologna sandwiches, and head south. To Mexico City.

10   We came back, of course. To yet another Chicago flat, another Chicago neighborhood, another Catholic school. Each time, my father would seek out the parish priest in order to get a tuition break, and complain or boast: "I have seven sons."

11   He meant *siete hijos*, seven children, but he translated it as "sons." "I have seven sons." To anyone who would listen. The Sears Roebuck employee who sold us the washing machine. The short-order cook where my father ate his ham-and eggs breakfasts. "I have seven sons." As if he deserved a medal from the state.

12   My papa. He didn't mean anything by that mistranslation, I'm sure. But some-how I could feel myself being erased. I'd tug my father's sleeve and whisper, "Not seven sons. Six! and *one daughter*."

13   When my oldest brother graduated from medical school, he fulfilled my father's dream that we study hard and use this—our heads, instead of this—our hands. Even now my father's hands are thick and yellow, stubbed by a history of hammer and nails and twine and coils and springs. "Use this," my father said, tapping his head, "and not this," showing us those hands. He always looked tired when he said it.

14   Wasn't college an investment? And hadn't I spent all those years in college? And if I didn't marry, what was it all for? Why would anyone go to college and then choose to be poor? Especially someone who had always been poor.

15   Last year, after ten years of writing professionally, the financial rewards started to trickle in. My second National Endowment for the Arts Fellowship. A guest pro-fessorship at the University of California, Berkeley. My book, which sold to a major New York publishing house.

16   At Christmas, I flew home to Chicago. The house was throbbing, same as always; hot tamales and sweet tamales hissing in my mother's pressure cooker, and everybody—my mother, six brothers, wives, babies, aunts, cousins—talking too loud and at the same time. Like in a Fellini[9] film, because that's just how we are.

2. **retrospect:** look back in the past

3. **putter about:** to do something in a relaxed way, without a specific purpose

4. **philandering:** unfaithful, having an affair with another woman

5. **mortar:** a heavy bowl used to smash or grind spices for cooking

6. **woo:** attract, make interested

7. **bouts:** episodes

8. **nostalgia:** homesickness

9. **Fellini:** Federico Fellini, 1920-1993, Italian film director

10. Chicano: Mexican American

11. Pedro Infante: 1917–1957, Mexican actor

12. Galavision: Spanish language television channel

17   I went upstairs to my father's room. One of my stories had just been translated into Spanish and published in an anthology of Chicano[10] writing and I wanted to show it to him. Ever since he recovered from a stroke two years ago, my father likes to spend his leisure hours horizontally. And that's how I found him, watching a Pedro Infante[11] movie on Galavision[12] and eating rice pudding.

18   There was a glass filmed with milk on the bedside table. There were several vials of pills and balled Kleenex. And on the floor, one black sock and a plastic urinal that I didn't want to look at but looked at anyway. Pedro Infante was about to burst into song, and my father was laughing.

19   I'm not sure if it was because my story was translated into Spanish, or because it was published in Mexico, or perhaps because the story dealt with Tepeyac, the *colonia* my father was raised in and the house he grew up in, but at any rate, my father punched the mute button on his remote control and read my story.

20   I sat on the bed next to my father and waited. He read it very slowly. As if he were reading each line over and over. He laughed at all the right places and read lines he liked out loud. He pointed and asked questions: "Is this so-and-so?" "Yes," I said. He kept reading.

21   When he was finally finished, after what seemed like hours, my father looked up and asked, "Where can we get more copies of this for the relatives?"

22   Of all the wonderful things that happened to me last year, that was the most wonderful.

CHECK YOUR COMPREHENSION

1. Which of the following would be the best alternative title for this essay?
   a. "Being a Successful Writer"
   b. "My Father's Approval"
   c. "Mexican-Americans in Chicago"
   d. "Mistranslations and Their Effects"

2. The main idea of this essay is that
   a. children of all ages desire the respect and approval of their parents.
   b. Mexican men do not treat their daughters fairly.
   c. writing is an important profession.
   d. most people don't pay attention to women.

3. Who is Cisneros's audience for this essay?
   a. Mexican Americans
   b. Catholic priests
   c. the general public
   d. her editors

4. Does this essay include the Four Basics of Narration? Be prepared to say why or why not.

5. Write sentences using the following vocabulary words: *retrospect* (para. 5); *woo* (8); *nostalgia* (9).

Illustration   71

READ CRITICALLY

1. What do you think is Cisneros's most likely purpose in writing this essay? Did she succeed in her purpose? Why or why not?

2. In paragraphs 6–11, what does Cisneros describe as her frustration? How does this frustration motivate her?

3. How does Cisneros describe her father in paragraph 13? How does this description help readers understand her father's attitude towards writing as a career?

4. What details does Cisneros provide in paragraphs 16–18 as she describes her family and her father? What do these details tell us about how her father has changed?

5. What does her father ask for at the end of the essay? Why was this question so important to Cisneros?

WRITE

1. In "Only Daughter," Cisneros describes how important a father's approval is for a daughter. Write a paragraph or an essay about your efforts to earn the approval or affection of someone important to you—a parent, teacher, coach, or friend. Present the major events in a clear order, and use details to show what you did and how the other person responded to your actions.

2. Write a narrative paragraph or an essay about a time when you overcame a challenge through hard work and sticking to your goal. Be sure to tell what the incident was, why it is important, when it occurred, and who or what was involved. Include vivid details to help your reader experience the event as you did, and explain how you benefited as a result of the challenge.

Illustration

Illustration uses examples to show, explain, or prove a point.

Four Basics of Illustration

1   It has a main point to illustrate.

2   It gives specific examples to show, explain, or prove the point.

3   It gives details to support the examples.

4   It uses enough examples to get the point across.

The numbers and colors in the following paragraph correspond to the Four Basics of Illustration.

1 Although people starting out in the nursing field may feel that they do not have any relevant work experience, they may actually have gained valuable and transferrable skills in other jobs, which they may possibly have held earlier. **2** For example, working in a restaurant does not sound as though it would be a job that would particularly help a person prepare for a career in nursing, but, in fact, it can. **3** Like nursing, restaurant work requires good listening skills, a sharp memory, and constant attention to detail. It builds experience in dealing with demanding customers who might not always be at their best. And working in a restaurant can also help a person develop the important skills of prioritizing and multitasking. **2** Caring for young children is another job that can provide some relevant background experience to a person who is entering the nursing profession. **3** Child-care workers as well as parents develop important communication skills, patience, and compassion that can be helpful if they enter a career in nursing. The steady and capable caregiving skills gained from work with children can help prepare nursing students for caring for others, of any age. **2** A third type of background, customer service, can also establish a groundwork of relevant experience for beginning nursing students. **3** A demanding job as a retail salesclerk, receptionist, cashier, or landscape worker requires the ability to do hard jobs, keep focused, and interact with many different kinds of people. **1** All of these skills—multitasking, caregiving, listening and communicating well, relating to people—are essential to being a good nurse, and they can all be learned in a variety of jobs.

4 Enough examples to make the writer's point

1. Underline the **topic sentence**.

2. In your own words, what is the point the writer wants to make?

   _____

   _____

3. Circle the **transitions**.

4. What is another example the writer might give?_____

   _____

   _____

Guided Outline: Illustration

Fill in the outline with examples and details that support the topic sentence. Try prewriting to get ideas.

Topic sentence: Today's college students have many _____

_____ (choices / stresses / roles . . .).

First example: _____

Details: _____

Illustration   **73**

Second example: _____

Details: _____

Third example: _____

Details: _____

Concluding sentence: Going to college is not easy, (and /but /so) _____

_____

_____ .

Write an Illustration Paragraph

Write an illustration paragraph using the outline you developed, one of the following topics, or a topic of your own. Then, complete the illustration checklist on page 74.

- Why you like certain music
- What makes a class good
- Some things that annoy you
- What you hope to get from a college education
- The benefits of something you do regularly

- Examples of junk e-mail
- Examples of bad television
- Examples of deceptive ads
- Dreams that you remember
- Examples of rude behavior

USE A VISUAL TO WRITE AN ILLUSTRATION PARAGRAPH

Look at the photo below. In a paragraph, illustrate what it is like to be a part of a large crowd.

The crowd at a Dave Matthews Band concert.

CHECKLIST

Evaluating Your Illustration Paragraph

☐ My writing style is appropriate for the audience and purpose. (Most college assignments should be written in formal English.)

☐ The paragraph has *all* the Four Basics of Illustration (p. 71).

  - My topic sentence presents my main point, is more than just a simple fact, and is confident (without *I think* or *I hope*).

  - I have included enough detailed examples to help readers understand my point.

☐ I have included transitions to move readers smoothly from one example to the next.

☐ I have reread the paragraph, making improvements and checking for grammar and spelling errors.

Explore Illustration Further: Family Ties

As you read the sample paragraphs and essays below, look for the Four Basics of Illustration (p. 71). Also, remember to use the 2PR strategy: preview, read, pause, and review (see pages 6-10).

Student Illustration Paragraph

Mary Adams

From Embarrassing Stories to Favorite Memories

Mary Adams is a student at Lord Fairfax Community College. She plans to transfer to Shenandoah University in Winchester, Virginia, to study nursing. In this paragraph, she uses the example of her sister, Reagan, to illustrate the funny memories she shares with her family.

I could write an entire book of embarrassing stories just about my eight-year-old sister, Reagan. One particular time I remember was when Reagan was about five years old. She cut herself with a pair of scissors on her finger, but not just any finger; it was her middle finger. Reagan was obsessed with this cut and wanted to show everyone what had happened to her. Whenever she saw someone or met someone new, she would proudly lift up her hand and shoot them the bird before any of us had time to explain why a five-year-old knew such a gesture. For about two weeks we had to constantly explain to friends, family, and her daycare teachers why she was flipping them off. This story has become a part of the silly happenings that help to shape our family's strange history, and although it made me cringe at the time, it has now become a funny memory.

Professional Illustration Paragraph

Arnold Brown

Relationships, Community, and Identity in the New Virtual Society

In this paragraph, Arnold Brown illustrates the positive effects that the Internet can have on family relationships. Brown is the chairman of Weiner, Edrich, and Brown, Inc., a consulting firm that helps businesses prepare for the future. He wrote this paragraph as part of a larger article about the ways that the Internet is changing relationships and communities.

The Internet can strengthen family ties because it provides a continuously connected presence. In Norway, for example, one study showed that college students were in touch with their parents on average 10 times a week. Young people use mobile devices to Skype, text, upload photos and videos to Facebook, and more, with increasing frequency. Cyberspace enables families and friends to converse, in effect, as if they were in the same room. This is part of the reason that the Millennial generation reported feeling closer to their parents than did their older siblings during adolescence, according to the Pew Internet and American Life Survey.

UNDERSTANDING ILLUSTRATION

After you have read the two illustration paragraphs, complete the following.

1. Underline the topic sentence (main idea) in each paragraph.

2. How many examples does Adams give to illustrate her point?

3. How many examples does Brown give to illustrate his point?

4. What strategy or strategies does each writer use to introduce examples?

Student Illustration Essay

Sabina Pajazetovic

My Mother, My Hero

Sabina Pajazetovic attended Sanford-Brown Institute for Medical Assisting and Florida State College for nursing. Because her essay "My Mother, My Hero" was written for an exit exam and not for a classroom assignment, Pajazetovic did not have a chance to revise it, but she writes that the piece "came from my heart." Even as a full-time student with a full-time job, Pajazetovic always found time in her demanding schedule for reading: "No matter how hard my day was, I find a little time before I go to bed to read for at least ten minutes. It just relieves all my stress and worries."

Guiding question What examples does Pajazetovic give of her mother's heroism?

Tip A guiding question can help you focus when you are reading. Make sure you can answer the guiding question when you have finished. For more information on reading and guiding questions, see Chapter 1.

1. **worthy:** having great value, honor, or use

2. **Bosnian War:** an armed conflict that took place between 1992 and 1995 in Bosnia and Herzegovina, regions that were formerly part of the southeastern European country of Yugoslavia

3. **conditions:** situation or circumstances that affect your well-being

4. **snipers:** people who shoot at others from hidden places

5. **diagnosed:** identified

1   The one person that I consider to be a true hero and role model is my mother. Throughout my life, my mother has shown me the value of meeting difficult challenges and working hard. She has shown me how to be a strong woman. She has also shown me how to be a good mother. I hope that I will be as good and strong a person as she has been: That is a worthy[1] goal.

2   My mother has bravely faced many challenges. When my sister and I were young, we lived with her and her family in Bosnia. The Bosnian War[2] broke out, and conditions[3] were very dangerous. Most people living in Bosnia at that time were shot at, including me. We lived in constant danger. We did not have enough food, and we had no water. Whenever we needed water, my mother carried huge, empty water jugs to the fountain where she could get safe water. The trip was dangerous, and she could have been shot by snipers[4] at any time along the route. Many people died getting water. While she was gone, my sister and I would wait by the window, occasionally looking out to see if we could spot her. We feared that she would be killed and we would never see her again. But she came back each time, loaded down with the heavy jugs. She never complained or let us see if she was scared. She risked her life so that we would survive. When we had an opportunity to leave Bosnia, my mother bravely took it and brought us safely to the United States. She had to leave her parents behind, but she wanted a better life for us.

3   Another example of my mother's heroism is her hard work. When we came to the United States, my mother worked two jobs, one of them at Burger King, where she was on her feet the whole time. She was also very ill, with a health problem that was not diagnosed[5] for ten years. She did not know what was wrong, but she knew she had to keep working to support us. Even when she finally had surgery, she returned to work right away.

4   My mother also showed me how to be a loving parent. After working two jobs and while she was sick, she still came home every night to cook, clean, and take care of my sister and me. I consider my mother a supermom and a true hero, living every day with bravery, strength, and love.

CHECK YOUR COMPREHENSION

1. Which of the following would be the best alternative title for this essay?

   a. "The Legacy of the Bosnian Civil War"

   b. "My Mother's Struggle for Good Health Care in the United States"

   c. "My Brave, Strong, and Loving Mother"

   d. "The Many Problems of Parenthood"

2. The main idea of this essay is that

   a. parents have many difficulties raising children in a war zone.

   b. the writer's mother has demonstrated much heroism.

   c. children need their parents to be good role models.

   d. a daughter will always admire her mother more than her father.

3. According to Pajazetovic, what did her mother sacrifice to come to the United States?

   a. She had to leave her fortune and her career behind in Bosnia.

   b. She had to leave some of her children in Bosnia when she came to the United States.

   c. She had to leave her parents behind in Bosnia.

   d. She had to leave her doctor and the Bosnian health-care system.

4. Does this essay include the Four Basics of Illustration? Be prepared to say why or why not.

5. Write sentences using the following vocabulary words: *worthy* (para. 1); *condition, sniper* (2); *diagnose* (3).

READ CRITICALLY

1. Do you think that Pajazetovic provides enough examples to support her main point about her mother?

2. How do the details that the writer provides affect your overall impression of her mother?

3. How is the heroism that Pajazetovic's mother showed in Bosnia different from the heroism she showed after coming to the United States? How is it similar?

4. Why would it have been important for Pajazetovic's mother not to complain or show fear during their time in Bosnia?

5. According to this essay, what are the characteristics of a "loving parent"?

WRITE

1. Pajazetovic writes that her mother showed her how to be a "loving parent." What is "loving" behavior? Write an illustration paragraph or essay demonstrating your idea of such an act or attitude, using an example to make your point.

2. Do you have a role model or hero in your life? Choose a person that you know—or know of—and write an illustration paragraph or essay that shows the qualities that you find heroic and gives examples of this person demonstrating those qualities.

Professional Illustration Essay

Wil Haygood

Underground Dads

Wil Haygood (b. 1954) is an award-winning journalist and author. He has written a number of books, including biographies of Adam Clayton Powell Jr., Sammy Davis Jr., and Sugar Ray Robinson, and he has worked for major newspapers including *The Boston Globe* and *The Washington Post*. Currently a professor at Miami University in Ohio, Haygood has gained much attention for his 2013 book, *The Butler: A Witness to History*, which was made into a film starring Forest Whitaker and Oprah Winfrey.

Guiding question   What examples does Haygood give of the men who were role models and substitute fathers in his life?

1   For years, while growing up, I shamelessly told my playmates that I didn't have a father. In my neighborhood, where men went to work with lunch pails, my friends thought there was a gaping[1] hole in my household. My father never came to the park with me to toss a softball, never came to see me in any of my school plays. I'd explain to friends, with the simplicity of explaining to someone that there are, in some woods, no deer, that I just had no father. My friends looked at me and squinted. My mother and father had divorced shortly after my birth. As the years rolled by, however, I did not have the chance to turn into the pitiful little black boy who had been abandoned by his father. There was a reason: other men showed up. They were warm, honest (at least as far as my eyes could see) and big-hearted. They were the good black men in the shadows, the men who taught me right from wrong, who taught me how to behave, who told me, by their very actions, that they expected me to do good things in life.

2   There are heartbreaking statistics tossed about regarding single-parent black households these days, about children growing up fatherless. Those statistics must be considered. But how do you count the other men, the ones who show up—with perfect timing, with a kind of soft-stepping loveliness—to give a hand, to take a boy to watch airplanes lift off, to show a young boy the beauty of planting tomatoes in the ground and to tell a child that all of life is not misery?

3   In my life, there was Jerry, who hauled junk. He had a lean body and a sweet smile. He walked like a cowboy, all bowlegged, swinging his shoulders. It was almost a strut. The sound of his pickup truck rumbling down our alley in Columbus, Ohio, could raise me from sleep.

4   When he wasn't hauling junk, Jerry fixed things. More than once, he fixed my red bicycle. The gears were always slipping; the chain could turn into a tangled mess. Hearing pain in my voice, Jerry would instruct me to leave my bike on our front porch. In our neighborhood, in the 60's, no one would steal your bike from your porch. Jerry promised me he'd pick it up, and he always did. He never lied to me, and he cautioned me not to tell lies. He was, off and on, my mother's boyfriend. At raucous[2] family gatherings, he'd pull me aside and explain to me the importance of honesty, of doing what one promised to do.

5   And there was Jimmy, my grandfather, who all his life paid his bills the day they arrived: that was a mighty lesson in itself—it taught me a work ethic.[3] He held two jobs, and there were times when he allowed me to accompany him on his night job,

1. **gaping:** open, wide, or obvious

2. **raucous:** loud, harsh, or unpleasant to the ears

3. **ethic:** a set of rules for personal behavior or conduct

when he cleaned a Greek restaurant on the north side of Columbus. Often he'd mop the place twice, as if trying to win some award. He frightened me too. It was not because he was mean. It was because he had exacting standards. He didn't like short-cutters. His instructions, on anything, were to be carried out to the letter. He believed in independence, doing as much for yourself as you possibly could. It should not have surprised me when, one morning while having stomach pains, he chose not to wait for a taxi and instead walked the mile to the local hospital, where he died a week later of stomach cancer.

My uncles provided plenty of good background music when I was coming of age. Uncle Henry took me fishing. He'd phone the night before. "Be ready. Seven o'clock." I'd trail him through woods—as a son does a father—until we found our fishing hole. We'd sit for hours. He taught me patience and an appreciation of the outdoors, of nature. He talked, incessantly,[4] of family—his family, my family, the family of friends. The man had a reverence[5] for family. I knew to listen.

6   I think these underground fathers simply appear, decade to decade, flowing through the generations. Hardly everywhere, and hardly, to be sure, in enough places, but there. As mystical, sometimes, as fate when fate is sweet.

7   Sometimes I think that all these men who have swept in and out of my life still couldn't replace a good, warm father. But inasmuch as I've never known a good, warm father, the men who entered my life, who taught me right from wrong, who did things they were not asked to do, have become unforgettable. I know the cold statistics out there. And yet, the mountain of father-son literature does not haunt me. I've known good black men.

4. **incessantly:** without stopping

5. **reverence:** deep respect

CHECK YOUR COMPREHENSION

1. Which of the following would be the best alternative title for this essay?

   a.   "Fathers and Mothers"

   b.   "The Good Men in My Life"

   c.   "Fishing: What Boys and Grandfathers Do"

   d.   "Disadvantages of Being Raised Without a Father"

2. The main idea of this essay is that

   a.   boys need a father in their lives.

   b.   it's important to teach young boys not to lie.

   c.   statistics about single-parent families cannot be trusted.

   d.   adult men who get involved in a boy's life can keep the boy on the right track.

3. According to Haygood, what did his grandfather Jimmy teach him?

   a.   how to find shortcuts

   b.   how to win awards for good work

   c.   how to work hard and be independent

   d.   how to clean a floor

4. Does this essay include the Four Basics of Illustration? Be prepared to say why or why not.

5. Write sentences using the following vocabulary words: *gaping* (para. 1), *raucous* (4), *work ethic* (5), *incessantly* (6).

READ CRITICALLY

1. Do you think that Haygood provides enough examples to support his main point about father figures?

2. In paragraph 1, Haygood says that the actions of the "underground dads" in his life showed him that they expected him "to do good things in life." What specific actions in paragraphs 2 through 6 illustrate this expectation?

3. Why does Haygood include details about his bicycle in paragraph 4?

4. What does Haygood mean when he says his uncles "provided plenty of good background music" (para. 6) when he was an adolescent?

5. According to this essay, what are the most important things a boy needs to learn from his father or the other adult men in his life?

WRITE

1. Haygood explains that Jerry taught him the importance of keeping promises. Write an illustration paragraph or essay demonstrating why it is important for adults to keep promises to children, using an example to make your point.

2. Some of the significant men in Haygood's life were relatives, including his grandfather and his uncles. Does an adult have to be a family member in order to make a significant impact on a child's life? Write a paragraph or an essay to answer this question, using two or more examples to illustrate your point.

Description

Description creates a strong impression of your topic: It shows how the topic looks, sounds, smells, tastes, or feels.

Four Basics of Description

1 It creates a main impression—an overall effect or image—about the topic.

2 It uses specific examples to create the impression.

3 It supports the examples with details that appeal to the senses—sight, hearing, smell, taste, and touch.

4 It brings a person, a place, or an object to life for the readers.

The numbers and colors in the following paragraph correspond to the Four Basics of Description.

1 Late at night, the ocean near my grandmother's house always fills me with wonder. **2** It is dark, lit only by the moon. **3** When the moon is full, the light reflects off the water, bouncing up and shining on the waves as they start to break. When the clouds cover the moon, the darkness is complete. The world stands still and silent for a moment. **2** Then, I hear the waves **3** coming toward me, swelling, breaking, and bursting into surf that I cannot see. I hear them gently go back, only to start again. **2** Gulls call in the distance. **3** During the day, their call sounds raw, but at night it softens and sounds like a plea. **2** Now that I am in touch with my senses, I am hit with a smell of salt and dampness that **3** seems to coat my lungs. **2** I stand completely still, just experiencing the beach, as if I have become a part of the elements. The experience always calms me and takes away the strains of everyday life.

4 Examples and details bring the subject to life.

1. What impression does the writer want to create? _____

   _____

2. Underline the **topic sentence**.

3. Double-underline the **example** that makes the strongest impression on you. Why did you choose this example? _____

4. Add another sensory detail to one of the examples. _____

   _____

5. Try rewriting the topic sentence. _____

   _____

Guided Outline: Description

Fill in the outline with examples and details that support the topic sentence. Try prewriting to get ideas.

Topic sentence: The _____ on this campus is _____.

First example: _____

   Details: _____

Second example: _____

   Details: _____

Third example: _____

   Details: _____

Concluding sentence: Every time I am there, I think _____

   _____

   _____.

Write a Description Paragraph

Write a description paragraph, using the outline you developed, one of the following topics, or a topic of your own. Then, complete the description checklist on the next page.

- A favorite food
- A photograph
- Your dream house
- A section of the college library
- An alien being

- A home of the future
- A scary person
- A scene that makes you feel threatened
- A pet

USE A VISUAL TO WRITE A DESCRIPTION

Look at the photo below. Write a paragraph describing this food stand.

A food stand at the Florida State Fair.

CHECKLIST

Evaluating Your Description Paragraph

☐ My writing style is appropriate for the audience and purpose. (Most college assignments should be written in formal English.)

☐ The paragraph has the Four Basics of Description (p. 80).

- My topic sentence includes the main impression that I want to create for readers.
- I include specific examples to create the impression.
- I have supported the examples with details that appeal to the senses.

☐ I have included transitions to move readers smoothly from one example to the next.

☐ I have reread the paragraph, making improvements and checking for grammar and spelling errors.

Explore Description Further: The People We Meet and the Places We Go

As you read the sample paragraphs and essays below, look for the Four Basics of Description (p. 80). Also, remember to use the 2PR strategy: preview, read, pause, and review (see pages 6-10).

Student Description Paragraph

Faye Phelps

The Bachelor Life

Faye Phelps is a wife, student, and mother who plans to complete an Office Assistant Certificate at Bay College in Michigan. Phelps wrote this paragraph in response to an assignment that required students to describe a place other than their own homes. She says she wanted to help the reader start at her uncle's front door and have a "clear, picture-perfect" view of his home.

My Uncle Steve is a terminal bachelor and always will be. His house is a direct reflection of his life and how he runs it The first thing that you need to know about him is that he lives, eats, and breathes deer hunting; nothing is more important to him. When you first walk into his house, your nose is assaulted with the smell of man. This is not the smell of an ordinary man but the smell of a Yooper[1] man, which is a combination of Old Spice, hamburger, and dirt. When you walk directly into the kitchen and look to the floor, it is covered with hunter green rugs to cover the linoleum, so mopping

1. **Yooper:** a person from the upper peninsula of Michigan

is not needed. A quick glance to your left, and there is a rug that is covered in every possible style of boot you could imagine: camouflage boots, work boots, mud boots, and waterproof boots. The counter to the left and farther ahead is covered with plastic cups, the same that I drank out of when I was a child. The dish rag draped over the sink appears to be a washcloth that has been retired to the kitchen. The stove, which is next to the sink, has a wide array of spices and seasonings that will be used to complement the latest kill. The kitchen table, which is directly in front of you, has a cutting board for a center piece, with salt, pepper, an ashtray, and the latest issues of *Cabela's*[2] magazine and *Buckmasters*.[3] The fridge that is directly opposite the stove is still covered with pictures of his son, my senior picture, and a fifth grade diploma awarded to my cousin, who is now twenty-two. Next to the fridge, closer to the door, is a counter top; on it is always a candy dish with a deer horn for the handle. To the left is the living room. Statues of bald eagles, bucks leaping over stumps, and randomly found deer horns cover the entertainment center that is directly to your right. In front of the entertainment center is a rocking chair that my grandfather uses. Directly behind the rocking chair is a sofa which I have only witnessed being used once. The lack of furniture and the placement suggests that a woman has never set foot inside this house. When you walk down the hallway, which is off the living room, there are three pictures hanging on the wall to your left: my grandparents' wedding photo, a picture of my late grandmother, and a picture of my Uncle Steve when he was a baby. The first door on the right is my Uncle Steve's bedroom. I have only ever set foot in there once, but it was hard to forget. The wall to my right, all along the floor, consists of a pile almost three feet tall of camouflage hunting bags, more boots, hunting clothes, and anything else directly related to hunting. His bed, which is opposite of the door, is thrown together with a compilation of mismatched pillows and a blanket that resembles a mover's blanket. My Uncle Steve was married once upon a time, and since he is no longer, his house is his. He's not scared of being judged and has no one to answer to. His one hobby in life is hunting and he takes pride in this, with not much worry about other things.

2. Cabela's: a hunting and fishing supply store

3. Buckmasters: name of an organization and magazine devoted to deer hunting

Professional Description Paragraph

Scott Russell Sanders

Excerpt from "The Men We Carry in Our Minds"

Scott Russell Sanders (b. 1945) is an American writer of essays and novels. His nonfiction works include *A Private History of Awe* (2006), *Writing from the Center* (1995), and *A Conservationist Manifesto* (2009). He retired in 2009 after more than 30 years of teaching at Indiana University, but he continues to write. His latest work, a novel entitled *Divine Animal*, was published in 2014.

1. maimed: wounded

The bodies of the men I knew were twisted and maimed[1] in ways visible and invisible. The nails of their hands were black and split, the hands tattooed with scars.

Some had lost fingers. Heavy lifting had given many of them finicky[2] backs and guts weak from hernias.[3] Racing against conveyor belts had given them ulcers. Their ankles and knees ached from years of standing on concrete. Anyone who had worked for long around machines was hard of hearing. They squinted, and the skin of their faces was creased like the leather of old work gloves. There were times, studying them, when I dreaded growing up. Most of them coughed, from dust or cigarettes, and most of them drank cheap wine or whiskey, so their eyes looked bloodshot and bruised. The fathers of my friends always seemed older than the mothers. Men wore out sooner. Only women lived into old age.

2. **finicky:** not consistent; frequently causing problems

3. **hernia:** a medical condition in which a body organ pushes through the walls around it, especially in the abdomen

UNDERSTANDING DESCRIPTION

After you have read the two description paragraphs, complete the following.

1. What is being described in each paragraph?

2. What specific examples or details are given, and what impression do they create?

3. How do the details appeal to the senses?

4. How does the author bring the people or place to life?

Student Description Essay

Andrew Dillon Bustin

Airports Are for People Watching

Andrew Dillon Bustin graduated from Indiana University Bloomington with a degree in geography. Bustin says his educational background has led him to be most interested in writing about the various ways in which people interact with their environment. Of writing itself, Bustin says, "The ability to write and communicate using language is such an amazing human quality. Not only are reading and writing unique to our species, but Americans especially have been granted the right to speak their minds freely. In my opinion, nothing is more powerful than that." His essay "Airports Are for People Watching" came about during a four-hour layover at the Hartsfield-Jackson International Airport in Atlanta.

Guiding question What details does Bustin use to bring to life the people whom he is describing?

1   While waiting for a delayed flight, I examine my fellow passengers. I sit across from the largest man I have ever seen. Everything bulges, sticking out over his wrinkled collar, belt, even his too-short socks. His sneakers are enormous and untied over his fleshy feet. The man has a round chubby face, which reacts to some imaginary conversation. On his left sits another man, shadily[1] whispering business into a cheap-looking cell phone. I imagine he gambles; that's just what his face tells me. A woman nearby plucks[2]

Tip A guiding question can help you focus when you are reading. Make sure you can answer the guiding question when you have finished. For more information on reading and guiding questions, see Chapter 1.

1. **shadily:** in a way that suggests dishonest or even criminal activities

2. **plucks:** picks, quickly removes from its place

3. **demolished:** destroyed

4. **slouch:** drooping posture

5. **monotone:** unchanging in pitch

6. **goes ballistic:** becomes very angry

7. **clout:** influence, power

8. **intimidated:** filled with fear

mascara clots from her eyes. She has just demolished[3] a chicken sandwich and has a glob of mayo on her left cheek. Farther down the row sits a man who looks exactly like an old history teacher of mine: bald, skinny, with a sour, disapproving expression. It takes me a moment to convince myself, with great relief, that it is not my old teacher, and I recover from my momentary slouch[4] of inferiority.

2   Approaching from my right is a pretty young lady with tight pants. She passes close by me, leaving a trail of perfume behind her. She is not quite my type but has a nice walk to her, a gentle, regular sway. Somehow unimpressed, I keep on looking about. There is so much going on here at once, so much activity. People are drifting along in their own worlds, ignorant of mine or anyone else's. They are reading papers, crossing and uncrossing their legs, shifting in their seats looking for a comfortable position, chewing gum, biting nails, nodding to music silently pulsing on their iPods. They are texting, typing, yawning, anything to pass the time. The clack of heels running down the hall and the sounds of suitcase wheels rolling keep an uneven beat. Women in wheelchairs have wandering eyes. We are a tired group, bored but expectant.

3   Suddenly, everyone turns and strains to hear a monotone[5] voice crackling bad news over the loudspeaker. We whine and moan, grind our teeth and groan. One dude just goes ballistic.[6] He yells and points, waves his arms all around. About every twenty seconds, he backs off from the counter and paces around in a circle, gathering his thoughts. Then, he renews his attacks. We all watch as two big security guys march up looking mean, heat and cuffs hanging by their belts with clout.[7] The argumentative one, who—judging by his thin beard really could not be more than seventeen—calms down immediately. Noticeably intimidated[8] by their obvious authority, the boy apologizes and nervously explains himself. We are all slightly disappointed that the drama is over.

4   If you pay attention, sitting in an airport can be like watching a movie, with all different kinds of people, activities, and emotions. As a dog barks and a baby wails, I shift my eyes to the gate next to ours, where lucky passengers are boarding. People circle the boarding area, straining for their numbers to be called. Children throw last waves and blow kisses to their grandparents. A soldier embraces his wife and shakes his young son's hand. Others stare straight ahead, faces blank. We all have our stories, some of which can be imagined from the momentary glimpses we get at the airport.

CHECK YOUR COMPREHENSION

1.   Which of the following would be the best alternative title for the essay?

    a.   "Today's Airport Delays Drive Me Crazy"

    b.   "Scenes from an Airport Departure Lounge"

    c.   "The Guy Who Went Ballistic at the Airport"

    d.   "Telling My Own Personal Story at the Airport"

2. The main idea of this essay is that

    a. when their flights get delayed, people at airports become rude and impatient.

    b. an airport is a good place to watch people and imagine their stories.

    c. air travel is much more entertaining than traveling by car or train.

    d. parents should watch their children carefully at airports.

3. How does Bustin describe himself and his fellow travelers?

    a. They are intimidated, angry, and apologetic.

    b. They are delayed, lucky, and obvious.

    c. They are ignorant, imaginary, and sour.

    d. They are tired, bored, and expectant.

4. Does this essay include the Four Basics of Description? Be prepared to say why or why not.

5. Write sentences using the following vocabulary words: *pluck, demolish, slouch* (para. 1); *clout, intimidate* (3).

READ CRITICALLY

1. How many of the five senses does Bustin appeal to in this essay? Find examples.

2. Bustin says that the face of the man with the cell phone "tells" him that the man gambles (para. 1). Do you think it is possible to "read" faces in this way and learn about people's lives?

3. Why do you think that the writer reacts as he does to the man who looks like his old history teacher?

4. What is Bustin's tone in this essay? Does he seem to be judging his fellow passengers, or does he appear to be a neutral observer? What gives you this impression, either way?

5. When the security guards arrive and the angry teenager calms down and apologizes, why are the writer and the other observers "slightly disappointed" (para. 3)?

WRITE

1. Bustin does his people watching at an airport, where he imagines people's stories from "momentary glimpses" of their lives (para. 4). Go to another place where you can watch many people, and write your own description about whom and what you see. Try to be as specific, vivid, and imaginative as possible.

2. In "Airports Are for People Watching," the writer looks at other people but does not consider how others see him. Reflect on how you look to others—your appearance, your clothing, your face, your actions—and then describe how other people might see you and imagine your personality or life.

Professional Description Essay

Amy Tan

Fish Cheeks

Amy Tan was born in 1952, the daughter of Chinese immigrants. She studied at San Jose State University, where she earned a B.A. in English and Linguistics and an M.A. in Linguistics. Her first novel, *The Joy Luck Club,* was published in 1989, and it was a finalist for the National Book Award. Since then, she has published *The Kitchen God's Wife* (1991), *The Hundred Secret Senses* (1995), *The Bonesetter's Daughter* (2000), *Saving Fish from Drowning* (2005), and *The Valley of Amazement* (2013).

Guiding question What details does Amy Tan use to describe herself and her family?

1   I fell in love with the minister's son the winter I turned fourteen. He was not Chinese, but as white as Mary in the manger. For Christmas I prayed for this blond-haired boy, Robert, and a slim new American nose.

2   When I found out that my parents had invited the minister's family over for Christmas Eve dinner, I cried. What would Robert think of our shabby Chinese Christmas? What would he think of our noisy Chinese relatives who lacked proper American manners? What terrible disappointment would he feel upon seeing not a roasted turkey and sweet potatoes but Chinese food?

3   On Christmas Eve I saw that my mother had outdone herself in creating a strange menu. She was pulling black veins out of the backs of fleshy prawns.[1] The kitchen was littered with appalling[2] mounds of raw food: A slimy rock cod with bulging eyes that pleaded not to be thrown into a pan of hot oil. Tofu, which looked like stacked wedges of rubbery white sponges. A bowl soaking dried fungus back to life. A plate of squid, their backs crisscrossed with knife markings so they resembled bicycle tires.

4   And then they arrived—the minister's family and all my relatives in a clamor[3] of doorbells and rumpled Christmas packages. Robert grunted hello, and I pretended he was not worthy of existence.

5   Dinner threw me deeper into despair. My relatives licked the ends of their chopsticks and reached across the table, dipping them into the dozen or so plates of food. Robert and his family waited patiently for platters to be passed to them. My relatives murmured with pleasure when my mother brought out the whole steamed fish. Robert grimaced.[4] Then my father poked his chopsticks just below the fish eye and plucked out the soft meat. "Amy, your favorite," he said, offering me the tender fish cheek. I wanted to disappear.

1. **prawns:** sea creatures similar to shrimp

2. **appalling:** causing shock or horror

3. **clamor:** a loud or disruptive noise

4. **grimaced:** made a face that shows disgust or pain

6   At the end of the meal my father leaned back and belched loudly, thanking my mother for her fine cooking. "It's a polite Chinese custom to show you are satisfied," explained my father to our astonished guests. Robert was looking down at his plate with a reddened face. The minister managed to muster up[5] a quiet burp. I was stunned into silence for the rest of the night.

5. **muster (up):** to summon; pull together

7   After everyone had gone, my mother said to me, "You want to be the same as American girls on the outside." She handed me an early gift. It was a miniskirt in beige tweed. "But inside you must always be Chinese. You must be proud you are different. Your only shame is to have shame."

8   And even though I didn't agree with her then, I knew that she understood how much I had suffered during the evening's dinner. It wasn't until many years later— long after I had gotten over my crush on Robert—that I was able to fully appreciate her lesson and the true purpose behind our particular menu. For Christmas Eve that year, she had chosen all my favorite foods.

CHECK YOUR COMPREHENSION

1. Which of the following would be the best alternative title for the essay?
   a. "Christmas Traditions Around the World"
   b. "The Lesson My Mother Taught Me"
   c. "Chinese vs. American Food and Customs"
   d. "Awkward Moments for Teenaged Girls"

2. The main idea of this essay is that
   a. immigrants to the United States should adopt American customs.
   b. immigrants to the United States should not adopt American traditions.
   c. people should not be ashamed of their culture and heritage.
   d. parents should make an effort not to embarrass their children.

3. According to Tan, as a teenager
   a. she did not enjoy Chinese food.
   b. she looked like other girls her age in the United States.
   c. she wanted to fit in with American children.
   d. she did not know how to eat with chopsticks.

4. Does this essay include the Four Basics of Description? Be prepared to say why or why not.

5. Write sentences using the following vocabulary words: *appalling* (para. 3); *clamor* (4); *grimaced* (5); and *muster* (6).

READ CRITICALLY

1. What is Tan's purpose in this essay?

2. Tan gives her reader very little information about her appearance in paragraph 1, but the details she does give are very important. What can the reader learn about her physical appearance from these details? Why is this information important to the essay?

3. In paragraph 3, Tan describes the traditional Chinese food that her mother prepares. What details bring this description to life for the reader? How do these details appeal to the senses?

4. Some of the details in paragraph 3 are written as sentence fragments (incomplete thoughts). Identify these fragments. What effect do these fragments have on the reader? Try rewriting these sentences so that they are complete thoughts. What effect do your changes make?

5. In the final paragraphs of the essay, Tan quotes her mother. Why is it important for the reader to "hear" the mother's voice? How do her words support the main idea of the essay?

WRITE

1. Amy Tan describes her family's traditional Chinese meal and her embarrassment as she realizes that the minister's family is not comfortable during this meal. In a paragraph, describe a place, a situation, or a person that made you feel embarrassed or uncomfortable. Be sure to provide details that will bring the place, situation, or person to life for your readers.

2. Describe yourself at an earlier time in your life. Provide details that will help your readers picture who you were and what was important to you at that time in your life.

Chapter Review

1. What does a narration paragraph do? _____

_____

_____

_____

2. What does an illustration paragraph do? _____

_____

_____

_____

3. What does a description paragraph do? _____

_____

_____

_____

REFLECTING ON THE JOURNEY

Skills Learned

Now that you've completed the chapter, share what you've learned about each skill by completing the following chart.

Skill	What I learned about this skill
Write a narration paragraph (tell a story to make a point)	
Write an illustration paragraph (use examples to make a point)	
Write a description paragraph (describe a topic to make an impression)	

7

Developing Process-Analysis, Classification, and Definition Paragraphs

Three More Ways to Present Your Ideas

Learning Objectives

Chapter Goal: Write paragraphs using different patterns of development: process analysis, classification, and definition.

Tools to Achieve the Goal

- Four Basics of Process Analysis (p. 93)
- Sample process-analysis paragraphs and essays (p. 95)
- Four Basics of Classification (p. 102)
- Sample classification paragraphs and essays (p. 106)
- Four Basics of Definition (p. 113)
- Sample definition paragraphs and essays (p. 116)

READING ROADMAP

Key Terms

Skim Chapter 7 before you begin reading. Can you find each of these words in **bold** type? Put a check mark next to each word once you have located it in the chapter.

_____ process analysis   _____ classification
_____ topic sentence   _____ definition
_____ transitions

Highlight or circle any of these words that you already know.

Before You Read

Before you begin reading this chapter, fill out the following chart. For each skill, think of a time when you have used this skill and what you would like to know on completing the chapter. At the end of the chapter, you will be asked to share what you learned about this skill.

Skill	When I have used this skill	What I want to know about this skill
Write a process analysis (explain how something works or how to do something)		
Write a classification paragraph (sort a topic into categories)		
Write a definition paragraph (explain what a topic means)		

In Chapter 6, you discovered three ways to develop a paragraph: narration, illustration, and description. In this chapter, you will learn about three additional patterns for developing paragraphs: process analysis, classification, and definition.

Process Analysis

Process analysis explains either how to do something (so that readers can do it) or how something works (so that readers understand it).

Four Basics of Process Analysis

> 1 It tells readers either how to do the steps of the process or how something works.
>
> 2 It includes the major steps in the process.
>
> 3 It explains each step in detail.
>
> 4 It presents the steps in the order they happen (time order).

The numbers and colors in the following paragraph correspond to the Four Basics of Process Analysis.

People always ask for the recipe for the simplest cookie that I make, and I am always a little embarrassed to give it to them. **1** Here is how to make delicious cookies with almost no effort. **2** First, buy two ingredients—a roll of sugar-cookie dough from your supermarket's refrigerated section and a bag of mini peanut butter cups. Cut the roll into half-inch slices, and then cut each slice in half. Next, roll the pieces into balls. Then, grease a mini-muffin pan and put the balls in the pan. Start baking the dough according to the directions on the sugar-cookie package. When the cookies are about three minutes from being done, take them out. Press a peanut butter cup into the center of each ball, and return the cookies to the oven until they are golden brown. When they are cool, pop them out of the muffin pans. These cookies are so easy to make that even little children can help. Enjoy!

> 1 Readers told how to do something
>
> 3 Steps explained in detail
>
> 4 Steps presented in the order they need to happen

1. Underline the **topic sentence**.

2. How many steps does the writer describe? _____

3. Could you perform the process after reading the paragraph? If not, where do you need more information? _____

4. Circle the **transitions**.

5. Which of the Four Basics does this paragraph lack? _____
   Revise the paragraph so that it includes this basic.

Guided Outline: Process Analysis

Fill in the outline with the steps in the process and detailed explanations of them. Try prewriting to get ideas, and organize the steps according to time order.

Topic sentence: Learning how to _____

(something you do well) is not hard if you _____

_____.

First step: _____

    Explanation: _____

Second step: _____

    Explanation: _____

Third step: _____

    Explanation: _____

Concluding sentence: _____ takes some practice

and concentration, but anyone can do it.

Write a Process-Analysis Paragraph

Write a process-analysis paragraph, using the outline that you developed, one of the following topics, or a topic of your own. Then, complete the process-analysis checklist on page 95.

- How to use a cell phone
- How to find a book in a library
- How to make someone (a partner, a coworker, a teacher) mad
- How to find information on the Web

- How to make something
- How to fail a test
- How to get a bargain
- How to make a good impression at a job interview
- How to find a job

USE A VISUAL TO WRITE PROCESS ANALYSIS

Look at the photo below. Write a paragraph that explains how to write a good resume.

VARTANOV ANATOLY/SHUTTERSTOCK

> **CHECKLIST**
>
> **Evaluating Your Process-Analysis Paragraph**
>
> ☐ My writing style is appropriate for the audience and purpose. (Most college assignments should be written in formal English.)
>
> ☐ The paragraph has the Four Basics of Process Analysis (p. 93).
>
> - My topic sentence tells readers what process I am writing about in this paragraph, and it is confident (without *I think* or *I hope*).
>
> - I have included all the major steps and details about them.
>
> - I have included time-order transitions to move readers smoothly from one step to the next.
>
> ☐ I have reread the paragraph, making at least three improvements and checking for grammar and spelling errors.

Explore Process Analysis Further: Skills for Success

As you read the sample paragraphs and essays below, look for the Four Basics of Process Analysis (p. 93). Also, remember to use the 2PR strategy: preview, read, pause, and review (see pages 6-10).

Student Process-Analysis Paragraph

Jonathan Simon-Valdez

Impossible, Difficult, Done

When his teacher asked him to write a process-analysis paragraph to illustrate the theme "Impossible, Difficult, Done," Jonathan Simon-Valdez chose to write about his own efforts to get in shape.

    A lot of people have done something in their lifetime that they originally deemed[1] impossible, whether it is playing a sport, achieving a good grade in school, or even training a pet. For the past three months, I have been doing something that I thought was impossible: getting in shape. It seemed impossible to me because of the fact that I have never been physically active. Just the thought of an exercise routine seemed impossible to me when I started. In fact, I needed to get in shape and be more physically active because I spent most of my time drinking, smoking, and eating unhealthy foods. My first step was changing the way I ate and other unhealthy habits. I started eating smaller meal portions and more fruits and vegetables; for example, when I woke up, I would eat apples or bananas. I also stopped smoking cigarettes and cut my drinking habits. Second, I needed to get physically active, and what better way to do that than go to the gym? Now I go to the Student Union Building to work out almost every

1. **deemed:** thought or held an opinion

day except Saturdays and Sundays, when it is closed. When I'm at the gym, I spend 30 minutes on the treadmill and 30 minutes lifting weights. Finally, I made my changes into a daily routine; now I make sure that I have time to work out, and I make sure that I eat healthy foods. Before I started this process, I weighed myself, and after three months passed, I weighed again: I lost 20 pounds. Losing weight has been the biggest reward for getting into shape. I feel more confident about myself, and the thought that I continue to lose weight makes me happy.

Professional Process-Analysis Paragraph

Federal Trade Commission

Building a Better Credit Report

The following paragraph is from **www.ftc.gov**, the Web site of the Federal Trade Commission, the consumer protection agency of the U.S. government. The paragraph is part of a larger discussion of how people can improve their credit report—a record of their financial habits and financial health. Among other purposes for these reports, lenders review them when deciding whether to extend credit to those who apply for it.

1. **assessment:** review

The first step toward taking control of your financial situation is to do a realistic assessment[1] of how much money you take in and how much money you spend. Start by listing your income from all sources. Then, list your "fixed" expenses—those that are the same each month—like mortgage payments or rent, car payments, and insurance premiums. Next, list the expenses that vary—like entertainment, recreation, and clothing. Writing down all your expenses, even those that seem insignificant,[2] is a helpful way to track your spending patterns, identify necessary expenses, and prioritize[3] the rest. The goal is to make sure you can make ends meet on the basics: housing, food, health care, insurance, and education.

2. **insignificant:** small; unimportant
3. **prioritize:** put in order of importance

UNDERSTANDING PROCESS ANALYSIS

After you have read the two process-analysis paragraphs, complete the following.

1. What process is being described in each paragraph?

2. Underline the major steps in each process.

3. What details are given to help explain the steps?

4. What is the result or purpose of completing these steps?

Student Process-Analysis Essay

Rashad Brown

When I Grow Up I Wanna Be . . .

Rashad Brown, who is pursuing a double major in communications and popular music at Catawba College, wrote the following essay for the college's student newspaper, the *Pioneer*. He says, "My passion for music and the arts was the force that inspired me to pursue music/entertainment journalism. It was the logical path for me to choose since it combined the two things I excelled at in school, music and writing." In addition to writing for the *Pioneer*, Brown is a music scholar for Catawba's Omwake-Dearborn Chapel and a music intern for the First United Church of Christ in Salisbury, North Carolina. He sings in five different musical groups, from choral to popular music.

The following piece, Brown says, "was inspired by my actual life."

Guiding question   What are the keys to success according to Brown?

1   How many times can you recall saying this famous phrase throughout your childhood: "When I grow up I want to be a fire fighter, no an astronaut, no a rock star!!!" It seems that during our youth the possibilities were endless. Now as young college students, we study to receive the credentials to pursue the careers we are interested in. But besides credentials, how do you actually achieve the career path of your choosing?

2   There are a set of steps that, if put into practice, can lead to immense success. They are to LOOK, KNOW, PERFECT, and BE the part.

Look the Part

3   A wise friend of mine once said . . . "When you wish to be in a specific industry, you must dress the part." This means dress for success. You would never see a person pursuing a career as a doctor walking into an interview dressed as an auto mechanic. Tailor your wardrobe so that it complements, not overshadows, you. Also, make it a habit of keeping up that appearance. Practice, for instance, dressing for your career each day. You never know who is watching you, so try to look your best at all times.

Know the Part

4   To truly be a success at any career, you must be knowledgeable about it. Last year, I was privileged to work with rock composer Eric Whitacre. He shared the story of how he decided to pursue a career in music. He went on to say, "I realized very early that music was my true calling, so the only option I had for myself was to work my butt off and be the best I could possibly be." This is the way everyone should think. To be as good as you can at what you do, know your industry inside and out. The more knowledgeable you are, the more sought after you will be in your industry.

Tip A guiding question can help you focus when you are reading. Make sure you can answer the guiding question when you have finished. For more information on reading and guiding questions, see Chapter 1.

Perfect the Part

5   It is said that practice makes perfect. So push yourself, don't just do the bare minimum. Find ways to challenge yourself in your industry. It will make your job much more fulfilling and help you to become better simultaneously.[1]

1. **simultaneously:** at the same time

Be the Part

6   Embrace your career; make it a part of yourself as a whole. A career is supposed to be something that makes you better; if it doesn't, then it's just a job. Everyone knows that though a job may pay the bills, most people do not care much for them. But a career is something that you can wake up each morning looking forward to.

7   If you follow these basic steps and work hard, the sky is the limit. Remember that nothing comes easy, but with a little hard work and dedication, you can have the career you've always dreamed of.

CHECK YOUR COMPREHENSION

1. Which of the following would be the best alternative title for this essay?
   a.   "Dress for Success"
   b.   "Steps to Success"
   c.   "Interviewing for Your Dream Job"
   d.   "How to Write a Cover Letter"

2. The main idea of this essay is that
   a.   if you work hard and set your mind to it, you can have the career you want.
   b.   most people don't like their work, so it is best to settle for the highest-paying job you can find.
   c.   if you dress appropriately, everything else will fall into place.
   d.   most children don't grow up to be what they thought they would.

3. According to the essay, a career is supposed to
   a.   make you lots of money.
   b.   pay the bills.
   c.   make you better.
   d.   provide you with nice clothes.

4. Does this essay include the Four Basics of Process Analysis? Be prepared to say why or why not.

5. Write a sentence using the following vocabulary word: *simultaneously* (para. 5).

1. Who is Brown's intended audience? Are his style and tone appropriate for this audience?

2. What point does Brown want the reader to get? What does he say to back up that point?

3. What are the major steps that Brown includes in his process-analysis essay?

4. How does Brown describe the difference between a job and a career? Do you agree or disagree with the author?

5. Reread the last paragraph of the essay. Based on your own experience and that of people you know, do you think Brown is right? What other factors might help a person get his or her dream career?

1. Write about a process that is familiar to you, either through first-hand experience (for example, changing a flat tire) or from reading about it (for example, how a microwave oven works). When you write, be sure to have a specific audience in mind, and keep your tone focused on that audience.

2. Brown's first piece of advice is to "Look the Part." Using a step-by-step guide, write about how you would, or perhaps already do, dress for your own career. (If you are unsure of your career choice, pick one you might like or one that a friend has chosen.)

Professional Process-Analysis Essay

Ron Friedman

When to Schedule Your Most Important Work

Ron Friedman, founder of the consulting firm ignite80, holds a Ph.D. in social psychology. His book *The Best Place to Work: The Art and Science of Creating an Extraordinary Workplace* was published in December 2014. Friedman wrote the following blog for the *Harvard Business Review*.

Guiding question How should we schedule important work during the day, according to Friedman?

1   If you work with a team, chances are your inbox is often flooded with invitations. Internal meetings, client conference calls, the occasional lunch request. Assuming you have some control over your calendar, how you respond to these

offers generally depends on two factors: the value of attending the meeting and your availability.

2   Rarely, however, do most consider a third factor in our decision-making criteria: the time of day when you are at your most productive.

3   By now, you've probably noticed that the person you are midway through the afternoon is not the same person who arrived first thing in the morning. Research shows our cognitive[1] functioning fluctuates[2] throughout the day. If you're like most people, you'll find that you can get a lot done between 9:00am and 11:00am. Not so at 2:30pm. Later in the day, it often feels like we're moving at a fraction of our morning pace.

4   That's not an illusion. Recent studies have found that on average, people are considerably worse at absorbing new information, planning ahead and resisting distractions as the day progresses.

5   The reason this happens is not merely motivational. It's biological. Our bodies run on a circadian[3] rhythm that affects our hormone production, brain wave activities, and body temperature. Each of these variations tinkers[4] with our energy level, impacting our alertness and productivity.

6   Importantly, we don't all follow identical patterns. While most people do their best work in the morning (and our preference for mornings tends to increase with age), others are night owls who are more productive later in the day. Research suggests that our fondness for morning or evenings isn't simply a personal preference— it's directly tied to the time of day when our physical and cognitive abilities peak. And one new study has even found that morning people are more ethical[5] in the morning—and night owls, more ethical later in the day.

7   To get the most out of every day, you need to guard the hours when you are at your most productive. Think back to yesterday and the day before. At which points of your day did you *feel* at your most energetic? Chances are, these are times with the highest productivity potential.

8   Once you've identified high-potential hours, consider treating them differently— for example, by blocking them off on your calendar. This discourages colleagues with access to your availabilities from suggesting these times for meetings. An additional advantage of having high-potential hours blocked off is that it prompts[6] you to think twice before suggesting your own nonessential meetings at that time.

9   Proactively[7] setting aside your best hours to get work done saves you from having to scramble later on to compensate.[8] Use these hours for working on high-priority projects, making decisions you've been avoiding, or initiating a difficult conversation.

10   And, if you're the owner of a dull, 10 a.m. staff meeting, do your team a favor and reschedule it for after lunch. The afternoon is when most people's energy levels naturally dip. Lower energy levels can be disastrous for work that requires deep focus, but is considerably less detrimental[9] in the context of other people. Having others around also naturally increases our alertness levels, helping counteract the slump in energy.

11   Fatigue, it's worth noting, is not all bad. In fact, the findings of a 2011 study suggest that when our minds are tired, we are more distractible and less adept[10] at filtering out seemingly irrelevant ideas. The free association that ensues[11] makes "off-peak" hours an ideal time for finding novel[12] solutions.

1. **cognitive:** related to the mind, thinking, or reasoning
2. **fluctuate:** change, move up and down

3. **circadian:** related to body patterns or rhythms occurring in 24-hour cycles
4. **tinker:** make small changes in something, often with unpredictable results

5. **ethical:** morally good

6. **prompt:** suggest or encourage an action

7. **proactively:** before or in advance of an expected problem
8. **compensate:** make up for or pay for what has been lost

9. **detrimental:** harmful

10. **adept:** capable of or skilled at
11. **ensues:** follows as a result of something
12. **novel:** new

12   Ultimately, the best way to schedule is to take our natural energy fluctuations into account. You can maximize your productivity by calibrating activities to the right time of day. If a task requires willpower and complex thinking, plan to do it when you are at your most alert. In contrast, if what you're after is a fresh perspective, use fatigue to your advantage by looking for solutions when your energy drops.

13   In either case, protect your best hours. If *you* don't do it, who will?

CHECK YOUR COMPREHENSION

1. Which of the following would be the best alternative title for this essay?
    a. "How to Stay Awake Throughout Your Day"
    b. "Night Owls and Morning People"
    c. "How to Avoid Stress At Work"
    d. "How to Make the Best Use of Your Time"

2. The main idea of this essay is that
    a. people do their best work in the morning.
    b. people should plan to do their most difficult work when their energy level is highest.
    c. being around other people helps us stay focused.
    d. you cannot change your body's preference for morning or evening.

3. According to the essay, people should not do which of the following when they are at a "high-potential" or high-energy time of day?
    a. start a difficult conversation
    b. work on an important project
    c. make major decisions
    d. schedule boring meetings

4. Does this essay include the Four Basics of Process Analysis? Be prepared to say why or why not.

5. Write a sentence using the following vocabulary words: *fluctuate* (para. 3); *tinker* (5), *proactively, compensate* (9); *adept* (11).

READ CRITICALLY

1. Who is Friedman's intended audience? How do his examples and word choice reflect his audience?

2. Does Friedman believe that fatigue is always a problem? Explain.

3. What are the major steps that Friedman includes in his process-analysis essay?

4. According to Friedman, how can a person discover his or her most productive time of day? What is your most productive time of day?

5. Can Friedman's advice be applied to students? How would your schedule for work, school, and study change if you followed his advice?

WRITE

1. All of the writing in this section explains how to make changes for success, from finances and health to the workplace. What is one part of your life you have changed successfully? Explain your process, making sure to show the major steps you followed to make the change.

2. Just as people are more productive at different times of the day, students may study most effectively in different ways: some work best by talking in groups and listening to information (auditory learners); some study successfully by reading, writing, and reviewing notes and diagrams (visual learners); and some perform well by moving their hands or feet while studying (kinesthetic learners). Write a paragraph or essay recommending steps for studying according to your preferred learning style. Be sure to identify your style, and provide at least three tips or strategies for studying successfully.

Classification

Classification sorts people or things into categories so that they can be understood.

Four Basics of Classification

1. It makes sense of a group of people or things by sorting them into useful categories.
2. It has a purpose for sorting.
3. It includes categories that follow a single organizing principle (for example, to sort by size, by color, by price, and so on).
4. It gives detailed examples or explanations of things that fit into each category.

The numbers and colors in the following paragraph correspond to the Four Basics of Classification.

1 Over the past several years, three kinds of diets have been 2 very popular in this country. 3 The first one was the low-fat diet. 4 Dieters had to limit their fat intake, so they stayed away from foods like nuts, fatty meats, ice cream, and fried foods. They could eat lots of low-fat foods like pasta, bread, fruits, and vegetables, as well as lean meat, fish, and chicken. 3 The second kind of diet was the low-carbohydrate plan. 4 The first popular low-carb diet was the Atkins plan. Under this plan, dieters could eat all the

fatty meats, butter, cheese, and nuts they wanted. Some people were eating a whole pound of bacon for breakfast with eggs and butter. However, they could not eat bread, pasta, or most fruits. On this plan, people lost a lot of weight quickly, but many found that they could not stick with a diet that did not allow carbs. The South Beach diet was also a low-carb plan, but not quite as strict as the Atkins diet, at least after the first two weeks. **3** The third diet plan, one that has been around for a long time, is Weight Watchers. **4** It requires that dieters eat smaller portions of most foods—everything in moderation. Points are assigned to foods, and dieters must stay within a certain number of points each day. High-calorie foods have a high number of points, and many vegetables have no points. Americans have spent millions on these diet plans, but the obesity rate continues to increase. It seems that the "right" kind of diet, one that allows people to lose weight and keep it off, has yet to be invented.

1. Underline the **topic sentence**.

2. What are the categories? _____

   _____

3. Circle the **transitions**.

4. What is the purpose of the classification? _____

5. What is the organizing principle? _____

6. Try rewriting the concluding sentence in your own words. _____

   _____

Guided Outline: Classification

Fill in the outline with the categories and detailed examples or explanations of what fits into them. Try prewriting to get ideas.

Topic sentence: Like most people, I have several different kinds of

_____ (collections / clothes / coworkers / moods . . .).

First category: _____

   Example/explanation of what fits into the category: _____

   _____

   _____

   _____

   _____

   _____

Second category: _____

    Example/explanation of what fits into the category: _____

    _____

    _____

Third category: _____

    Example/explanation of what fits into the category: _____

    _____

    _____

Concluding sentence: Even though my _____ are

different, they are all _____ to me.

Write a Classification Paragraph

Write a classification paragraph, using the outline that you developed, one of the following topics, or a topic of your own. Then, complete the classification checklist below.

- Kinds of music
- Kinds of attitudes
- Kinds of television programs
- Kinds of drivers
- Kinds of cars

- Kinds of clutter in your room or home
- Kinds of students
- Kinds of movies
- Kinds of smells

CHECKLIST

Evaluating Your Classification Paragraph

☐ My writing style is appropriate for the audience and purpose. (Most college assignments should be written in formal English.)

☐ The paragraph has the Four Basics of Classification (p. 102).

- My topic sentence states what I am sorting and shows my purpose for classifying.

- I have an organizing principle.

- I have stated the categories and given examples of what is in them.

- I have included transitions to move readers smoothly from one category to the next.

☐ I have reread the paragraph, making improvements and checking for grammar and spelling errors.

USE A VISUAL TO WRITE CLASSIFICATION

Look at the photos below. Write a paragraph that classifies at least four types of weddings. Then, complete the classification checklist on page 104.

© MIKE WATSON/MOODBOARD/CORBIS

© BEN PIPE/ROBERT HARDING WORLD IMAGERY/CORBIS

© ROY MCMAHON/CORBIS

BARRIE NEIL/ALAMY

Explore Classification Further: Types of People We Meet

As you read the sample paragraphs and essays below, look for the Four Basics of Classification (p. 102). Also, remember to use the 2PR strategy: preview, read, pause, and review (see pages 6-10).

Student Classification Paragraph

Kristy Fouch

Servers

Kristy Fouch grew up in a military family, and she traveled extensively, living for a time in Okinawa, Japan, and Taif, Saudi Arabia. She is currently a student in the Medical Billing and Coding Program at Lord Fairfax Community College in Virginia.

There are several different types of servers in restaurants: the forgetful servers, the overly crowding servers, the unhappy servers who don't really like their jobs, and the good servers. The forgetful server is, of course, the one to whom you have to say the same thing multiple times, such as asking him or her to bring the lemons for your water. Next, the overly crowding server is the one who seems to be almost on top of you every time you turn around, standing right next to you as you are eating. It is easy to pick out the third kind of servers, the ones who really do not like their job and just want to go home. With their eye on the clock, they make you feel as if they are rushing you out. Lastly, there are your overall good servers. These servers check back at just the right time, keep your drinks full, and have a pleasurable attitude. In their line of work, in fact, their service is reflected in the amount of money they bring home. Being a server in the past has helped me identify different types of servers, given me a different outlook, and definitely played a part in determining the amount of tip I leave.

Professional Classification Paragraph

Marvin Montgomery

Types of Salespeople

Marvin Montgomery is an author, trainer, and motivational speaker. His blog, "Ask the Sales Doctor," appears in *Smart Business Blog*. In this paragraph, Montgomery categorizes types of sales people.

When I look back over the last 46 years of my career in sales and professional sales training, I have noticed that there are three different types of salespeople. The first type is "Those who let it happen." They are not organized, nor are they in control of the sales process. The second type is "Those who wonder what happened." This type does no follow-up or follow-through after the initial appointment. They are still waiting for the prospect to contact them and close the sale themselves. Then there is the third type, which is also the minority—"Those who make it happen." This is the type that doesn't wait for their ship to come in; they swim out to it. They have the self-discipline to do what is required when it's required, whether they feel like it or not. It's no coincidence that they are also the ones that consistently achieve (and exceed) their sales goals. The question is: Which one are you?

UNDERSTANDING CLASSIFICATION

After you have read the two classification paragraphs, complete the following.

1. Underline the broad subject that the writers are classifying in each paragraph.

2. Double-underline the categories that each paragraph uses to sort the broad subject.

3. Does each writer provide definition, examples, or description for the categories? Identify one supporting detail from each paragraph.

4. What is the purpose of each paragraph?

Student Classification Essay

Lauren Woodrell

Cheating

Lauren Woodrell began her studies at Lord Fairfax Community College in Middletown, Virginia. She is currently a student at the University of Virginia. In this essay, Woodrell addresses three types of cheating that she has encountered in her school career.

Guiding question What are the three categories of cheating Woodrell introduces?

1   The test was excruciatingly[1] painful. Arianna studied for hours over the weekend but she still couldn't figure out how to solve this rate of change problem. She threw her head back in exasperation[2] and let out a hefty sigh. How could she be so stupid? She glanced over and noticed David lifting up his paper and looking under it. That cheater wrote the formulas and things to remember on his desk! She turned in her test, which was destined to be an F, and on the way out the door she told David, "I can't believe you cheated!" He just looked at her, shrugged his shoulders, and walked away.

2   The next day in class, Arianna got her paper back with a 54 written in blood red ink. Glancing to her side, she noticed that Cheater David got a 92. Maybe cheaters really do succeed.

Tip A guiding question can help you focus when you are reading. Make sure you can answer the guiding question when you have finished. For more information on reading and guiding questions, see Chapter 1.

1. **excruciatingly:** causing intense suffering, to the point of being unbearable

2. **exasperation:** a state of great frustration

3. **escalate:** cause to grow

3   Cheating is depressingly common among students. We live in a world where cheating engulfs us. It is so much a part of society that we have become immune to it. If we can deceive just a little more than someone else, we believe we accomplish so much more and use our deception to escalate[3] our success above our competition. Society has taught us to cheat. Where will this form of deception lead us? Cheating in the academic world is not going to kill us, but there can only be harm in the long run, with no positive outcomes.

4   Cheating is defined by dictionary.com as:

—**verb** (when *intransitive usually followed by "on"*)

1. to deceive or practice deceit, especially for one's own gain; trick or swindle (someone)

2. (*intransitive*) to obtain unfair advantage by trickery

This definition supports the idea that cheating, especially in scholastic situations, has many different forms.

Home-No-Work

4. **divvy up:** divide (informal)

5   Home-no-work is when a student takes the concept of "work" out of homework. Home-no-work occurs in two different situations: when a group of close friends divvy up[4] the work then circulate their papers to copy down the answers that they didn't get themselves and when people make "friends" with smart people so that they can copy their homework.

6   Most people may not view this as cheating but as some version of "group work." Of course there are major advantages to working in groups for studying or doing homework and, if done right, the advantage gained is surprisingly big. Group work, however, is not home-no-work, because we are actually doing work. When we practice home-no-work, any work is too much work. We all know that in group work we have to sit together, look at each individual question, discuss possible answers, then write something down in our own words. Phew. Even the thought is exasperating. If we just split it up or beg that nice nerd in the front row, we can get the same grade. What's wrong with doing less work and getting the same grade? Everybody wins. Think about it this way, though: that girl in the front row who did her own homework will receive the same grade as the group that did a fraction of the work she did, but she may actually remember it. Did everyone truly win?

Clever Testing

7   Today, the idea of the clever tester has dramatically changed since when our grandparents and parents went to school. Instead of being someone who tests really well, the clever tester is the person who can use his or her surroundings to get a very good grade. Examples of taking advantage of surroundings range from discreetly looking at posters in the rooms to writing on desks and leaving binders open under desks to sneak a look. Clever testers may even progress to more serious cheating strategies: putting answers in mechanical pencils or water bottles and even creating

codes to communicate with friends across the room. These aren't even all of the strategies clever testers use! David got a higher grade because he was clever, and poor Arianna received a low grade because she wasn't clever enough to use her surroundings to get a good grade. All that matters to the clever testers, however, is the grade, so they believe this type of prevarication[5] is harmless. Students are either clever enough to use their surroundings as resources, or dumb enough not to. But is clever testing really clever in the end?

5. **prevarication:** lying

Plagiarism

8   We all know what plagiarism is: taking someone else's work, copying it, then putting our name on it. We have all heard it before: "Plagiarism is unacceptable and will not be tolerated. There will be major consequences to anyone who plagiarizes anything." Plagiarism is the one form of cheating that can be caught a fair amount of the time thanks to the tools on the Internet. However, it may not always be so obvious. What if someone gave another individual a very enlightened idea orally, and then the listener wrote it down? Is this not plagiarism? These perpetrators[6] go unpunished and, in most cases, receive great accolades[7] for their breakthrough or insight.

6. **perpetrators:** people who commit crimes

7. **accolades:** praise or rewards for doing something well

9   The people who cheat have no confidence; if they did, they wouldn't feel the need to cheat. At the same time, cheating is arrogant, because the cheaters feel they are entitled to the good grade. Why does it continue? Society has encouraged it to spread through its wide acceptance of the deceitful action.

10   A recent discovery shows that doctors have begun to share the answers to their certification exams. If these doctors feel the need to cheat to get their certification, how can patients feel comfortable getting treated by one? We could end up with a generation of doctors who really don't know what they need to do in order to treat their patients sufficiently. Doctors can end a life with the most minuscule but incorrect motion or the slightest wrong prescription; can we afford doctors who have cheated their way to success?

11   In the end, society as a whole will be what suffers the most from cheating. We need to stand up and say "no." How much will our society have to suffer before we do just that? Cheating hurts everyone involved. The teacher thinks that the student understands and moves on to the next subject, the student gets a good grade without learning anything, and society acquires a generation of people who use cheating as a resource to excel. Cheating will ultimately destroy the integrity of our society.

CHECK YOUR COMPREHENSION

1. Which of the following would be the best alternative title for this essay?
    a. "Cheating vs. Group Work"
    b. "The Ways We Cheat"
    c. "How to Cheat and Get Away with It"
    d. "Ways to Address Cheating in the Classroom"

2. The main idea of this essay is that

   a.   most cheating is harmless.

   b.   cheating has changed over the past few decades.

   c.   no matter what form it takes, cheating causes problems for students and for society.

   d.   there are many creative ways students can cheat and not get caught.

3. According to the essay, home-no-work occurs when

   a.   students work together to solve assigned problems.

   b.   students refuse to do homework assignments at all.

   c.   students copy answers from the Internet.

   d.   students divide assignments and copy from others so that they don't have to do as much work.

4. Does this essay include the Four Basics of Classification? Be prepared to say why or why not.

5. Write a sentence using the following vocabulary words: *exasperation* (para.1); *escalate* (3).

READ CRITICALLY

1. Who is Woodrell's intended audience? How do the questions she asks throughout the essay appeal to her audience?

2. Woodrell begins her essay with a short narrative about two students, Arianna and David. What is the effect of this story on the reader? How does it relate to the thesis of her essay?

3. Is there a type of cheating Woodrell does not include in her essay? Explain.

4. According to Woodrell, what will happen to society if cheating is not addressed? Do you agree with her? Why or why not?

5. Why does Woodrell include a dictionary definition of *cheating* in paragraph 4? How does the definition help prepare readers for her classification?

WRITE

1. Cheating is a form of deception or lie. Write a paragraph or essay in which you classify types of lies (or liars). To limit your topic, choose a specific focus area: lies parents tell children, lies in romantic relationships, or lies on the Internet. Define each category, and provide examples and details to support your classification.

2. With your classmates, collect examples of homework assignments from different instructors and different classes. After reviewing the examples, sort them into categories. Write a paragraph or an essay that defines and illustrates your classification of homework assignments.

Professional Classification Essay

Stephanie Dray

Five Kinds of Friends Everyone Should Have

Stephanie Dray, a former lawyer, teacher, and game designer, holds a B.A. in government from Smith College and a law degree from Northwestern University. Currently, she is focused on writing novels that blend history and fantasy and that seek, in Dray's words, "to illuminate the stories of women in history and inspire the young women of today." Her most recent books, *Lily of the Nile* and *Song of the Nile* (both published in 2011), follow the adventures of Cleopatra's daughter after the fall of Egypt to the Romans.

Dray wrote this essay about friends for Associated Content (now Yahoo! Voices; **voices .yahoo.com**) because she was thinking about the many good friends that she has and wanted to show her respect for their individual value in her life.

Guiding question What kinds of friends do you have, and how would you classify them?

1   We all know we need friends, and we all know the basics. Our friends should be loyal, supportive, loving, and kind—and we should give that loyalty, support, love, and kindness back in return. But it's not just how many friends you have; it is also the kind of friends you keep that will make or break your happiness in life. Here is a list of the top five kinds of friends we should cultivate.[1]

2   *The Listener.* Everyone needs a shoulder to lean on sometimes, and some of our friends are better at listening than others. Sure, your beer buddy might be a great listener when it comes to your endless droning about baseball stats, but will he fidget impatiently if you need to talk about your family troubles? Not every friend is cut out to sit quietly and let you vent[2] without getting judgmental[3] or offering too much advice, but if you find a friend that can do that for you, hold on to them for dear life.

3   *The Geek.* Face it. We live in the Information Age, and if you don't have a Geek[4] for a friend, you are going to get left behind. This type of friend isn't just useful for helping you when your laptop goes on the fritz.[5] The Geek often has a unique perspective[6] on the world around you and can open up new guilty pleasures that you've never thought of before. The Geek is someone who will allow you to gush[7] about your enthusiasms, while being entirely unselfconscious about his own. Best of all, Geek Loyalty is a bond that is hard to break. Even your love life could use a little tech support from time-to-time, so cultivate a friendship with someone who knows more than you do!

4   *The Twin.* Have you ever met someone who seems to share every single interest that you have? The moment you connect with this kind of friend, all kinds of sparks fly. You can bond over your obscure[8] love of ancient cookery or re-runs of Buck Rogers.[9] Maybe you're both night owls, maybe you're both addicted to Coldstone

1. **cultivate:** acquire or develop

2. **vent:** release, pour out, express
3. **judgmental:** disapproving, critical
4. **geek:** a person who knows a lot about technology
5. **on the fritz:** temporarily not working
6. **perspective:** a viewpoint
7. **gush:** pour forth

8. **obscure:** not well known or understood
9. **Buck Rogers:** a fictional adventure character who traveled in space

10. cherish: hold dear

Creamery's cake batter ice cream. Whatever your passion, this kind of friend will share it. In short, the twin is a kind of friend that's just like you. Cherish[10] your bond with this kind of friend, and if you don't have one already, find one as soon as you can!

11. validated: proved accurate or true

5   *The Opposite.* We all try to cultivate friends who are just like us because it helps us feel validated,[11] and having our enjoyment reflected back at us is a great feeling. But for every friend you have that is a twin, you should also look for an opposite. Life's perspective is limited when your friends are all the same. When you find the kind of friend who has a personality just the opposite of your own, she can teach you to have a new perspective. This kind of friend is not only horizon broadening, but can often earn your respect in ways no one else can. For a well-rounded life, seek out an opposite for friendship and your point of view will be enriched.

12. motivate: inspire or activate

6   *The Motivator.* Sometimes we wish our friends would just accept us for exactly who we are, but sometimes it's better to have the kind of friends who motivate[12] us to change and love us even if we don't. You know the type: She's the friend who will get your butt up in the morning to go running. He's the kind of friend who prompts you to write a list of everything you want to accomplish in life, and dares you every so often to do it. Motivators are great friends to have, and they should be tolerated

13. frenetic: fast in a wild way

even when their frenetic[13] pace gets on your nerves.

7   There are all kinds of people in this world, and we benefit from having many types of them be our friends. Our diverse friends help us grow as people, and we do the same for them. As the author Anaïs Nin once wrote, "Each friend represents a world in us, a world possibly not born until they arrive, and it is only by this meeting that a new world is born."

CHECK YOUR COMPREHENSION

1. Which of the following would be the best alternative title for the essay?
   a. "We All Need Friends"
   b. "Our Best Friends Are Most Like Us"
   c. "The Best Kinds of Friends You Can Have"
   d. "We Need Friends Who Are Different from Us"

2. The main idea of this essay is that
   a. having different kinds of friends is valuable.
   b. having lots of friends is valuable.
   c. people should be careful about the friends they choose.
   d. we do not have to be like the people who are our friends.

3. According to the essay, the "listener" is the kind of friend who
   a. can keep a secret.
   b. does not talk about himself very much.
   c. can listen without being critical.
   d. is good at helping to solve problems.

4. Does this essay include the Four Basics of Classification? Be prepared to say why or why not.

5. Write sentences using the following vocabulary words: *cultivate* (para. 1); *judgmental* (2); *perspective* (3); *obscure* (4); *validate* (5).

READ CRITICALLY

1. What is Dray's purpose for writing this essay? Why does she use classification to achieve her purpose?

2. What does Dray use as transitions to move the reader from one category to the next?

3. In your opinion, which of the kinds of friends that Dray describes are people *least* likely to have? Why?

4. Why do you think that Dray ends with the specific quotation she uses? How does it relate to her purpose?

5. What types of friends can you think of that Dray does not include?

WRITE

1. Think about the various kinds of friends that you have, and write about the categories that they fit into, as Dray does. Include at least two categories that are not in Dray's essay. Give details about each category, as Dray does.

2. Write a classification paragraph or essay describing the kinds of relatives that you have. To move from one category to another, use transitional sentences rather than labels, as Dray does. Give details about each kind of relative.

Definition

Definition explains what a term or concept means.

Four Basics of Definition

1	It tells readers what is being defined.
2	It gives a clear definition.
3	It gives examples to explain the definition.
4	It gives details about the examples that readers will understand.

The numbers and colors in the following paragraph correspond to the Four Basics of Definition.

1 Propaganda **2** is information that is promoted to support certain views or messages. It can come in many forms, but its purpose is to persuade us to see things a certain way. **3** For example, the president of the United States may give televised speeches to convince us that some policy or action he supports is right. **4** We may get mailings on the subject. People who agree with the president's message may speak in favor of it on talk shows or in interviews. **3** Religious organizations may spread propaganda about the importance of certain actions (or avoiding certain actions). **4** For example, many churches sent positive messages to their members about the religious importance of the movie *The Chronicles of Narnia*. Churches urged their members to see the movie and even had their own showings, hoping the film would increase church attendance. **3** Propaganda can be good, as when a health organization sends information about how to avoid unhealthy behavior and follow good habits, or bad, as when one political group publishes false or exaggerated information to attack another group. Because we are surrounded by propaganda, it is important that we think about who is behind the message and whether we believe the information.

1. Underline the **topic sentence**.

2. What is the term being defined? _____

3. In your own words, what does the term mean? _____

   _____

   _____

4. Give another example that would help define the term. _____

   _____

   _____

5. Add a **transition** that would be useful. _____

   _____

   _____

Guided Outline: Definition

Fill in the outline with a definition and examples and details that explain the definition. Try prewriting to get ideas.

Topic sentence: A *family* is a group of people who _____.

First example: _____

Details: _____

Second example: _____

Details: _____

Third example: _____

Details: _____

Concluding sentence: Families are _____

_____ .

(Do not repeat the definition from your topic sentence.)

Write a Definition Paragraph

Write a definition paragraph, using the outline you developed, one of the following terms, or a topic of your own. Then, complete the definition checklist on page 116.

- Mentor
- Success
- A good student
- Ethical

- Frugal
- Fantasy
- Collaboration
- Education

USE A VISUAL TO WRITE A DEFINITION

Look at the photo below. Using the photo as the basis for your definition, write a paragraph that defines *democracy*.

Voters at the polls in Boise, Idaho

CHECKLIST

Evaluating Your Definition Paragraph

☐ My writing style is appropriate for the audience and purpose. (Most college assignments should be written in formal English.)

☐ The paragraph has the Four Basics of Definition (p. 113).

- My topic sentence tells readers what is being defined and gives a basic definition.

- I have given examples and details that show readers what the term means as I am defining it.

☐ I have included transitions to move readers smoothly from one example to the next.

☐ I have reread the paragraph, making improvements and checking for grammar and spelling errors.

Explore Definition Further: Identity

As you read the sample paragraphs and essays below, look for the Four Basics of Definition (p. 113). Also, remember to use the 2PR strategy: preview, read, pause, and review (see pages 6-10).

Student Definition Paragraph

Sydney Tasey

Sex vs. Gender

Student Sydney Tasey wrote the following paragraph as part of a longer article called "Finding One's Gender Identity" for *The Centurion*, the student newspaper of Bucks County Community College in Pennsylvania.

1. **physiological:** having to do with the body and its parts

2. **constructed:** built or created by a group of people, not by nature

A person's sex is defined by a person's biological and physiological[1] characteristics. For example, women menstruate and men do not, women have ovaries while men have testicles, women can get pregnant and men cannot—in other words, a person's sex is considered to be either male or female. On the other hand, a person's gender is defined by the constructed[2] roles, behaviors, activities and things that a society considers to be appropriate for men and women, making gender vary from country to country. For example, nursing is seen as a woman's job in the U.S., making it a feminine role, although many men enter the profession. Similarly, women usually wear tighter jeans in the U.S., so people see that as a feminine style, though many men today wear tight jeans. In other words, gender is considered to be either masculine or feminine.

Professional Definition Paragraph

Douglas Main

Who Are the Millennials?

Douglas Main, a journalist and staff writer for the science Web sites LiveScience.com and OurAmazingPlanet.com, wrote the following paragraph as part of a reference article.

The term *Millennials* generally refers to the generation of people born between the early 1980s and the early 2000s. Perhaps the most commonly used birth range for this group is 1982-2000. The Millennial Generation is also known as Generation Y, because it comes after Generation X—those people born between the early 1960s and the 1980s. It has also been called the Peter Pan or Boomerang Generation because of the propensity[1] of some to move back in with their parents, perhaps due to economic constraints, and a growing tendency to delay some of the typical adult-hood rites of passage[2] like marriage or starting a career. The publication *Ad Age* was one of the first to coin the term[3] "Generation Y," in an editorial in August 1993. But the term didn't age well, and "Millennials" has largely overtaken it. But the terms basically mean the same thing.

1. **propensity:** a tendency to do something

2. **rite of passage:** important events or ceremonies to show when a person moves to the next stage of life

3. **coin a term:** create a new word or term for something

UNDERSTANDING DEFINITION

Read the two sample paragraphs, and then complete the following.

1. What is being defined in each paragraph?

2. Is the definition clear? In your own words, can you define each term?

3. Do the paragraphs give examples to support the definition?

4. What supporting details does each paragraph give to explain the terms being defined?

Student Definition Essay

Spencer Rock

Mask-ulinity: The Price of Becoming a Man

Spencer Rock was managing editor of *The Current*, the student newspaper of Green River Community College in Washington state, when he wrote this piece about what it means to be a man.

Guiding question How does our society define *man*, according to the author?

1   Being a man in America is not the easiest thing to do. Throughout our lives we're told over and over again what it means to be a man. Many

Tip A guiding question can help you focus when you are reading. Make sure you can answer the guiding question when you have finished. For more information on reading and guiding questions, see Chapter 1.

people don't take into account the social pressure of being a man. Our society does not seem to see that the expectations of masculinity we put on our young men might be the cause of unneeded and unwanted stress.

2   Growing up I was a sensitive kid. I cried a lot; I got angry a lot; I got scared a lot; I got made fun of a lot. By the time I was a teenager, I had learned to hide those emotions, and ever since then that has been my charge as a man: in order to fit in and be accepted by society, I need to hide the negative things I feel.

3   Men are commonly told that they are supposed to bottle up their emotions because that's what a man does. Any emotions that are not positive should not exist anywhere outside of the mind. If emotions are released, a man becomes the subject of judgment and possibly contempt,[1] due to the fact that he has emotions that he cannot hold in anymore. Through this logic, a man's strength is generally based on his ability to appear pleasant even though the way he's actually feeling is being stifled.[2]

4   There's also tremendous social pressure from women. All women want their ideal guy and that's understandable, but we've all heard the usual lines. "I'm tired of dating a**-holes, I want a sensitive guy." It's a nice thought in theory, but in reality such a man is practically nonexistent.

5   In our ever-changing world, women who've been fighting for equality have found themselves in a world where female masculinity has become more socially acceptable. However, men are still constricted by social pressure to hide qualities that might be considered feminine in nature.

6   Any guy who cries in front of a woman or shows some form of sadness becomes sexually unappealing. Any guy who shows anger in front of a woman is a monster. Any guy who shows fear is weak. As long as emotions are expressed in the context of entertainment, they're okay, but actually expressing them in real life is practically forbidden. But we still hear the women of America say that they want a sensitive guy, and then they get one and realize that it is easier to just be with an a**-hole because there's less baggage.

7   From what I've seen and experienced, if a woman is upset, the man is supposed to be there for her, which is understandable. It's a good thing to support one another. Yet, I've never seen that same kind of regard from women towards men's feelings, or even from men towards men's feelings, whether it's due to genuine misunderstanding or a lack of sympathy.

8   There's also the fact that there are men out there who are slaves to their emotions and use them as excuses to do awful things. While I don't think this fact should make us afraid of our emotions, there is some merit[3] in considering this reality. Lack of control or taking things too far is part of the reason why society has pushed for men to be so masculine and emotionless.

9   If there's one thing I've learned from being a man in America, it is that to prosper you must lock your emotions in a cage and never let them come out. With the eyes of the world watching every step you take there has never been so much pressure to publicly display masculinity at a constant rate. But at what point will masculinity be evaluated without a mask to hide behind?

1. **contempt:** strongly negative feelings

2. **stifled:** covered up; smothered; crushed

3. **merit:** worth, reason to be accepted

CHECK YOUR COMPREHENSION

1. Which of the following would be the best alternative title for this essay?

   a. "Society Says Men Should Hide Emotions"

   b. "Men Are Jerks"

   c. "Why Women Dislike Sensitive Men"

   d. "Men Are from Mars; Women Are from Venus"

2. The main point of this essay is that

   a. men don't know how to express emotions as well as women do.

   b. women pressure men to show emotion in relationships.

   c. society pressures men to stifle their emotions.

   d. men face difficult stresses in the 21st century.

3. According to Rock,

   a. men should not be emotionally available to women.

   b. women should not be emotionally available to men.

   c. men's hidden emotions are always dangerous.

   d. men and women should be emotionally open to each other.

4. Does this essay include the Four Basics of Definition? Why or why not?

5. Write sentences using the following vocabulary words: *contempt, stifled* (para. 3).

READ CRITICALLY

1. Do you think Rock was writing primarily for women, for men, or for both? Explain.

2. Rock focuses on showing how society defines *masculinity*. Is that definition clear? Explain.

3. Rock suggests that society's definition of "masculinity" actually causes problems for men. Do you believe Rock has accurately captured society's definition? If not, why not? Do you think he has accurately captured women's views of men? If not, why not?

4. In paragraph 8, Rock implies that there is a reason that society wishes to keep emotions out of masculinity. What is that reason?

5. In paragraph 5, Rock says that "female masculinity" is acceptable in society. What do you think he means? Can you give an example?

WRITE

1. Rock looks at a term that describes a person based on gender. Choose a term that defines a person based on profession (nurse, athlete, mechanic), hobby (hunter, crafter, snowboarder), or other passions (Cowboys fan, Trekkie, shop-a-holic). Write a paragraph or essay in which you define this term, giving examples and details to support your definition.

2. Rock suggests that society's definition of *masculine* causes problems for many men. Do you think society has defined any other term in an unfair or problematic way? Write a paragraph or an essay in which you explore society's definition of that word, giving examples and details to explain the definition and the problems with it.

Professional Definition Essay

Roque Planas

Chicano: What Does the Word Mean and Where Does It Come From?

Roque Planas is an editor of the Latino Voices section of *The Huffington Post*. He writes about Latino culture, politics, and other topics. In this article, he explores the meaning of the word *Chicano*.

Guiding question   How does this essay change your understanding of the word *Chicano*?

1   Lots of people use the word "Chicano," but what exactly does it mean?

2   Scholars can't pinpoint the word's origins, but there are at least two theories, according to Tejano[1] historian Arnoldo de León. Some think the word may trace its roots all the way back to the Nahuatl[2] term "Meshico," the indigenous[3] word better known for evolving into the modern-day word "Mexico." Others think "Chicano" is just a variation of the Spanish "mexicano."

3   Whatever its origins, Mexican Americans have used the word "Chicano" to describe people of Mexican origin living in the United States since the early twentieth century, de León writes. Originally wealthier Mexican-Americans used the term as a pejorative,[4] a way to describe Mexican-Americans of lower social standing (likely with some racial overtones).

4   But it wasn't until the outbreak of the civil rights movement in the 1960s that the term "Chicano" became popular. Students walked out in protest at public schools from Crystal City, Texas, to East Los Angeles. The United Farm Workers under the leadership of Cesar Chavez[5] and Dolores Huerta[6] held marches and led the Delano grape strike.

5   When university students joined those and other political movements of the era, they adopted the term "Chicano" as a point of pride, upending its historically derogatory[7] meaning. In his poem "I am Joaquín," poet Rodolfo "Corky" Gonzalez ruminated[8] on the Chicano cultural experience. Today, politicians like former Texas State Rep. Paul Moreno proudly refer to themselves as "Chicanos," and several universities boast Chicano Studies programs.

1. **Tejano:** from the Spanish for "Texan," describing Texans of Mexican descent and their culture

2. **Nahuatl:** language spoken by some of the native peoples of Central America

3. **indigenous:** native to a particular place

4. **pejorative:** a word that is negative, hateful, or belittling

5. **Cesar Chavez:** 1927-1993, American civil rights leader and activist for farm workers

6. **Dolores Huerta:** b. 1930, American labor activist and civil rights leader

7. **derogatory:** negative; intentionally hurtful or offensive

8. **ruminated:** thought about or meditated on

6   While the term refers broadly to Mexican-Americans, some people avoid the label because of its ties to leftwing politics. But for those who embrace it, like actor Cheech Marin, many feel that "Chicano" more accurately describes them than generic terms such as "Hispanic" or "Latino":

> Hispanic is a census term that some dildo[9] in a government office made up to include all Spanish-speaking brown people. It is especially annoying to Chicanos because it is a catch-all term that includes the Spanish conqueror. By definition, it favors European cultural invasion, not indigenous roots.

9. **dildo:** stupid person (slang)

7   "Chicano" isn't the only alternate term Mexican-Americans have adopted to describe themselves over the years. As Francisco Arturo Rosales writes in his book *Chicano! The History of the Mexican American Civil Rights Movement*:

> Francisco P. Ramírez, through his Los Angeles Spanish-language weekly "El Clamor Público," proposed the term "la raza"[10] to denote Mexican Californians. Other self-identifiers were *la población*,[11] *la población California* and *nuestra raza española*.[12] Richard Griswold del Castillo, however, noted that, in the Mexican culture in California, "the increasing use of 'La Raza' as a generic term in the Spanish-language press was evidence of a new kind of ethnic consciousness.

10. *la raza:* Spanish for "the race"

11. *la población:* Spanish for "the population"

12. *nuestra raza española:* Spanish for "our Spanish Race"

8   The Chicano movement also embraced the term. Today, one of the most prominent Latino political organizations is called the National Council of La Raza.

CHECK YOUR COMPREHENSION

1. Which of the following would be the best alternative title for this essay?
    a. "Mexican Americans"
    b. "Spanish Speakers in the United States"
    c. "Chicano and other terms for Mexican Americans"
    d. "Hispanic Names"

2. The main point of this essay is that
    a. the word *Chicano* has changed from a negative term to a widely accepted name for Mexican Americans.
    b. only left-wing politicians use the term *Chicano* in the 21st century.
    c. no one really knows where the word *Chicano* comes from.
    d. *Chicano* is a term that was used by student protestors.

3. According to Planas, Mexican-Americans prefer *Chicano* to words like *Latino* or *Hispanic* because
    a. all Spanish speakers in the United States today are the same.
    b. *Chicano* is too political.
    c. *Latino* and *Hispanic* focus on the influence of Europe, not native people.
    d. *Hispanic* is too negative.

4. Does this essay include the Four Basics of Definition? Be prepared to say why or why not.

5. Write sentences using the following vocabulary words: *indigenous* (para. 2); *pejorative* (3); *derogatory* (5).

READ CRITICALLY

1. How have the connotations of the word *Chicano* changed over the years? Can you think of other words that have had similar shifts in meaning?

2. For whom is Planas writing? How do you know?

3. Planas includes two longer quotations from other writers in his essay. What do those quotations add to his definition?

4. Why do some people reject the word *Chicano* to identify themselves? What words do you prefer to identify yourself? Which words do you reject, and why?

5. Compare Planas's definition of *Chicano* with one you find in a contemporary wiki, such as Wikipedia (www.wikipedia.org) or the Urban Dictionary (www.urbandictionary.com). What differences do you find? Which definition do you find more reliable? Why?

WRITE

1. Planas defines a term used to describe a group of people in the United States. What is a term that is used to define a group with which you identify? Explore what that term means in a paragraph or an essay. Be sure to write a clear definition and give examples and details to support your main idea.

2. *Chicano* is a word that refers to both a people and a culture; similarly, the word *Tejano* can describe people, culture, or music, specifically. Choose a word that describes a culture, music style, or food that is familiar to you. In a paragraph, define that word, using examples and descriptive details to illustrate your definition.

Chapter Review

1. What does a process analysis paragraph do? _____

_____

2. What does a classification paragraph do? _____

_____

3. What does a definition paragraph do? _____

_____

REFLECTING ON THE JOURNEY

Skills Learned

Now that you've completed the chapter, share what you've learned about each skill by completing the following chart.

Skill	What I learned about this skill
Write a process-analysis paragraph (explain how something works or how to do something)	
Write a classification paragraph (sort a topic into categories)	
Write a definition paragraph (explain what a topic means)	

8

Developing Comparison-and-Contrast, Cause-and-Effect, and Argument Paragraphs

Additional Ways to Present Your Ideas

Learning Objectives

Chapter Goal: Write paragraphs using different patterns of development: comparison and contrast, cause and effect, and argument.

Tools to Achieve the Goal

- Four Basics of Comparison and Contrast (p. 125)
- Sample comparison-and-contrast paragraphs and essays (p. 128)
- Four Basics of Cause and Effect (p. 137)
- Sample cause-and-effect paragraphs and essays (p. 139)
- Four Basics of Argument (p. 147)
- Sample argument paragraphs and essays (p. 150)

READING ROADMAP

Key Terms

Skim Chapter 8 before you begin reading. Can you find each of these words in **bold** type? Put a check mark next to each word once you have located it in the chapter.

_____ comparison	_____ cause
_____ contrast	_____ effect
_____ point-by-point	_____ argument
_____ whole-to-whole	

Highlight or circle any of these words that you already know.

Before You Read

Before you begin reading this chapter, fill out the following chart. For each skill, think of a time when you have used this skill and what you would like to know on completing the chapter. At the end of the chapter, you will be asked to share what you learned about this skill.

Skill	When I have used this skill	What I want to know about this skill
Write a comparison-and-contrast paragraph (show how two things are similar or different)		
Write a cause-and-effect para-graph (explain why something happens or what the results of something are)		
Write an argument paragraph (give reasons and evidence to support a position)		

In Chapters 6 and 7, you discovered six ways to develop a paragraph: narration, illustration, description, process analysis, classification, and definition. In this chapter, you will learn about three additional patterns for developing paragraphs: comparison and contrast, cause and effect, and argument.

Comparison and Contrast

Comparison shows the similarities among people, ideas, situations, and things; **contrast** shows the differences.

Four Basics of Comparison and Contrast

> **1** It has subjects (usually two) that are enough alike to be usefully compared or contrasted.
>
> **2** It serves a purpose—to help readers either make a decision about two subjects or understand them.
>
> **3** It gives several points of comparison and/or contrast.
>
> **4** It uses one of two organizations—**point-by-point** or **whole-to-whole**.

Point-by-Point	Whole-to-Whole

1. First point of comparison
    Subject 1
    Subject 2
2. Second point of comparison
    Subject 1
    Subject 2
3. Third point of comparison
    Subject 1
    Subject 2
	1. Subject 1
	    First point of comparison
	    Second point of comparison
	    Third point of comparison
	2. Subject 2
	    First point of comparison
	    Second point of comparison
	    Third point of comparison

The numbers and colors in the following paragraph correspond to the Four Basics of Comparison and Contrast.

1 Greenline Bank **2** suits my needs much better than **1** Worldly Bank does. **3** For one thing, there are not any hidden charges at Greenline. For example, customers get free checking even if they keep a low balance in their accounts. Since I do not usually have much in my checking account, this is important for me. In contrast, to get free checking at Worldly Bank, customers must have a minimum balance of $3,000. That would mean that I pay for every check I write, and I do not need that charge. **3** Another way that Greenline Bank is better is that it offers low interest rates on loans. If I need a loan for

4 Uses one type of organization throughout.

4 Uses one type of organization throughout.

something like a new car, for example, the bank's rate of interest on that would be 9 percent. Worldly Bank would charge 17.5 percent for the same loan. Over a three-year period, the difference between 9 percent and 17.5 percent is huge.

3 Another difference between the two banks is that Greenline Bank is a small, local bank. People know me when I walk in, and I feel that I can trust them. I also believe that giving Greenline my business helps the local economy in some small way. In contrast, Worldly Bank is huge. The people in the local office are polite in a businesslike way, but I do not feel as if I know them. Worldly Bank as a whole is the fourth-largest bank in the country, so I know that my little account means nothing to it. Because of these differences, I am a loyal Greenline Bank customer.

1. Underline the **topic sentence**.

2. Is the purpose to help readers make a choice or to help them understand?

   _____

3. Does the paragraph compare or contrast? _____

4. What kind of organization does it use? _____

5. What are the points of comparison? _____

   _____

Guided Outline: Comparison and Contrast

Fill in the outline with the points of comparison between the two subjects. Try prewriting to get ideas, and save the most important point of comparison for last.

Topic sentence: _____ (falling in love/learning to drive/the first week of a new job . . .) can be just like

_____

_____.

Subject 1 _____

    First point of comparison: _____

    Second point of comparison: _____

    Third point of comparison: _____

Subject 2 _____

    First point of comparison: _____

    Second point of comparison: _____

    Third point of comparison: _____

Concluding sentence: The important thing about both is that _____

_____

_____

_____ .

Write a Comparison-and-Contrast Paragraph

Write a comparison or contrast paragraph, using the outline you developed, one of the following topics, or a topic of your own. Then, complete the comparison-and-contrast checklist on page 128.

- Yourself and a sister or brother
- The job that you have/the job that you want
- Two bosses
- Two places where you have lived
- Clothes for a job interview/clothes for a weekend
- Yourself now/yourself ten years ago
- Your life now/what you want it to be
- Two friends
- Two photographs of your family
- A good student/a bad student
- Two types of pets

USE A VISUAL TO WRITE COMPARISON AND CONTRAST

Look at the photos below. Write a paragraph that compares and contrasts online and traditional classes.

CHECKLIST

Evaluating Your Comparison-and-Contrast Paragraph

☐ My writing style is appropriate for the audience and purpose. (Most college assignments should be written in formal English.)

☐ The paragraph has the Four Basics of Comparison and Contrast (p. 125).

- My topic sentence tells readers what my subjects are and shows my purpose for comparing, contrasting, or both.

- I have detailed points of comparison or contrast between the two subjects.

- I have included transitions to move readers smoothly from one point or subject to the next.

☐ I have reread the paragraph, making improvements and checking for grammar and spelling errors.

Explore Comparison and Contrast Further: Our Changing Culture

As you read the sample paragraphs and essays below, look for the Four Basics of Comparison and Contrast (p. 125). Also, remember to use the 2PR strategy: preview, read, pause, and review (see pages 6-10).

Student Comparison-and-Contrast Paragraph

Yolanda Castaneda Vasquez

Classroom Culture, Past and Present

Yolanda Castaneda Vasquez, originally from Guatemala, has been living in the United States since 2008, and she hopes to return to her country someday. She is studying now to improve her English so that she can begin taking classes to become a paralegal.

    Time has influenced our culture; although some people try to keep the culture, it inevitably changes as time passes. In my home country of Guatemala, for example, time has influenced the classroom atmosphere. I remember when I was in elementary school; every time we saw a teacher come into our classroom, we had to stand up and say, "Good morning, Teacher" followed by his or her name. This custom was not only for the professors; we also had to stand up and say "Good morning" to each person who came into our classroom. In that room, we had one small desk for each student. As a result, we each had our own space to do all the work we needed. And there was a lot of work! We had to memorize the multiplication tables quickly; the next day of class, the teacher would ask the answer for nine times nine, and if we gave the wrong answer, the result was an automatic F for our grade. Moreover, we weren't allowed to use the calculator on a math test, or even in our homework. Nowadays the custom of greeting every person who comes to the classroom is completely lost; for instance, I went to my brother's classroom one day, and all the students were talking or writing while I was there. They never paid attention to me, and the teacher did not say anything to them because, as she told me, "They are working on their projects." We have lost some respect for other people, especially if they are older than us. Also, the classes now have tables that are for at least three students together, so when students sit down, they have to limit the space they use. They are allowed to use a calculator while they are taking a math test, and they are not required to memorize the multiplication tables because the teacher never quizzes them about that in class. As a result, we have some students who never worry about their grades or their work because they believe that it is easy to get good grades. On the other hand, sharing space with other students can help young people become more sociable. In conclusion, even though some of us disagree with all the changes that time has made in our culture, we can still find some value in those changes.

Professional Comparison-and-Contrast Paragraph

CNN iReport

Brick and Mortar vs. Online Shopping

This paragraph comes from an article that looks at the pros and cons of shopping online and shopping in stores.

Brick and mortar shopping, in most cases, gives you the option of paying with cash, check or credit/debit card. And of course when you need something in a hurry or need items like gas, food, or medicine, you have to go to a store. The downsides are that you have to spend money on gas or public transportation to get to a store, in most cases. It can also take a considerable amount of time if you are shopping for gifts or hard to find items. You have to go from store to store sometimes and it can be exhausting. Increasingly, more and more items can be purchased online, even cars, furniture, computers and houses. If you are looking for something obscure, chances are you can find it with a quick search in your favorite search engine rather than driving all around town. So you save time and gas by shopping online. The downside is that you can't physically inspect the product or try it on, if it's a clothing item. So you'll need to make sure the website has a generous return policy. For example, Zappos lets customers return shoes at no cost to the customer if the shoes don't fit properly. Most online clothing websites have generous return policies and provide return shipping labels. Make sure this is the case before you order. Also, unless you're willing to pay for overnight shipping, you can't get the product instantly when you shop online and have to pay a shipping charge. But the convenience of ordering from home and the ability to find discount prices online often outweigh this. And most websites make fast shipping a high priority, so you'll usually get your item in less than a week. Many websites, such as Amazon, have customer reviews and testimonials, and this will give you a good idea how reliable the shipping and product quality are. A final advantage to online shopping: there is now a way to instantly find the best prices on everything, and it doesn't cost a thing.

UNDERSTANDING COMPARISON AND CONTRAST

1. What two subjects are being compared in each paragraph? Are the subjects being compared, contrasted, or both?

2. What is the main idea of each paragraph?

3. What are the points of comparison used by the writer?

4. Does the paragraph use a point-by-point or whole-to-whole organization?

Student Comparison-and-Contrast Essay

James Sellers

His and Hers

James Sellers wrote this essay for an in-class writing assignment. Students were asked to select two advertisements for a similar product and compare or contrast them according to their intended audiences.

Tip A guiding question can help you focus when you are reading. Make sure you can answer the guiding question when you have finished. For more information on reading and guiding questions, see Chapter 1.

1. stereotyping: defining a person based on the common view of a particular group of people

Guiding question What are the differences between advertisements targeting women and advertisements targeting men?

1   Television advertisements are prone to stereotyping[1] when trying to reach a particular group of people. For instance, advertisements that target men are very different from advertisements that target women. An example of these stereotypes can be observed by viewing two television commercials that are both for the same exact make and model vehicle. As we will see, advertisers know the stereotypical differences in men and women all too well.

2   In the two television commercials, the advertisers are selling Volvo SUVs. The commercial for men has three male musicians. It shows them on stage with bright lights and cheering crowds. Then the commercial shows the three men in separate parts of the world having adventures in solitude while a song about leaving the world behind plays in the background. In contrast, the commercial for women begins with a woman in a black Mercedes SUV stopped at a red light. The woman uses her rearview mirror to check her hair and makeup. She is very proud of how she looks, and it is obvious that she spends a lot of time on her appearance. Then, a woman in a white Volvo SUV pulls up next to her at the light. The woman in the Volvo briefly checks her appearance and then uses her mirror to make silly faces so her two children in the backseats laugh. Then a narrator says "the Volvo XC60, designed for real people."

3   Advertisers are very good at knowing what to say and show their intended audience. The messages in the two commercials are very different. The message in the ad for men suggests that the Volvo XC60 will allow men to escape their daily lives and take an adventure, while the message in the ad for women suggests that real people are people with families and they drive Volvos. Advertisers know people and they know how to sell a product to people. The use of gender stereotypes is nothing new. In fact, advertisers have been using them since the 40's, giving them plenty of time to refine their use of gender stereotypes. Advertisers know that the majority of men like excitement and adventure, so showing them a concert with bright lights and loud music will catch their attention very fast and effectively. In the commercial for women, the advertisers target family-oriented women with sunny weather and laughing children. Even the appearance of the men and women in both commercials are different. The men look rugged and unshaven. They have no concern about how they look. The women, in contrast, are well groomed and dressed nicely.

4   The commercial also shows the driving capabilities of the vehicle in different ways. The women are in an urban setting. They are driving in normal conditions with sunny weather. The commercial has the women in the urban setting because that is a more appealing driving situation for most women. The men, on the other hand, are driving on bad terrain in bad weather conditions. This commercial shows that the vehicle is ideal for both urban driving and off road conditions. The commercial shows the men driving through rough terrain because a stereotypical man likes to go off road.

5   I don't think that advertisers will change how they use gender stereotypes to sell products to men and women. Men like adventure, and most men would like to escape their lives to go on an adventure; women are social, and they like to interact with one another. As the world changes, so do men and women. Even though they adapt to the same types of environments, men and women still remain very different, and advertisers are vigilant[2] in monitoring these adaptations so that they too can adapt and exploit those changes to sell their products.

2. **vigilant:** very careful about watching or monitoring

CHECK YOUR COMPREHENSION

1. Which of the following would be the best alternative title for this essay?

    a.   "Why Women Buy Volvos"

    b.   "Advertisements for Men and Women"

    c.   "The Differences Between Male and Female Drivers"

    d.   "Stereotypes on Television"

2. The main point of this essay is that

    a.   men like adventure, but women prefer social interactions.

    b.   men are less likely to care about their appearance than women.

    c.   advertisers unfairly stereotype men and women.

    d.   advertisers use gender stereotypes to market their products to men and women.

3. According to Sellers,

   a. city driving in clear conditions is more likely to appeal to women.

   b. heavy traffic and bad weather are more likely to appeal to men.

   c. women like to put on make-up while they are driving.

   d. men like to drive when there are other men in the car to talk to.

4. Does this essay include the Four Basics of Comparison and Contrast? Be prepared to say why or why not.

5. Write sentences using the following vocabulary word: *vigilant* (para. 5).

READ CRITICALLY

1. Sellers claims advertisers use stereotypical differences between men and women to market their products, and he offers two commercials as examples to support his point. Can you find other television, online, or print advertisements that illustrate his claim?

2. What are three points of comparison that Sellers uses to contrast the two Volvo commercials?

3. Does Sellers use a point-by-point or whole-to-whole organization for the essay? How does the organization of his essay help him make his point?

4. Does Sellers seem critical or accepting of the use of gender stereotypes in advertising? Explain.

5. Do you think advertising strategies such as those described by Sellers are effective? Why or why not?

WRITE

1. Sellers suggests that marketers change advertisements based on the target audience, and he uses two television commercials to make his point. Choose two print or online advertisements that have different target audiences and write a compare-and-contrast essay. In your essay, focus on points of comparison that highlight the difference in target audience.

2. Compare and contrast two versions or brands of technology (two tablets, computers, smart phones, etc.). Which would you recommend and why? Write a paragraph or essay in which you present your recommendation and your points of comparison, following either a point-by-point or a whole-to-whole organization.

Professional Comparison-and-Contrast Essay

Jenny Deam

E-books vs. Print: What Parents Need to Know

Jenny Deam is a writer who covers family issues for a number of different publications. She lives in Colorado with her husband and three children, and she wrote this essay for scholastic.com**.**

Guiding question What are the advantages and disadvantages of e-readers and print books for children?

1   When Maggie Moore, a suburban Denver mom, was literally weighing her packing options for a family trip, she was stumped by her 4-year-old son's stack of favorite books. He had dozens, and she knew they'd be too heavy to take along. But they would be away for a few weeks—how could she bring only a few?

2   That's when she reluctantly bought a Nook, loading titles for both of them onto it. She wasn't a big fan of the extra screen time it would mean for her preschooler, but Moore justified the purchase as a stopgap[1] solution. What happened next surprised her: From the moment her son held the device and began to scroll through a book, he was transfixed.[2] "He was in heaven," says Moore.

3   E-reading devices have been around only a few years, but it's already hard to imagine life without them. And like all things tech, what started as a product for adults is now targeted at a younger audience. In fact, according to Scholastic's new *Kids & Family Reading Report*, the percentage of children who have read an e-book has almost doubled since 2010, jumping to 46 percent. And e-books for kids and teens became the fastest-growing segment in 2011, according to the Association of American Publishers and the Book Industry Study Group.

4   "We are not going to stop this train," says psychologist Jim Taylor, Ph.D., author of *Raising Generation Tech*. But should we try to slow it down? When it comes to the youngest readers, some experts are skittish[3] about putting tablets into tiny hands. Parents are conflicted, too—68 percent prefer that their 6- to 8-year-olds read print books, Scholastic found. Since there's not much research out there, it may be years before we understand the impact of tech devices on young readers.

5   Still, there are signs that e-readers can have a positive effect on newbie readers, especially when it comes to targeted learning based on each child's ability. But don't give those storybooks the heave-ho[4] just yet. "It doesn't have to be an either-or. You don't build a house with only one tool," says Otis Kriegel, a fifth-grade teacher in New York City and the author of *Covered in Glue: What New Elementary School Teachers Really Need to Know*. Here's how you can inspire your reader with both options.

Print May Be Better For . . .

6   **The hands-on experience.** Some experts, including Taylor, worry that devices can distance little kids from the real world. If they're only exposed to e-readers, kids

1. **stopgap:** temporary solution.

2. **transfixed:** too excited or amazed to move

3. **skittish:** uncertain, hesitant

4. **heave-ho:** rejection; act of throwing away

lose the tactile experience of handling a traditional book, turning its pages, or sharing their favorites with friends. "Technology is a beautiful box but it is still a box," he says.

7   **Falling in love with reading.** Cuddling with a parent over a book or gathering around the teacher for storytime helps kids associate reading with nurturing. "These reading experiences can set the stage for later reading success," says Julia Parish-Morris, a post-doctoral fellow[5] at the University of Pennsylvania who studies how young children interact with e-books. While she thinks e-books are great for independent readers, she's not as sure how good they are for preschoolers and kindergartners. Her research has found that parents often become more controlling, concentrating more on what their child is doing with the device instead of talking about the story.

8   **Focusing a child's attention.** The music, animation, and games that are loaded into kids' e-books can end up being more distracting than useful, says Lisa Guernsey, director of the early education initiative at the New America Foundation. "The technology is so exciting that the conversation focuses on what button to push instead of the content," she says. What's better is when those bells and whistles lead back to the story, instead of just entertaining.

Digital Matches Print For . . .

9   **Boosting early reading skills.** For the past four years the Center for Literacy at the University of Akron has been studying how to integrate e-readers into classrooms. Jeremy Scott Brueck, director of the school's Digital Text Initiative, found that animation and audio in e-books did seem to help young kids identify printed words. When Brueck tested pre-K students, a third knew the words before reading the story with a grown-up on an e-reader. After reading the e-book, the number shot up to 54 percent. It's unclear whether the results would have come out the same with traditional books; it might have been the shared reading experience—a known vocabulary-builder—rather than the device that helped kids learn. But what they did find: "The kids were extremely engaged," says Brueck.

Digital May Trump[6] Print Because . . .

10   **It's more interactive.** While add-ons can distract, they are extremely useful for beginning readers, who can zoom in on unfamiliar words or click links that help make connections to their world, says Guernsey. Plus, the touchscreen or buttons on an e-reader can hone[7] a preschooler's fine-motor skills.

11   **It's more rewarding.** When kids see printed words light up as they sound out the words, they're encouraged. Kim Floyd has been teaching kindergarten in Napa Valley, CA, for 24 years and using iPads loaded with books for the last three. The proof of e-reading success is in front of her every day when she sees how excited her students are the second she pulls out the tablets. Because the devices help children understand words by highlighting and defining those they struggle with, their vocabulary increases. Her kindergartners have vocabularies more typical of second graders, she notes. Floyd even studied the vocab-building phenomena[8] for her master's degree last year, testing pre-kindergartners who were not native English speakers and had no preschool experience. By the end of three weeks, their vocabularies had jumped from roughly 200 words into the thousands.

5. **post-doctoral fellow:** a person who has completed the Ph.D. degree and is working on research, usually at a university.

6. **trump:** win or beat; be better than

7. **hone:** sharpen or improve

8. **phenomenon:** an impressive fact or occurrence

12   **It caters to a kid's unique learning style.** Floyd also likes that the anonymity[9] of the device helps struggling readers feel less embarrassed. "It lets children find a book that fits their interest and skill without the entire class knowing what they are reading," she says. Erika Alexander, a suburban Detroit mother, agrees. Her fourth-grade son is a reluctant[10] reader, even though books were part of his routine when he was younger. Recently when they were shopping, he picked up a Nook that was loaded with a graphic novel. Attracted at first to the gadgetry, he stood in the aisle and inhaled the story. Alexander still plans to encourage a love of old-fashioned books. But she also recognizes that her son is a visual person, and a high-tech device hooks him in ways that were missing before.

9. **anonymity:** being unknown or not identified

10. **reluctant:** unwilling

The Bottom Line . . .

13   Kids have a lot to gain from *both* reading tools. Even though she's a huge e-reader fan, Floyd believes that children should be exposed to print first or at least simultaneously. Her students switch off easily, and there are surprisingly few squabbles over who gets the iPad. "After the novelty wears off, they become nonchalant,[11]" she says. Plus, technology will never replace good parenting and good teachers. So when you read to your child—regardless of whether it's a traditional or e-book—keep the conversation lively. Talk about what he sees on the page. Ask what he thinks will happen next. Because as researchers and educators all agree, the most important app, especially for little kids, is human.

11. **nonchalant:** not excited; uninterested

CHECK YOUR COMPREHENSION

1. Which of the following would be the best alternative title for this essay?
   a. "The Screen or the Paper: Which Is Better for Kids?"
   b. "How to Make Your Child Love Reading"
   c. "Should Elementary Classrooms Use E-readers?"
   d. "Finding the Best Books for Your Child"

2. The main point of this essay is that
   a. kids who have e-readers have bigger vocabularies than children who don't.
   b. children can benefit from early exposure to both books and e-readers.
   c. parents should teach children to read before starting school.
   d. features in e-books can be distracting for children.

3. According to Deam, which of the following is NOT an advantage of digital readers?
   a. They can help children with fine-motor skills.
   b. They can help children focus their attention.
   c. They are encouraging because students are rewarded for progress.
   d. They can build vocabulary.

4. Does this essay include the Four Basics of Comparison and Contrast? Be prepared to say why or why not.

5. Write sentences using the following vocabulary words: *skittish* (para. 4); *hone* (10); *anonymity* (11); *reluctant* (12); *nonchalant* (13).

READ CRITICALLY

1. What are the points of comparison that Deam uses in her essay?

2. What organizational strategy does she use, point-by-point or whole-to-whole?

3. Deam ends her essay by saying, "Kids have a lot to gain from both reading tools." Do the points of comparison and organizational strategy support this conclusion? Explain.

4. Deam introduces each section of the comparison and contrast with a subtitle that is part of a sentence, and then she completes the sentence in different ways to open each paragraph. How could Deam have introduced each paragraph without using this strategy? With a group, rewrite one section of the paper without using subtitles (you will need to revise the topic sentence in each paragraph). Is the essay still effective? Why or why not?

5. Who is Deam's intended audience? How do the examples she gives help her connect to her target audience?

WRITE

1. Deam compares and contrasts print and screen readers for children. What are the advantages and disadvantages of print and electronic textbooks for college students? Explore this question in a compare-and-contrast essay. Make sure you have a clear organizational structure, and develop your points of comparison with clear transitions between each one.

2. There are many computer-based products designed to help students learn a variety of skills in addition to reading: interactive art and music programs, math skill-builders, engineering and science virtual labs, sports programs, and more. Choose a skill or subject matter you have studied, and write a comparison-and-contrast paragraph or essay about practicing that skill traditionally and online. What are the advantages and disadvantages of each?

Cause and Effect

A **cause** is what makes something happen. An **effect** is what happens as a result of something.

A ring diagram is useful to show causes and effects of something.

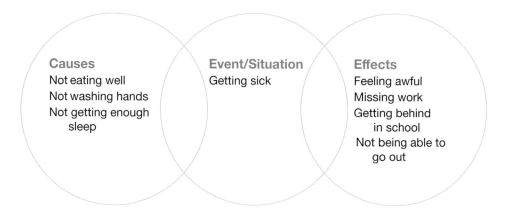

Causes	Event/Situation	Effects
Not eating well	Getting sick	Feeling awful
Not washing hands		Missing work
Not getting enough sleep		Getting behind in school
		Not being able to go out

Four Basics of Cause and Effect

1 The main point reflects the writer's purpose—to explain causes, effects, or both.

2 If the purpose is to explain causes, it gives real causes, not just things that happened before. For example, eating a hot dog before getting a speeding ticket does not mean that the hot dog causes the ticket.

3 If the purpose is to explain effects, it gives real effects, not just things that happened after. For example, getting a speeding ticket was not the effect of eating the hot dog; it simply happened after you ate the hot dog.

4 It gives readers detailed examples or explanations of the causes and/or effects.

The numbers and colors in the following paragraph correspond to the Four Basics of Cause and Effect.

1 Apple iPods and other portable listening devices may cause hearing loss in several ways, if people are not careful. **2** First, these devices often use earbuds. Earbuds come in many different varieties, and some have built-in microphones for phone calls. **4** Because these snug-fitting headphones deliver the music directly into the ear canal, **3** they can damage the eardrum. **2** Second, people listening to portable devices often turn the volume up to unsafe levels. **4** Some experts say volume levels that are higher than 80 percent of maximum **3** can harm the delicate parts of the inner ear. **2** The third, and perhaps most surprising, way that portable devices cause hearing loss is that people listen to them for too long. Before MP3 players and iPods, portable listening devices could hold only one tape or CD at a time, and hearing loss was rarely a problem. Now, with so many hours of music available on one small device, we can listen for many hours without taking a break. **4** In order to prevent permanent hearing damage, physicians recommend listening for no more than ninety minutes per day. Taking good care of your ears now, by listening at safe volumes for limited periods of time, will allow you to continue enjoying music throughout your life.

1. Underline the **topic sentence**.

2. What is the writer's purpose? _____

   _____

3. What are three causes of iPod hearing loss? _____

   _____

4. What are two effects explained in the paragraph?_____

   _____

5. Circle the sentence that is neither a cause nor an effect of iPod hearing loss.

Guided Outline: Cause and Effect

Fill in the outline with the detailed examples or explanations of effects. Try prewriting to get ideas, and save the most important effect for last.

Topic sentence: I never expected so much to happen as a result of my

decision to _____.

First effect: _____

    Details: _____

Second effect: _____

    Details: _____

Third effect: _____

    Details: _____

Concluding sentence: All of this reminded me that _____

   _____.

Write a Cause-and-Effect Paragraph

Write a cause-and-effect paragraph, using the outline that you developed, one of the following topics, or a topic of your own. Then, complete the cause-and-effect checklist on page 139.

- Causes of laughter
- Causes of cheating
- Causes of stress
- Causes of anxiety
- Causes of being late
- Causes of lying
- Causes of obesity
- Effects of overeating

- Possible effects of cheating
- Effects of getting a degree
- Effects of having a job you like
- Effects of being late to work
- Effects of lying to a partner
- Effects of obesity
- Effects of exercise

USE A VISUAL TO WRITE CAUSE AND EFFECT

Look at the photo below. Write a paragraph that discusses either the causes or effects of traffic congestion in cities.

AP PHOTO/RIC FRANCIS

CHECKLIST

Evaluating Your Cause-and-Effect Paragraph

☐ My writing style is appropriate for the audience and purpose. (Most college assignments should be written in formal English.)

☐ The paragraph has the Four Basics of Cause and Effect (p. 137).

• My topic sentence includes my topic and whether I am writing about causes, effects, or both.

• I have presented real causes (not just things that happened before), real effects (not just things that happened after), or both.

• I have given details so that my reader will understand the causes or effects.

☐ I have included transitions to move readers smoothly from cause or effect to the next.

☐ I have reread the paragraph, making improvements and checking for grammar and spelling errors.

Explore Cause and Effect Further: Health

As you read the sample paragraphs and essays below, look for the Four Basics of Cause and Effect (p. 137). Also, remember to use the 2PR strategy: preview, read, pause, and review (see pages 6-10).

Student Cause-and-Effect Paragraph

Kendal Rippel

We Need Sleep

Kendal Rippel wrote this paragraph for a health blog at *The Quill*, the student newspaper of Carroll Community College in Maryland. She addresses a problem many college students encounter: lack of sleep.

There are many risks to not getting enough sleep. When you do not get enough, your days can start to be affected. Sleeping allows you to relax and recover from the stress of the day. When you neglect to sleep it causes your body more stress. This stress can affect your life in many forms. It can cause you to be moody, drowsy, and very irritable. Your job and school work can also be affected, considering that you won't be able to focus as well as you would normally.

Professional Cause-and-Effect Paragraph

Wayne Weiten and Margaret Lloyd

What Makes Us Happy

This paragraph comes from Wayne Weiten and Margaret Lloyd's psychology textbook *Psychology Applied to Modern Life: Adjustment in the 21st Century*. The paragraph is part of a larger section addressing why people are happy and what research tells us about the causes of happiness.

The best predictor of individuals' future happiness is their past happiness. Some people seem destined to be happy and others unhappy, regardless of their triumphs or setbacks. Several studies suggest that happiness does not depend on external circumstances—having a nice house, good friends, and an enjoyable job—as much as internal factors, such as one's outlook on life. With this reality in mind, researchers have begun to look for links between personality and subjective[1] well-being, and they have found some relatively strong connections. For example, self-esteem is one of the predictors of happiness. Not surprisingly, people who like themselves tend to be happier than those who do not. Other personality correlates[2] of happiness include extraversion,[3] optimism, and a sense of personal control over one's life.

1. **subjective:** related to the thinking of an individual

2. **correlates:** two things that are related to each other

3. **extraversion:** a personality type that is focused primarily on the environment and other people and not on one's own thoughts or feelings

UNDERSTANDING CAUSE AND EFFECT

After you have read the two cause and effect paragraphs, complete the following.

1. Underline the main point in each paragraph.

2. In each paragraph, what cause or causes are explained?

3. In each paragraph, what effect or effects are explained?

4. What details or examples are given to support either the causes or the effects?

Student Cause-and-Effect Essay

Delia Cleveland

Champagne Taste, Beer Budget

Delia Cleveland attended New York University, where she majored in media studies. Her essay "Champagne Taste, Beer Budget" was written while she was a student at NYU and first appeared in the March 2001 issue of *Essence* magazine. Cleveland has also had her work published in *Black Elegance* and *Spice* magazines.

Guiding question   What effects did Cleveland's "champagne taste" have on her life?

1   My name is Dee, and I'm a recovering junkie. Yeah, I was hooked on the strong stuff, stuff that emptied my wallet and maxed-out my credit card during a single trip to the mall. I was a fashion addict. I wore a designer emblem on my chest like a badge of honor and respect. But the unnatural high of sporting a pricey label distorted[1] my understanding of what it really meant to have "arrived."

2   At first, I just took pride in being the best-dressed female at my high school. Fellows adored my jiggy[2] style; girls were insanely jealous. I became a fiend[3] for the attention. In my mind, clothes made the woman, and everything else was secondary. Who cared about geometry? Every Friday, I spent all my paltry[4] paycheck from my part-time job on designer clothes. Life as I knew it revolved around a classy façade.[5] Then, slowly my money started getting tight, so tight I even resorted to borrowing from my mother. Me, go out looking average? Hell no! I'd cut a class or wouldn't bother going to school at all, unable to bear the thought of friends saying that I had fallen off and was no longer in vogue.

3   Out of concern, my mother began snooping around my bedroom to see where my paycheck was going. She found a telltale receipt I'd carelessly left in a shopping bag. Worse, she had set up a savings account for me, and I secretly withdrew most of the money—$1,000—to satisfy my jones.[6] Then, I feverishly[7] charged $600 for yet another quick fashion fix.

4   "Delia, you're turning into a lunatic, giving all your hard-earned money to multimillionaires!" she screamed.

5   "Mama," I shrugged, "you're behind the times." I was looking fly,[8] and that was all that mattered.

6   Until I got left back in the tenth grade.

7   The fact that I was an A student before I discovered labels put fire under my mother's feet. In her eyes, I was letting name brands control my

Tip A guiding question can help you focus when you are reading. Make sure you can answer the guiding question when you have finished. For more information on reading and guiding questions, see Chapter 1.

1. **distorted:** twisted or bent out of shape

2. **jiggy:** slang for exciting and stylish

3. **fiend:** an obsessive or fanatical person

4. **paltry:** small, lacking in importance

5. **façade:** a false front

6. **jones:** a craving or desire for something

7. **feverishly:** in an excited, out-of-control way

8. **fly:** cool

life, and I needed help. Feeling I had no other choice, she got me transferred to another school. I had screwed up so badly that a change did seem to be in order. Besides, I wanted to show her that labels couldn't control me. So even though everyone, including me, knew I was "smart" and an excellent student, I found myself at an alternative high school.

8   Meanwhile, I began looking at how other well-dressed addicts lived to see where they were headed. The sobering reality was this: They weren't going anywhere. In fact, the farthest they'd venture[9] was the neighborhood corner or a party—all dressed up, nowhere to go. I watched them bop around in $150 hiking boots—they'd never been hiking. They sported $300 ski jackets—they'd never been near a ski slope. I saw parents take three-hour bus trips to buy their kids discount-price designer labels, yet these parents wouldn't take a trip to make a bank deposit in their child's name. Watching them, I was forced to look at myself, at my own financial and intellectual stagnation,[10] at the soaring interest on my overused credit card.

9   That's when it all came clear. At my new high school, I attended classes with adults—less emphasis on clothes, more emphasis on work. Although the alternative school gave me invaluable work experience, I never received the kind of high school education I should have had—no sports, no prom, no fun. I realized I had sacrificed an important part of my life for material[11] stuff that wasn't benefiting me at all.

10   That was twelve years ago. Today, I'm enjoying a clean-and-sober lifestyle. Armed with a new awareness, I've vowed to leave designer labels to people who can truly afford them. I refuse to tote a $500 bag until I can fill it with an equal amount of cash. I'm not swaggering[12] around in overpriced Italian shoes until I can book a trip to Italy. On my road to recovery, I have continued to purchase clothing—sensibly priced. And every now and then, the money I save goes toward a Broadway play or a vacation in the sun. I'm determined to seek the culture my designer clothes once implied[13] I had. I no longer look the part—because I'm too busy living it.

9. venture: go out, explore

10. stagnation: a dullness; a state without growth or motion

11. material: of the physical world, not of the spiritual

12. swaggering: walking around in a boastful, cocky, or arrogant way

13. implied: suggested without directly stating

CHECK YOUR COMPREHENSION

1. Which of the following would be the best alternative title for this essay?

   a. "How to Save Money on Brand-Name Products"

   b. "America's Financial Crisis"

   c. "Confessions of a Former Fashion Junkie"

   d. "Alternative School Was the Only Alternative"

2. The main idea of this essay is that

   a. teenagers need to build good credit while they are young.

   b. out-of-control spending and obsessions with brand names can have damaging consequences for teenagers.

   c.   today's high school students are not willing to work as hard as students in the past but are good at saving money.

   d.   Cleveland's parents did not provide enough rules when she was growing up, which led to her financial problems.

3. According to the article,

   a.   Cleveland always had trouble in school but made up for this by buying fashionable clothes.

   b.   only students with bad grades can get caught up in irresponsible shopping and credit card problems.

   c.   Cleveland's mother set a poor financial example for her daughter.

   d.   Cleveland was an A student before she discovered designer labels.

4. Write sentences using the following vocabulary words: *distort* (para. 1); *paltry, façade* (2); *feverishly* (3); *stagnation* (8).

READ CRITICALLY

1. What values and desires caused Cleveland to become a brand-name "junkie"?

2. What were the effects of the writer's spending habits?

3. Cleveland uses some slang in her essay. Why, considering the audience and purpose, is this appropriate?

4. Paragraph 6 is a fragment. What effect does this one-fragment paragraph have on the reader?

5. What finally caused Cleveland to change her attitude and spending habits?

WRITE

1. Have you ever had a conflict with a parent like the one that Cleveland includes here? What caused it? What effects did it have?

2. Cleveland writes about an experience that caused her to change her values, attitudes, and behavior. Has any experience made you alter your own point of view or your habits? Write a cause-and-effect paragraph or essay about what happened and how the experience changed you.

Professional Cause-and-Effect Essay

Natalie McGill

Caffeine: Don't Let Your Pick-Me-Up Drag You Down

Natalie McGill is a reporter for *The Nation's Health*, a publication of the American Public Health Association.

Guiding question What are the effects of consuming too much caffeine?

1   You may feel like you need a cup of coffee to wake you up in the morning or an energy drink to keep you awake during the day. Those beverages have one thing in common to keep you coming back for more: caffeine.

2   Caffeine is a substance that can be found in drinks such as soda, coffee and tea or in foods such as chocolate. It stimulates[1] your central nervous system, making you more alert and focused. But there is such a thing as too much caffeine, and if you think you need two energy drinks instead of one, it's important to recognize signs of a problem—and the ways you can cut back.

3   With many adult Americans consuming caffeine regularly, people should be aware of how caffeine affects them, says Steven Meredith, PhD, a postdoctoral research fellow[2] at the Johns Hopkins University School of Medicine's Behavioral Pharmacology[3] Research Unit.

4   Meredith says a 12-ounce can of soda usually contains 40 milligrams of caffeine, while a 16-ounce energy drink could contain 160 milligrams or more. Cups of coffee bought at a coffee house can contain 300 milligrams or more of caffeine, he says. And that's on top of added sweeteners and calories.

5   Healthy adults can have 400 milligrams or more of caffeine per day, but consuming excessive amounts can lead to health concerns such as heart issues, Meredith says. Other side effects can include elevated blood pressure, dehydration[4], dizziness and trouble sleeping, according to the U.S. Food and Drug Administration.

6   "Certain individuals—especially children, the elderly, people with heart conditions, women who are pregnant and breastfeeding or individuals with anxiety problems or other psychological problem—should avoid excessive consumption[5] or check with their physician before consuming too much caffeine," he says.

7   While people can have side effects from too much caffeine, they can also have withdrawal[6] symptoms when they don't have their usual amount. The symptoms are the "exact opposite of the direct effects of caffeine," Meredith says.

8   "So if caffeine makes you feel energized and alert, then caffeine withdrawal may make you feel tired or foggy," he says. "And consciously or not, many people try to relieve or avoid the withdrawal symptoms by just consuming more caffeine."

Tips for Cutting Back on Caffeine

9   If you think you consume too much caffeine and that the best route is stop cold turkey, think again.

---

1. **stimulate:** excite; cause to be active

2. **Postdoctoral Research Fellow:** a researcher who has completed a doctoral degree
3. **pharmacology:** the study of drugs and their effects on people

4. **dehydration:** a dangerous loss of water from the body

5. **consumption:** eating or drinking

6. **withdrawal:** the process or results of stopping use of a drug

10   Meredith says the best way to reduce your need for caffeine is to wean[7] yourself off of it. If you usually have three caffeine drinks each day, cut back to two, he recommends. Avoid drinking caffeine in the afternoon or the evening, because that could affect your sleep. Regular exercise and a healthy diet can also help you reduce your need for caffeine.

11   "If you brew your own coffee, or if you buy it from a coffee house, make it 75 percent regular and 25 percent decaf during the first week of your quit attempt, and then slowly kind of mix in more decaf during subsequent[8] weeks," Meredith says.

12   Gradually reducing your need for caffeine is better than bringing your consumption to a grinding halt. Stopping abruptly may worsen withdrawal symptoms such as fatigue, irritability, nausea and vomiting.

7. **wean:** to separate from something or stop using something gradually

8. **subsequent:** following

Keep Caffeine away from Kids

13   While caffeine can be common in drinks aimed at kids, it's best to keep it out of their diets. Pediatricians say that kids younger than 12 shouldn't have caffeine in their diets because there are no benefits to having caffeine at an early age, Meredith says. Consuming caffeine at a young age may lead to slower brain development in teens, a recent study found.

14   "Children now have access to not only a greater number of caffeine-containing products, but some of these products contain more caffeine than what most of us were exposed to when we were children," Meredith says. "A caffeinated drink might contain three or more times the amount of caffeine that's contained in the serving size of soda."

15   In addition to knowing how much their children consume, parents should consider either reducing their caffeine intake or cutting it out of their diet to be good role models for their kids.

16   Instead of relying on caffeine to wake up early in the morning or find more energy in the afternoon, "We might want to teach out kids that there are other ways to solve these problems, like exercising or getting more sleep," he says.

CHECK YOUR COMPREHENSION

1. Which of the following would be the best alternative title for this essay?
    a. "Caffeine Addiction: America's Health Crisis"
    b. "How to Brew a Perfect Cup of Decaf"
    c. "How Caffeinated Beverages Have Changed"
    d. "Caffeine: How Much Is Too Much?"

2. The main point of this essay is that
    a. children should not be given caffeine.
    b. energy drinks can be dangerous.
    c. people should be careful how much caffeine they consume.
    d. two cups of coffee is enough for anyone.

3. According to McGill,

   a.   heavy caffeine drinkers should stop all at once.

   b.   caffeine withdrawal can make people feel tired and sluggish.

   c.   caffeine at night helps people sleep better.

   d.   caffeine does not affect blood pressure.

4. Does this essay include the Four Basics of Cause and Effect? Be prepared to say why or why not.

5. Write sentences using the following vocabulary words: *withdrawal* (para. 7); *wean* (10); *subsequent* (11).

READ CRITICALLY

1. Who is McGill's intended audience? How do you know?

2. Why is too much caffeine dangerous, according to the essay?

3. McGill discusses not only the effects of too much caffeine but also the effects of caffeine withdrawal when people try to eliminate or reduce caffeine intake too quickly. What are the effects of caffeine withdrawal, and how do they relate to the main point of the essay?

4. What evidence does McGill use to convince her readers of the dangers of too much caffeine? Is her evidence convincing? Why or why not?

5. McGill uses short paragraphs in her article; paragraph 15, for example, is a single sentence. What is McGill's purpose? How do the short paragraphs in the article help her accomplish that purpose?

WRITE

1. According to McGill, caffeine is dangerous only if you have too much of it. We may often ask ourselves how much is too much of something. Explore that question for another food, substance, or activity. What happens when you have too much?

2. In paragraph 15, McGill recommends that parents change their behavior in order to be good role models for their children. Have you ever changed your behavior for the benefit of a child, parent, or friend? Has someone ever changed his or her behavior for your benefit? What happened? Write about the experience, making sure that you emphasize the effects of the change in behavior.

Argument

Argument takes a position on an issue and gives detailed reasons that defend or support it. You use argument to persuade someone to see things your way and/or to take an action. Being able to argue well is important in every area of your life.

Four Basics of Argument

1 It takes a strong and definite position.

2 It gives good reasons and evidence to defend the position.

3 It considers opposing positions.

4 It has enthusiasm and energy from start to finish.

The numbers and colors in the following paragraph correspond to the Four Basics of Argument.

1 Rap singers should change what they talk about. 2 One reason that they should change is that they talk about women in a disrespectful way. Rap singers should stop calling women "hos" and other negative terms. Most women resent being called these terms, and calling women names encourages men to treat them badly. Rap songs also make violence toward women seem manly and reasonable. 2 Another reason to change topics is that the lyrics promote violence, crime, and drugs in general. When young people are shooting each other in cities around the country, something is wrong, and no one should be making it seem glamorous, courageous, or manly. That is what rap lyrics do. 3 Some people say that rap songs are just music, not causes of anything but enjoyment. But I disagree: Many young people listen carefully to rap lyrics and are affected by the words. 2 The most important reason that rap singers should change topics is that they have a chance to make things better rather than glorifying violence. Rap singers could be a strong force for positive change. They could help our cities and our country. Rap singers can sing about whatever they like: Why can't they sing for the good of all?

4 Argument has energy from start to finish.

1. Underline the **topic sentence**.

2. What is the topic? _____

   What is the writer's position? _____

   _____

3. What three reasons does the writer give to support the position? _____

   _____

   _____

4. Name one detail that the writer could add to make the paragraph
    stronger. _____

    _____

    _____

5. Rewrite the topic sentence to make it stronger. _____

    _____

Guided Outline: Argument

Fill in the outline with reasons, and details about the reasons, that support the position in the topic sentence. Try prewriting to get ideas, and save the most important reason for last.

Topic sentence: It should be legal/illegal for the government to listen in on

U.S. citizens' phone conversations without having to get a warrant.

First reason: _____

    Details: _____

Second reason: _____

    Details: _____

Third reason: _____

    Details: _____

Concluding sentence: _____

_____.

Write an Argument Paragraph

Write an argument paragraph, using the outline that you developed, one of the following topics, or a topic of your own. Then, complete the argument checklist on page 149.

- Why you should get a raise
- Why you should get a higher grade
- Banning/allowing junk food in schools
- Why people should recycle
- Why college athletes should/should not get special treatment
- Lowering/raising the drinking age
- Making smoking illegal
- Your college should have more . . .

- Why you should be allowed to retake a test
- Why someone should finish high school
- The practice of taking photos of strangers in public places, and then posting these photos on social Web sites with admiring notes and comments

USE A VISUAL TO WRITE AN ARGUMENT PARAGRAPH

Look at the photos below. Write a paragraph arguing that students should (or should not) be allowed to have cell phones, laptops, and other electronic devices in class.

CHECKLIST

Evaluating Your Argument Paragraph

- [ ] My writing style is appropriate for the audience and purpose. (Most college assignments should be written in formal English.)
- [ ] The paragraph has the Four Basics of Argument (p. 147).
    - My topic sentence presents my topic and a strong position on that topic.
    - I have given solid reasons and details to support my position.
    - I have considered the opposing point of view.
    - I have written with enthusiasm and energy.
- [ ] I have included transitions to move readers smoothly from reason or example to the next.
- [ ] I have reread the paragraph, making improvements and checking for grammar and spelling errors.

Explore Argument Further: How We Eat and the Language We Speak

As you read the sample paragraphs and essays below, look for the Four Basics of Argument (p. 147). Also, remember to use the 2PR strategy: preview, read, pause, and review (see pages 6-10).

Professional Argument Paragraph

Michael Pollan

Vegetarians and Human Culture

The following paragraph by environmental journalist Michael Pollan came from his 2006 book *The Omnivore's Dilemma: A Natural History of Four Meals.* In this passage, he describes a loss he feels after becoming a vegetarian.

1. **trivial:** minor

2. **virtuous:** righteous; honorable

3. **alienated:** separated

Even if the vegetarian is a more highly evolved human being, it seems to me he has lost something along the way, something I'm not prepared to dismiss as trivial.[1] Healthy and virtuous[2] as I may feel these days, I also feel alienated[3] from traditions I value: cultural traditions like the Thanksgiving turkey, or even franks at the ballpark, and family traditions like my mother's beef brisket at Passover. These ritual meals link us to our history along multiple lines—family, religion, landscape, nation, and, if you want to go back much further, biology. For although humans no longer need meat in order to survive (now that we can get our B-12 from fermented foods or supplements), we have been meat eaters for most of our time on earth. This fact of evolutionary history is reflected in the design of our teeth, the structure of our digestion, and, quite possibly, in the way my mouth still waters at the sight of a steak cooked medium rare. Meat eating helped make us what we are in a physical as well as a social sense. Under the pressure of the hunt, anthropologists tell us, the human brain grew in size and complexity, and around the hearth where the spoils of the hunt were cooked and then apportioned, human culture first flourished.

UNDERSTANDING ARGUMENT

1. Underline the main position that is being argued.

2. Double-underline the reasons that are given to defend the position. What details and examples are used to explain those reasons?

3. Are any opposing positions acknowledged? If so, circle them.

4. Does the author's argument convince you of his point? Why or why not?

Professional Argument Paragraph

Physicians Committee for Responsible Medicine

Eating Healthfully

The following paragraph is from **www.nutritionmd.org**, a Web site sponsored by the Physicians Committee for Responsible Medicine. This nonprofit organization, which has more than 6,000 member physicians, seeks to improve the prevention and treatment of conditions like diabetes and cancer through educational programs, clinical research, and other measures. The paragraph is part of a larger discussion of how particular dietary changes can reduce the risk of certain diseases.

Abundant[1] evidence suggests that the most healthful diets set aside animal products and also reduce fats in general, while including large amounts of vegetables and fruits. Eliminating meat and dairy products from your diet is a powerful step in disease prevention. These products are typically high in saturated fat and cholesterol and completely devoid of fiber. They have also been specifically linked to an increased risk of certain types of cancers. Eating a low-fat, plant-based diet rich in whole grains, beans, fruits, and vegetables is the best way to prevent disease and increase chances of survival.

1. **abundant:** plentiful; large amounts of

> **UNDERSTANDING ARGUMENT**

1. Underline the main position that is being argued.

2. Double-underline the reasons that are given to defend the position.

3. Are any opposing positions acknowledged? If so, circle them.

4. Are you convinced of this paragraph's main argument? Why or why not?

Student Argument Essay

Sheena Ivey

English as an Official Language: One Language for One Nation

Sheena Ivey wrote this essay while she was a student at the University of South Alabama. This essay and the piece that follows it were featured in the student newspaper, *The Vanguard,* to provide opposing opinions on the topic "English as an Official Language."

Guiding question   What reasons does Ivey give to support her position?

Tip A guiding question can help you focus when you are reading. Make sure you can answer the guiding question when you have finished. For more information on reading and guiding questions, see Chapter 1.

1. **political correctness:** excessive concern about diversity

2. **irrelevant:** not important

3. **fluent:** able to speak a language fully and easily

1   Political correctness[1] has gotten the best of some people in our nation on the question as to whether to make English the official language of the United States. The fact that our Constitution is in English, along with the foundations of our law, seems to be irrelevant[2] to certain citizens and lawmakers.

2   Our country was founded by English-speaking men. All of our presidents have been fluent[3] in English. Every congressional session has been spoken in English. The United States, as a superpower in the world today, has largely influenced the spread of English (not Spanish) throughout the world. We have much influence as an English-speaking nation. However, some people question how we dare to propose English as our official language, even when doing so would benefit the United States by making it more unified and efficient.

3   America could easily be divided and cease to be a superpower if we do not adopt English as our official language. We would open ourselves up to state or local governments adopting other languages as their "official language" by a simple majority vote of the people in that area, as we see in Canada, which now has two official languages (English and French) and is a divided nation.

4   Having an official language will unify the United States by helping to prevent cultural divisions. Classes in American schools should have to be taught in only one language. Imagine what kind of division would be created if some students attended classes taught only in Spanish, while others attended classes taught only in English.

5   What about someone running for the presidency or some other public position? He or she would need to speak in a language that everyone in the United States could understand, but even this will become impossible if English does not become our official language and America's culture is divided into different language groups.

4. **mandatory:** necessary, required

5. **notoriously:** in a well-known manner

6   Making it mandatory[4] for immigrants to learn English will help them become more successful in the United States. The kinds of jobs available in America to people who cannot speak English are notoriously[5] poorly paid, difficult, and dead-end. Learning English would also help people to protect themselves better legally and to communicate better with emergency medical technicians, doctors, waiters, and corporate personnel directors, along with the vast majority of American citizens.

6. **sectors:** parts of a society

7   Not having English as our official language has already opened us up to lawsuits demanding interpreters and translators in our governmental and educational sectors.[6] Where does it end when the attempt is made by legislators to make everyone happy?

8   We, of course, welcome people of all cultures and languages to the United States, as long as they meet a certain standard, part of which should be to speak English relatively well. Should we as American taxpayers have to provide all non-English-speaking people with translators? It is not fair to provide services only to Hispanics just because there are more Hispanic immigrants living here than other groups. They should have to conform to U.S. standards, just as all other immigrants must conform. By having

everything from street signs to shampoo bottles in multiple languages is cumbersome[7] and counterproductive.

9   The cost to American taxpayers for not making English the official language of the United States will be enormous. The workforce in the United States already bears a heavy tax burden, and it should not be increased by having to provide the funding necessary to staff all of our governmental agencies, including every city hall and license office, with multiple interpreters. Doing so would be the equivalent of saying that we as taxpayers have to pay more taxes because foreigners want to come to the United States. Others are welcome to come as assets to the country but not as burdens or detriments[8] to U.S. citizens.

10   The legislation that pushed for English as an official language keeps being watered down from an "official" language to a "national" language to a "common and unifying" language of America. About half of the world's countries have an official language. How can such a powerful nation as the United States become so feeble[9] as to beat around this topic, minimizing the importance of the issue? Some may say that pushing for an official language is creating a problem that does not exist. However, even though it may not be an immediately pressing issue, it is important to take preventive measures. We need an official national identity. People from all over the world already see us as an English-speaking nation, and we should make that official.

11   Having said this, it is also important that we begin teaching our children more languages in schools, in order to better understand and communicate with other parts of the world while remaining unified as an English-speaking nation. Having an official national language—English—will benefit our nation for both symbolic[10] and practical purposes, as will having citizens who know other languages in order to work more efficiently with the rest of the world.

7. **cumbersome:** heavy, troublesome, and difficult to handle

8. **detriments:** losses, damages, or disadvantages

9. **feeble:** weak

10. **symbolic:** representing or standing for something else

CHECK YOUR COMPREHENSION

1. Which of the following would be the best alternative title for this essay?
   a. "American Students Need to Learn Foreign Languages"
   b. "English: One Official Language for All Americans"
   c. "America: A Nation Divided against Itself"
   d. "The American Workforce Is Overtaxed"

2. The main idea of this essay is that
   a. lawmakers should make English the official language of the United States to increase efficiency and unity.
   b. people who come to the United States should not have to leave their culture or their language behind them.
   c. the United States has become feeble compared with other countries.
   d. interpreters and translators are overpaid and unnecessary.

3. Ivey makes the point that

   a. English is not the official language of Mexico.

   b. Americans are generally unwelcoming of immigrants and immigrant cultures.

   c. the people who wrote the U.S. Constitution originally planned to make English the official language of the country.

   d. there will be an enormous financial cost to Americans for not making English the official language.

4. Does the essay include the Four Basics of Argument? Be prepared to say why or why not.

5. Write sentences using the following vocabulary words: *irrelevant* (para. 1); *mandatory* (6); *cumbersome* (8); *detriment* (9); *symbolic* (11).

READ CRITICALLY

1. According to Ivey, what are the bad or undesirable effects of not making English the official language of the United States?

2. What examples does she provide to support her argument that English should be the official language?

3. Does Ivey do an effective job of considering and addressing opposing arguments?

4. According to Ivey, what attitude should Americans and American society take toward immigrants to the United States?

5. How effective is Ivey's concluding paragraph? Why do you think that she includes this in her argument?

WRITE

1. Ivey writes that making English the national language would have symbolic value as well as practical value for the United States. Do you think that national symbols are important for national unity? Write an argument for why or why not, using an example of a national symbol.

2. According to Ivey, "political correctness" is a major reason that the United States has not made English its official language. Do you agree that the United States has generally become too concerned with diversity and too sensitive on subjects like race, immigration, and cultural differences? Write an argument paragraph or essay presenting your position on this question.

Student Argument Essay

Tony Felts

English as an Official Language: The Injustice of One Language

Tony Felts graduated from the University of South Alabama with a degree in geography and currently works as a city planner. During the revision of his essay, which he wrote as a student for the student newspaper, *The Vanguard,* Felts says that his goals were "first and foremost, to correct any grammatical and spelling errors, and two, to make my ideas and arguments more cogent and effective." With experience in writing on controversial topics, Felts advises other writers, "Do not compromise your views, but also do not appear to be arrogant. Always put the reader at ease, and relate a story that they can identify with to give the issue a personal touch."

Guiding question   What reasons does Felts give to support his position?

1   The color of this country is changing. According to the United States Census Bureau, some 35.5 million Americans are of Hispanic descent. That represents 12.5 percent of the country's population. Perhaps nowhere in Alabama is this change more evident than it is in the city of Albertville.

2   Albertville, by all outward appearances, is a typical Alabama town, but look closer. As you drive down Highway 205, you will notice that road signs and shopping center signs include language proclaiming "tiendas," "joyerías," "mercados," and "iglesias." Everywhere you look, you will notice the presence of the Spanish language. Spanish advertisements fill the yellow pages and the local newspaper. Even the local court system has added Spanish-speaking officials to keep the wheels of justice moving. Hispanics have created a vibrant[1] home and community within the city of Albertville.

3   But is this influx[2] of Hispanics a bad thing? According to Jared Stewart, a bilingual court referral officer in the Marshall County court system, most of the Hispanics in the Marshall County area, and indeed the rest of the country, are hard workers. They hold jobs in the agricultural industry; some own businesses, and all pay taxes. But from talking to non-Hispanic people in the area, one gets the impression that the Hispanics are the worst thing that ever happened to Albertville. Indeed, since the influx of Hispanics began, many of the white residents have relocated. In no uncertain terms, what Albertville is experiencing is rural "white flight." What is the root cause of this? It is the by-product of ignorance, fear, and quite frankly, racism. And it is not even well-veiled.

4   In no issue is the racism so clearly conveyed[3] as with the discussion about making English the official language. The original language of Senator James Inhofe's (R-Oklahoma) amendment to the Senate Immigration Reform Bill stipulated[4] that no government body would have any obligation to provide government documents or assistance in any language other than English. Such a stipulation would have caused this county to come to a grinding halt. Many

1. **vibrant:** lively, energetic, active
2. **influx:** the process of flowing in

3. **conveyed:** carried or presented

4. **stipulated:** promised or required, in making an agreement

areas, where cash-strapped governments are cutting corners in anywhere they can find, would see this as an invitation to cut costs by deleting Spanish language services. Such a move would send hardworking individuals down a slippery slope[5] into the shadows, removing them from society altogether, instead of integrating them into the melting pot of America.

5. slippery slope: a small step leading to a chain reaction

5   Imagine a Spanish speaker with little skill in English being charged with a crime that he or she did not commit. Then imagine being summoned to court to face charges and arguments in a language that he or she cannot understand. This is not American and not moral. But the accused doesn't even have to be a Spanish speaker. Consider the many Vietnamese right here in Mobile County or in Biloxi, Mississippi. Consider Tagalog[6] speakers in Rhode Island. Senator Inhofe's amendment affects all Americans and harshly impacts the lives of hardworking immigrants.

6. Tagalog: a language spoken in the Philippines

6   Ultimately, new language was added to Senator Inhofe's amendment that stipulated that English would be the "national" language, not the "official" language, and that the English-only mandates would negate existing laws.

7   Should immigrants learn English? Yes. Should immigrants have to be functionally[7] literate in English before becoming a citizen? Yes. Should we deny non-English speakers their rights to due process[8] and access to assistance because they do not understand the language? No. It is wrong, racist, and, most important, immoral.

7. functionally: in a way that allows someone to do basic, essential, and practical tasks

8. due process: fair treatment in the courts

8   Our country has historically been a melting pot of new people. Except for the 4.1 million of us who describe ourselves as Alaska Native or American Indian, each and every one of us is the descendant[9] of an immigrant. Many immigrants had little knowledge of English when they arrived in this country in the huge wave of immigration in the nineteenth century. Historically, there have been colonies of Spanish speakers, French speakers, Italian speakers, German speakers, and so on in this country. In fact, Puerto Rico, a United States territory with some 4 million American citizens, is almost exclusively Spanish speaking. What about these people and their language?

9. descendant: a person related to a family member who existed at an earlier point in history

9   The bottom line is that our country is as diverse as it is large. We have historically been a melting pot of cultures, ideas, and languages. We cannot become a people who say that it is our way or the highway. We must reject that nationalist[10] form of ignorance. We must continue to accept and understand the needs of our citizens and our immigrants. We must reject the idea of cutting off services to people and, instead, adopt a spirit of helpfulness. Perhaps we should also consider learning a foreign language ourselves, instead of being stubborn about speaking only English. We have to have open arms in the United States: That is the very foundation of our country.

10. nationalist: devoted to your own nation over the interests of all others

CHECK YOUR COMPREHENSION

1. Which of the following would be the best alternative title for this essay?

    a. "Spanish Is Already Our Unofficial National Language"

    b. "Cash-Strapped Governments Cut Corners in Bad Economy"

    c. "Hispanics Build Vibrant Home in Alabama"

    d. "We Should Reject Nationalist Ignorance in Language Debate"

2. The main idea of this essay is that
    a. immigrants tend to be hard workers, even if they cannot speak English.
    b. having an official national language would be unjust and un-American.
    c. immigrants need to learn English or return to their home countries.
    d. America was once a melting pot but no longer is one.

3. Felts claims some whites are leaving Albertville, Alabama, because
    a. they want more satisfying and better-paying jobs in other towns.
    b. of their ignorance, fear, and racism.
    c. housing prices in the town have become too high.
    d. the town has made Spanish its official language.

4. Does the essay include the Four Basics of Argument? Why or why not?

5. Write sentences using the following vocabulary words: *vibrant* (para. 2); *influx* (3); *stipulate* (4); *functional* (7); *nationalist* (9).

READ CRITICALLY

1. How does Felts's essay describe most immigrant workers? How does this help his argument?

2. According to Felts, what will happen if the government passes legislation such as Senator Inhofe's amendment to the Immigration Reform Bill?

3. What points does Felts make in paragraph 5?

4. Does Felts consider and address the arguments of those who disagree with his point of view? How effectively does he do this?

5. How does Felts appeal to American history and ideals in his essay?

WRITE

1. Felts takes a definite position against making English the official language of the United States. What is your own view of this issue? Write an argument in which you make your own case either for or against making English an official language.

2. Write an argument about another national problem dealing with immigration, race, American identity, or a related subject that interests you. Like Felts, take a clear position, and provide examples and details to support your case.

3. If you have read both Felts's and Ivey's essays, write an argument that draws from both of those essays—one to support your position, the other to consider the opposing view. You may want to quote the authors directly. If so, see Chapter 28 for information about how to use quotation marks correctly.

Chapter Review

1. What does a comparison-and-contrast paragraph do? _____

   _____

2. What does a cause-and-effect paragraph do? _____

   _____

3. What does an argument paragraph do? _____

   _____

REFLECTING ON THE JOURNEY

Skills Learned

Now that you've completed the chapter, share what you've learned about each skill by completing the following chart.

Skill	What I learned about this skill
Write a comparison-and-contrast paragraph (show how two things are similar or different)	
Write a cause-and-effect paragraph (explain why something happens or what the results of something are)	
Write an argument paragraph (give reasons and evidence to support a position)	

9

Moving from Paragraphs to Essays

How to Write Longer Papers

Learning Objectives

Chapter Goal: Write an essay with five paragraphs.

Tools to Achieve the Goal

- Parts of an essay (p. 160)
- The writing process for essays (p. 162)
- Four Basics of a Good Draft (p. 167)
- Checklist for evaluating an essay (p. 169)

Key Terms

Skim Chapter 9 before you begin reading. Can you find each of these words in **bold** type? Put a check mark next to each word once you have located it in the chapter.

_____ introduction   _____ conclusion
_____ body   _____ thesis statement

Highlight or circle any of these words that you already know.

Before You Read

Before you begin reading this chapter, fill out the following chart. For each skill, think of a time when you have used this skill and what you would like to know upon completing the chapter. At the end of the chapter, you will be asked to share what you learned about this skill.

Skill	When I have used this skill	What I want to know about this skill
Narrow a topic for an essay		
Write a thesis statement for an essay		
Support the thesis statement with topic sentences for paragraphs		

Understand Essay Structure

An essay has multiple paragraphs and three necessary parts:

Essay Part	Contents / Purpose of the Part
1. An **introduction**	includes a thesis statement that states the main point. The introduction is usually the first paragraph.
2. A **body**	includes at least three paragraphs. Each paragraph usually begins with a topic sentence that supports the thesis statement. Each topic sentence is supported by examples and details in the rest of the paragraph.
3. A **conclusion**	reminds readers of the main point, just as the concluding sentence of a paragraph does. The conclusion in an essay is usually the last paragraph. It summarizes the support and makes an observation.

The following diagram shows how the parts of an essay relate to the parts of a paragraph.

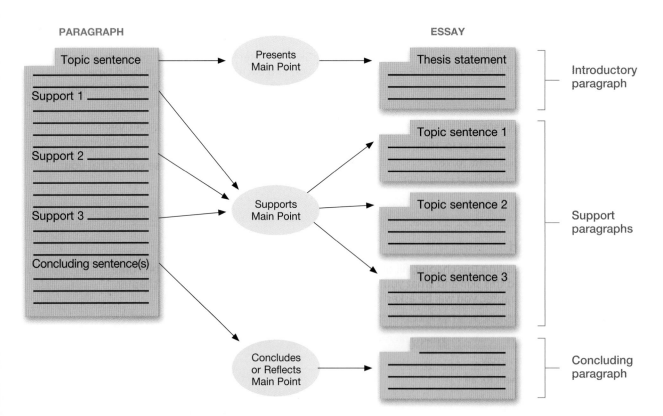

Read the following essay, noticing how the introduction, body, and conclusion paragraphs differ from each other.

Demand for medical professionals is high, and it is expected to grow over the next decade. Although physicians are always needed, medicine offers many other kinds of jobs that provide satisfaction and good salaries.

Thesis statement
Introduction

One of the high-demand professions is that of radiology technician. These professionals perform ultrasounds, take X-rays, and do mammograms and magnetic resonance imaging (MRI) tests. Radiology technicians must operate expensive, sensitive machines with great care and accuracy. They must also have good people skills because they will encounter patients who are nervous about tests. The average starting salary for these technicians is $44,000.

Another high-demand profession is nursing. With the average age of Americans on the rise, many more nurses are needed to supply good health care to the aging population. Registered nurses are in short supply all over the United States, and hospitals are competing with one another to hire them. These nurses provide a wide range of patient care, such as documenting symptoms, administering medicines, and working with physicians. Registered nurses' average starting wage is $24 an hour, and many nurses can expect to be offered large bonuses when they agree to accept a position.

Body paragraphs

Another high-demand job in the medical field is physician's assistant, or PA. Physician assistants work in doctors' offices, hospitals, or clinics, where they are supervised by a doctor. They do many of the routine tasks that used to be performed only by doctors: they examine patients, prescribe medications, and order additional tests. Physician assistants may do other jobs as well, depending on where they work. They may assist with surgery, give vaccinations, or monitor patients in a hospital. Because many healthcare facilities are hiring physician assistants to support the work of doctors, there is a great demand for PAs, whose average starting salary is $71,000.

Medical careers offer many advantages, including the ability to find a job in almost any area of the country as well as good salaries and benefits. Trained radiology technicians, nurses, and pharmacists are likely to remain in high demand as the population ages, as scientists discover new cures, and as technology advances.

Conclusion

Essays can be short or long, depending on the writer's purpose and on the assignment. In this course, you may be asked to write essays that have five paragraphs—an introduction, three body paragraphs, and a conclusion.

Write an Essay

The process of writing an essay is the same process you have used to write a paragraph. The steps in this section will help you write an essay, but if you need more explanations and practices, go back to Chapters 3–5, which have more details about each of the steps.

> **Get Ideas**
> **(See Chapter 3.)**
>
> • Narrow and explore your topic (prewrite).

↓

> **Write**
> **(See Chapter 4.)**
>
> • State your main point (thesis statement).
> • Write topic sentences for each major point supporting the thesis statement, and write paragraphs that support each topic sentence.
> • Make an outline or plan of your ideas.
> • Write a draft.
> • Reread your draft, taking notes about what would make it better.

↓

> **Rewrite**
> **(See Chapter 5.)**
>
> • Rewrite your draft, making the changes you noted (and more).
> • Reread the new draft, making sure it is as good as you can make it.

↓

> **Edit**
> **(See Parts 2–7.)**
>
> • Read your paper for grammar, punctuation, and spelling errors.

Narrow Your Topic

Just as you have done for paragraphs, you often need to narrow a general essay topic to a smaller one.

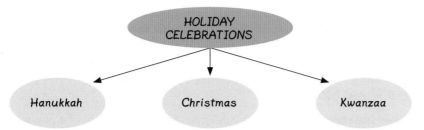

Because essays are longer than paragraphs, essay topics can be a little more general than paragraph topics, but not a lot more. The topic still needs to be narrow enough that you can make your main point about it in a manageable number of paragraphs. Use prewriting (see Chapter 3) to narrow and explore your topic as necessary.

The following examples show how the topic for an essay is a little broader than one for a paragraph.

Assigned general topic		Narrowed for an essay		Narrowed for a paragraph
Student stress	→	Managing work and college	→	Studying for a test
Television programs	→	Reality TV	→	*American Idol*
Gender differences	→	Male/female speech patterns	→	Male/female responses to a James Bond movie

PRACTICE 1

Narrow the following five general topics to good essay topics. Think about whether you could make a point about the topic and support that point in three paragraphs.

1. Professional sports

   Narrowed essay topic: _____

2. Vacation

   Narrowed essay topic: _____

3. Personal goals

   Narrowed essay topic: _____

4. Helping others

   Narrowed essay topic: _____

5. Things that annoy you

   Narrowed essay topic: _____

As you narrow your topic, you usually get some ideas about why that topic is impor-tant to you (or what is interesting about it) and what you want to say about it. Make a note of those ideas so that you can use them to write a thesis statement.

Write a Thesis Statement

The **thesis statement** of an essay is similar to the topic sentence of a paragraph. It usually introduces the narrowed topic that the essay will focus on, and it includes the main point of the essay in a clear and confident statement.

Narrowed topic + Main point = Thesis statement

Banks that invest irresponsibly should be held accountable for their own losses.

PRACTICE 2

Write a thesis statement for each of the following essay topics. After you have written each thesis statement, circle the topic and underline the main point.

1. How drinking affects driving ability

   Thesis: _____

2. Annoying things about public transportation

   Thesis: _____

3. Kinds of fast-food restaurants

   Thesis: _____

4. Some differences between what men like and what women like

   Thesis: _____

5. Kinds of summer activities

   Thesis: _____

PRACTICE 3

Write a thesis statement for each of the narrowed topics you wrote for Practice 1.

1. Narrowed topic: _____

   Thesis: _____

2. Narrowed topic: _____

   Thesis: _____

3. Narrowed topic: _____

   Thesis: _____

4. Narrowed topic: _____

   Thesis: _____

5. Narrowed topic: _____

   Thesis: _____

You may have to rewrite your thesis statement several times, first after you write it and again as you read and revise your essay. Because the thesis statement sets up the whole essay, it must clearly state the main point that the essay will support.

PRACTICE 4

Rewrite three of the thesis statements that you wrote for Practice 3. Think about how someone else would react to the original statement, and strongly state what you want to show, explain, or prove about your topic.

1. _____

2. _____

3. _____

Support Your Thesis Statement and Write Topic Sentences

Each body paragraph in an essay presents a different point that supports your thesis statement. The point of each paragraph is expressed in a topic sentence. Then, the rest of the sentences in the paragraph show, explain, or prove the topic sentence.

Using a prewriting technique is an excellent way to find support. You practiced these ways to get ideas (freewriting, brainstorming, mapping or clustering, journal writing, and using the Internet) in Chapter 3. If you need to review them, go back to that chapter.

When you have completed your prewriting, read what you have written and select the ideas that will best support your thesis; you will turn these ideas into topic sentences. You also need details and examples that will show, explain, or prove the support.

PRACTICE 5

On a separate piece of paper, use a prewriting technique to get ideas to support your thesis and explain the support. Use one of the thesis statements you wrote for Practice 4.

Tip For a review of prewriting, see Chapter 3.

PRACTICE 6

Choose three points from your prewriting that support your thesis. Turn each support point into a topic sentence, and add details that explain the topic sentences.

1. Support point: _____

   Topic sentence: _____

   Details that explain the topic sentence: _____

   _____

2. Support point: _____

   Topic sentence: _____

   Details that explain the topic sentence: _____

   _____

3. Support point: _____

   Topic sentence: _____

   Details that explain the topic sentence: _____

   _____

Make a Plan

After you have chosen the best support for your thesis and have written topic sentences for each major support point, decide the order in which you should present the support. Three common ways to organize your ideas are time order, space order, and order of importance. For a review of these organization methods, see Chapter 5. Also, you will need to think of ideas for your introduction and your conclusion.

The planning stage is a good time to think of ideas for your introduction and conclusion. The introduction includes your thesis statement and previews what you will show, explain, or prove in the rest of your essay. It should let readers know what your purpose is and make them want to read the rest of the essay. The conclusion should both remind readers of your main point and make an observation based on what you have written. For examples of an introduction and conclusion, see the essay on page 161.

PRACTICE 7

Using your work from Practices 4 and 6, fill in the blanks that follow. For each topic sentence, write sentences for the supporting details. At the top, indicate what order of organization you are using and why.

   Order of organization: _____

   Reason for using this order: _____

Thesis statement: _____

    Other ideas for introductory paragraph: _____

_____

Topic sentence 1: _____

    Supporting details (1 sentence for each detail): _____

_____

Topic sentence 2: _____

    Supporting details (1 sentence for each detail): _____

_____

Topic sentence 3: _____

    Supporting details (1 sentence for each detail): _____

_____

Conclusion reminding readers of main point and making an

observation: _____

Write, Revise, and Edit

The next step is to write your essay, using the outline you created and referring to the following basics of a good draft. Make sure to indent each paragraph. (If you are using a computer, you can do this with the tab key.)

Four Basics of a Good Draft

1. It has an introduction that gets readers interested and includes a thesis statement.
2. It has a topic sentence for each paragraph supporting the thesis.
3. It has examples and details to support each topic sentence.
4. It has a conclusion that reminds readers of the main point and makes an observation.

PRACTICE 8

Using your outline from Practice 7, write a draft essay.

Get feedback on your draft by asking another student to answer the Questions for a Peer Reviewer checklist on page 44. After taking a break, reread your draft essay, thinking about the feedback you received.

PRACTICE 9

Revise your draft, using the checklist on page 169 as a guide. Or, if you prefer, write and revise an essay based on one of the Fifty Popular Essay Topics in the list below.

Fifty popular essay topics

Family traditions

Identity theft

Greediness

Cheating

Something that I think is wrong

Moral values

Society today

Why college students do not vote

What I read in a month

Religious traditions

Effects of being popular/unpopular

A first date

Belongings that I would save from a fire

When does a child become an adult?

What I really care about

I wish that someone would . . .

Vivid dreams

Something that I would go to jail for

The kind of person that I want to be

Mistakes

First love

Becoming (or being) a parent

Family feuds

Things that frighten me (or make me laugh)

My first best friend

Something that I will remember for a long time

Procrastination

Why do I need to learn grammar?

Things that I want to gain from college

How to stand up for your rights

Pets

When I was not treated fairly

What I expect in a friend

If I won the lottery, . . .

Losing gracefully

If I could be anyone, . . .

Something that I will regret for a long time

How to waste time

Things I save

Things that I would put in a time capsule

Star athletes' salaries

A statement of my beliefs

When I graduate, I hope . . .

Dear Mr. President, . . .

Job interviews

Favorite Web sites

A news event that got my attention

The generation gap

How to fight stress

I wish I had more time to . . .

> **CHECKLIST**
>
> **Evaluating Your Essay**
>
> ☐ My essay fulfills the assignment and includes all of the Four Basics of a Good Draft (above).
>
> ☐ My writing style is appropriate for the audience and purpose. (Most college assignments should be written in formal English.)
>
> ☐ In the introduction, my thesis statement expresses my main point with confidence.
>
> ☐ The body paragraphs have good topic sentences that support the thesis statement.
>
> ☐ Detailed examples show, explain, or prove the points made in the topic sentences.
>
> ☐ The paragraphs are organized logically, and I have included transitions to move readers smoothly from one idea to the next.
>
> ☐ My concluding paragraph reminds readers of my main point and ends on a strong note.
>
> ☐ I have reread the essay, making improvements and checking for grammar and spelling errors.

Chapter Review

1. What are the three parts of an essay? _____

   _____

2. A thesis statement includes _____

   _____

3. The major support for the main point is expressed in _____

   _____

4. What are three ways to organize an essay? _____

   _____

5. What are some ways to improve an essay when you revise? _____

   _____

   _____

   _____

REFLECTING ON THE JOURNEY

Skills Learned

Now that you've completed the chapter, share what you've learned about each skill by completing the following chart.

Skill	What I learned about this skill
Narrow a topic for an essay	
Write a thesis statement for an essay	
Support the thesis statement with topic sentences for paragraphs	

Part 2

Grammar Basics

The Parts of Speech

READING ROADMAP

Learning Objectives

Chapter Goal: Identify all the major parts of speech.

Tools to Achieve the Goal

- Reference chart: personal pronouns (p. 177)
- Reference chart: indefinite pronouns (p. 180)
- Reference chart: intensive/reflexive pronouns (p. 182)
- Reference charts: other types of pronouns (p. 182)
- Reference chart: common linking verbs (p. 186)
- Reference chart: common helping verbs (p. 187)
- Reference chart: common prepositions (p. 192)
- Reference chart: coordinating conjunctions (p. 193)
- Reference chart: subordinating conjunctions (p. 194)

Key Terms

Skim Chapter 10 before you begin reading. Can you find each of these words in **bold** type? Put a check mark next to each word once you have located it in the chapter.

____ noun	____ verb
____ pronoun	____ action verb
____ personal pronoun	____ linking verb
____ indefinite pronoun	____ helping verb
____ intensive/reflexive pronoun	____ adjective
____ object pronoun	____ adverb
____ possessive pronoun	____ preposition
____ relative pronoun	____ prepositional phrase
____ interrogative pronoun	____ coordinating conjunction
____ reciprocal pronoun	____ subordinating conjunction

Highlight or circle any of these words that you already know.

The chapters in this unit focus on basic grammar that will help you understand the later chapters in this book. This chapter offers a brief review of the parts of speech.

Nouns

A **noun** is a word that names a general or specific person, place, thing, or idea. Nouns that name a specific person, place, thing, or idea need to begin with capital letters.

	General (Common nouns)	Specific (Proper nouns)
Person	politician	Barack H. Obama
Place	city	Chicago
Thing	shoe	Nike
Idea	peace	Nobel Peace Prize

LaunchPadSolo

Visit **LaunchPad Solo for Readers and Writers > Parts of Speech** for more practice recognizing nouns, pronouns, adjectives, adverbs, prepositions, and conjunctions.

Most nouns can be **singular**, meaning *one*, or **plural**, meaning *more than one*.

Singular	Plural	Singular	Plural
politician	politicians	dish	dishes
window	windows	tax	taxes
apple	apples	city	cities
shoe	shoes	key	keys
bus	buses	wife	wives
man	men	tooth	teeth

For rules and instructions on how to form plural nouns, see Chapter 25, Spelling.

 Language note: Standard English usually requires an *-s* or *-es* ending for plurals of nouns that can be counted (for instance, *computers*, *inches*). For nouns that cannot be counted, usually abstract ideas such as *information* or *advice*, the plural form does not change

Example	The library has many <u>computers</u> for public use.
	The library has <u>information</u> available on how to use the Internet.

For more on count versus noncount nouns, see pages 508–510.

PRACTICE 1

Underline all the nouns you can find in the paragraph below.

Example: Since ancient <u>times</u>, <u>bread</u> has been an important <u>part</u> of <u>people's lives</u>.

1 Archaeologists have found loaves of bread in the tombs of ancient Egyptians. 2 Sometimes the bread was in the shape of animals or human figures. 3 Originally, bread was baked only in the home by women. 4 Soon, however, men set up bread-baking shops, and bakeries were born. 5 In ancient Greece, cities competed to make the best bread. 6 Politicians in Athens insisted that authors record the names of the greatest bakers. 7 Through these records, we have come to know the importance of bread in early societies.

Pronouns

Pronouns replace nouns or other pronouns in a sentence so that you do not have to repeat them.

        his
Earl loaned me ~~Earl's~~ lawn mower.
[The pronoun *his* replaces *Earl's*.]

        she
You know Tina. ~~Tina~~ is my best friend.
[The pronoun *she* replaces *Tina*.]

   their
After ~~the singers'~~ final performance, the singers celebrated.
[The pronoun *their* replaces *the singers'*.]

The noun or pronoun that a pronoun replaces is called the **antecedent**. In many cases, a pronoun refers to a specific antecedent nearby.

Antecedent

I removed my photo albums and papers from the basement. It flooded just an hour later.

Pronoun replacing antecedent

Personal Pronouns

Personal pronouns take the place of specific persons or things.

Singer Amy Winehouse died young. She was only twenty-seven years old.

The Boston Bruins won the Stanley Cup in 2011. They had not won it since 1972.

When rescuers found the young boy, his pulse was weak.

> **Language note:** Most singular third-person pronouns (*he/she*, *him/her*, *his/hers*) show gender. *He*, *him*, and *his* are masculine. *She*, *her*, and *hers* are feminine. If the pronoun replaces a masculine noun, the pronoun must be masculine. A pronoun that replaces a feminine noun must be feminine.

Gloriana is my cousin. She lives in Buenos Aires.

[Gloriana is female, so the pronoun must be feminine: *she*.]

The jacket belongs to David. Janice gave it to him.

[David is male, so the pronoun must be masculine: *him*.]

Personal pronouns may not have an antecedent if the meaning is clear.

I remember seeing that movie last summer.
It was very thoughtful of the class to send you flowers.
That laptop is mine.
Our project took three weeks to finish.

Personal pronouns can act like nouns, serving as the subjects or objects in a sentence, or they can be possessives, describing the ownership of a noun.

Personal Pronouns

	Subject		Object		Possessive	
	Singular	**Plural**	**Singular**	**Plural**	**Singular**	**Plural**
First Person	I	we	me	us	my/mine	our/ours
Second Person	you	you	you	you	your/yours	your/yours
Third Person	he she it	they	him her it	them	his her/hers its	their/theirs

SUBJECT PRONOUNS

A **subject pronoun** serves as the subject, or the main noun, that does the action of a verb.

> She plays on the softball team.
> I changed the oil.
> We ate the cake.

 Language note: Some languages omit subject pronouns, but English sentences always have a stated or written subject.

Incorrect	Hates cleaning.
Correct	He hates cleaning.

OBJECT PRONOUNS

An **object pronoun** either receives the action of the verb (it is the object of the verb) or is part of a prepositional phrase (it is the object of the preposition).

Object of the verb	Roberto asked me to copy the report.
	[*Me* receives the action of the verb *asked*.]
	Roberto gave me the report.
	[*Me* receives the action of the verb *gave*.]
Object of the preposition	Roberto gave the report to me.
	[*Me* is part of the prepositional phrase *to me*.]

POSSESSIVE PRONOUNS

Possessive pronouns refer to an antecedent and show that antecedent's ownership of something.

The students will choose their class president on Tuesday.

[The antecedent of the pronoun *their* is *students*; the president belongs to the students.]

Denise left her watch at the hotel.

[The antecedent of the pronoun *her* is *Denise*; the watch belongs to Denise.]

As with all personal pronouns, possessives may not have an antecedent if the meaning is clear.

My handwriting is hard to read.

[The handwriting belongs to me; no antecedent is needed.]

The winning project was ours.

[The project belongs to us; no antecedent is needed.]

Because possessive pronouns already show ownership, you never need to put an apostrophe in them.

Incorrect	That job is *your's*.
Correct	That job is *yours*.

> **PRACTICE 2**
>
> In each of the following sentences, circle the personal pronoun, underline the noun that it refers to, and draw an arrow from the pronoun to the noun. For possessive pronouns, draw a dotted arrow to the noun that is owned by the pronoun.
>
> Example: The <u>seahorse</u> was so named because its head is shaped like a horse's.
>
> 1. Many people are fascinated by seahorses because they are such interesting underwater creatures.
>
> 2. Seahorses wrap their tails around coral and sea grass while feeding.
>
> 3. Perhaps the most unusual thing about this underwater creature is the way it reproduces.

4. Among seahorses, the female produces eggs, but she is not responsible for carrying the fertilized eggs.

5. After the eggs are fertilized, the female deposits them into the male.

6. As the eggs enter the male, his belly grows as the female's belly shrinks.

7. The young seahorses hatch inside the male, where they will grow for two to four weeks before emerging.

8. During these weeks, the female visits her mate each morning.

9. The male carries the young until he is ready to give birth.

10. Without any protection or nurturing from their parents, the offspring must survive alone in the ocean.

PRACTICE 3

In each of the following sentences, fill in the blank with an appropriate pronoun. In some cases, there may be more than one correct choice. The clues in parentheses indicate what type of pronoun is needed.

Example: **Last week my aunt Carmen sent me one of** ___*her*___ *(possessive)*
              special gifts.

1. Aunt Carmen never remembers our birthdays, but she always gives

     _____ *(object)* surprises during the year.

2. In our family, her gifts are famous for _____ *(possessive)*

   originality.

3. _____ *(subject)* somehow finds things that no one expects.

4. When the box arrived, _____ *(possessive)* label had nearly

   peeled off.

5. I knew that it was for _____ *(object)*, however, because Aunt

   Carmen had called and said a gift would arrive soon.

6. I tried to guess what _____ *(subject)* had sent me.

7. I asked my brother Mikey for _____ *(possessive)* opinion.

8. _____ *(subject)* thought that the box was big enough for

   a statue.

9. My sister hoped that Aunt Carmen had sent _____ (*object*) sweaters that she could borrow.

10. _____ (*subject*) laughed when we opened the box and discovered six tins of cookies.

Indefinite Pronouns

An **indefinite pronoun** does not refer to a specific person, place, thing, or idea, so it does not have an antecedent. Most indefinite pronouns function only as nouns (subjects or objects).

Someone in the audience was smoking.

Everyone clapped when the bride and groom were announced.

The volunteers are not allowed to accept anything for their work.

Some indefinite pronouns can function either as nouns or as adjectives describing a noun.

All are welcome to join the club.

All classes were canceled because of the fire.

Few could argue with the judge's decision.

The mechanic had seen few cars as run-down as mine.

Indefinite Pronouns

all	everybody	nobody
another	everyone	none
any	everything	nothing
anybody	few	one
anyone	many	several
anything	most	some
both	much	somebody
each	neither	someone
either	no one	something

PRACTICE 4

In the sentences below, fill in the blank with an appropriate indefinite pronoun. (There may be more than one correct answer.)

Example: ___*Anyone*___ **who is entering the job market must have good writing skills.**

1 Even the most qualified candidate may know little or _____ about how to look good on paper. 2 _____ should start by having a carefully proofread résumé. 3 _____ potential employers say that it takes only six to eight seconds to decide whether to seriously consider a résumé. 4 If _____ on a résumé suggests that the candidate was too lazy to proofread, that person may be eliminated from consideration. 5 In addition, _____ should send a résumé without a cover letter. 6 Although _____ people are tempted to use the same cover letter for every job application, that reuse of letters is not a good idea. 7 Managers want to hire _____ who shows interest and experience in a specific position. 8 Finally, _____ potential employer might also ask you to fill out an application form. 9 _____ who fills out these forms should use neat handwriting. 10 _____ wants to lose a job offer because of a problem with a résumé, cover letter, or job application, so it is worth the time and effort to make these documents flawless.

Other Types of Pronouns

REFLEXIVE AND INTENSIVE PRONOUNS

Reflexive pronouns are used when the person receiving the action is the same as the actor in the sentence. They end with the suffix *-self* or *-selves*.

Louis taught himself how to speak Italian.

We forced ourselves to study on weekends.

Intensive pronouns also end with *-self* or *-selves*, but they are used to emphasize the noun or pronoun being referenced.

The queen herself would envy my grandmother's herb garden.

The billionaires themselves have offered to pay higher taxes.

Intensive/Reflexive Pronouns

	Singular	**Plural**
First Person	myself	ourselves
Second Person	yourself	yourselves
Third Person	herself himself itself	themselves

RELATIVE PRONOUNS

Relative pronouns refer to a noun already mentioned in a sentence, and they introduce a group of words that describe that noun.

The chef who wins the competition will receive $10,000.
[Which chef? The one who wins the competition.]

Basketball, which was invented in 1891, is my favorite sport.
[How is basketball being described? As a sport invented in 1891.]

The house that was almost torn down is now a historic landmark.
[Which house? The one that was almost torn down.]

Relative Pronouns

who	which
whom	that
whose	

INTERROGATIVE PRONOUNS

Interrogative pronouns are used to begin questions.

> [Which] sport was invented in 1891?
> [What] was the jury's verdict?
> [Whom] were you speaking to?

Interrogative Pronouns

who	which
whom	what
whose	

DEMONSTRATIVE PRONOUNS

Demonstrative pronouns specify which noun is being referred to.

> [This] restaurant looks better than [that] one across the street.
> Use [these] new dishes, not [those] old ones.

Demonstrative Pronouns

this	these
that	those

RECIPROCAL PRONOUNS

Reciprocal pronouns are used to refer to individuals when the antecedent is plural.

> My lab partner and I could not see [each other] through all the smoke.

> The tigers glared at [one another] through the glass.

Reciprocal Pronouns

each other	one another

PRACTICE 5

Circle the pronouns in the sentences that follow. All sentences contain more than one pronoun, and (not counting the example) there are fifty pronouns in all.

Example: When **I** graduated from high school two years ago, **many** people asked **me**, "**What** do **you** want to do with **your** life?"

1. Few people know the answer to this question when they are 18 years old, but many decide to go to college anyway.

2. I did not feel ready to take this route, so I delayed spending any money on college applications.

3. My parents said they would understand if I took a year off to see for myself what full-time work was like.

4. Some of my friends were also staying home after graduation, but my girlfriend went to college out of state.

5. We knew it would be hard on our relationship to live far away from one another.

6. There are, however, many ways to stay in touch, such as e-mail, texting, video chatting, and regular phone calls, so we agreed to use one of these methods to contact each other every day.

7. My uncle, who owns a furniture factory, said I could work for him until I found something else.

8. As it turned out, I really liked making furniture and I decided this was the career I wanted for myself.

9. My uncle suggested I take part-time classes in business administration, which would help me become assistant manager at his factory.

10. Now when somebody asks me, "What do you want to do with your life?" I can give an answer that I am proud of.

Verbs

All sentences have at least one **verb** that explains the action or state of being of a noun.

> I drive to school.
> The car is black.

Verbs can change form depending on the subject (see Chapter 15, Subject-Verb Agreement Problems).

I <u><u>drive</u></u> to school every day, but Shane <u><u>drives</u></u> only one day a week.

Verbs also change tense depending on when the action took place (see Chapter 16, Verb Tense Problems).

I <u><u>walk</u></u> to school every day this year, but last year I <u><u>walked</u></u> only once.

Action Verbs

Action verbs show the subject *doing* something.

My mother <u><u>calls</u></u> me at least three times per week.
On Saturdays, Maya <u><u>feeds</u></u> the ducks by the river.
Last year, we <u><u>hiked</u></u> Mount Washington.

> **PRACTICE 6**
>
> In the following paragraph, double-underline the action verb in each sentence.
>
> 1 I lost most of my hair years ago. 2 Upset about my baldness, I complained to my close friends. 3 Some friends teased me about my shiny head. 4 However, most people ignored it. 5 After a while, I forgot about my embarrassment. 6 Then, I heard an ad on the radio for a new miracle drug. 7 According to the ad, the drug replaces lost hair. 8 Then, I read about a new laser treatment for baldness. 9 I rejected both ideas as too good to be true. 10 I now accept my baldness, my right-handedness, my poor eyesight, and the rest of myself as well.

Linking Verbs

Linking verbs connect the subject of the sentence to a word or words that describe it.

Even fake fur coats <u><u>feel</u></u> soft.
Jose <u><u>looked</u></u> older with a beard.
The children <u><u>are</u></u> quiet this morning.

Some words can be either action verbs or linking verbs, depending on how they are used.

Action verb	Mario tasted the lasagna.
	[Mario *does* something: he *tasted* the lasagna.]
Linking verb	The lasagna tasted delicious.
	[The lasagna doesn't *do* anything. *Tasted* links lasagna to a word that describes it: *delicious*.]

Common Linking Verbs

Forms of *be*	Forms of *become* and *seem*	Forms of sense verbs
am	become/becomes/became	appear/appears/appeared
are	seem/seems/seemed	feel/feels/felt
is		look/looks/looked
was		smell/smells/smelled
were		taste/tastes/tasted

PRACTICE 7

Either by yourself or with a partner, write sentences using the words in the chart of common linking verbs above. Make sure you use them as linking verbs, not action verbs. Double-underline the linking verbs. Draw an arrow from the word that describes the subject to the subject noun.

1. (form of *be*) _____

2. (form of *seem*) _____

3. (form of *become*) _____

4. (form of *appear*) _____

5. (form of *feel*) _____

6. (form of *look*) _____

7. (form of *smell*) _____

8. (form of *taste*) _____

Main Verbs and Helping Verbs

A complete verb may consist of more than one part: a **main verb** and a **helping verb**. In the sentences below, the complete verbs are double-underlined, and the helping verbs are circled.

I am driving to school right now.

Mauricio might call this evening.

They will be eating lunch at 12:00.

In questions or negative sentences, some words may interrupt the helping verb and the main verb.

Did you wait for the bell to ring?

Chloe has not studied for two days.

Common Helping Verbs

Forms of *be*	Forms of *have*	Forms of *do*	Other
be	have	do	can
am	has	does	could
are	had	did	may
been			might
being			must
is			shall
was			should
were			will
			would

 Language note: The words in the "Other" column above are also called *modal auxiliaries*. If you have trouble using them correctly, see Chapter 32.

Incorrect   His dog ~~will~~ might bark.

Correct   His dog might bark.

Using helping verbs in negative statements and questions can also be tricky. Chapter 32 shows how to form such statements.

PRACTICE 8

In each of the following sentences, double-underline the complete verb (the helping verb plus the main verb), and circle the helping verb.

Example: **My great-aunt Gertrude will be 103 this month.**

1. She has seen many changes in her lifetime.

2. Not many people can remember a world without electricity, airplanes, or telephones.

3. Like many people in the early twentieth century, Gertrude's family could not afford many luxuries.

4. Gertrude had been playing the school's piano for years before the age of fifteen.

5. Eventually, she did save enough money for a piano of her own.

Adjectives

Adjectives describe nouns and pronouns. They add information about what kind, which one, or how many.

The five new students shared a two-floor house.

The funny movie made the sad little girls laugh.

Two large gray birds stood in the water.

Language note: In English, adjectives are never plural unless they are numbers.

Incorrect	The three babies are *adorables*.
	[The adjective *three* is fine because it is a number, but the adjective *adorables* should not end in -s to indicate a plural noun.]
Correct	The three babies are *adorable*.

Adjectives can come either before or after the nouns that they describe.

Many inexpensive homes are for sale in that area.

The homes for sale in that area are inexpensive.

Sometimes words that look like nouns act like adjectives.

The computer technician repaired Shania's laptop.

 Language note: Adjectives are often followed by prepositions. Here are some common examples:

afraid of	fond of	proud of
ashamed of	full of	responsible for
aware of	happy about	scared of
confused by	interested in	sorry about/sorry for
excited about	jealous of	tired of

Peri is afraid *of* snakes.

We are happy *about* Dino's promotion.

PRACTICE 9

Double-underline the adjectives in the sentences below, and draw an arrow to the noun or pronoun being described.

Example: Books about vampires have become popular recently.

1. The books focus on the lives of high school students who are vampires.

2. The vampires face the problems of ordinary teenagers.

3. Of course, they also have supernatural abilities.

4. They are immortal, and they can fly.

5. But they can survive only by drinking fresh blood.

PRACTICE 10

In each sentence, underline the word that is being described, and fill in an appropriate adjective.

Example: Today almost anyone can create ___unusual___ **pictures on a computer.**

1. Before computers, _____ photographers used their imagination to make postcard pictures.

2. Simple photographs could be changed to make the subject look _____ .

Tip For more on verbs and other sentence parts, see Chapter 11.

3. Parts of _____ pictures were then pieced together.

4. The results were _____ .

5. For example, one postcard shows a _____ grasshopper riding on the back of a donkey.

6. Another picture shows a _____ child riding on a hen.

7. The _____ postcards also had amusing messages.

8. A picture of gigantic corn stalks came with the message "The stalks are so _____ , they are cutting them into railroad ties."

9. Most of the postcards were made in the Midwest, where people loved to tell _____ stories that amazed their friends and family.

10. Best of all, they hoped that someone back east would be silly enough to believe that a family could live in a _____ pumpkin in Nebraska.

Adverbs

Adverbs describe verbs, adjectives, or other adverbs. They add information about how, how much, when, where, or why. Adverbs often end with *-ly*.

Describing a verb	Mira sings beautifully. [*Beautifully* describes the verb *sings*.]
Describing an adjective	The extremely talented singer entertained the crowd. [*Extremely* describes the adjective *talented*.]
Describing another adverb	Mira sings very beautifully. [*Very* describes the adverb *beautifully*.]

Like adjectives, adverbs can come either before or after the words they modify, and more than one adverb can be used to modify a word.

PRACTICE 11

In each sentence, underline the word that is being described, and fill in an appropriate adverb. Draw an arrow from the adverb to the word being described.

Example: **When my brother called and invited me to his house for dinner, I ___*happily*___ accepted his offer.**

1. He asked _____ if I could bring dessert.

2. Knowing that I am helpless in the kitchen, I _____ stopped at the bakery and bought a large cake.

3. When I arrived at my brother's house, I _____ took the cake from the car.

4. I was late, so I _____ walked to the door.

5. I rang the doorbell and waited _____ for him to answer.

6. Much to my surprise, a _____ barking dog began pawing at the door.

7. When my brother opened the door, a black dog rushed out and began _____ sniffing my shoes.

8. My brother _____ told the dog to sit, but it continued sniffing.

9. I _____ handed my brother the cake, fearful that I would drop it because of the dog.

10. My brother proudly introduced me to his new "roommate," Henry, who had begun chewing _____ on my shoes.

Prepositions

A **preposition** is a word (such as *of, above, between, about*) that comes before a noun or pronoun and helps show how that noun or pronoun relates to another part of a sentence. The group of words in combination with the preposition is called a **prepositional phrase**.

The cow jumped over the moon.

[*Over* is the preposition; *over the moon* is the prepositional phrase describing where the cow jumped.]

When you observe an unusual event, you should write about it.

[*About* is the preposition; *about it* is the prepositional phrase describing what you should write. (The pronoun *it* refers to *event*.)]

The prepositional phrase may contain more than one noun or pronoun, and it contains all the adjectives related to those nouns or pronouns.

I quit school and joined a rock band against my parents' will.

After a year of all work and no play, I finally got my diploma.

Sentences may contain several prepositional phrases, sometimes in a row.

The pendant dangled ⬚from⬚ a shiny gold chain ⬚with⬚ a small diamond ⬚in⬚ each link.

Common Prepositions

about	before	except	of	to
above	behind	for	off	toward
across	below	from	on	under
after	beneath	in	out	until
against	beside	inside	outside	up
along	between	into	over	upon
among	by	like	past	with
around	down	near	since	within
at	during	next to	through	without

 Language note: *In* and *on* can be tricky prepositions for people whose native language is not English. Keep these definitions and examples in mind:

> *in* = inside of (in the box, in the office) or within a period of time (in January, in the fall, in three weeks)

> *on* = on top of (on the table, on my foot), located in a certain place (on the page, on Main Street), or at a certain time (on January first)

If you get confused by what prepositions to use in common English phrases, see Chapter 30.

Note that even though the word *to* can be a preposition, it is often used as part of a verb's infinitive: *to walk, to run, to drive.* These are not prepositional phrases, and the word *to* is not a preposition when it is used in an infinitive.

PRACTICE 12

Circle the prepositions and underline the prepositional phrases in the sentences below. Sentences may have more than one preposition.

Example: Basketball was invented ⬚in⬚ Massachusetts ⬚in⬚ the late 1800s.

1. During the cold winter weather, people wanted to play a sport inside the gymnasium.

2. Baskets were placed on tall poles at either end of the gym.

3. The players had to get the ball into the other team's basket.

4. The court was surrounded by large metal cages.

5. The game has changed over the years, but basketball players are still sometimes called *cagers*.

Conjunctions

Conjunctions are used to connect words and word groups. There are two main types of conjunctions: coordinating and subordinating.

Coordinating Conjunctions

Coordinating conjunctions join two or more words or word groups that have the same function in a sentence.

Dogs and cats are common household pets.

[The conjunction *and* joins the two nouns *dogs* and *cats*.]

I knew I would have to drop a class, quit the swim team, or cut back on work.

[The conjunction *or* joins the three phrases *drop a class, quit the swim team,* and *cut back on work*.]

The semester begins tomorrow, but the school is still under construction.

[The conjunction *but* joins two complete thoughts: *The semester begins tomorrow* and *the school is still under construction*.]

Remember the seven coordinating conjunctions by using the acronym *fanboys:* (**for, and, nor, but, or, yet, so**).

Coordinating Conjunctions

for	and	nor	but	or	yet	so

PRACTICE 13

Circle the coordinating conjunctions in the following sentences, and underline the words or word groups being joined.

Example: Most people realize that eating well and exercising
regularly are both good choices.

1. Some people wonder which is more important: diet or exercise.

2. The body needs nutrients, so a healthy diet is essential.

3. Healthy habits can prevent disease and lead to a longer life.

4. Everyone knows obesity is unhealthy, yet many people have trouble losing weight.

5. Activities such as dancing, playing tennis, and bicycling are all enjoyable forms of exercise.

Subordinating Conjunctions (Dependent Words)

Subordinating conjunctions are words that help explain when or under what circumstances an event occurred.

[When] Sam opened the refrigerator, he smelled the moldy cheese.

The smell was overwhelming [when] Sam opened the refrigerator.

In this book, subordinating conjunctions are also called **dependent words** because they can turn a complete thought (or an independent clause) into an incomplete thought (or a dependent clause).

Sam opened the refrigerator.
[The words above form a complete thought.]

[When] Sam opened the refrigerator
[The addition of the dependent word *when* makes the thought incomplete. (What happened when Sam opened the refrigerator?)]

Common Subordinating Conjunctions (Dependent Words)

after	if	what(ever)
although	since	when(ever)
as	so that	where(ver)
because	that	whether
before	though	which
even though	unless	while
how	until	who/whose

PRACTICE 14

Circle the subordinating conjunction (dependent word) in each sentence below.

Example: **Vertigo is a condition [that] makes a person feel dizzy.**

1. After spinning around on a playground, many children experience vertigo.

2. They feel like they are moving even though they are still.

3. Adults experience this feeling because they have inner ear problems.

4. When an attack of vertigo comes on, a person may also feel like vomiting.

5. If a person experiences vertigo regularly, he or she should consult a doctor.

Interjections

Interjections are words that show excitement or emotion. They are not typically used in formal English.

Oh, did you need that report today?

Wow! This is the best cupcake I ever tasted!

Write and Edit Your Own Work

Write a paragraph describing the movie poster for *Invasion of the Saucer Men*, a 1957 science fiction film (see photo). When you have finished, mark all of the parts of speech you can identify in the paragraph. Look for nouns, pronouns, verbs, adjectives, adverbs, prepositions, conjunctions, and interjections.

© FOUND IMAGE PRESS/CORBIS

Chapter Review

1. A _____ is a word that names a general or specific person, place, thing, or idea.

2. Pronouns replace _____ or other _____ in a sentence.

3. _____ pronouns serve as the subject of the verb. Give an example:

   _____

4. _____ pronouns receive the action of a verb or are part of a prepositional phrase. Give an example: _____

5. _____ pronouns show ownership. Give an example: _____

   _____

6. List three indefinite pronouns: _____

   _____

7. List five relative pronouns: _____

8. Write three sentences, one using an action verb, one using a linking verb, and one with a helping verb and main verb. _____

9. _____ describe nouns, and _____ describe verbs, adjectives, or other adverbs.

10. Adverbs often end in _____.

11. List five prepositions: _____

12. _____ conjunctions join two or more words or word groups that have the same function in a sentence. List three of these conjunctions:

    _____

13. _____ conjunctions are words that help explain when or under what circumstances an event occurred. These conjunctions are also called _____. List three of these conjunctions:

    _____

REFLECTING ON THE JOURNEY

Skills Learned

Now that you've completed the chapter, look again at this sentence.

> John was unhappy because some noisy children sat next to him in the theater, and he quickly moved to the balcony.

Using what you've learned in this chapter, identify the part of speech (noun, verb, adjective, adverb, pronoun, preposition, and conjunction) of each word in the sentence, and answer the questions below.

1. Are you confident that you can identify the parts of speech correctly?
2. Which part(s) of speech is the most difficult for you to identify?
3. What questions do you have about the parts of speech?

11

Simple Sentences

READING ROADMAP

Key Terms

Skim Chapter 11 before you begin reading. Can you find each of these words in **bold** type? Put a check mark next to each word once you have located it in the chapter.

____ sentence
____ subject
____ verb
____ complete thought
____ independent clause
____ noun
____ pronoun
____ simple subject
____ complete subject
____ plural subject
____ prepositional phrase
____ action verb
____ linking verb
____ helping verb
____ dependent clause
____ direct object
____ indirect object

Highlight or circle any of these words that you already know.

Learning Objectives

Chapter Goal: Identify the parts of a simple sentence.

Tools to Achieve the Goal
- Reference chart: prepositions (p. 203)
- Reference chart: six basic English sentence patterns (p. 207)

Before You Read

Study the following sentences and complete the chart. At the end of the chapter, you will examine the sentences again and reflect on what you have learned.

1. I recently rented an apartment with very small rooms.

2. Built for a young family in the 1950s.

3. The appliances in the kitchen and the boiler in the basement are old and unreliable.

Put a check mark by each statement in the chart that is true for you.

Statement	
I know which sentence is not a complete thought.	
I can identify the simple subject and the complete subject for each independent clause.	
I can identify one action verb and one linking verb.	
I can identify a direct object.	

Understand What a Sentence Is

A **sentence** is the basic unit of written communication. A complete sentence in formal English has a **subject** and a **verb** and expresses a **complete thought**. Sentences are also called **independent clauses** because they make sense by themselves, without other information.

None of the following examples is a sentence:

Invented the telephone in 1876.

The Great Wall of China the largest man-made structure in the world.

The movie *Slumdog Millionaire*, which won several Oscars.[1]

The first example is missing a subject, the second is missing a verb, and none express a complete thought. Here they are rewritten as complete sentences:

Alexander Graham Bell **invented** the telephone in 1876.

The Great Wall of China *is* the largest man-made structure in the world.

The movie *Slumdog Millionaire*, which won several Oscars, *is about a young Indian boy.*

1. **Oscars:** Film-industry awards given every year in the categories of best movie, best actor, best screenwriter, and others.

Tip In the sentence examples in this chapter, subjects are blue and verbs are red.

Find Subjects

A **subject** is the word or words that a sentence is about. Subjects can be **nouns** (people—Alexander Graham Bell; places—the Great Wall of China; things—the movie *Slumdog Millionaire*). They can also be **pronouns** (like *I*, *you*, *he/she*, *it*, *we*, *they*).

 Language note: In English, subjects cannot be left out of sentences.

| Incorrect | Called Stephan last night. |
| Correct | I called Stephan last night. |

Subject Nouns

The **noun as subject** is the person, place, thing, or idea that either performs the action or is the main focus of the sentence. In the examples in this chapter, subjects appear in bold blue.

Janine tripped on the sidewalk.

[Janine performs the action, *tripped*.]

Carlo looked great in his new glasses.

[Carlo is the focus of the sentence.]

Tip For more on nouns, see Chapter 10.

PRACTICE 1

Underline the noun subjects in each of the following sentences. Remember, the noun subject either performs the action or is the main focus of the sentence. The sentence might have other nouns that are not the subject.

Example: **The battered old car broke down.**

1. The owner of the car called for help.

2. After an hour, the tow truck had not appeared.

3. Sick of waiting and late for an appointment, the owner left the car.

4. The driver of the tow truck arrived a few minutes later.

5. By that time, the owner had arrived at the appointment on foot.

6. The tow truck driver called the dispatcher at his company and went on to another call.

7. An hour later, a police officer noticed the abandoned car.

8. After walking around the car, the officer wrote a ticket.

9. The owner returned later in the day.

10. The old car had caused a lot of trouble and expense.

Subject Pronouns

Tip For more on pronouns, see Chapter 10.

Like a noun subject, the **subject pronoun** is the person, place, thing, or idea that performs the action or is the main focus of the sentence. The subject pronouns are *I, you* (singular), *he, she, it, we, you* (plural), and *they*.

PRACTICE 2

Underline the subject pronouns or subject nouns in the following sentences. Some sentences may have pronouns and nouns that are not the subject of the sentence. Keep in mind that the subject either performs the action or is the focus of the sentence.

Example: **After getting a degree, I want to be a physician assistant.**

1. Physician assistants are in high demand.

2. They can go wherever they want to live.

3. Because of the high demand, physician assistants make good salaries.

4. In March, I will apply to the physician assistant program.

5. The program at the local college has a waiting list of two years, though.

6. I can find out what courses I need and take those.

7. Colleges want to expand the programs but cannot find instructors.

8. Physician assistants make more money than college instructors.

9. After getting a degree, they can start at about $100,000.

10. It is worth the hard work.

Simple and Complete Subjects

A **simple subject** is just the one noun or pronoun that the sentence is about.

The summer-school **students were taking** final exams.

A **complete subject** includes all the words that describe the simple subject.

The summer-school students were taking final exams.

PRACTICE 3

In each of the following sentences, underline the complete subject.

Example: **The common mosquito is one of the most unpopular creatures on earth.**

1. These annoying insects have bothered people for thousands of years.

2. The female mosquitoes are the ones that bite.

3. The hungry pests are attracted to body heat and certain chemicals.

4. Human sweat contains one of these chemicals, lactic acid.

5. Mosquitoes also like the smell of perfume.

6. Some scientists recently made an interesting discovery.

7. Their discovery, however, is good news for only some people.

8. Some lucky people produce certain chemicals.

9. These special chemicals keep mosquitoes away from them.

10. For the rest of us, bug spray is the best defense.

Singular and Plural Subjects

Singular means one, and *plural* means more than one. Sentences can have singular or **plural subjects**.

Singular	Elizabeth Blackwell **was** the first woman doctor in the United States.
	[There is one noun: *Elizabeth Blackwell*.]
Plural	Elizabeth Blackwell and **her sister Emily were** both doctors.
	[There are two separate nouns: *Elizabeth Blackwell* and *her sister Emily*.]
	The Blackwell **sisters started** a women's medical college in the late 1800s.
	[There is one plural noun: *The Blackwell sisters*.]

Language note: In the present tense, regular verbs for third-person singular subjects (like *Bob, he, she,* or *it*) end in *-s* or *-es*.

Singular   Singular
subject   verb

Perry hates vegetables.

Plural   Plural
subject   verb

The **boys hate** vegetables.

For more on subject-verb agreement and verb tense, see Chapters 13 and 14.

PRACTICE 4

In each of the following sentences, underline the complete subject. In the space to the left of each item, write **S** if the subject is singular. If the subject is plural, write **P**.

Example: _P_ **Many people use the Internet every day.**

1. ____ College students spend an average of 15.1 hours online weekly, according to one survey.

2. ____ On average, male students spend slightly more time online than female students do.

3. ____ Google.com and ESPN.com are among students' most frequently visited Web sites.

4. ____ Despite its many advantages, the Internet makes some people nervous.

5. ____ Some Internet users are concerned about losing their privacy.

6. ____ My mother and my grandmother refuse to make online purchases.

7. ____ My mother likes to see a product before buying it.

8. ____ Grandma and many other people feel uncomfortable using their credit cards online.

9. ____ Eventually, online shopping sites may become more popular than traditional retail stores.

10. ____ For now, though, many people prefer to go online just for information.

PRACTICE 5

Write five sentences using plural subjects. Underline the subjects.

Prepositional Phrases

A common mistake is to think that the subject of the sentence is in a **prepositional phrase**, which starts with a **preposition** and ends with a noun (the object of the preposition).

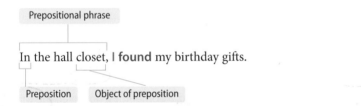

Prepositional phrase

In the hall closet, I **found** my birthday gifts.

Preposition   Object of preposition

You might think that the words *hall closet* are the subject of the sentence, but— *and this is very important*—**the subject of a sentence is never in a prepositional phrase.**

To find prepositional phrases, look for prepositions.

Common Prepositions

about	before	except	of	to
above	behind	for	off	toward
across	below	from	on	under
after	beneath	in	out	until
against	beside	inside	outside	up
along	between	into	over	upon
among	by	like	past	with
around	down	near	since	within
at	during	next to	through	without

To make sure that you do not confuse the noun in the prepositional phrase (the object of the preposition) with the subject of the sentence, try crossing out the prepositional phrase.

~~In the hall closet,~~ I **found** my birthday gifts.

Many sentences have more than one prepositional phrase. To find the subject, cross out all the prepositional phrases.

~~At the Apollo Theater in New York City,~~ many famous African American musicians **got** their start.

Some ~~of the big future stars~~ **were** Count Basie, Billie Holiday, Ella Fitzgerald, and Aretha Franklin.

~~In the 1970s, after some years of slow business,~~ the **theater closed**.

~~After major remodeling,~~ the **theater reopened** ~~in 1985~~.

PRACTICE 6

In the following paragraph, cross out any prepositional phrases and underline the subject of each sentence.

1 Without a doubt, crows are intelligent birds. 2 Crows in the Pacific Northwest steal food using both violence and trickery. 3 Crows from this region violently attack other crows for food. 4 Sometimes, however, the thief simply sneaks a bite of another bird's food. 5 Curious about this behavior, scientists at the University of Washington observed a group of fifty-five crows. 6 After thirty months, the researchers made an interesting discovery. 7 The crows are rough and aggressive while stealing from distant relatives and nonrelatives. 8 However, crows in the same family steal by using trickery instead of violence. 9 Like most humans, these birds are nicer to members of their family than to nonrelatives.

Find Verbs

For a review of what a verb is, see Chapter 10.

Every sentence has a **verb** that either tells what the subject does or connects the subject to another word that describes it. In the examples in this chapter, the subject's verb is shown in bold red.

Clarence Birdseye **invented** frozen foods in 1923.

[The verb *invented* tells what Birdseye, the subject, did.]

By 1930, **he was** ready to sell his product.

[The verb *was* connects the subject to a word that describes him: *ready*.]

Action verbs show the subject *doing* something.

The **players dumped** the cooler of ice water on their coach's head.

Linking verbs connect the subject of the sentence to a word or words that describe it. In the following sentence, the linking verb is red and the words describing the subject are in italics.

Joseph McCarthy was *a powerful senator from Wisconsin.*

 Language note: The verb *be* is required in English to complete sentences like the following:

Incorrect	Tonya well now.
Correct	Tonya is well now.

Helping verbs are joined with main verbs to make a complete verb.

Thumbelina can hold her breath for one hundred seconds.

[*Can* is the helping verb, and *hold* is the main verb.]

PRACTICE 7

In each of the following sentences, double-underline the complete verb (the linking verb or the helping verb plus the main verb), and circle the linking or helping verb.

Example: In my nursing class this semester, I am learning some interesting facts about famous people.

1. Alexander the Great, Benjamin Franklin, and other familiar figures throughout history have suffered from gout.

2. Gout is a common form of arthritis.

3. The condition is most common among men over the age of forty.

4. People with gout are troubled by terrible pain in their big toes and other joints.

5. The number of people with gout has doubled since 1969.

6. People from all parts of society can have gout, not just the rich.

7. Gaining thirty pounds or more after the age of twenty-one can double a person's risk for gout.

8. According to a recent study, gout is seen most often among men with a diet high in meat and seafood.

9. People with gout should watch their diets carefully.

10. Gout is treated with medications and rest.

Decide If There Is a Complete Thought

Even when a group of words has a subject and a verb, it may not express a complete thought.

> Because their **team won** the championship.
>
> [There is a subject (*team*) and a verb (*won*), but you cannot tell what is going on without more information.]

In the following examples, the added words (in italics) create a complete thought.

> *The students went wild* because their team won the championship.
>
> Because their team won the championship, *the students went wild*.

Read the following sentences and ask if there is a complete thought.

> Who **sat** next to me in class.
>
> Damon **saved** the game.

Tip For more on dependent clauses, see Chapter 12.

A word group that has a subject and a verb but that is not a complete thought is called a **dependent clause**. It is not a sentence because it is *dependent* on another set of words for meaning.

PRACTICE 8

Two of the following items contain complete thoughts, and eight do not. In the space to the left of each item, write **C** for complete thought or **I** for incomplete thought. If you write **I**, add words to make a sentence.

Example: __I__ *I got several* ~~Several~~ speeding tickets last year.

1. __I__ The cost of my car insurance. *is high*

2. __I__ After I paid the speeding tickets.

3. __I__ The speed limit in my town. *is 25 mph*

4. __C__ It is twenty-five miles per hour.

5. __I__ Even though my friends make fun of me. *I didn't care*

6. __C__ If they had paid $225 in speeding fines.

7. __I__ Another speeding ticket. *I got*

8. __I__ When aggressive drivers follow me too closely. *I get scared*

9. __C__ Sometimes, impatient drivers honk their horns at me.

10. __I__ Continue driving exactly at the speed limit. *add "I"*

PRACTICE 9

Write five sentences of your own. Each should have a subject and a verb, and each should express a complete thought.

Six Basic English Sentence Patterns

In English, there are six basic sentence patterns, some of which you have already studied in this chapter. Although there are other patterns, they build on these six.

1. Subject-Verb (S-V)

```
S     V
|     |
Dogs bark.
```

2. Subject-Linking Verb-Noun (S-LV-N)

```
S    LV    N
|    |     |
They are animals.
```

3. Subject-Linking Verb-Adjective (S-LV-ADJ)

```
S    LV   ADJ
|    |     |
Cats seem quiet.
```

4. Subject-Verb-Adverb (S-V-ADV)

```
S     V    ADV
|     |     |
They meow softly.
```

5. **Subject-Verb-Direct Object (S-V-DO)**

A **direct object** directly receives the action of the verb.

Dogs **fetch** sticks.

6. **Subject-Verb-Indirect Object-Direct Object (S-V-IO-DO)**

An **indirect object** does not directly receive the action of the verb.

My **dog brings** me sticks.

PRACTICE 10

Using the sentence pattern indicated, write a sentence for each of the following items.

1. (subject-verb-direct object) _____

   _____

2. (subject-linking verb-noun) _____

   _____

3. (subject-verb-adverb) _____

   _____

4. (subject-verb-indirect object-direct object) _____

   _____

5. (subject-verb-indirect object-direct object) _____

   _____

Write and Edit Your Own Work

Tell about a time in your life when something did not happen the way that you expected it to. What was good about the experience, and what was bad about it? How did it change you? When you are done, check that each sentence has a subject, a verb, and a complete thought.

Chapter Review

1. What are the three necessary elements of a sentence in formal written English?

   _____ Write a complete sentence, identifying

   the complete subject and the complete verb.

2. What is the difference between a simple subject and a complete subject?

   _____

   _____ Underline where these terms are first

   defined in the chapter.

3. The subject of a sentence is never in _____ .

4. Highlight where action verbs, linking verbs, and helping verbs are defined in this chapter, and write a sentence for each kind of verb.

5. A dependent clause has a _____ and a _____ but

   is not _____ .

REFLECTING ON THE JOURNEY

Skills Learned

Now that you've completed the chapter, look again at these sentences.

1. I recently rented an apartment with very small rooms.

2. Built for a young family in the 1950s.

3. The appliances in the kitchen and the boiler in the basement are old and unreliable.

Using what you've learned in this chapter, identify two independent clauses, one incomplete thought, a compound subject, a linking verb, an action verb, and a direct object. Then answer the questions below.

1. Are you confident that you can identify complete and incomplete thoughts?

2. Are you confident that you can identify the parts of a sentence (independent clause)?

3. What questions do you have about the parts of a simple sentence?

12

Longer Sentences

READING ROADMAP

Learning Objectives

Chapter Goal: Join related ideas to form longer sentences correctly.

Tools to Achieve the Goal

- Diagram of a compound sentence (p. 211)
- Diagram of a complex sentence (p. 212)
- Reference chart: common dependent words (p. 213)

Key Terms

Skim Chapter 12 before you begin reading. Can you find each of these words in **bold** type? Put a check mark next to each word once you have located it in the chapter.

____ compound sentence

____ independent clause

____ complex sentence

____ dependent clause

____ subordinating conjunction

____ compound-complex sentence

Highlight or circle any of these words that you already know.

Before You Read

Study the following sentences and complete the chart. At the end of the chapter, you will examine these sentences again and reflect on what you have learned.

1. Many Americans are unhappy about their weight, so they are turning to fitness and calorie-counting apps for their mobile devices.

2. Because these apps can connect directly with restaurant menus and product bar codes, dieters can quickly and easily calculate their calorie intake.

Put a check mark by each statement in the chart that is true for you.

Statement	
I can identify one compound sentence and one complex sentence.	
I can identify one coordinating conjunction.	
I can identify one subordinating conjunction.	
I can identify the subject and verb in the independent clauses.	
I can identify the subject and verb in the dependent clause.	

Chapter 10 reviews the parts of speech, and Chapter 11 discusses the basic building blocks of English sentences. Chapter 12 shows you how these basic elements work in longer sentences with multiple ideas.

Compound Sentences

A **compound sentence** contains two complete thoughts (**independent clauses**), usually joined by a comma and a coordinating conjunction (*and, but, for, nor, or, so, yet*).

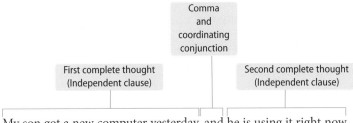

My son got a new computer yesterday, and he is using it right now.

You can remember the coordinating conjunctions by thinking of *fanboys:* **f**or, **a**nd, **n**or, **b**ut, **o**r, **y**et, **s**o.

In a compound sentence, the complete thoughts being joined are related, and they are equal in importance.

Texting is a great way to stay in touch with friends, and it is fun.

I wanted to go swimming after work, but the pool was closed.

You can drive to work with me, or you can wait for the bus.

PRACTICE 1

Underline the two complete thoughts in the compound sentences below, and circle the comma and coordinating conjunction that joins them.

Example: **A smoothie can be a healthy snack, but it can also contain many calories.**

1. Smoothies from restaurants usually have lots of sugar, and they are rarely made from all-natural ingredients.

2. The menu may not provide a list of ingredients, so you may want to ask your server for details.

3. Homemade smoothies are not necessarily lower in sugar, nor are they always better for you.

4. Your recipe might call for ice cream, or it might include high-calorie additives such as flavored syrups.

5. The best smoothies avoid excess calories, and they use fresh fruit for natural sweetness.

PRACTICE 2

Complete the compound sentences below by adding a complete thought after the coordinating conjunction. Be sure that your complete thought contains a subject and a verb.

Example: **Classes were canceled, so** ___*I went to the beach*___ .

1. The waves were high, and _____ .

2. It started to rain, but _____ .

3. No lifeguards were on duty, nor _____ .

4. It was getting late, yet _____ .

5. I had a great day, but _____ .

Complex Sentences

A **complex sentence** contains two ideas, but one of those ideas is dependent on (or subordinate to) the other. The complete thought (also called the **independent clause**) can stand on its own as a sentence, but the dependent idea (also called a **dependent clause** or a **subordinate clause**) cannot. The dependent clause begins with a dependent word (also called a **subordinating conjunction**) such as *after, although, because,* or *when*.

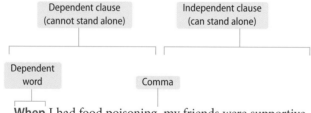

When I had food poisoning, my friends were supportive.

The dependent clause can come before or after the independent clause. Note that when the independent clause comes before the dependent clause, no comma is used to join the two sentences.

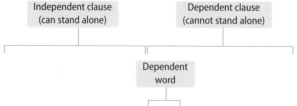

My friends were supportive **when** I had food poisoning.

After I raked the entire yard, I was tired.

You must drive with an adult **even though** you have your driver's license.

If Patti works overtime, she will make an extra $200 this week.

Common Dependent Words (Subordinating Conjunctions)

after	if	what(ever)
although	since	when(ever)
as	so that	where(ver)
because	that	whether
before	though	which
even though	unless	while
how	until	who/whose

PRACTICE 3

In the following sentences, circle the dependent word, underline the dependent clause, and double-underline the independent clause.

Example: Because I am a good mechanic, my friends bring their cars to me.

1. When my best friend's car broke down, she had it towed to my house.

2. Since I take apart old cars all the time, I had the right parts to fix her car.

3. She gave me a gift certificate for Best Buy after I made the repairs.

4. Although she did not have to do this, I appreciated her kindness.

5. I am always happy to help out when I can.

PRACTICE 4

Fill in the blanks below with an independent clause to complete each complex sentence. Be sure that your independent clause is a complete thought with a subject and a verb.

Example: **After we lost the final game,** _our coach took us out for pizza_.

1. Although it is easy to celebrate when you win, _____.

2. _____ when you lose the last game of the season.

3. _____ even though we had won almost every game.

4. While the winning team was basking in glory, _____.

5. _____ because we gave it our best.

Fill in the blanks below with a dependent clause to complete each complex sentence. Be sure to begin each dependent clause with a dependent word.

Example: _When my brother called me in the middle of the night_ , **I thought**

something was wrong.

1. _____ , he told me the reason for his call.

2. He was up all night playing a video game _____.

3. He said he couldn't stop playing the game _____.

4. _____ , he reminded me that I had given him the game.

5. He was calling to blame me for his lack of sleep _____.

Compound-Complex Sentences

A **compound-complex sentence** is a compound sentence (two or more independent clauses) that also has one or more dependent clauses.

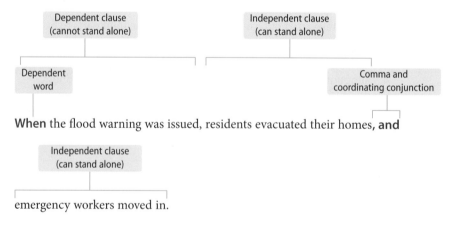

The dependent clause(s) can come before or after the independent clauses.

Residents evacuated their homes, **and** emergency workers moved in **when** the flood warning was issued.

PRACTICE 6

Write five compound-complex sentences. Be sure each sentence includes at least two independent clauses, joined by a comma and a coordinating conjunction, and at least one dependent clause, introduced by a dependent word.

Write and Edit Your Own Work

Imagine you are standing in a long line, as in the photo below. Write a paragraph about what you and the others in the line are doing as you wait. Make sure your paragraph includes at least one compound, one complex, and one compound-complex sentence.

Chapter Review

1. A compound sentence contains two complete thoughts or _____ clauses, which are joined by a comma and a _____ conjunction.

2. A complex sentence contains one _____ clause and one _____ clause.

3. Dependent clauses are introduced by _____ words, which are also called _____ conjunctions.

4. A compound-complex sentence has two or more _____ clauses and one or more _____ clauses.

REFLECTING ON THE JOURNEY

Skills Learned

Now that you've completed the chapter, look again at these sentences.

1. Many Americans are unhappy about their weight, so they are turning to fitness and calorie-counting apps for their mobile devices.

2. Because these apps can connect directly with restaurant menus and product bar codes, dieters can quickly and easily calculate their calorie intake.

Using what you've learned in this chapter, identify three independent clauses, one dependent clause, one subordinating conjunction, one coordinating conjunction, one compound sentence, and one complex sentence. Then answer the questions below.

1. Are you confident that you can identify independent clauses and dependent clauses?

2. Are you confident that you can identify compound sentences and complex sentences?

3. What questions do you have about the structure of longer sentences?

13

Fragments

READING ROADMAP

Learning Objectives

Chapter Goal: Find and correct sentence fragments in writing.

Tools to Achieve the Goal

- Trouble Spot 1: prepositional phrase fragments (p. 221)
- Trouble Spot 2: dependent word fragments (p. 224)
- Trouble Spot 3: *ing* verb fragments (p. 226)
- Trouble Spot 4: *to* + verb fragments (p. 228)
- Trouble Spot 5: example or explanation fragments (p. 231)
- Find and Fix chart (p. 235)

Key Terms

Skim Chapter 13 before you begin reading. Can you find each of these words in **bold** type? Put a check mark next to each word once you have located it in the chapter.

____ fragment   ____ *ing* verb fragment

____ prepositional phrase fragment   ____ *to* + verb fragment

____ dependent-word fragment   ____ example or explanation fragment

Highlight or circle any of these words that you already know.

Before You Read

Before you begin reading this chapter, read the following paragraph and complete the chart that follows.

> Though I had a credit card for several years. I had to give it up. I always owed a lot of money when I had the card. I worked hard. To keep track of what I was spending. Still, I always managed to increase my debt. I decided I needed a new strategy. No credit cards until I had paid back all my debt. I am happy now to be debt-free. After seven years of hard work.

This paragraph has a problem with sentence fragments. Put a check mark by the statement that best describes you.

Skill Statement	
I understand what the mistakes are, and I know how to fix them.	
I understand what the mistakes are, but I am not sure how to fix them.	
I think I understand what the mistakes are.	
I don't understand what the mistakes are.	

The Four Most Serious Errors

Visit **LaunchPad Solo for Readers and Writers > Fragments** for practice recognizing and correcting fragments.

This unit focuses on four major grammar errors that people most often notice in writing.

The four most serious errors

1. Fragments (Chapter 13)

2. Run-ons and comma splices (Chapter 14)

3. Subject-verb agreement problems (Chapter 15)

4. Verb-tense problems (Chapter 16)

Tip For a review of the parts of speech and basic grammar, see Chapters 10 and 11.

If you can avoid these four—just four—kinds of errors, your writing will improve.

Understand What Fragments Are

A **fragment** is a group of words that is missing one or more parts of a complete sentence.

Fragment	To the store.
	[*Who* is doing *what*? You cannot tell without more information.]
Sentence	Dara **drove** to the store.
	[A subject, *Dara,* and an action verb, *drove*, make the fragment a complete sentence. Now you know *who did what*.]

Read the following word groups, pausing at the periods. Is there a difference in the way you read the fragment (in italics) and the sentence? If you read only the words in italics, would they be a complete thought?

Tip In the sentence examples in this chapter, subjects are blue and verbs are red.

Fragment	I am going to a concert on Friday. *At Memorial Arena.*
Sentence	I am going to a concert on Friday at Memorial Arena.
Fragment	Jack loves Florida. *Because it is warm.*
Sentence	Jack loves Florida because it is warm.
Fragment	Penny broke her leg. *Snowboarding last week.*
Sentence	Penny broke her leg snowboarding last week.

In the Real World, Why Is It Important to Correct Fragments?

In writing, a fragment is one of the grammar errors that people notice most, and it can make a bad impression on bosses, clients, and instructors.

Read aloud Jeremy Trail's written response to the following job-interview question, pausing at all periods. Can you hear the fragments?

How would you complete and support the statement "I am a good
_____"?

Jeremy Trail's answer:

I am a good listener. This trait serves me well in all areas of my life. At work, for example. I listen carefully to directions. To do the job right. I listen to all customers, even older people. Who talk slowly and repeat themselves. Listening carefully takes patience. I listen quietly and wait for people to finish. I also listen to my colleagues. To hear what they think and how we can work together. Being a good listener is key to being a good worker. I believe this ability to listen makes me a good candidate. For the position at Stillmark Company.

Employer's response to Jeremy's answer:

Jeremy's writing had several errors. He may be able to listen, which is important, but he cannot write correctly, and that is important in the job, too. When I read applicants' answers, I am looking for ways to narrow the field of candidates. With Jeremy's answer, I found a way. He would not be hired.

Learning how to avoid or correct fragments is important because it will prevent you from being in a situation such as Jeremy's, in which he was ruled out for a job right away.

> **PRACTICE 1**
>
> There are five fragments in Jeremy's writing. Looking for subjects, verbs, and complete thoughts in each word group, underline what you think are the fragments.

Tip To do this chapter, you need to understand the following terms: *sentence, subject, verb, preposition,* and *prepositional phrase.* (For review, see Chapters 10 and 11.)

The following section will explain how to find and fix five common types of fragments.

Find and Correct Fragments

Trouble Spot 1: Fragments That Start with a Prepositional Phrase

Watch for word groups that begin with prepositions but do not contain subjects or verbs.

Tip For a list of common prepositions, see page 203.

Prepositional-phrase fragments

Last week, I **found** a starfish. *At the beach.*

Free **parking is** available. *Behind the mall.*

I **met** Joe on Chester Street. *By the stop sign.*

Fragment joined to sentences

Last week, I **found** a starfish at the beach.

Free **parking is** available behind the mall.

I **met** Joe on Chester Street by the stop sign.

Prepositional-phrase fragments

I **visited** the Super Duper Dollar Store. *In the Emerald Square Mall.*

I **am taking** a three-week luxury cruise with Carnival Cruise Lines. *With my mother.*

Fragments made into their own sentences

I **visited** the Super Duper Dollar Store. **It is** in the Emerald Square Mall.

I **am taking** a three-week luxury cruise with Carnival Cruise Lines. My **mother is coming** along.

The word groups in italics have no subject (remember that the subject is *never* in the prepositional phrase). Also, they have no verb and no complete thought.

PRACTICE 2

In the following items, circle any preposition that appears at the beginning of a word group. Then, correct fragments by connecting them to the previous or the next sentence.

Example: ⬭During⬭ a ten-year study of people ages seventy and older, ∧
A group of scientists reached some interesting conclusions.

1. Among older people. Those with close friends tend to live longer.

2. Through their research. The scientists also learned that the older people with the most good friends lived the longest.

3. Having close family ties did not affect the life span. Of the people in the study.

4. This finding may come as a surprise. To most of us.

5. Before the study. Many people believed that staying close to family members would help a person live longer.

6. The researchers interviewed more than fourteen hundred people. During the study.

7. They interviewed participants every year. For the first four years of the study.

8. Over the remaining six years. Researchers talked with the participants twice.

9. This study sends a clear message. About our older relatives and friends.

10. For a long, healthy life. Friendship is important.

PRACTICE 3

In the following paragraph, eight of the ten items include a fragment that starts with a prepositional phrase. Underline each fragment, and then correct it either by adding the missing sentence elements or by connecting it to the previous or the next sentence. Two items are correct; write **C** next to them.

1 You should wait for a while before going swimming. After a meal. 2 Most of us have heard this warning since we were young. We might even repeat it to our own children. 3 At the pool. Children wait impatiently for their food to digest. 4 They take the warning seriously, believing that muscle cramps caused by food might lead to drowning. 5 From a review of the available statistics. It now appears that this warning is a myth. 6 Of drownings in the United States. Less than 1 percent occurred right after the victim ate a meal, according to one study. 7 With alcohol use involved. The story is different. 8 Among one hundred drowning deaths in the state of Washington one year. Twenty-five percent had been drinking heavily. 9 In California. Forty-one percent of drowning deaths one year were alcohol-related. 10 So you should no longer be afraid of swimming after eating, unless you had some alcohol. With your meal.

PRACTICE 4

Using the list of common prepositions on page 203, write five complete sentences that either start or end with a prepositional phrase. Underline the prepositional phrases.

Trouble Spot 2: Fragments That Start with a Dependent Word

Watch for word groups that begin with one of the following words. You might find a fragment.

Tip To learn more about dependent words (subordinating conjunctions), see Chapter 10, page 194.

Common Dependent Words (Subordinating Conjunctions)

after	if	what(ever)
although	since	when(ever)
as	so that	where(ver)
because	that	whether
before	though	which
even though	unless	while
how	until	who / whose

Dependent-word fragments

Amy **got** to the club. *After I went home.*

She **went** home to change. *Because she was uncomfortable.*

Fragments joined to a sentence

Amy **got** to the club after I **went** home.

She **went** home to change because **she was** uncomfortable.

Dependent-word fragments

I **went** to the Web site of IBM. *Which is the company I want to visit.*

Rob **is** known for having tantrums at airports. *Whenever his flight is delayed.*

Fragments made into their own sentences

I **went** to the Web site of IBM. **IBM is** the company I **want** to visit.

Rob **is** known for having tantrums at airports. **He gets** upset whenever his **flight is** delayed.

Tip To learn more about dependent clauses (subordinate clauses), see Chapter 12.

The word groups in italics have a subject and a verb, but they do not make sense alone; they are **dependent**, meaning that they depend on other words for their meaning. They are called *dependent clauses.*

PRACTICE 5

In the following items, circle any dependent word or words that appear at the beginning of a word group. Then, correct any fragment by connecting it to the previous or the next sentence. Four sentences are correct; write **C** next to them.

Example: If monkeys live on the rock of Gibraltar, ~~T~~the rock will stay under

British rule.

1. Even though it is just a legend, the British take this statement seriously.

2. The government of Gibraltar pays for the care and feeding of the colony's nearly 240 monkeys. Which the legend calls "Barbary apes."

3. The legend says that the monkeys must be allowed to wander freely. Therefore, they are not confined to any specific area.

4. Whether they are in search of candy bars, fruit trees, shady places, or human toys. The monkeys wander everywhere.

5. They have even learned to entertain tourists so that they can get bits of food.

6. Because tourists love it. The monkeys pose for cameras and act like they are snapping a picture.

7. They also steal ice cream cones from children. When the kids are not careful.

8. The monkeys particularly enjoy potato chips, candy, and ice cream. Although they now suffer from tooth decay.

9. Because they are Europe's last free-ranging monkeys, they are also Gibraltar's biggest tourist attraction.

10. While some Gibraltar residents think the monkeys are pests. Others feel they just have to live with them.

PRACTICE 6

All but one of the numbered items in the following paragraph include a fragment that begins with a dependent word. Underline the fragments, and then correct them either by adding the missing sentence elements or by connecting them to the previous or the next sentence. Write **C** next to the one correct item.

1 Because my cousin majored in zoology. He knows a lot about animals. 2 He was also an Eagle Scout. Which means he is familiar with many outdoor survival techniques. 3 He says that many people have an irrational fear of snakes. Even though most snakes are quite harmless. 4 Usually a snake will avoid contact. If it hears someone approaching. 5 Whenever most people see a snake. They freeze. 6 If a person does get bitten by a snake. It probably is not a deadly bite. 7 Although a shot of antivenom is probably not needed. It is a good idea to call 911 and get to the nearest hospital just in case. 8 It is also a good idea to remember what the snake looked like. Since the doctors and animal-control workers will want a description of it. 9 A snake bite can certainly be scary. However, remember that only six people die from snake bites in the United States each year.

> **PRACTICE 7**

Using the list of common dependent words on page 224, write five complete sentences that either start or end with a dependent clause. Underline the dependent clauses.

Trouble Spot 3: Fragments That Start with an -ing Verb

Make sure any word groups with an *-ing* verb also contain a subject.

-ing verb fragments

I **will be** up late tonight. *Studying for finals.*

I **get** plenty of daily exercise. *Walking to the bus stop.*

Fragments joined to sentences

I **will be** up late tonight studying for finals.

I **get** plenty of daily exercise walking to the bus stop.

-ing verb fragments

Gerard **swims** for three hours each day. *Training for the regionals.*

Maya **took** a plane instead of the bus. *Wanting to get home as fast as possible.*

Fragments made into their own sentences

Gerard **swims** for three hours each day. **He is training** for the regionals.

Maya **took** a plane instead of the bus. **She wanted** to get home as fast as possible.

 Language note: English uses both *-ing* verb forms (**Juliana loves** *dancing*) and *infinitives* (**Juliana loves** *to dance*). If these two forms confuse you, pay special attention to this section, and see also Chapter 32.

PRACTICE 8

In the following items, circle any *-ing* verb that appears at the beginning of a word group. Then, correct any fragment either by adding the missing sentence elements or by connecting it to the previous or the next sentence. One item contains no fragment; write **C** next to it.

Example: Writing in his spare time, Albert Einstein published four

important physics papers while working at a patent[1] office

in Switzerland.

1. patent: Protection of ownership rights to an invention.

1. Working an eight-hour shift six days a week. Einstein somehow found time to follow his true passion.

2. Examining patents by day. He revised the basic laws of physics at night.

3. Einstein's day job may have helped his scientific career. Remaining outside the academic community had its advantages.

4. Being at a university. He might have found others ignoring his advanced ideas.

5. Reviewing inventions at the patent office might also have been helpful. In keeping his mind active.

6. Taking a university job. He eventually entered the academic world, where he produced the general theory of relativity.

7. The Nobel Prize committee found Einstein's theory of relativity too extreme. Refusing Einstein the prize for that accomplishment.

8. Awarding him the Nobel Prize for his other contributions. The committee told Einstein not to mention relativity in his acceptance speech.

9. Ignoring the committee. He mentioned it anyway.

10. Perhaps people should pay more attention to dreamers. Forming brilliant ideas where they are least expected.

PRACTICE 9

In the following paragraph, eight items include a fragment that begins with an *-ing* verb form. Underline any fragment, and then correct it either by adding the missing sentence elements or by connecting it to the previous or the next sentence. Write **C** next to the two correct items.

1 Tens of millions of Americans try online dating every year. Making it one of the most popular paid services on the Internet. 2 Three economists recently researched an online dating service. Revealing some interesting facts. 3 Filling out a personal profile is one of the first steps in online dating. The information that people provide is often hard to believe. 4 Describing their appearance. Only 1 percent of those studied said their looks were less than average. 5 Looks were the most important personal feature. Ranking first for both women and men. 6 Hearing this fact. Most people are not surprised. 7 Women who posted photos got higher interest. Receiving twice as many e-mail responses as those who did not post photos. 8 Having plenty of money seems to increase men's chances of finding a date. Men who reported high incomes received nearly twice the e-mail responses as men with low incomes. 9 Going beyond looks and income. Most relationships last because of the personalities involved. 10 Accepting online dating despite some participants' focus on looks and money. Many single people say that it is no worse than other ways of meeting people.

PRACTICE 10

Write five complete sentences that either start or end with an *-ing* verb. Underline the *-ing* verbs.

Trouble Spot 4: Fragments That Start with *to* and a Verb

Word groups consisting of only *to* and a verb are also called **infinitives**. They do not function as a verb.

Word groups that contain an infinitive must be connected to a clause with a subject and a verb.

To + Verb fragments

Christiane **went** home last week. *To help her mother move.*

Hundreds of people **were waiting** in line. *To get tickets.*

Fragments joined to sentences

Christiane **went** home last week to help her mother move.

Hundreds of people **were waiting** in line to get tickets.

To + Verb fragments

Barry **spent** an hour on the phone waiting. *To talk to a customer-service representative.*

Leah **wrote** several letters to politicians. *To build support for the pedestrian-rights bill.*

Fragments made into their own sentences

Barry **spent** an hour on the phone waiting. **He wanted** to talk to a customer-service representative.

Leah **wrote** several letters to politicians. **She hoped** to build support for the pedestrian-rights bill.

 Language note: Do not confuse *to* + a verb with *that*.

| Incorrect | My brother wants **that** his girlfriend cook. |
| Correct | My brother wants his girlfriend **to cook**. |

PRACTICE 11

In the following items, circle any infinitive (*to* + a verb) at the beginning of a word group. Then, correct fragments by connecting them to the previous or the next sentence. Two items contain no fragments; write **C** next to them.

Example: **At the age of twelve, Paul G. Allen used an aluminum tube.**
            ⌐t⌐
            〔**To build**〕 **his first rocket.**
                ∧

1. To fuel the rocket. He used zinc and sulfur from his chemistry set.

2. To launch the rocket. He lit the fuel mixture.

3. Unfortunately, he should have used a stronger metal. To prevent the burning fuel from melting the rocket.

4. To get on with his life. Allen accepted the failure.

5. He later achieved success as a cofounder of Microsoft. To become a billionaire must have been satisfying for Allen, who never lost his interest in rockets.

6. His wealth has made it possible for him to pursue his interest. To build bigger and better rockets, it takes a lot of money.

7. To help build the rocket *SpaceShipOne*. Allen invested a large amount of money.

8. *SpaceShipOne* won a $10 million prize for being the first privately financed vehicle. To send a person into space.

9. What Allen learned as a businessman may have helped him. To find the designer and test pilots who made *SpaceShipOne* a success.

10. To create the best spacecraft. He knew he had to hire the best people for the job.

PRACTICE 12

In the following paragraph, most items include a fragment that begins with an infinitive (*to* + a verb). Underline any fragment and then correct it either by adding the missing sentence elements or by connecting it to the previous or next sentence. Two items are correct; write **C** next to them.

1 To make cars more comfortable and convenient to drive. Engineers have designed many high-tech features. 2 Seat heaters were invented. To keep people warm while driving in cold weather. 3 However, some seat heaters are programmed. To switch off after fifteen minutes without warning the driver. 4 To stay warm on a long trip. The driver must remember to keep turning the seat heater back on. 5 To some people, these cars may be too convenient. One car's computer has seven hundred possible commands. 6 To avoid bothering their neighbors at night. Some people want to stop their cars from honking when they lock the doors. 7 Many people do not know that it is fairly easy.

To turn off some of a car's features. 8 Some people carefully study their cars' systems. To change the programming. 9 To make programming changes on one's own car is risky. It may cause the car's warranty to be invalid. 10 It is probably easiest for people who own these complicated cars. To simply enjoy their high-tech conveniences.

> **PRACTICE 13**
>
> Write five complete sentences that begin or end with *to* and a verb. Underline the sentences that begin with *to* and a verb.

Trouble Spot 5: Fragments That Start with an Example or Explanation

Watch for word groups beginning with *for example, like, especially,* and *such as.* If the word group does not contain a subject and a verb, it is a fragment.

Fragments starting with an example or explanation

I **would like** to get new boots. *Like the ones that Sheila wore last night.*

I **get** lots of offers from credit card companies. *Such as Visa and MasterCard.*

Fragments joined to sentences

I **would like** to get new boots like the ones that Sheila wore last night.

I **get** lots of offers from credit card companies such as Visa and MasterCard.

Fragments starting with an example or explanation

It **is** hard to stay in and study. *Especially during the summer.*

Some **people cook** entirely from scratch, even if it takes all day. *For example, Bill.*

Fragments made into their own sentences

It **is** hard to stay in and study. It **is** especially hard during the summer.

Some **people cook** entirely from scratch, even if it takes all day. **Bill does** that.

> **PRACTICE 14**
>
> In the following paragraph, most items include a fragment that begins with an example or an explanation. Underline any fragment, and then correct it either by adding the missing sentence elements or by connecting it to the previous

or the next sentence. Two items contain no fragment; write **C** next to them.

1 One major fast-food chain is making changes to its menu. Like offering fresh apple slices. 2 The company still mostly sells traditional fast food. For example, double cheeseburgers. 3 The company is trying to offer its customers healthier food. Such as fresh fruit and salads. 4 The cause of the change seems to be public opinion. Like complaints about high-calorie fast-food meals. 5 Many people are blaming fast-food companies for Americans' expanding waistlines. Especially those of children. 6 Consumers love to eat fatty foods. However, they also like to blame fast-food restaurants when they gain weight. 7 This particular restaurant is discovering that healthy food can be profitable. Such as earning about 10 percent of its income from fresh salads. 8 There are limits to how far the company will go to make its food healthier. For instance, with its apple slices. 9 Apple slices are certainly healthy. However, they are less healthy when dipped in the sugary sauce that the company packages with the slices. 10 The company followed the advice of its taste testers. For example, preferring the slices dipped in the sugary sauce.

PRACTICE 15

Write five complete sentences that include examples or explanations. Underline the examples or explanations.

Edit Fragments in Everyday Life

Complete the editing reviews as instructed, referring to the chart on page 235.

EDITING PARAGRAPHS 1

In the following business letter, underline the fragments and correct them either by adding the missing sentence elements or by connecting the fragment to the previous or the next sentence. Write **C** next to the one item that is correct. The first item has been edited for you.

October 12, 2015

Alexis Vallecillo

Humane Society of Riverside County

2343 Monterey Road

St. Lucie, FL 34897

Dear Ms. Vallecillo:

1 Thank you for talking with me on the phone last week, Regarding your organization's Pup Parade next March. 2 I have confirmed that we will be able to accommodate your event at the Bridge Road Estate and Park. On March 15. 3 Reviewing our calendar. I can see that we are currently free for both our morning and afternoon time slots. 4 Be sure to let me know which time you prefer. Because spring is our busiest season.

5 I have calculated the total amount for the use of the facility for four hours. With a parking attendant, a tent, and 200 folding chairs. 6 The normal fee is $4,500. However, we give a 10% discount to nonprofit organizations such as yours. 7 If the fee of $4,050 is acceptable to you. Be sure to submit your deposit before December 15. So that we can guarantee your reservation.

8 Thank you. For thinking of Bridge Road Estate and Park for your organization's needs. 9 If you have any questions or concerns. Please contact me at (516) 555-9670. 10 I look forward to working with you. On your fun and worthwhile event.

Sincerely,

Jean Scott, Facilities Manager

EDITING PARAGRAPHS 2

A friend of yours wants to send the following letter about problems on her street to a city councilor. Before she does, she wants your help in revising it so that she will make the best impression possible. Underline the fragments that you find. Then, correct them and revise informal or inappropriate language so that it is suitable to address a public official. The first numbered item has been edited for you. In addition to this item, you should find eight cases of informal language.

Tip For advice on using formal English, see Chapter 2. For advice on avoiding slang, see Chapter 23.

Dear Councilor Thompson,

    1 As a longtime resident of 5 Rosemont Way in this city, I have seen my
decline.
neighborhood go down the toilet. 2 But not one damn person in the city
government seems to care. Although different residents on this street have
complained at least ten separate times to city councilors.

    3 The sidewalks are messed up bad and have caused several residents
to injure themselves. Such as my son. 4 Also, trash pickup is unreliable and
inconsistent. With the trucks coming at 8:00 a.m. one time and at noon
another time. 5 As a result, residents do not know the right time. To leave out
their trash. 6 If they leave it out too late. It sits around all day getting smelly.
7 It ain't pretty!

    8 Worst of all, most streetlights are busted up bad and never get re-
paired. Even when only one or two are left burning. 9 Hanging out at the bus
stop in the morning darkness. My daughter is afraid. 10 Because of her fears, I
have driven her to school myself. On several occasions.

    11 Thirty residents of the Rosemont neighborhood, including me, have
organized. To draw up a full list of our beefs. 12 We gonna go to the press with
the list. Unless we get a satisfactory response from your office within
seven days.

Sincerely,

Sheree Niles

Write and Edit Your Own Work

ASSIGNMENT 1   **Write**

Write a paragraph about the two most important things that you hope to gain
from going to college. Then, read your writing carefully, stopping at periods
and looking for the five fragment trouble spots. Use the chart on page 235 to
help you revise any fragments that you find.

ASSIGNMENT 2   **Edit**

Using the chart on page 235, correct fragments in a paper that you are writing
for this course or another course or in a piece of writing from your work or
everyday life.

Chapter Review

1. What are the five fragment trouble spots? Highlight where they first appear in this chapter.

2. The two ways to correct a fragment are _____ _____. Highlight where this information appears in the book.

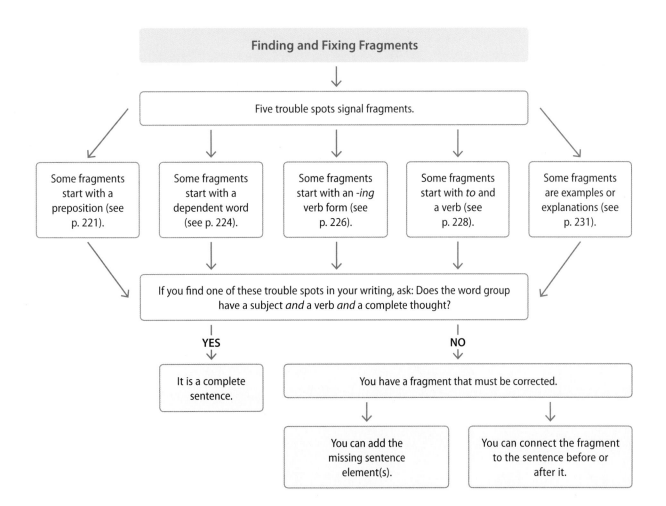

Finding and Fixing Fragments

↓

Five trouble spots signal fragments.

| Some fragments start with a preposition (see p. 221). | Some fragments start with a dependent word (see p. 224). | Some fragments start with an *-ing* verb form (see p. 226). | Some fragments start with *to* and a verb (see p. 228). | Some fragments are examples or explanations (see p. 231). |

If you find one of these trouble spots in your writing, ask: Does the word group have a subject *and* a verb *and* a complete thought?

YES → It is a complete sentence.

NO → You have a fragment that must be corrected.

- You can add the missing sentence element(s).
- You can connect the fragment to the sentence before or after it.

REFLECTING ON THE JOURNEY

Skills Learned

Now that you've completed the chapter, look again at this paragraph.

> Though I had a credit card for several years. I had to give it up. I always owed a lot of money when I had the card. I worked hard. To keep track of what I was spending. Still, I always managed to increase my debt. I decided I needed a new strategy. No credit cards until I had paid back all my debt. I am happy now to be debt-free. After seven years of hard work.

Using what you've learned in this chapter, edit this paragraph for sentence fragments and answer the questions below.

1. Are you confident that you have identified the fragments?

2. Are you confident that you have corrected the fragments?

3. What questions do you have about finding and fixing sentence fragments?

14

Run-Ons and Comma Splices

READING ROADMAP

Learning Objectives

Chapter Goal: Find and correct sentence run-ons and comma splices in writing.

Tools to Achieve the Goal

- Strategy 1: Add a period or semicolon (p. 240)
- Strategy 2: Add a comma and a coordinating conjunction (p. 242)
- Strategy 3: Add a dependent word (p. 244)
- Find and Fix chart (p. 250)

Key Terms

Skim Chapter 14 before you begin reading. Can you find each of these words in **bold** type? Put a check mark next to each word once you have located it in the chapter.

____ sentence	____ run-on
____ comma splice	____ dependent word
____ coordinating conjunction	

Highlight or circle any of these words that you already know.

Before You Read

Before you begin reading this chapter, study the following paragraph and complete the chart. At the end of the chapter, you will examine the paragraph again and reflect on what you have learned.

> The business of toy making has changed over the past 50 years. Large discount chains are keeping toy prices low this makes it difficult for toy companies to make a profit. Also, children still like traditional toys, but new gadgets are often more popular. For example, many kids play video games, they also spend a lot of time on the internet. While dolls are still popular, children prefer dolls that sing, dance, tell jokes, and play games. Some children do ask for simple, traditional toys large chain stores can copy these toys and sell them for a cheaper price. The original toys cannot compete with the cheap price of the copies the toy companies lose money.

This paragraph has problems with comma splices and run-on sentences. Put a check mark by the statement that best describes you.

Skill Statement	
I understand what the mistakes are, and I know how to fix them.	
I understand what the mistakes are, but I am not sure how to fix them.	
I think I understand what the mistakes are.	
I don't understand what the mistakes are.	

Understand What Run-Ons and Comma Splices Are

LaunchPadSolo

Visit **LaunchPad Solo for Readers and Writers > Run-ons and Comma Splices** for more practice with finding and fixing run-ons and comma splices.

Tip In the sentence examples in this chapter, subjects are blue and verbs are red.

Sometimes, two complete **sentences** (or independent clauses) can be joined to make one sentence.

Two complete sentences joined correctly

Independent clause   Independent clause

The **bus was** late, so many **people went** home.

Independent clause   Independent clause

Drivers were on strike, but few **passengers knew** it.

Complete sentences that are not joined correctly are either run-ons or comma splices. A **run-on** occurs when two complete sentences are joined without any punctuation.

Run-on

Independent clause   Independent clause

My **aunt has** several dogs **she has** no other pets.

A **comma splice** occurs when two complete sentences are joined by only a comma instead of a comma and one of the following words: *and, but, for, nor, or, so, yet.*

Comma splice

Independent clause   Independent clause

My **aunt has** several dogs, **she has** no other pets.

In the Real World, Why Is It Important to Correct Run-Ons and Comma Splices?

Although run-ons and comma splices may not be noticeable in spoken language, they are confusing in writing. Like fragments, they make a bad impression.

Read Jenny Kahn's answer to the following question, which was on an application for a job as a veterinarian's assistant.

Why do you think that you are qualified to work with people and their pets?

Jenny Kahn's answer:
Growing up, I had many pets, there were always dogs and cats in our house. My parents made sure I was responsible for my animals I had to

feed, comb, and bathe them regularly. I also had to take them to the vet once a year for their shots, I often talked to other people in the waiting room about their pets. Some people were upset about their sick pets, I tried to calm them down with reassuring words. Pets, too, get nervous in the vet's waiting room, so they have to be calmed down. If you work with animals, you have to have some experience you also have to be quiet and gentle or you are going to scare the pet and its owner.

Veterinarian's response to Jenny's answer:

My assistants work with animals and their owners in my office, but they also have to do a good deal of writing. They write up the patients' histories, and they update files. They also write memos to our clients and to companies that sell us supplies. Jenny's answer has many confusing sentences. Her writing might reflect badly on me. It might even be dangerous if I could not understand what she has written. I cannot hire her.

> **PRACTICE 1**

There are five run-ons or comma splices in Jenny's answer to the job-application question. Looking for complete sentences, underline what you think are the errors.

> **PRACTICE 2**

Five of the following sentences are correct, and the others are either run-ons or comma splices. In the blank to the left of each sentence, write **C** if the sentence is correct, **CS** if it is a comma splice, and **RO** if it is a run-on.

Example: _CS_ **Two young scientists met in a conference room in 1973, they were working in the new field of computer networks.**

1. ____ They wanted to connect separate computer networks this connection was not possible at the time.

2. ____ They argued out loud, wrote on a chalkboard, and sketched on a yellow pad.

3. ____ Two days later, they felt they had the start of a good technical paper, they did not realize that it was the beginning of today's Internet.

4. ____ Vinton G. Cerf and Robert E. Kahn received the 2004 A. M. Turing Award for their work, the Turing Award is like the Nobel Prize for the computer field.

5. ____ The Turing Award is named for a British mathematician who cracked German codes during World War II.

6. ____ Few people have ever heard of Cerf and Kahn; some believe the Internet was invented by a large company like Microsoft.

7. ____ Cerf and Kahn developed a way to group computer data into packages, each package could be sent to any computer in the world.

8. ____ To decide whose name would appear first on their research article, they tossed a coin.

9. ____ Other scientists have also been given credit for helping to develop the Internet, these scientists' inventions were important as well.

10. ____ Cerf and Kahn did not gain much fame for their invention, and they earned no money from it.

Tip Before going on in this chapter, you may want to review the following terms from Chapter 11: *sentence, subject,* and *verb*.

Find and Correct Run-Ons and Comma Splices

The rest of this chapter explains three ways to fix run-ons and comma splices.

Add a Period or a Semicolon

Notice how periods and semicolons are used between complete sentences.

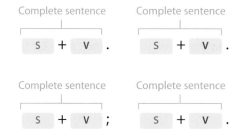

Correct a run-on or comma splice by adding a period or a semicolon.

Run-on	Students **crowded** the tiny library **they were studying** for final exams.
Corrected with a period	Students **crowded** the tiny library. **They were studying** for final exams.
Corrected with a semicolon	Students **crowded** the tiny library; **they were studying** for final exams.

Comma splice	Children **played** in the park, **they loved** the merry-go-round.
Corrected with a period	Children **played** in the park. **They loved** the merry-go-round.
Corrected with a semicolon	Children **played** in the park; **they loved** the merry-go-round.

PRACTICE 3

For each of the following items, indicate in the space to the left whether it is a run-on (**RO**) or a comma splice (**CS**). Then, correct the sentence by adding a period or a semicolon. Capitalize letters as necessary to make two sentences.

Example: <u>RO</u>   **At an art auction in 2005, three paintings sold for more than $26,000 . T the artist was neither Renoir nor Andy Warhol.**

1. _____ The artist was a chimpanzee named Congo, he created the three abstract paintings in 1950.

2. _____ Animal artists are not new on the art scene many zoos around the country are teaching different animals to paint.

3. _____ Ruby, an Asian elephant at a zoo in Arizona, loves to paint, one of her works sold for $5,000.

4. _____ When she first came to the zoo, she lived with a goat and some chickens, she got bored and started drawing with a stick.

5. _____ Ruby quickly learned to paint she chooses her colors, and they go together well.

6. _____ Many different animals have been handed a paintbrush, an art lover can find paintings by kangaroos, ocelots, red pandas, and even sea lions.

7. _____ The animals learn quickly painting helps eliminate the boredom the animals face in captivity.

8. _____ The artistic talents of animals seem to differ some really enjoy painting while others refuse to lift a claw or trunk or paw.

9. ____ Then, too, some of the animals are temperamental, they refuse to paint and will just walk away or, in the case of sea lions, swim away.

10. ____ People are able to buy beautiful animal paintings to decorate their homes at the same time, the money spent on the paintings helps animals.

Add a Comma and a Coordinating Conjunction

Tip To learn more about coordinating conjunctions, see Chapter 10.

You can add a comma and a **coordinating conjunction** between two complete sentences. Remember the seven coordinating conjunctions by using the acronym *fanboys* (**f**or, **a**nd, **n**or, **b**ut, **o**r, **y**et, **s**o).

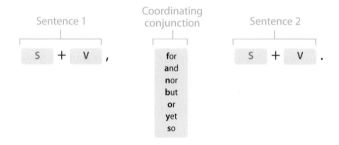

Run-ons

His used **cars are** too expensive **I bought** mine from another dealer.

Computers are her first love **she spends** a lot of time gardening.

Corrected

His used **cars are** too expensive, *so* **I bought** mine from another dealer.

Computers are her first love, *yet* **she spends** a lot of time gardening.

Comma splices

I would spend an extra day in Chicago, I simply **do** not **have** the free time.

Jane is in charge of billing, her **sister runs** the lingerie department.

Corrected

I would spend an extra day in Chicago, *but* I simply **do** not **have** the free time.

Jane is in charge of billing, *and* her **sister runs** the lingerie department.

Language note: Coordinating conjunctions connect two complete sentences.

Incorrect

Not a complete sentence | Complete sentence

Although he said he was going home, **but** he never did.

Correct

Complete sentence | Complete sentence

He said he was going home, **but** he never did.

PRACTICE 4

All of the following items are run-ons or comma splices. First, underline the subject, and double-underline the verb in each part. Then, correct the error by adding a comma, if necessary, and the appropriate coordinating conjunction from the two choices in parentheses.

Example: The black-capped chickadee's <u>name</u> <u><u>makes</u></u> perfect sense *, for* its <u>song</u> <u><u>sounds</u></u> like "chick-a-dee." (but, for)

1. Most birds use their songs to attract mates the chickadee also sings for another reason. (or, but)

2. The chickadee has many enemies, the hawk and the owl are two of the most dangerous. (so, and)

3. Chickadees are protective of their flock they use their song to warn other chickadees of danger. (so, for)

4. The song tells other chickadees of a nearby enemy it also tells more than that. (nor, yet)

5. The chickadee's call can have a different number of "dees" at the end the number of "dees" sends a message to the rest of the flock. (but, and)

6. A call might end with many "dees," it might end with just a few. (for, or)

7. A call ending with many "dees" warns of a small enemy fewer "dees" signal a larger enemy. (and, nor)

8. Chickadees are small and fast, larger and slower animals are not a big threat. (for, so)

9. A call ending with a large number of "dees" brings many chickadees to the area to dive-bomb the enemy fewer "dees" draw fewer chickadees. (yet, and)

10. The chickadee is good at driving enemies out of its territory it knows how to use its song for protection. (so, for)

PRACTICE 5

Some items in the following paragraph are run-ons or comma splices. Correct each error by adding a comma, if necessary, and a coordinating conjunction. Two sentences are correct; write **C** next to them.

1 Bette Nesmith Graham was a secretary in the 1950s her typing skills were poor. 2 She needed more income she took a second job decorating bank windows for the holidays. 3 While painting windows, she noticed some artists painting over their mistakes. 4 She realized she could paint over her typing errors she brought a small bottle of paint to her secretarial job. 5 She soon needed more paint the other secretaries wanted to use the fluid, too. 6 She experimented with other fluids at home, she also asked her son's chemistry teacher for advice. 7 She started selling an improved fluid in 1956, she called it Mistake Out. 8 In the 1960s, she changed the name to Liquid Paper it was the same product. 9 Graham eventually sold her Liquid Paper business for $47.5 million in 1979. 10 Hardly anybody today uses a typewriter, reports show that people still use correction fluid on about 42.3 million pages a year.

Add a Subordinating Conjunction (Dependent Word)

Finally, to fix a run-on or comma splice, you can add a **dependent word** (also called a *subordinating conjunction*) to one of the two complete sentences to make it a dependent clause.

Tip To learn more about dependent words (subordinating conjunctions), see Chapter 10.

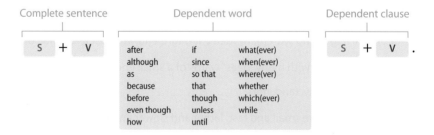

Complete sentence	Dependent word			Dependent clause
S + V	after	if	what(ever)	S + V .
	although	since	when(ever)	
	as	so that	where(ver)	
	because	that	whether	
	before	though	which(ever)	
	even though	unless	while	
	how	until		

Run-ons

Day care is free at our college **I can afford** to go to school.

She lost her job her **company outsourced** her position.

Corrected

Because day care **is** free at our college, **I can afford** to go to school.

She lost her job *after* her **company outsourced** her position.

Comma splices

He was nervous, **he stayed** in the delivery room.

The **deck will be built**, **they return** from their vacation in June.

Corrected

Even though **he was** nervous, **he stayed** in the delivery room.

The **deck will be built** *before* **they return** from their vacation in June.

When the dependent clause starts the sentence, add a comma after it, as in the first corrected examples in each of the previous groups. When the dependent word is in the middle of the sentence, you do not need a comma.

> **PRACTICE 6**
>
> All of the following items are run-ons or comma splices. First, underline the subject and double-underline the verb in each part. Then, correct the error by adding the appropriate subordinating conjunction from the two choices in parentheses. If a dependent clause starts the sentence, it should be followed by a comma.
>
> Example: *If you*
> You feel tired all the time, you are not alone. (if, that)
>
> 1. Most people understand the importance of a good night's rest, about half of all Americans do not get enough sleep. (because, even though)
>
> 2. We are busy sleep often becomes our least important concern. (how, when)
>
> 3. You have had a long week with little sleep, you might sleep late on the weekend. (after, so that)
>
> 4. Many people try to catch up on lost sleep this is not possible, according to doctors. (although, if)
>
> 5. Coffee, tea, and soda can keep you alert they contain caffeine. (because, after)
>
> 6. Studies have not proven that caffeine is harmful to most people's health, it is a poor substitute for sleep. (though, when)

7. Your pillow might be the problem you have trouble sleeping. (until, if)

8. You prefer a soft or a firm pillow, it should not be too flat. (whether, because)

9. A supportive pillow is important for restful sleep, pillow experts suggest a simple test. (before, because)

10. You fold a pillow in half, it should unfold itself instantly. (after, whichever)

PRACTICE 7

In the following paragraph, correct any run-ons or comma splices by adding a subordinating conjunction. Two sentences are correct; write **C** next to them.

1 Emergency medical technicians are often the first to arrive at the scene of an emergency, they are trained to follow certain procedures. 2 The first thing they need to do is survey the scene and make sure it is safe. 3 Hazardous materials, fire, or other dangers may be present, technicians must immediately take care to protect themselves. 4 The technician carefully assesses the patient, she determines whether the patient is conscious and alert. 5 The patient shows any signs of spinal cord injuries the technician must be extra careful to prevent further damage. 6 The next thing the technician does is look for an airway she can be sure the patient can breathe. 7 The airway is blocked, the technician must immediately find a way to unblock it. 8 The airway has been established, the technician checks to see if the patient's breathing is normal. 9 Then, the technician stops any major external bleeding and checks the patient's pulse. 10 These important initial steps have been taken, the technician can more thoroughly examine, reassure, and comfort the patient until further help can be given.

Edit Run-Ons and Comma Splices in Everyday Life

Complete the editing reviews as instructed, referring to the chart on page 250.

EDITING PARAGRAPHS 1

The following paragraph is similar to one that you might find in a science textbook. Revise the paragraph, correcting run-ons and comma splices. In addition to the first sentence, which has been marked for you, three more sentences are correct; write **C** next to them.

C

1 Watching cows may not be most people's idea of a fun-filled afternoon, but scientists have a different opinion. 2 Researchers recognize that many smaller animals seem to understand the earth's magnetic lines, they have discovered that large mammals seem to have a sense of direction as well. 3 A study of satellite images shows that herds of cattle almost always face in the north-south directions these directions are not geographic north-south. 4 Almost without exception, they align with the magnetic north or south lines of the earth. 5 The scientists considered environmental factors time of day or wind direction seemed to have no influence on the cattle's position. 6 In 308 locations in different parts of the world, 8,510 cattle stood in the north-south position, however, cows are not the only animals that align with the magnetic lines of the earth. 7 In the Czech Republic, other researchers personally observed 2,974 deer. 8 These scientists studied where the deer slept and where they sought shelter deer also faced the magnetic north-south. 9 Other animals such as salmon, birds, and turtles have a sense of direction that relies on magnetic lines for example, a species of bat has a magnetic compass. 10 Now it is up to scientists to discover why this magnetic alignment occurs and how they can use the information to benefit mankind.

EDITING PARAGRAPHS 2

Find and correct the run-ons and comma splices in the following paragraph, which might appear in a medical brochure about skin cancer. Then, revise informal language. Aside from the first sentence, which has been marked for you, two sentences are correct. Write **C** next to them. In addition, you should find three cases of informal language.

Tip For advice on using formal English, see Chapter 2. For advice on avoiding slang, see Chapter 23.

1 Skin cancer is most commonly diagnosed as one of three types they are basal cell carcinoma, squamous cell carcinoma, and melanoma. 2 Basal cell carcinoma (BCC) is the most common type of skin cancer it is also the most

curable. 3 BCC looks like a smooth, pearly bump on the skin, it is most often found on the face, neck, and shoulders. 4 BCC can usually be removed surgically, without even leaving a scar. 5 The second most common type of skin cancer is squamous cell carcinoma (SCC). 6 SCC, like BCC, is most often found on the head and shoulders, it looks like a gross scab or a scaly red patch of skin. 7 SCC is curable, if you don't deal with it, the cancer could spread to other parts of the body. 8 The least common type of skin cancer is melanoma it usually has a dark brown or black color and an asymmetrical shape. 9 In men, melanomas typically appear on the head, back, and chest, in women, melanomas most often occur on the lower legs. 10 Melanoma is not as common as BCC and SCC, it is the most likely form of skin cancer to spread throughout the body and cause death. 11 Everyone should have regular checkups to detect weird-looking things that might be one of the three types of skin cancer.

Write and Edit Your Own Work

ASSIGNMENT 1   **Write**

Write a paragraph describing an exciting activity you have done. You may use the photographs below and on the next page to generate ideas. When you have finished, read your paragraph carefully, using the chart on page 250 to correct any run-ons or comma splices you find.

| ASSIGNMENT 2 | **Edit**

Using the chart on page 250, correct run-ons or comma splices in a paper you are writing for this course or another course or in a piece of writing from your work or everyday life.

Chapter Review

1. A _____ is two complete sentences joined without any punctuation.

2. A _____ is two complete sentences joined by only a comma instead of a comma and *and, but, for, nor, or, so,* or *yet*.

3. What are the three ways to fix a run-on or comma splice? _____
_____
_____

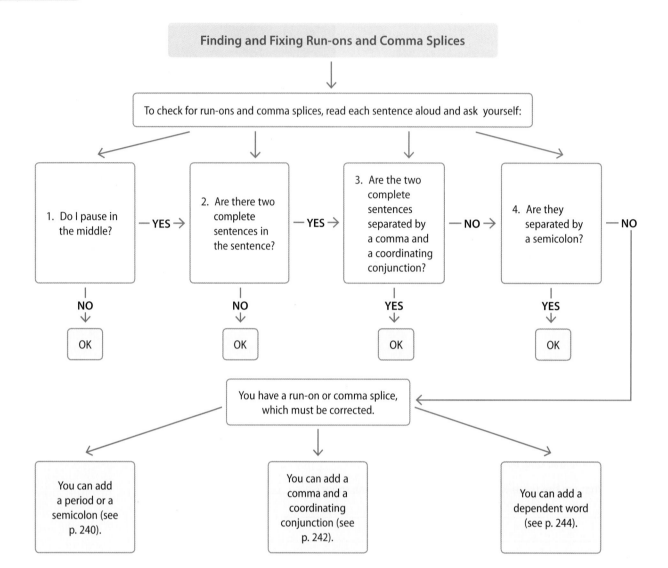

Finding and Fixing Run-ons and Comma Splices

To check for run-ons and comma splices, read each sentence aloud and ask yourself:

1. Do I pause in the middle? —YES→ 2. Are there two complete sentences in the sentence? —YES→ 3. Are the two complete sentences separated by a comma and a coordinating conjunction? —NO→ 4. Are they separated by a semicolon? —NO

1. NO ↓ OK

2. NO ↓ OK

3. YES ↓ OK

4. YES ↓ OK

You have a run-on or comma splice, which must be corrected.

You can add a period or a semicolon (see p. 240).

You can add a comma and a coordinating conjunction (see p. 242).

You can add a dependent word (see p. 244).

REFLECTING ON THE JOURNEY

Skills Learned

Now that you've completed the chapter, look again at this paragraph.

The business of toy making has changed over the past 50 years. Large discount chains are keeping toy prices low this makes it difficult for toy companies to make a profit. Also, children still like traditional toys, but new gadgets are often more popular. For example, many kids play video games, they also spend a lot of time on the internet. While dolls are still popular, children prefer dolls that sing, dance, tell jokes, and play games. Some children do ask for simple, traditional toys large chain stores can copy these toys and sell them for a cheaper price. The original toys cannot compete with the cheap price of the copies the toy companies lose money.

Using what you've learned in this chapter, edit this paragraph for comma splices and run-on sentences. Then answer the questions below.

1. Are you confident that you have identified the mistakes?
2. Are you confident that you have corrected the mistakes?
3. What questions do you have about comma splices and run-ons?

15

Subject-Verb Agreement Problems

READING ROADMAP

Learning Objectives

Chapter Goal: Find and correct sentences with subject-verb agreement problems.

Tools to Achieve the Goal
- Reference chart: forms of *be* in the present tense (p. 257)
- Reference chart: forms of *be* in the past tense (p. 257)
- Reference chart: forms of *have* in the present tense (p. 258)
- Reference chart: forms of *do* in the present tense (p. 260)
- Agreement when words come between the subject and verb (p. 261)
- Agreement when the sentence has a compound subject (p. 264)
- Agreement when the subject is an indefinite pronoun (p. 266)
- Agreement when the verb comes before the subject (p. 268)
- Find and Fix chart (p. 273)

Key Terms

Skim Chapter 15 before you begin reading. Can you find each of these words in **bold** type? Put a check mark next to each word once you have located it in the chapter.

_____ subject
_____ verb
_____ agree
_____ irregular verbs
_____ prepositional phrase

_____ dependent clause
_____ compound subject
_____ indefinite pronoun

Highlight or circle any of these words that you already know.

Before you begin reading this chapter, study the following paragraph and complete the chart. At the end of the chapter, you will examine the paragraph again and reflect on what you have learned.

> Here are the farm stand we were telling you about. It sells the freshest fruits and vegetables that you will ever taste. The corn is picked every morning. You may be asking, "Where is the fields where the corn is grown?" The fields are located behind the main barn, where you will find tomatoes that is loaded with flavor and watermelons that is too big for one person to carry. There are also homemade ice cream, fresh from the freezer. The owners also sells prize-winning pies, including apple pies hot from the oven. There is baskets for customers to carry everything to the car, but I never have enough room!

This paragraph has problems with subject-verb agreement. Put a check mark by the statement that best describes you.

Skill Statement	
I understand what the mistakes are, and I know how to fix them.	
I understand what the mistakes are, but I am not sure how to fix them.	
I think I understand what the mistakes are.	
I don't understand what the mistakes are.	

Understand What Subject-Verb Agreement Is

In any sentence, the **subject and the verb must match—or agree**—in number. If the subject is singular (one person, place, thing, or idea), then the verb must also be singular. If the subject is plural (more than one), the verb must also be plural.

Singular   The library **computer crashes** often.

> [The subject, *computer*, is singular—just one computer—so the verb must take the singular form: *crashes*.]

Plural   The library **computers crash** often.

> [The subject, *computers*, is plural—more than one computer—so the verb must take the plural form: *crash*.]

In the present tense, verbs for third-person singular subjects (like *Bob, he, she,* or *it*) end in *-s* or *-es*.

Third-person singular subject	Present-tense verb
he she it (computer)	→ crashes

Visit **LaunchPad Solo for Readers and Writers > Subject-Verb Agreement** for more practice with making subjects and verbs agree.

Tip In the sentence examples and charts in this chapter, subjects are blue and verbs are red.

Verbs for other subjects (*I, you, we, they*) do not add an *-s* or *-es* ending.

Other subjects	Present-tense verb
I	
you	
we	crash
they	

🌐 **Language note:** You may hear nonstandard usage in informal, spoken English, but for formal, written English, make sure subjects and verbs agree. Remember to add *-s* or *-es* to regular verbs that go with third-person singular subjects (*she, he, it*).

Incorrect	She know the manager.
Correct	She know**s** the manager.

PRACTICE 1

In each of the following sentences, circle the correct form of the verb. Then, write the subject and verb in the blank next to the sentence.

Example: _*people want*_ Many people (want/wants) to understand and communicate with whales.

1. _____ In Japan, a professor (believe / believes) that he can talk to a beluga whale.

2. _____ He (say/says) that he uses sound to help a whale understand the meaning of objects and sounds.

3. _____ Whales (communicate/communicates) with each other by using sounds.

4. _____ This whale's name (is/are) Nack.

5. _____ The professor (show/shows) Nack an object and plays a sound.

6. _____ Eventually, the animal (make/makes) the sound when it sees the object.

7. _____ Nack also (choose/chooses) an object when hearing the correct sound.

8. _____ Scientists (want/wants) whales to be able to express their likes and dislikes.

9. _____ However, humans (need/needs) to develop better equipment to hear the sounds that whales make.

10. _____ Researchers (hope/hopes) that whale language will
   be understood someday.

PRACTICE 2

For each subject, fill in the blank with the correct present-tense form of the verb.

Example: (to write) I   _____write_____

he   _____writes_____

they   _____write_____

1. **(to ride)**   he   _____

we   _____

they   _____

2. **(to play)**   we   _____

I   _____

he   _____

3. **(to give)**   they   _____

she   _____

you   _____

4. **(to clean)**   he   _____

she   _____

they   _____

5. **(to drive)**   he   _____

we   _____

they   _____

6. **(to lose)**   we   _____

he   _____

I   _____

7. **(to bring)**   they   _____

you   _____

she   _____

8. **(to let)**   you   _____

she   _____

they   _____

In the Real World, Why Is It Important to Correct Subject-Verb Agreement Errors?

When Danny Alvarez filled out his application for admission to Eastside College, he had to write about his reasons for choosing that particular college. Read his paragraph aloud. Can you hear the problems with subject-verb agreement?

Briefly tell us why you chose Eastside College.

Danny's answer:

I knows Eastside College is the best college in the area. My sister Beth and my sister Angel attends it now. My older sister study in the nursing school, and my younger sister want to be a paralegal in a lawyer's office. Both sisters likes the college fine and feels they gets a good education there. I hopes to get an associate's degree in drafting; my drafting teacher in high school and my high school counselor also recommends Eastside College for this line of work.

The response of Eastside College's registrar to Danny's answer:

We get hundreds of applications each semester, and, of course, we cannot accept them all. Therefore, we must choose those candidates who seem most prepared for college work. The mistakes in Danny's response make me think that he is not ready for college at this time.

PRACTICE 3

There are nine subject-verb agreement errors in Danny's response. Looking at the subjects and verbs in each sentence, underline what you think are the errors.

Find and Correct Errors in Subject-Verb Agreement

Tip To do this chapter, you need to understand the following terms: *subject, verb, prepositional phrase, dependent clause,* and *pronoun.* (For review, see Chapters 10 and 12.)

To avoid subject-verb agreement errors, identify the subject and verb in each sentence. Make sure that verbs agree with subjects, especially when you have trouble spots like those listed below.

The Verb Is a Form of Be, Have, or Do

The verbs *be, have,* and *do* do not follow the regular patterns for forming singular and plural forms; they are **irregular verbs**.

Forms of the Verb *Be* in the Present Tense (Happening Now)

	Singular (one only)		Plural (two or more)	
	If the subject is	. . . then the verb is	If the subject is	. . . then the verb is
First person	I	am	we	are
Second person	you	are	you	are
Third person	he/she/it	is	they	are

Forms of the Verb *Be* in the Past Tense (Happening before Now)

	Singular (one only)		Plural (two or more)	
	If the subject is	. . . then the verb is	If the subject is	. . . then the verb is
First person	I	was	we	were
Second person	you	were	you	were
Third person	he/she/it	was	they	were

 Language note: Some nouns that do not end in -*s* are plural and need plural verbs. For example, *children* and *people* do not end in -*s,* but they indicate more than one, so they are plural.

| **Incorrect** | These children is making me crazy. |
| **Correct** | These children **are** making me crazy. |

For more on irregular plural forms of nouns, see Chapter 10.

Incorrect

You *is* the fastest driver.

Most **books** in this library *is* hard.

Correct

You *are* the fastest driver.

[The second-person singular, *you,* takes *are* as the verb.]

Most **books** in this library ***are*** hard.

[The third-person plural, *books,* takes *are* as the verb.]

PRACTICE 4

In each of the following sentences, fill in the correct form of *be*. Make sure that the verb agrees with the subject.

Example: **My friend Corey and I** *are* **members of the drama club at my college.**

1. Corey _____ a theater major who has been acting since he _____ five years old.

2. I _____ new to acting and singing, but I enjoy being in the shows.

3. Last semester, I _____ in a production of *Les Miserables,* a famous musical about France in the early 1800s.

4. Anyone could try out for the show, but members of the drama club _____ specially coached before the auditions.

5. Because I _____ still learning how to act and sing, I got only a small role.

6. Corey, who is an excellent singer, _____ offered the lead role of Jean Valjean.

7. We _____ both expected to attend all rehearsals, which took away from our study time.

8. Next semester's play _____ *Chicago,* which I saw on Broadway.

9. Corey and I _____ both going to try out.

10. I _____ working to improve my singing so I can get a bigger part in the next play.

Forms of the Verb *Have* in the Present Tense (Happening Now)

	Singular (one only)		Plural (two or more)	
	If the subject is	. . . then the verb is	If the subject is	. . . then the verb is
First person	I	have	we	have
Second person	you	have	you	have
Third person	he/she/it	has	they	have

Incorrect

I *has* the right to see my records.

They *has* the parking permit.

Correct

I *have* the right to see my records.

[The first-person singular, *I*, takes *have* as the verb.]

They *have* the parking permit.

[The third-person plural, *they*, takes *have* as the verb.]

PRACTICE 5

In each of the following sentences, fill in the correct form of *have*. Make sure that the verb agrees with the subject.

Example: I __*have*__ a job at the new burrito restaurant in town.

1. It _____ a small menu, but the ingredients are fresher than the ones you find in most fast-food restaurants.

2. Customers _____ the choice of burritos, tacos, or salads.

3. We also _____ side items such as soups, tortilla chips, and freshly made pies for dessert.

4. The restaurant _____ good choices for people with special dietary needs, such as gluten-free, dairy-free, and meat-free items.

5. At our restaurant, people _____ to order from the counter and get their own drinks.

6. They _____ no problem with this setup.

7. All employees _____ to pitch in and serve customers at the counter, cook in the kitchen, and even clean the tables and the bathroom.

8. For each shift, we _____ a list of responsibilities posted by the time clock.

9. My boss _____ a philosophy that employees will work better together if they understand what everyone does.

10. Although I _____ my favorite parts of the job, I _____ no complaints about the way the restaurant is run.

Forms of the Verb *Do* in the Present Tense (Happening Now)

	Singular (one only)		Plural (two or more)	
	If the subject is	. . . then the verb is	If the subject is	. . . then the verb is
First person	I	do	we	do
Second person	you	do	you	do
Third person	he/she/it	does	they	do

Incorrect

She always *do* her assignments on time.

They *does* not like to swim.

Correct

She always *does* her assignments on time.

[The third-person singular, *she,* takes *does* as the verb.]

They *do* not like to swim.

[The third-person plural, *they,* takes *do* as the verb.]

PRACTICE 6

In each of the following sentences, fill in the correct form of *do*. Make sure that the verb agrees with the subject.

Example: I ___*do*___ **everything at the last minute, unlike my friend Kevin.**

1. He _____ all his assignments early.

2. My other friends are like me; they _____ their work late, too.

3. We _____ understand the importance of starting early.

4. When you _____ an entire paper the night before a deadline, you run out of time for revising and editing.

5. I _____ my best to start assignments early, but it is easy to get distracted.

6. Thinking that the paper can wait, I _____ the dishes or the laundry instead.

7. We _____ not understand how Kevin is so good at managing his time.

8. In addition to night classes and his full-time job, he even _____ volunteer work on weekends.

9. He _____ not have a secret way of adding extra hours to the day; he simply creates a written schedule and sticks to it.

10. He _____ well in all of his classes, so it really _____ pay to be organized.

PRACTICE 7

In the following paragraph, correct problems with subject-verb agreement. If a sentence is correct as written, write **C** next to it. There are five correct sentences.

1 My family have trouble finding time to eat dinner together. 2 We do our best. 3 Our busy schedules is hard to work around, however. 4 We are aware of the importance of regular family meals. 5 Scientists has found interesting benefits to such meals. 6 One study are especially revealing. 7 According to this study, teenagers does less drinking and smoking if they eat with family members an average of five to seven times weekly. 8 Family mealtime also has a link to eating disorders. 9 A teen girl are less likely to be anorexic or bulimic if she regularly eats meals with her family. 10 Family dinners even does wonders for children's language development. 11 Mealtime is more important to children's vocabulary than play, story time, and other family activities. 12 Of course, long discussions is more useful for vocabulary skills than comments like "Eat your vegetables." 13 Vegetables is certainly important, too, and children eat more of them when dining with their families. 14 Like most people, you probably has a busy schedule. 15 Nevertheless, family dinners are clearly well worth the time.

 Language note: The verbs *be, have,* and *do* cause problems for people who use only one form of the verb in casual conversation: *You is the nicest* (incorrect); *He is the nicest* (correct); *She be upset* (incorrect); *She is upset* (correct). In college and at work, use the correct form of the verbs as shown in this chapter.

Words Come between the Subject and the Verb

A prepositional phrase or a dependent clause often comes between the subject and the verb. Even when the subject and the verb are not next to each other in the sentence, they still must agree.

A **prepositional phrase** starts with a preposition and ends with a noun or pronoun:

Tip For a list of common prepositions, see page 203.

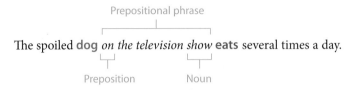

The spoiled **dog** *on the television show* **eats** several times a day.

A **dependent clause** has a subject and a verb but does not express a complete thought. When a dependent clause comes between the subject and the verb, it usually starts with the word *who, whose, whom, that,* or *which.*

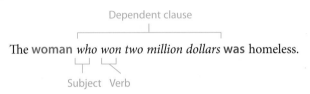

The **woman** *who won two million dollars* **was** homeless.

Remember, the subject of a sentence is never in a prepositional phrase or dependent clause.

Read the following sentences, emphasizing the subject and the verb and mentally crossing out the words between them.

Incorrect

The best **deal** with the greatest savings *are* at that store.

Items for sale *includes* a baby carriage.

The **chef** who studied at one of their schools *make* good money.

Some county **records** that burned in the fire *was* replaced.

Correct

The best **deal** ~~with the greatest savings~~ *is* at that store.

Items ~~for sale~~ *include* a baby carriage.

The **chef** ~~who studied at one of their schools~~ *makes* good money.

Some county **records** ~~that burned in the fire~~ *were* replaced.

PRACTICE 8

In each of the following sentences, underline the subject, and cross out the prepositional phrase between the subject and the verb. Then, circle the correct form of the verb.

Example: __Apples__ ~~around the world~~ (come/comes) in more than 7,500 varieties.

1. Certain varieties of apples (make/makes) good cider.

2. Apples of other types (work/works) well in pies.

3. The fruit by itself (is/are) what I enjoy most.

4. An apple without any added toppings (fill/fills) you up without a lot of calories.

5. My dentist over by the new shopping center (tell/tells) me that apples are good for the teeth and gums.

PRACTICE 9

In each of the following sentences, underline the subject, and cross out the dependent clause. Then, circle the correct form of the verb.

Example: <u>People</u> who travel a lot (appreciates/(appreciate)) helpful advice.

1. Tips that save money or improve comfort (is/are) always welcome.

2. Flights that are overbooked (is/are) common around holidays.

3. Passengers who volunteer to travel on a later flight (receives/receive) a free ticket.

4. Travel agents who save you money (is/are) worth their fees.

5. The people who sit near you on a plane (is/are) important to your comfort.

PRACTICE 10

In each sentence of the following paragraph, cross out any prepositional phrases or dependent clauses that come between the subject and the verb. Then, correct all verbs that do not agree with their subjects. Two sentences are correct; write **C** next to them.

1 Visitors to the ruins at Chichen Itza in Mexico is impressed with the ancient Mayan city. 2 A ninety-foot-tall pyramid with steps on each of its four sides stand in the center of the site. 3 This central pyramid, the largest of all Chichen Itza's structures, were built more than 1,500 years ago. 4 A temple that was built at the top of the pyramid honors the Mayan god Kukulcan. 5 A throne that was discovered inside the temple in the 1930s are carved in the shape of a jaguar. 6 The Sacred Cenote, where the ancient Mayans made sacrifices to the gods, lie a short distance from the main pyramid. 7 A small road off to the side of the ruins lead to the Sacred Cenote. 8 The Main Ball Court, which has a long narrow playing field, is also located near the temple. 9 Carved images of ball players on the walls next to the ball court was made

centuries ago. 10 Archaeologists who want to learn more about the Mayan culture continues to study the ruins at Chichen Itza.

The Sentence Has a Compound Subject

If two (or more) subjects are joined by *and,* they form a **compound** (plural) **subject,** which requires a plural verb.

Plural subject

The fire **truck** and the **ambulance take** the freeway.

If two (or more) subjects are connected by *or* or *nor,* they are actually considered separate, and the verb agrees with the closer subject.

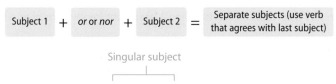

Singular subject

The fire **truck** or the **ambulance takes** the freeway.

Plural subject

Neither the fire **truck** nor the **ambulances take** the freeway.

Incorrect

The **Girl Scouts** and their **leader** *buys* the leftover cookies.

Neither his **children** nor his **dog** *like* him.

Correct

The **Girl Scouts** and their **leader** *buy* the leftover cookies.
[The subject is plural.]

Neither his **children** nor his **dog** *likes* him.
[The verb agrees with the closest subject, *dog.*]

PRACTICE 11

In each of the following sentences, circle the word that joins the two parts of the compound subject. Then, choose the correct form of the verb.

Example: **My bedroom and the library (is/are) two places that I expect to be**

fairly quiet.

1. Loud conversations or blaring music (makes/make) it hard to study.

2. Rock music and loud voices (is/are) common in my house every night.

3. My sister and I (runs/run) downstairs to see who is being so loud.

4. As usual, my brother Leo and his friend (is/are) listening to the stereo and playing a video game at the same time.

5. The stereo and the television (is/are) so loud that I can barely hear myself think.

6. My sister and I (looks/look) at each other thinking about how to handle the situation.

7. An angry complaint or a dirty look (is/are) not a good solution to the problem.

8. A bribe or a gentle request (works/work) much better with my little brother.

9. Leo and his friend (agrees/agree) to my offer without giving it much thought.

10. A new video game and a new CD (is/are) their prize for being quiet the rest of the evening.

PRACTICE 12

In the following paragraph, correct problems with subject-verb agreement. Three sentences are correct; write **C** next to them.

1 Diet and exercise is important parts of a healthy lifestyle. 2 Unfortunately, laziness or bad habits controls the way we eat in many cases. 3 Doctors and nutritionists recommends starting every day with a healthful breakfast.

4 On busy mornings, however, a doughnut or a muffin seem easier than more nutritious options. 5 A healthy lunch or dinner are easier to prepare than many people think. 6 However, frozen food or fast food seems easier than preparing a fresh, healthful meal. 7 As a result, our health and wallets suffer.

8 At a fast-food restaurant, fries and a drink comes in a combination meal.

9 Most children and adults orders the combination meal, even when they want only a hamburger. 10 In many cases, the easiest choice or the most familiar choice is not the best choice for our health.

The Subject Is an Indefinite Pronoun

Indefinite pronouns, which refer to unspecified people or objects, are often singular, although there are exceptions.

Indefinite Pronouns

Always singular (use the *is* form of *be*)

anybody	everyone	nothing
anyone	everything	one (of)
anything	much	somebody
each (of)	neither (of)	someone
either (of)	nobody	something
everybody	no one	

Always plural (use the *are* form of *be*)

both	many

May be singular or plural (use the *is* or *are* form of *be*)

all	none
any	some

Nobody **wants** to tell him the bad news.

[*Nobody* is always singular, so it takes the singular verb *wants*.]

Some of the soldiers **stay** on base over the weekend.

[In this case, *some* is plural, referring to some (more than one but less than all) of the *soldiers,* so it takes the plural verb *stay*.]

When you give makeup as a gift, remember that **some is** hypoallergenic.

[In this case, *some* is singular, so it takes the singular verb *is*.]

Often, an indefinite pronoun is followed by a prepositional phrase or a dependent clause; remember that the subject of a sentence is never found in either of these. To choose the correct verb, you can cross out the prepositional phrase or dependent clause to focus on the indefinite pronoun.

Incorrect

Anyone in the choir *sing* better than I do.

Both of them *is* graduates of this college.

Someone, whom I cannot remember at the moment, always *leave* early.

Many who buy tickets early *feels* cheated when a concert is canceled.

Correct

Anyone ~~in the choir~~ *sings* better than I do.
[The subject is *anyone,* which takes a singular verb.]

Both ~~of them~~ *are* graduates of this college.
[The subject is *both,* which always takes a plural verb.]

Someone, ~~whom I cannot remember at the moment,~~ always *leaves* early.
[*Someone* is always singular.]

Many ~~who buy tickets early~~ *feel* cheated when a concert is canceled.
[The subject is *many,* which is always plural.]

PRACTICE 13

In each of the following sentences, circle the verb that agrees with the subject.

Example: One of my daughters (wants/want) her own pet.

1. Everyone (thinks/think) that this is a good chance to teach her responsibility.

2. No one (knows/know) why, but she is not interested in puppies and kittens.

3. Someone in her class (owns/own) a goldfish and some Sea Monkeys.

4. Either (makes/make) a good first pet.

5. Everybody who has raised Sea Monkeys (tells/tell) me that they are inexpensive and easy to care for.

6. One of my daughter's friends (thinks/think) that the small creatures are related to monkeys.

7. Neither of my children (believes/believe) this.

8. Each of the tiny animals (is/are) actually a type of shrimp.

9. Everybody (loves/love) to watch the little shrimp wiggle around in the water.

10. Everyone who (enjoys/enjoy) Sea Monkeys can thank Harold von Braunhut, who started selling the shrimp eggs in 1957.

The Verb Comes before the Subject

In most sentences, the subject comes before the verb. However, the verb comes *before* the subject in questions and in sentences that begin with *here* or *there*. To find the subject and verb, turn these sentences around.

> Which **is** the prize that you won? The prize that you won **is** . . .

> Where **are** the envelopes? The envelopes **are** . . .

Notice that turning a question around means answering it.

> Here **is** the magazine that I promised to bring you. The magazine that I promised to bring you **is** here.

> There **are** several pictures on the wall. Several pictures **are** on the wall.

Incorrect

Which company *deliver* your boxes?

There *is* the paintbrushes I brought you.

Correct

Which company *delivers* your boxes?
[Answer: UPS *delivers* . . .]

There *are* the paintbrushes I brought you.
[The paintbrushes *are* there.]

> ### PRACTICE 14

In each of the following sentences, underline the subject, and circle the correct verb.

Example: **Here (are /is) our cabin.**

1. There (is/are) a lake around the corner.

2. Here (is/are) the boat that we can use on the lake.

3. Where (is/are) the keys to the boat?

4. There (is/are) a family of birds nesting on the lake.

5. (Is/Are) their cries what we hear every night?

6. There (is/are) the small kitchen where we will cook.

7. Here (is/are) the phone number of the cabin's owner.

8. There (is/are) some maps of the area.

9. (Is/Are) there good hiking trails around?

10. Here (is/are) the bed that I want to nap on before we do anything else.

PRACTICE 15

In the following paragraph, correct problems with subject-verb agreement. Three sentences are correct; write **C** next to them.

1 Here is some common questions about traveling to New York City: 2 Do a trip to the city have to be expensive? 3 How much does most hotels cost? 4 Is cheap hotels available in safe areas? 5 Where does travelers on a tight budget stay? 6 People who worry about these questions are often pleasantly surprised to learn about hostels. 7 A hostel is an inexpensive type of lodging in which travelers share dormitory-style rooms. 8 There is many benefits of staying in a hostel. 9 Most hostels are quite safe, clean, and affordable; plus, they offer you the chance to meet interesting travelers from all over the world. 10 What else does budget-minded travelers need?

PRACTICE 16

Write five questions or sentences that begin with *here* or *there,* making sure that the verb agrees with the subject.

Edit Subject-Verb Agreement Problems in Everyday Life

Complete the editing reviews as instructed, referring to the chart on page 273.

EDITING PARAGRAPHS 1

Correct the subject-verb agreement errors in the following grant-application letter. Then, revise informal language. The first sentence has been corrected for you. In addition to this sentence, you should find four cases of informal language.

Tip For advice on using formal English, see Chapter 2. For advice on avoiding slang, see Chapter 23.

February 10, 2015
Maura Vogel
Grant Manager
Tri-State Foundation
429 Woodland Ridge Boulevard
Fort Wayne, IN 46803

Dear Ms. Vogel:

1 The Volunteer Center of Northern Indiana ~~wish~~ *wishes* to apply for a Tri-State Foundation Community Development Grant.

Our Mission: 2 The Volunteer Center, which serves Allen, Whitley, Noble, and DeKalb counties, are a nonprofit organization. 3 The center supports volunteerism in the area by hooking up various organizations with volunteers. 4 The 150 organizations that turn to us for help includes animal shelters, youth programs, hospitals, and soup kitchens. 5 There is many people who are unsure about where to volunteer their time and energy. 6 Everyone who come to us are referred to an organization that need their help.

Purpose of Grant: 7 The Volunteer Center seek a $10,000 grant from the Tri-State Foundation. 8 How does we plan to spend the dough? 9 The Volunteer Center now operate on an $800,000 annual budget. 10 One-eighth of our funds come from grants. 11 Currently, however, no funds is used for training our volunteers or communications staff. 12 Newsletters and our Web site gives potential volunteers the 411 on volunteer opportunities. 13 With a Tri-State Foundation Community Grant, we plan to train our peeps to communicate this information more effectively. 14 We also hopes to purchase new software and computers to improve the quality of our newsletters and Web site.

15 I looks forward to your response.

Sincerely,

Marcus Owens

EDITING PARAGRAPHS 2

Correct problems with subject-verb agreement in the following essay. Eight sentences are correct; write **C** next to them. The first sentence has been edited for you.

1 There *are* is few natural disasters more destructive than a hurricane. 2 The winds of a hurricane usually forms over a warm ocean into a spiral shape. 3 A typical hurricane measures about three hundred miles across. 4 The hurricane's center, which is usually twenty to thirty miles wide, are called the *eye*. 5 The eye of a hurricane is its calmest spot. 6 The winds near the eye of a hurricane is the strongest. 7 In fact, some hurricanes has winds of up to 250 miles per hour near the eye.

8 Major hurricanes, like Hurricane Katrina, has destroyed entire communities. 9 Hurricane winds cause much of the damage. 10 However, floods that are caused by a hurricane is often more destructive than the wind. 11 A wall of water called a storm surge build up in front of a hurricane. 12 The tide sometimes rises more than twenty-five feet when the storm surge reaches land. 13 The violent waves and high water is extremely dangerous.

14 The amount of damage from a hurricane depend on the storm's strength. 15 There is five categories of hurricanes. 16 Category 1 is the weakest. 17 A Category 1 hurricane have wind speeds of 74 to 95 miles per hour. 18 Hurricanes in this category causes some flooding but generally only minor damage. 19 Roofs and trees is damaged during a Category 2 hurricane. 20 However, most buildings does not receive much damage. 21 Anything over a Category 2 are considered a major hurricane. 22 These hurricanes result in major damage and severe flooding. 23 With wind speeds over 150 miles per hour, a Category 5 hurricane result in widespread destruction.

24 How does scientists measure the strength of a hurricane? 25 There is several methods. 26 Satellites and ground stations measure hurricane conditions whenever possible. 27 At other times, people flies small planes right into a hurricane. 28 Air Force members who fly into a storm is called Hurricane

Hunters. 29 They collect information on wind speeds, rainfall, and air pressure. 30 The National Hurricane Center in Miami, Florida, use this information to predict the hurricane's strength and path. 31 Anyone who understands the incredible power of hurricanes admire the bravery of these men and women.

Write and Edit Your Own Work

ASSIGNMENT 1   **Write**

Write a paragraph about an important purchase you have made or hope to make. Then, edit the paragraph to make sure that all subjects and all verbs agree. Revise any subject-verb agreement problems that you find using the chart on page 273.

ASSIGNMENT 2   **Edit**

Using the chart on page 273, edit subject-verb agreement errors in a paper you are writing for this course or another course, or in a piece of writing from your work or everyday life.

Chapter Review

1. In any sentence, the subject and the verb must match—or agree—in _____ .

2. What are the five trouble spots for subject-verb agreement? _____

   _____

   _____

   _____

3. Write three subjects and present-tense forms of *be, have,* and *do* that agree with the subjects. _____

4. Write four examples of indefinite pronouns. _____

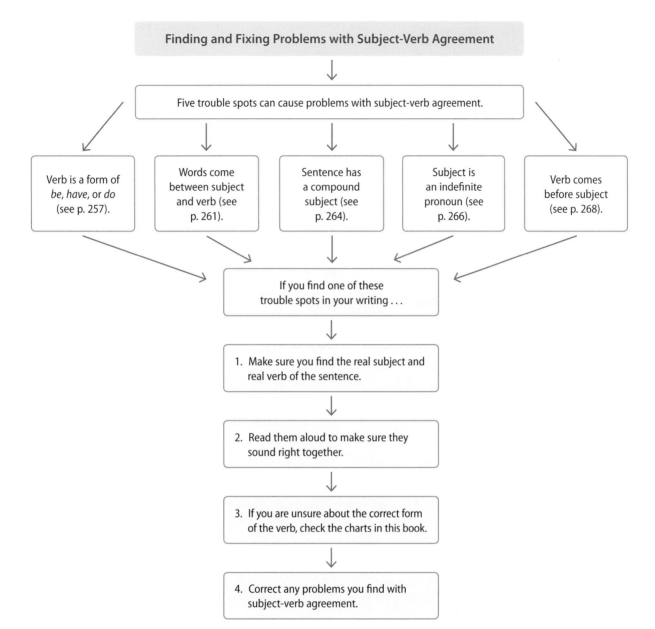

Finding and Fixing Problems with Subject-Verb Agreement

Five trouble spots can cause problems with subject-verb agreement.

Verb is a form of *be*, *have*, or *do* (see p. 257).

Words come between subject and verb (see p. 261).

Sentence has a compound subject (see p. 264).

Subject is an indefinite pronoun (see p. 266).

Verb comes before subject (see p. 268).

If you find one of these trouble spots in your writing . . .

1. Make sure you find the real subject and real verb of the sentence.

2. Read them aloud to make sure they sound right together.

3. If you are unsure about the correct form of the verb, check the charts in this book.

4. Correct any problems you find with subject-verb agreement.

REFLECTING ON THE JOURNEY

Skills Learned

Now that you've completed the chapter, look again at this paragraph.

Here are the farm stand we were telling you about. It sells the freshest fruits and vegetables that you will ever taste. The corn is picked every morning. You may be asking, "Where is the fields where the corn is grown?" The fields are located behind the main barn, where you will find tomatoes that is loaded with flavor and watermelons that is too big for one person to carry. There are also homemade ice cream, fresh from the freezer. The owners also sells prize-winning pies, including apple pies hot from the oven. There is baskets for customers to carry everything to the car, but I never have enough room!

Using what you've learned in this chapter, edit this paragraph for errors in subject-verb agreement. Then answer the questions below.

1. Are you confident that you have identified the mistakes?

2. Are you confident that you have corrected the mistakes?

3. What questions do you have about subject-verb agreement?

Verb-Tense Problems

READING ROADMAP

Learning Objectives

Chapter Goal: Find and correct sentences with verb-tense problems.

Tools to Achieve the Goal

- Reference chart: regular verbs in the past tense (p. 277)
- Reference chart: irregular verbs in the past tense (p. 279)
- Reference chart: forms of *be* in the present and past tenses (p. 282)
- Reference chart: forms of *have* in the present and past tenses (p. 283)
- Reference chart: forms of *can* and *will* in the present and past tenses (p. 284)
- Reference chart: past participles of regular verbs (p. 286)
- Reference chart: past participles of irregular verbs (p. 287)
- Present-perfect tense (p. 291)
- Past-perfect tense (p. 294)
- Passive and active voice (p. 297)
- Reference chart: verb tenses (p. 301)
- Forming the past and perfect tenses (p. 309)

Key Terms

Skim Chapter 16 before you begin reading. Can you find each of these words in **bold** type? Put a check mark next to each word once you have located it in the chapter.

____ verb tense	____ present-perfect tense
____ past tense	
____ regular verb	____ past-perfect tense
____ irregular verbs	____ passive voice
____ past participle	____ active voice

Highlight or circle any of these words that you already know.

Before you begin reading, study the following paragraph and complete the chart. At the end of the chapter, you will examine the paragraph again and reflect on what you have learned.

      The first humans use tools as early as 2.5 million years ago. The fork, however, not been around until fairly recently. For most of human history, people have simply eat with their fingers. The first forks, which were invented in ancient Greece, was not for eating. When Greek servers carved meat, food sometimes slipped and fall off the plate. With a fork, however, the servers can firmly hold the meat in place.

This paragraph has problems with verb tense. Put a check mark by the statement that best describes you.

Skill Statement	
I understand what the mistakes are, and I know how to fix them.	
I understand what the mistakes are, but I am not sure how to fix them.	
I think I understand what the mistakes are.	
I don't understand what the mistakes are.	

Understand Regular Verbs in the Past Tense

LaunchPadSolo
Visit **LaunchPad Solo for Readers and Writers > Verbs** for more practice with verb tenses.

Verb tense tells when the action of a sentence occurs. The **past tense** describes actions that began and ended in the past. To form the past tense of most **regular verbs,** add *-ed.* For verbs that end in *e,* just add a *-d.*

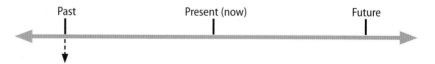

Past	Present (now)	Future

We **moved** last week.

Language note: Remember to include the *-d* or *-ed* endings on regular past-tense verbs, even if they are not noticed in speech or if they are not used in informal, spoken English.

Incorrect	Nate **listen** to his iPod while he walk**ed** the dog.
Correct	Nate **listened** to his iPod while he walk**ed** the dog.
Incorrect	Gina **work** late last night.
Correct	Gina **worked** late last night.

Remember the -d ending on the past tense of *use to*.

| Incorrect | I use to smoke. |
| Correct | I used to smoke. |

Regular Verbs in the Past Tense

Present/past		
Regular verbs → add -ed	Regular verbs ending with -e → add -d	Regular verbs ending with a consonant + y → change -y to -i and add -ed
learn/learn**ed**	move/move**d**	worry/worr**ied**
pass/pass**ed**	smoke/smoke**d**	cry/cr**ied**
finish/finish**ed**	hire/hire**d**	try/tr**ied**
start/start**ed**	stare/stare**d**	hurry/hurr**ied**
work/work**ed**	rescue/rescue**d**	party/part**ied**
play/play**ed**	excuse/excuse**d**	study/stud**ied**

Tip Consonants are *b, c, d, f, g, h, j, k, l, m, n, p, q, r, s, t, v, w, x, z,* and sometimes *y.*

In the Real World, Why Is It Important to Use the Correct Tense?

Stanley Mahoney works as a unit supervisor for Zapp's Electronics, a manufacturing company. Recently, he applied for an opening in the company's management-training program. Stanley followed up his interview with the company's vice president by sending this e-mail:

Stanley's e-mail:

Dear Mr. Kirby,

Thank you for meeting with me. I know you examine my qualifications thoroughly before our discussion. I hope yesterday you also learn personally how much I want to be a manager. I work hard to get this far in our company, but as a manager, I need to know more than what I experience over the years.

I am ready to begin!

Thank you,

Stanley Mahoney

▶

The Vice President's response:
Both management and the employees under Stanley respect him. He is smart, fair, and dedicated, but his poor grammar has always been a problem. The errors in this e-mail convince me that, as a manager, Stanley would not represent the company's high overall standards. Reluctantly, I have denied Stanley's application to this year's management-training program.

Tip To do this chapter, you may want to review Chapters 10 and 11.

PRACTICE 1

Find and underline the four verb-tense errors in Stanley's e-mail.

PRACTICE 2

In each of the following sentences, underline the main verb. Then, in the blank next to each sentence, write **present** if the verb is in the present tense; write **past** if the verb is in the past tense.

Example: ___*Present*___ **Believe it or not, spit, otherwise known as saliva, deserves respect.**

1. _____ Saliva protects your teeth by killing bacteria and viruses.

2. _____ Police use saliva tests to solve crimes and to find out if someone is driving under the influence of alcohol.

3. _____ Doctors test saliva to determine a diagnosis of certain diseases or to see if a woman is pregnant.

4. _____ Scientists conducted studies on the various properties of human saliva.

5. _____ In recent years, experts researched the link between a person's saliva and the risk of developing cavities.

6. _____ They hope to use this information to help dentists pinpoint the patients who might need extra dental care.

7. _____ Professor Mahvash Navazesh dedicated her professional life to studying saliva, earning her the nickname "Spit Queen."

8. _____ Although she jokes about her work, she takes the ingredients of saliva seriously.

9. _____ Her research demonstrated that while the main substance in saliva is water, saliva does contain other elements.

10. _____ It also contains proteins that clean teeth and gums.

PRACTICE 3

In the following paragraph, underline the verb in each sentence. Then, change each verb to the past tense.

1 Last winter I visit Costa Rica. 2 I enjoy the scenery and the adventure. 3 I live with my cousin's family on a large coffee plantation. 4 Every morning we walk out to the garden. 5 We pick some fresh fruit for breakfast. 6 We also listen to the tropical birds singing in the treetops. 7 I especially like the two-mile trail down to the ocean. 8 At the beach, I surf in waves larger than my house. 9 One day, I zipline over the jungle for a great thrill. 10 I hate for my Central American vacation to end.

Understand Irregular Verbs in the Past Tense

Irregular verbs do not follow the regular pattern of adding *-d* or *-ed* for the past tense. Practice using these verbs.

Irregular Verbs in the Past Tense

Base verb	Past tense	Base verb	Past tense
be (am/are/is)	was/were	dive	dived/dove
become	became	do	did
begin	began	draw	drew
bite	bit	drink	drank
blow	blew	drive	drove
break	broke		
bring	brought	eat	ate
build	built		
buy	bought	fall	fell
		feed	fed
catch	caught	feel	felt
choose	chose	fight	fought
come	came	find	found
cost	cost	fly	flew ▶

Base verb	Past tense
forget	forgot
freeze	froze
get	got
give	gave
go	went
grow	grew
have/has	had
hear	heard
hide	hid
hit	hit
hold	held
hurt	hurt
keep	kept
know	knew
lay	laid
lead	led
leave	left
let	let
lie	lay
light	lit
lose	lost
make	made
mean	meant
meet	met
pay	paid
put	put
quit	quit
read	read
ride	rode
ring	rang

Base verb	Past tense
rise	rose
run	ran
say	said
see	saw
sell	sold
send	sent
shake	shook
show	showed
shrink	shrank
shut	shut
sing	sang
sink	sank
sit	sat
sleep	slept
speak	spoke
spend	spent
stand	stood
steal	stole
stick	stuck
sting	stung
strike	struck
swim	swam
take	took
teach	taught
tear	tore
tell	told
think	thought
throw	threw
understand	understood
wake	woke
wear	wore
win	won
write	wrote

PRACTICE 4

In each sentence of the following paragraph, fill in the correct past-tense forms of the irregular verbs in parentheses.

1 After high school, I _____ (think) college would get in the way of all my fun. 2 I _____ (spend) most of my time working and partying, and no time thinking about college or my future. 3 I worked as a waitress and _____ (make) enough money to pay my bills. 4 After three years of waitressing, however, I _____ (feel) that I was accomplishing nothing. 5 That is when I _____ (begin) taking classes at our local college. 6 I _____ (take) three classes that first semester, in reading, math, and English. 7 Although it was hard to get back into the routine of going to class and doing homework, I _____ (stick) with it. 8 I gradually _____ (become) better at managing my workload and still finding some free time to have fun. 9 By the time finals _____ (come) at the end of the year, I was nervous but ready. 10 I _____ (get) two A's and a B that first semester back at college, and I was glad to know that all my hard work had paid off.

PRACTICE 5

In the following paragraph, change each irregular present-tense verb to the past tense.

1 A few years ago, I fall into debt. 2 Unfortunately, my computer's printer breaks just then. 3 Through a quick Internet search, I find a company that sells printers at a very low cost. 4 I give the company a call and speak to one of its sales representatives. 5 Then, I understand the reason for the low prices. 6 The salesperson says that the company puts new parts into used printers. 7 I buy one of these printers from the company. 8 At that time, I tell everyone about my possible mistake. 9 But over the last few years, my wonderful printer make me a believer in used products.

Understand Four Very Irregular Verbs

Some irregular verbs cause confusion and require special attention: *be, have, can,* and *will.*

The Verb Be

Be is tricky because its singular and plural forms are different, in both present and past tenses.

Present- and Past-Tense Forms of *Be*

	Singular		Plural	
	Present →	Past tense	Present →	Past tense
First person	I am →	I was	we are →	we were
Second person	you are →	you were	you are →	you were
Third person	he/she/it is →	he/she/it was	they are →	they were

Tip In the chart above, and in later charts and sentence examples, subjects are blue and verbs are red.

PRACTICE 6

In the following paragraph, fill in each blank with the correct past-tense form of *be.*

1 When our electricity bill for last month arrived, we _____ surprised. 2 The bill _____ for $3,218. 3 I _____ sure that this impossibly high amount _____ wrong. 4 Right away, my roommate and I _____ on the phone with the electric company. 5 The representatives with whom we spoke _____ of no help. 6 Each of them said that we _____ wrong and had to pay the bill. 7 A friend of mine who works for a cable company _____ much more helpful. 8 She _____ eager to give us advice. 9 If we continued complaining politely and regularly, she _____ sure that the company would correct the bill. 10 After a month of polite complaints and letters, we _____ pleased to receive a corrected bill of $218, which we immediately paid.

The Verb Have

Present- and Past-Tense Forms of *Have*

	Singular		Plural	
	Present →	Past tense	Present →	Past tense
First person	I have →	I had	we have →	we had
Second person	you have →	you had	you have →	you had
Third person	he/she/it has →	he/she/it had	they have →	they had

PRACTICE 7

In each of the following sentences, circle the correct form of *have:* present or past tense.

Tip *Have* is used with the past participle, covered on pages 286-299.

Example: **More than 90 percent of the people in the United States (have/ had) a cell phone today.**

1. Across the planet, more than four billion people (have/had) one.

2. Unfortunately, according to several different studies, a cell phone (has/ had) a number of risks associated with it.

3. First of all, many drivers (have/had) their attention on their phones and not on the road.

4. A person (has/had) to keep his eyes and mind on traffic rather than on a conversation.

5. Statistics (have/had) shown that drivers who talk on the phone run a much higher risk of having an accident than drivers who do not use phones.

6. Other concerns about cell phone use (have/had) some researchers worried.

7. Radiation is emitted from these phones, and doctors (have/had) evidence that these emissions can be harmful to humans.

8. One doctor at a prominent cancer research institute (have/had) a number of serious warnings for people.

9. He (have/had) to tell his own staff that he felt it was better to be safe now than sorry later.

10. In addition, the doctor (have/had) special warnings for cell phone use by young children since their brains are still developing.

Can/Could *and* Will/Would

Tip For a chart showing how to use *can, could, will, would,* and other modal auxiliaries, see pages 494–499.

People mix up the past- and present-tense forms of these tricky verbs. The verb *can* means *able*. Its past-tense form is *could*. The verb *will* expresses a plan. Its past-tense form is *would*.

Present tense	He **can play** poker daily.
	[He is able to play poker daily.]
	He **will play** poker daily.
	[He plans to play poker daily.]
Past tense	He **could play** poker daily.
	[He was able to play poker daily.]
	He **would play** poker daily.
	[He planned to play (and did play) poker daily.]

In these examples, *can, could, will,* and *would* are helping verbs followed by the main verb *play*. Notice that the main verb is in the base form (*play*). It does not change from present to past.

Present- and Past-Tense Forms of *Can* and *Will*

	Can/could		Will/would	
	Present	Past tense	Present	Past tense
First person	I/we can	I/we could	I/we will	I/we would
Second person	you can	you could	you will	you would
Third person	he/she/it can they can	he/she/it could they could	he/she/it will they will	he/she/it would they would

PRACTICE 8

In each of the following sentences, circle the correct verb.

Example: **This morning, Dane said that he (can/(could)) teach himself how to use our new digital camera.**

1. He always thinks that he (can/could) do everything on his own.

2. I told Dane that I (will/would) read the manual for him.

3. He answered that I (will/would) be wasting my time.

4. Several hours and many fuzzy pictures later, he admitted that he (can/could) not figure out how to use the camera's fancy features.

5. I decided that I (will/would) help him.

6. Next week, it (will/would) not be my fault if our vacation photographs turn out fuzzy.

7. I wish that he (will/would) have listened to me in the first place.

8. After reading the manual myself, I showed him how he (can/could) take better pictures.

9. Now he (can/could) use the camera like a professional.

10. On our vacation, he (will/would) appreciate my help.

PRACTICE 9

In the following paragraph, fill in each blank with the correct form of the helping verb *can/could* or *will/would*.

1 Learning to ride a bike _____ be difficult for a child. 2 When my daughter Carlita started learning, she _____ fall over every time. 3 Even with training wheels, she _____ not keep her balance. 4 I hoped that she _____ keep trying, but I did not want to force her. 5 Luckily, Carlita refused to quit and said that she _____ practice every day. 6 Soon, she _____ balance with the help of the training wheels. 7 Bikes like Carlita's _____ have their training wheels easily removed. 8 This morning, I asked Carlita if I _____ take the training wheels off. 9 She said that she _____ be ready for the challenge. 10 This afternoon, I _____ take off the training wheels.

11 As she tries to balance without them, I _____ hold her shoulders and run alongside her. 12 When I first let go, I know that she _____ probably fall. 13 We will keep trying until she _____ zip around the neighborhood all by herself. 14 I wish that I _____ keep her from falling, but I know that it is just part of the learning process. 15 Soon, I _____ have to go through this whole process again with Carlita's younger sister.

Understand the Past Participle

The **past participle** is a verb form that is used with a helping verb, such as *has* or *have*.

Helping verb   Past participle

Bees have swarmed around the hive all summer.

Past Participles of Regular Verbs

To form the past participle of a regular verb, add *-d* or *-ed*. For regular verbs, the past-participle form looks just like the past tense.

Regular Verbs and Their Past Participles

Base form	Past tense	Past participle
(Usually I . . .)	*(Yesterday I . . .)*	*(Over time, I have . . .)*
collect	collected	collected
dine	dined	dined
talk	talked	talked

> **PRACTICE 10**

In each of the following sentences, underline the helping verb *has* or *have*, and double-underline the past participle.

Example: **In many ways, computers have replaced handwriting.**

1. In recent years, communication has focused on speed rather than on thoroughness.

2. Instead of using envelopes and stamps, people have shared messages by tapping keys and using wireless technology.

3. Despite these changes, some have remained faithful to letter writing.

4. Some schools, but not all, have stopped requiring quality penmanship.

5. Still, some students have learned the pleasure of sitting down to write a letter by hand.

Tip To do this chapter, you may want to review the terms *subject, verb,* and *helping verb* from Chapters 10 and 11.

Past Participles of Irregular Verbs

The past participles of irregular verbs do not match their past-tense form, and they do not follow a regular pattern.

Irregular Verbs and Their Past Participles

Base form	Past tense	Past participle
(Usually I . . .)	*(Yesterday I . . .)*	*(Over time, I have . . .)*
drive	drove	driven
see	saw	seen
throw	threw	thrown

Irregular Verbs and Their Past Participles

Present tense (base form of verb)	Past tense	Past participle (used with helping verb)
be (am/are/is)	was/were	been
become	became	become
begin	began	begun
bite	bit	bitten
blow	blew	blown
break	broke	broken
bring	brought	brought
build	built	built
buy	bought	bought ▶

Present tense (base form of verb)	Past tense	Past participle (used with helping verb)
catch	caught	caught
choose	chose	chosen
come	came	come
cost	cost	cost
dive	dived, dove	dived
do	did	done
draw	drew	drawn
drink	drank	drunk
drive	drove	driven
eat	ate	eaten
fall	fell	fallen
feed	fed	fed
feel	felt	felt
fight	fought	fought
find	found	found
fly	flew	flown
forget	forgot	forgotten
freeze	froze	frozen
get	got	gotten
give	gave	given
go	went	gone
grow	grew	grown
have/has	had	had
hear	heard	heard
hide	hid	hidden
hit	hit	hit
hold	held	held
hurt	hurt	hurt
keep	kept	kept
know	knew	known
lay	laid	laid
lead	led	led

Present tense (base form of verb)	Past tense	Past participle (used with helping verb)
leave	left	left
let	let	let
lie	lay	lain
light	lit	lit
lose	lost	lost
make	made	made
mean	meant	meant
meet	met	met
pay	paid	paid
put	put	put
quit	quit	quit
read	read	read
ride	rode	ridden
ring	rang	rung
rise	rose	risen
run	ran	run
say	said	said
see	saw	seen
seek	sought	sought
sell	sold	sold
send	sent	sent
shake	shook	shaken
show	showed	shown
shrink	shrank	shrunk
shut	shut	shut
sing	sang	sung
sink	sank	sunk
sit	sat	sat
sleep	slept	slept
speak	spoke	spoken
spend	spent	spent
stand	stood	stood
steal	stole	stolen
stick	stuck	stuck ▶

Present tense (base form of verb)	Past tense	Past participle (used with helping verb)
sting	stung	stung
strike	struck	struck, stricken
swim	swam	swum
take	took	taken
teach	taught	taught
tear	tore	torn
tell	told	told
think	thought	thought
throw	threw	thrown
understand	understood	understood
wake	woke	woken
wear	wore	worn
win	won	won
write	wrote	written

PRACTICE 11

In each of the following sentences, fill in either *has* or *have* plus the past-participle form of the verb in parentheses.

Example: Many people _____*have grown*_____ **(grow) to enjoy photography.**

1. Few of them _____ (understand) how to take the best pictures, however.

2. Instead, they _____ (take) mediocre pictures that could have been fantastic.

3. Perhaps a person _____ (catch) a perfectly candid shot of a friend.

4. If he _____ (choose) an angle where the sun is not behind him, the photo may turn out too dark.

5. Perhaps he _____ (hold) the camera too loosely, and the photo turns out blurry.

6. Others _____ (find) that when they do not get close enough to the person that they are photographing, the picture appears cluttered.

7. A zoom lens _____ (give) some photos a concise, tight look that is appealing.

8. A quality camera _____ (cost) some novice photographers a great deal of money.

9. The photos that they _____ (make) are often worth every penny, though.

10. The money that they _____ (spend) is nothing compared to the memories that they have captured.

Use the Past Participle Correctly

The **past participle** is used in both the present-perfect and past-perfect tenses. It is also used to form the passive voice.

Present-Perfect Tense

Use the **present perfect** to show two different kinds of actions:

1. An action that started in the past and is still going on:

    The **families have vacationed** together for years.

2. An action that has just happened or was completed at some unspecified time in the past.

    The **package has arrived**.

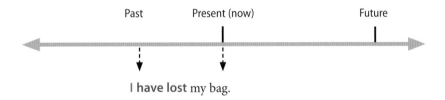

Form the present-perfect tense as follows:

Note the difference in meaning between the past tense and present-perfect tense.

Past-tense verb

Past tense   **He stole** bases.

[His stealing of bases began and ended in the past.]

Helping verb   Past participle

Present-perfect tense   **He has stolen** bases for years.

[He stole bases in the past and may continue to steal them.]

Helping verb   Past participle

He has recently **stolen** bases.

[At some unspecified point in the past, he stole bases.]

Language note: Be careful not to leave out *have* when it is needed for the present perfect. Time-signal words like *since* and *for* may mean that the present perfect is required.

Incorrect   I been driving since 1985.

We been waiting for two hours.

Correct   I **have** been driving since 1985.

We **have** been waiting for two hours.

Present-Perfect Tense (*have* + past participle)

	Singular	**Plural**
First person	I have finished	we have finished
Second person	you have finished	you have finished
Third person	he/she/it has finished	they have finished

Incorrect

Since 2009, **he** *traveled* to five continents.

We worked together for three years now.

Antiwar **protests** *became* common in recent years.

Correct

Since 2009, **he** *has traveled* to five continents.

[He completed his traveling at some unspecified point in the past.]

We *have worked* together for three years now.

[They still work together.]

Antiwar protests *have become* common in recent years.

[They continue to be common.]

PRACTICE 12

In each of the following sentences, circle the correct verb tense—past or present perfect.

Example: **Lately, fantasy camps (became/have become) popular among people who can afford them.**

1. Many people (went/have gone) to summer camp when they were children.

2. Now, fantasy camps (gave/have given) people a chance to attend camp as adults.

3. In 1988, a camp called Air Combat USA (opened/has opened) to the public.

4. Since then, it (offered/has offered) more than twelve thousand campers the opportunity to fly a fighter jet with the assistance of an experienced combat pilot.

5. In recent years, the Rock 'n' Roll Fantasy Camp (was/has been) one of the most well-attended adult camps.

6. There, campers (played/have played) their musical instruments with world-famous rock stars from the 1960s and '70s.

7. Many of these campers (played/have played) an instrument for many years.

8. The Rock 'n' Roll Camp (allowed/has allowed) them to perform with legendary musicians.

9. Other adults (always wanted/have always wanted) to shoot hoops with a professional basketball player, and basketball camps give them a chance to do just that.

10. These camps (found/have found) that people will pay a lot of money to live out their fantasies for a few days.

PRACTICE 13

In the following paragraph, fill in each blank with the correct tense—past or present perfect—of the verb in parentheses.

1 Before there were health clubs, people rarely _____ (have) problems getting along with one another during workouts. 2 Back then, in fact, most people _____ (work) out by themselves. 3 Today, health clubs and gyms _____ (become) popular places to exercise. 4 In these physically stressful settings, some people _____ (forget) how to be polite to others. 5 When we were young, we all _____ (learn) to take turns when playing with other children. 6 Our parents _____ (tell) us to treat others as we would like to be treated ourselves. 7 But in health clubs, some people _____ (complain) about customers who refuse to share the equipment. 8 Gym employees say that they _____ (notice) an increase in the number of arguments between members. 9 Yesterday, I _____ (see) one woman push another woman off a treadmill. 10 To create a more pleasant atmosphere, some gyms _____ (post) rules and suggestions for their customers. 11 Most people always _____ (consider) it to be common courtesy to clean up after themselves. 12 Now, health clubs _____ (begin) to require that exercisers wipe up any perspiration that they leave on equipment. 13 It seems that the need to stay in shape _____ (create) mental as well as physical stress for some people. 14 However, it is important to always keep in mind the basic rules of polite behavior that our parents _____ (teach) us when we were young.

Past-Perfect Tense

Use the **past-perfect tense** to show an action that was started and completed in the past before another action in the past.

Kara **had eaten** before she went to class.

Form the past-perfect tense as follows:

Subject	+	*had*	+	Past participle	=	Past-perfect tense

Note the difference in meaning between the past tense and past perfect tense.

Tip For a verb reference chart on the perfect tenses, see pages 303–305.

Past-tense verb

Past tense In March 1954, runner **Roger Bannister broke** the four-minute mile threshold.

[One action (breaking the four-minute mile) occurred in the past.]

Helping verb   Past participle

Past-perfect tense Within a month, **John Landy had broken** Bannister's record.

[Two actions (Bannister's and Landy's races) occurred in the past, but Bannister's action was completed before Landy's action started.]

Past-Perfect Tense (*had* + past participle)

	Singular	**Plural**
First person	I **had driven**	we **had driven**
Second person	you **had driven**	you **had driven**
Third person	he/she/it **had driven**	they **had driven**

PRACTICE 14

In each of the following sentences, circle the correct verb tense.

Example: **Before we left for our camping trip, we (talked/had talked) about the wildlife at Moosehead Mountain.**

1. I decided not to mention the rattlesnake that (scared/had scared) me on last year's trip.

2. I never (was/had been) afraid of snakes until I came that close to one.

3. On this year's trip, we (saw/had seen) something even more frightening than a snake.

4. As my friends and I (planned/had planned), we took a long hike after setting up our tent.

5. By the time we returned to the campsite, the sun (went/had gone) down.

6. Near the tent, we (heard/had heard) a low growl.

7. Suddenly, we (saw/had seen) a dark shadow running into the woods.

8. We realized that a bear (visited/had visited) our campsite.

9. Frightened but tired, we (tried/had tried) to get some rest.

10. When the sun finally came up, we saw that the bear (stayed/had stayed) away, but we (got/had gotten) little sleep.

PRACTICE 15

In the following paragraph, fill in each blank with the correct form of the verb in parentheses. Use whichever form of the verb is logical—simple past tense, present-perfect tense, or past-perfect tense.

1 Ever since he learned to talk, our six-year-old son, Christopher, _____ (show) an interest in the business world. 2 Last week, he said that he _____ (decide) to start a business of his own. 3 We _____ (become) used to eager statements like this.

4 When Christopher was five years old, he _____ (ask) for a larger allowance. 5 In return, he _____ (offer) to do more chores. 6 Before I decided what extra chores to give him, he already _____ (make) all the beds in the house. 7 So by the time that Christopher asked for his own business, I _____ (be) expecting it. 8 I _____ (tell) him that he could open a lemonade stand. 9 Before I even finished telling him my ideas, he _____ (come) up with a plan of his own. 10 For his products, Christopher _____ (choose) fresh lemonade and cookies. 11 With my help, he _____ (make) the lemonade and _____ (bake) the cookies. 12 I asked whether he _____ (decide) on a price for his products. 13 He _____ (settle) on twenty-five cents for each cup of lemonade and a dime for each cookie. 14 He set up the stand on a corner where he _____ (notice) many dog walkers. 15 To increase his business, he _____ (add) free dog biscuits to give to

his customers. 16 So far this week, he _____ (earn) $14.75.

17 I _____ (enjoy) watching Christopher run the lemonade stand.

18 He _____ (learn) that work can be fun and rewarding. 19 I also

_____ (notice) an improvement in his math and people skills. 20

For many years, lemonade stands _____ (teach) children valuable

lessons.

Passive versus Active Voice

In sentences that use the **passive voice**, the subject is acted on: It receives the action of the verb. The passive voice is formed as follows:

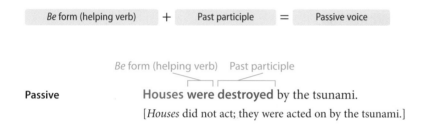

| *Be* form (helping verb) | + | Past participle | = | Passive voice |

Be form (helping verb)   Past participle

Passive   **Houses were destroyed** by the tsunami.

[*Houses* did not act; they were acted on by the tsunami.]

In sentences that use the **active voice**, the subject performs the action.

Passive   The **tsunami destroyed** the houses.

Whenever possible, use the active voice. Use the passive voice only when you do not know the specific performer of an action or when you want to emphasize the receiver of the action.

Examples of the correct use of active and passive voice

Active   After the fight, the **police took** him away.

[We know that the police took him away.]

Passive   After the fight, **he was taken** away.

[We do not know who took him away.]

Passive   The old **bridge was demolished** this morning by engineers.

[The important point is that the bridge was demolished.]

Passive   The chemical **elements are arranged** by their atomic weights.

[Scientific and technical reports frequently use the passive since the focus is often on the idea or thing being acted upon.]

Language note: Do not confuse the passive voice with the present-perfect or past-perfect tenses. The passive uses a form of the verb *be* (*is, was, were*), and the subject does not perform any action. Subjects in the present-perfect and past-perfect tenses perform an action, and they use a form of the verb *have* (*have* or *had*).

Passive, correct	The **dogs were trained** by professionals.
Passive, incorrect	The **dogs were been trained** by professionals.
	[The verb *trained* uses only four forms of *be: is, are, was,* and *were*. It does not use the form *been*.]
Present perfect	Professionals **have trained** the dogs.
	[The present-perfect tense uses the present form of *have*, which is *have*.]
Past perfect	Professionals **had trained** the dogs.
	[The past-perfect tense uses the past form of *have*, which is *had*.]

PRACTICE 16

In each of the following sentences, underline the verb. In the blank space provided, write **A** if the sentence is in the active voice or **P** if the sentence is in the passive voice.

Example: ___A___ **Many parents assume** that their children will stop eating when they are full.

1. ___ Scientists recently studied this assumption.

2. ___ In the study, children were given more food than necessary.

3. ___ The children almost always ate all the food on their plates.

4. ___ Their level of hunger made no difference.

5. ___ In another study, similar conclusions were drawn.

6. ___ Parents and their children were observed during a typical meal.

7. ___ The parents of overweight children served much larger portions.

8. ___ Often, the overweight children were told to finish everything on their plates.

9. ___ Healthier children were given much smaller amounts of food.

10. ___ The children who served themselves ate the most appropriate amount of food.

PRACTICE 17

Each of the following sentences is in the passive voice. Rewrite each sentence in the active voice.

The three of us made plans for the outdoor concert.
Example: ~~The plans for the outdoor concert were made by the~~
              ^
         ~~three of us.~~

1. The tickets to the concert at the campground were gotten by Matthew.

2. The dinner was planned by me.

3. The driving was done by Sean.

4. Unfortunately, the wrong directions were gotten by him.

5. Several wrong turns were made.

6. When we arrived, our tent was set up by Sean and Matthew.

7. Meanwhile, dinner was prepared by me.

8. The three-course meal was enjoyed by everyone.

9. While we waited for the concert to begin, we were joined by several other friends.

10. Wonderful music was played all evening by the band.

Edit Verb-Tense Errors in Everyday Life

Complete the editing reviews as instructed, referring to the charts on pages 309–310.

EDITING PARAGRAPHS 1

The following paragraphs are similar to those that you might find in a history-of-science textbook. Correct problems with the use of past tense, past participles in the present-perfect and past-perfect tenses, and passive voice. The first sentence has been edited for you.

created
1 Few scientific theories have ~~create~~ as much controversy as the theory
                                      ^
of evolution. 2 In 1860, Charles Darwin write *The Origin of Species*. 3 The book presented evidence that Darwin has collected on a five-year voyage along the coast of South America. 4 Darwin argued that life on earth begun slowly and gradually. 5 He believe that each species of animals, including humans, has developed from previous species. 6 This theory will have important effects on the study of biology, but it goed against the Bible's account of creation.

7 Ever since Darwin's theory became knowed, people had been divided on whether evolution should be taught in public schools. 8 Some parents worried that their children will get confused or upset by these teachings. 9 The first court trial on evolution is in 1925. 10 Earlier, in the small town of Dayton, Tennessee, a biology teacher named John T. Scopes assigned a textbook that described the theory of evolution. 11 The book said that humans had came from earlier forms of life. 12 Earlier that year, the state's Butler Law has banned the teaching of evolution, so Scopes was arrested. 13 Although Scopes's lawyer maked an impressive case against the constitutionality of the Butler Law, Scopes were found guilty, and the law remained intact. 14 In 1967, the Butler Law was ruled unconstitutional by the U.S. Supreme Court. 15 However, recent court cases in Kansas, Ohio, and Pennsylvania have showed that the teaching of evolution in public schools was still a controversial issue. 16 Ever since the Scopes trial, people fought over the issue in courtrooms across the country.

EDITING PARAGRAPHS 2

Tip For advice on using formal English, see Chapter 2. For advice on avoiding slang, see Chapter 23.

In the following business report, correct problems with the use of past tense, past participles in the present-perfect and past-perfect tenses, and passive voice. Then, revise the five cases of informal language. The first sentence has been corrected for you.

STATUS REPORT: Lydia Castrionni

Date: 9/18/15

I. NEW DATABASE TRAINING

1 On Monday, a new database system. *the Information Technology Department installed* ~~was installed by the Information Technology Department.~~ 2 This week, I have spended mucho time becoming familiar with the new system. 3 After I have studyed the user's manual, I attended the all-day training session on Tuesday. 4 On Wednesday, I done all the tutorials that the software company posted for us earlier.

5 Thursday morning, I help Ajay Shah with the new system because he blew off the training session. 6 I have maked a lot of progress learning the system. 7 However, this has took a lot of time away from my regular projects.

II. CUSTOMER-SERVICE TASKS

8 By the end of last week, I have logged thirty-five customer-service calls. 9 Twenty-five of the beefs involved problems with software. 10 All the software

problems are addressed at the time of the call. 11 The other ten complaints was from people who haved problems with their hardware. 12 So far, I have resolve half of these calls. 13 Five of these complaints were handled by me at the time of the call. 14 I submitted service requests for the other five calls, but I had no time to follow up on those requests yet. 15 I have expected to take care of all the customer-service calls last week, but the database training slowed me down big time. 16 I is certain the remaining problems would be resolved early next week. 17 OK?

III. HIRING A NEW RECEPTIONIST

18 We had received thirty apps for the receptionist position, and I has gathered the top five applicants for you to review. 19 Last week I start calling applicants to set up F2F interviews. 20 As you requested, I told monster.com that we will like to pull the job posting from the featured listings for now. 21 Job seekers could still find our posting in the regular listings.

Verb-Tense Reference Chart

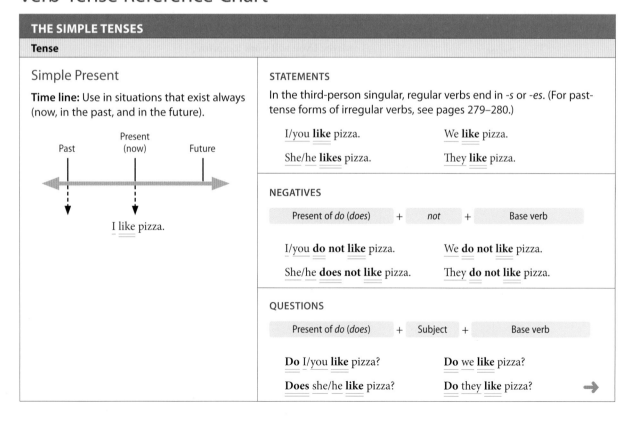

THE SIMPLE TENSES	
Tense	

Simple Present

Time line: Use in situations that exist always (now, in the past, and in the future).

Past — Present (now) — Future

I like pizza.

STATEMENTS

In the third-person singular, regular verbs end in *-s* or *-es*. (For past-tense forms of irregular verbs, see pages 279–280.)

I/you **like** pizza.   We **like** pizza.

She/he **likes** pizza.   They **like** pizza.

NEGATIVES

Present of *do* (*does*) + *not* + Base verb

I/you **do not like** pizza.   We **do not like** pizza.

She/he **does not like** pizza.   They **do not like** pizza.

QUESTIONS

Present of *do* (*does*) + Subject + Base verb

Do I/you **like** pizza?   **Do** we **like** pizza?

Does she/he **like** pizza?   **Do** they **like** pizza?

Tense

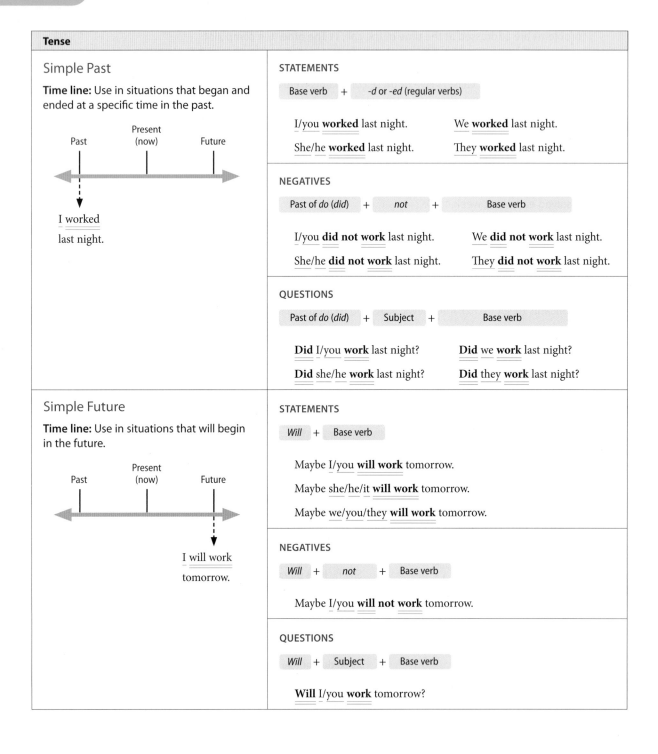

Simple Past

Time line: Use in situations that began and ended at a specific time in the past.

Past — Present (now) — Future

I worked
last night.

STATEMENTS

Base verb + -*d* or -*ed* (regular verbs)

I/you **worked** last night.   We **worked** last night.

She/he **worked** last night.   They **worked** last night.

NEGATIVES

Past of *do* (*did*) + *not* + Base verb

I/you **did not work** last night.   We **did not work** last night.

She/he **did not work** last night.   They **did not work** last night.

QUESTIONS

Past of *do* (*did*) + Subject + Base verb

Did I/you **work** last night?   **Did** we **work** last night?

Did she/he **work** last night?   **Did** they **work** last night?

Simple Future

Time line: Use in situations that will begin in the future.

Past — Present (now) — Future

I will work
tomorrow.

STATEMENTS

Will + Base verb

Maybe I/you **will work** tomorrow.

Maybe she/he/it **will work** tomorrow.

Maybe we/you/they **will work** tomorrow.

NEGATIVES

Will + *not* + Base verb

Maybe I/you **will not work** tomorrow.

QUESTIONS

Will + Subject + Base verb

Will I/you **work** tomorrow?

THE PERFECT TENSES

Tense

Present Perfect

Time line: Use in a situation that began in the past and either is still happening or ended at an unknown time in the past.

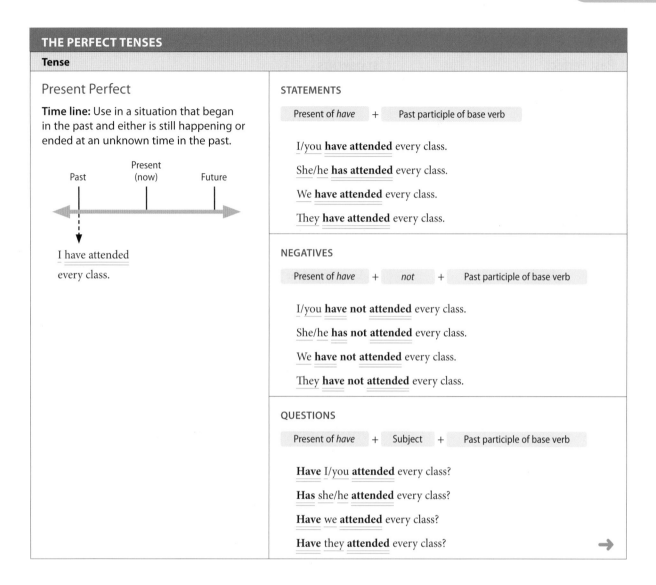

Past

Present (now)

Future

I have attended every class.

STATEMENTS

Present of *have* + Past participle of base verb

I/you **have attended** every class.

She/he **has attended** every class.

We **have attended** every class.

They **have attended** every class.

NEGATIVES

Present of *have* + *not* + Past participle of base verb

I/you **have not attended** every class.

She/he **has not attended** every class.

We **have not attended** every class.

They **have not attended** every class.

QUESTIONS

Present of *have* + Subject + Past participle of base verb

Have I/you **attended** every class?

Has she/he **attended** every class?

Have we **attended** every class?

Have they **attended** every class?

Tense	
Past Perfect	**STATEMENTS**

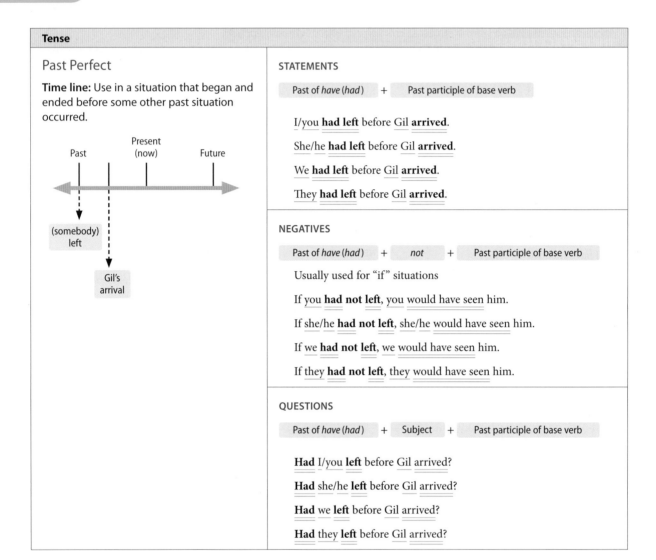

Past Perfect

Time line: Use in a situation that began and ended before some other past situation occurred.

STATEMENTS

Past of *have* (*had*) + Past participle of base verb

I/you **had left** before Gil **arrived**.

She/he **had left** before Gil **arrived**.

We **had left** before Gil **arrived**.

They **had left** before Gil **arrived**.

NEGATIVES

Past of *have* (*had*) + *not* + Past participle of base verb

Usually used for "if" situations

If you **had not left**, you would have seen him.

If she/he **had not left**, she/he would have seen him.

If we **had not left**, we would have seen him.

If they **had not left**, they would have seen him.

QUESTIONS

Past of *have* (*had*) + Subject + Past participle of base verb

Had I/you **left** before Gil arrived?

Had she/he **left** before Gil arrived?

Had we **left** before Gil arrived?

Had they **left** before Gil arrived?

Tense

Future Perfect

Time line: Use in a situation that will be completed in the future before another future situation.

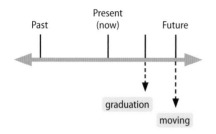

STATEMENTS

Will have + Past participle of base verb

I/you **will have graduated** before I/you move.

She/he **will have graduated** before she/he moves.

We **will have graduated** before we move.

They **will have graduated** before they move.

NEGATIVES

Will not have + Past participle of base verb

I/you **will** not **have graduated** before I/you move.

She/he **will** not **have graduated** before she/he moves.

We **will** not **have graduated** before we move.

They **will** not **have graduated** before they move.

QUESTIONS

Will + Subject + *have* + Past participle of base verb

Will I/you **have graduated** before I/you move?

Will she/he **have graduated** before she/he moves?

Will we **have graduated** before we move?

Will they **have graduated** before they move?

THE PROGRESSIVE TENSES

Tense

Present Progressive

Time line: a situation that is in progress now but started in the past

Past — Present (now) — Future

I am typing.

STATEMENTS

| Present of *be* (*am/is/are*) | + | Base verb ending in *-ing* |

I **am typing**.   We **are typing**.

You **are typing**.   They **are typing**.

She/he **is typing**.

NEGATIVES

| Present of *be* (*am/is/are*) | + | *not* | + | Base verb ending in *-ing* |

I **am not typing**.   We **are not typing**.

You **are not typing**.   They **are not typing**.

She/he **is not typing**.

QUESTIONS

| Present of *be* (*am/is/are*) | + | Subject | + | Base verb ending in *-ing* |

Am I **typing**?   **Are** we **typing**?

Are you **typing**?   **Are** they **typing**?

Is she/he **typing**?

Past Progressive

Time line: a situation started in the past and was in progress in the past

Past — Present (now) — Future

raining

arrival at restaurant

STATEMENTS

| Past of *be* (*was/were*) | + | Base verb ending in *-ing* |

It **was raining** when I got to the restaurant at seven o'clock.

The students **were studying** all night.

NEGATIVES

| Past of *be* (*was/were*) | + | *not* | + | Base verb ending in *-ing* |

It **was not raining** when I got to the restaurant at seven o'clock.

The students **were not studying** all night.

QUESTIONS

| Past of *be* (*was/were*) | + | Subject | + | Base verb ending in *-ing* |

Was it **raining** when I got to the restaurant at seven o'clock?

Were the students **studying** all night?

Tense

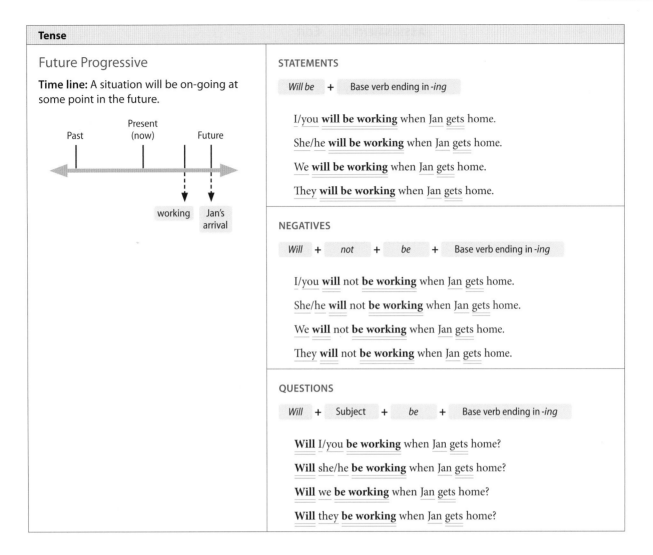

Future Progressive

Time line: A situation will be on-going at some point in the future.

Past — Present (now) — Future

working   Jan's arrival

STATEMENTS

Will be + Base verb ending in *-ing*

I/you **will be working** when Jan gets home.

She/he **will be working** when Jan gets home.

We **will be working** when Jan gets home.

They **will be working** when Jan gets home.

NEGATIVES

Will + *not* + *be* + Base verb ending in *-ing*

I/you **will** not **be working** when Jan gets home.

She/he **will** not **be working** when Jan gets home.

We **will** not **be working** when Jan gets home.

They **will** not **be working** when Jan gets home.

QUESTIONS

Will + Subject + *be* + Base verb ending in *-ing*

Will I/you **be working** when Jan gets home?

Will she/he **be working** when Jan gets home?

Will we **be working** when Jan gets home?

Will they **be working** when Jan gets home?

Write and Edit Your Own Work

ASSIGNMENT 1   **Write**

Write a paragraph describing what happened in the photo shown here (or write about an embarrassing situation that has happened to you). What happened before the photo was taken? What has happened since? Pay attention to the verbs as you write, and use the charts on pages 309-310 to revise any errors you find.

R. GINO SANTA MARIA/SHUTTERSTOCK

> **ASSIGNMENT 2** **Edit**
>
> Using the charts on pages 309–310, correct verb errors in a paper you are writing for this course or another course or in a piece of writing from your work or everyday life.

Chapter Review

1. The past tense is used to describe _____ .

2. To form the past tense of most regular verbs, add _____ or _____ .

3. The past tense of *can* is _____ , and the past tense of *will* is _____ .

4. _____ do not follow a regular pattern in the present, past, and past-participle forms.

5. Write the formula for the present-perfect tense: _____
   _____

6. The past-perfect tense is used to show _____ , one before the other.

7. In the passive voice, the subject _____ of the verb.

Forming the Simple Past Tense

Regular Verbs

Use an *-ed* ending for most regular verbs.

Base verb + *-ed*

clean	→	clean**ed**
explain	→	explain**ed**
toss	→	toss**ed**

Use a *-d* ending for verbs that end in *e*.

Base verb + *-d*

excite	→	excit**ed**
like	→	lik**ed**
promote	→	promot**ed**

For verbs that end with a consonant + *y*, change the *y* to an *i* before adding *-ed*.

Base verb − *y* + *-ied*

comply	→	compl**ied**
cry	→	cr**ied**
rely	→	rel**ied**
supply	→	suppl**ied**

Irregular Verbs

Irregular past tense

grew
rode
went

For a list of irregular verbs in the past tense, see pages 279–280. Be careful with very irregular verbs: *be, have, can/could,* and *will/would*. See the charts on pages 282, 283, and 284.

Forming the Perfect Tenses

Step 1: Form the Past Participle

Regular Verbs

Base verb + *-d* or *-ed*

listened
walked
promoted

The past participle of regular verbs looks just like the simple past.

Irregular Verbs

Irregular past participle

eaten
sat
known

For a list of irregular past participles, see pages 287–290.

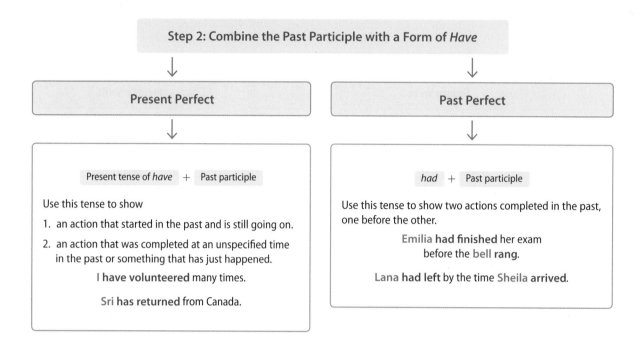

Step 2: Combine the Past Participle with a Form of *Have*

↓   ↓

Present Perfect   **Past Perfect**

↓   ↓

Present tense of *have* + Past participle

Use this tense to show

1. an action that started in the past and is still going on.

2. an action that was completed at an unspecified time in the past or something that has just happened.

I **have volunteered** many times.

Sri **has returned** from Canada.

had + Past participle

Use this tense to show two actions completed in the past, one before the other.

Emilia **had finished** her exam before the **bell rang**.

Lana **had left** by the time Sheila **arrived**.

REFLECTING ON THE JOURNEY

Skills Learned

Now that you've completed the chapter, look again at this paragraph.

> The first humans use tools as early as 2.5 million years ago. The fork, however, not been around until fairly recently. For most of human history, people have simply eat with their fingers. The first forks, which were invented in ancient Greece, was not for eating. When Greek servers carved meat, food sometimes slipped and fall off the plate. With a fork, however, the servers can firmly hold the meat in place.

Using what you've learned in this chapter, edit this paragraph for verb-tense problems. Then answer the questions below.

1. Are you confident that you have identified all the mistakes?

2. Are you confident that you have corrected the mistakes?

3. What questions do you have about verb-tense errors?

Editing for Other Errors and Sentence Style

17

Pronoun Problems

Learning Objectives

Chapter Goal: Find and correct sentences with pronoun problems.

Tools to Achieve the Goal

- Pronoun-antecedent agreement (p. 314)
- Reference chart: indefinite pronouns (p. 315)
- Reference chart: collective nouns (p. 317)
- Pronoun reference (p. 318)
- Pronoun case (p. 321)
- Reference chart: personal pronouns (p. 321)
- Pronouns used in comparisons (p. 324)
- Who and whom (p. 325)
- Find and Fix chart (p. 329)

READING ROADMAP

Key Terms

Skim Chapter 17 before you begin reading. Can you find each of these words in **bold** type? Put a check mark next to each word once you have located it in the chapter.

____ indefinite   ____ compound
     pronoun   ____ comparison
____ collective noun

Highlight or circle any of these words that you already know.

Before You Read

Before you begin reading this chapter, study the following paragraph and complete the chart. At the end of the chapter, you will examine the paragraph again and reflect on what you have learned.

> In March, a major corporation made their decision to relocate to a new production facility in our town. The mayor, who we elected just last year, gave his approval to the project. He knew they would help the town's economy. A construction company was chosen to build the factory, and workers broke ground in late May. Me and my dad have been offered jobs in the new factory. It's a great opportunity, since the company would offer great benefits to both he and I. For example, each company employee can have their families covered under the medical insurance program for a cheap rate. Also, the president of the company likes to get to know the employees. In fact, the president hisself interviewed my dad and me.

This paragraph has problems with pronouns. Put a check mark by the statement that best describes you.

Skill Statement	
I understand what the mistakes are, and I know how to fix them.	
I understand what the mistakes are, but I am not sure how to fix them.	
I think I understand what the mistakes are.	
I don't understand what the mistakes are.	

 **LaunchPad**Solo

Visit **LaunchPad Solo for Readers and Writers > Pronouns** for more practice with finding and fixing pronoun errors.

This chapter explains how to find and fix common pronoun errors. For a review of pronoun types, see pages 175–184.

Make Pronouns Agree with Their Antecedents

A pronoun must agree with (match) the noun or pronoun that it refers to in number: Both must be singular (one) or plural (more than one).

The Riccis opened *their* new store yesterday.

[*Their* agrees with *Riccis* because both are plural.]

If a pronoun refers to a singular noun, it must also match that noun in gender: *he* for masculine nouns, *she* for feminine nouns, and *it* for genderless nouns. Do not use *their,* a plural pronoun, when the noun that it replaces is singular. To avoid this common pronoun error, use a singular pronoun for a singular noun or make the noun plural.

Incorrect	A new student must get *their* college identification card.
	[*Student* is singular; the pronoun that refers to *student* (*their*) is plural.]
Correct	A new student must get *his or her* college identification card.
	[*Student* and *his or her* are singular.]
Correct	New *students* must get *their* college identification cards.
	[Both *students* and *their* are plural.]

Although using a masculine pronoun alone (*A new student must get* his *college identification card*) is grammatically correct, it is considered sexist language. Avoid it.

> 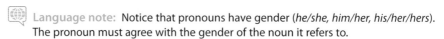 **Language note:** Notice that pronouns have gender (*he/she, him/her, his/her/hers*). The pronoun must agree with the gender of the noun it refers to.

Incorrect	My sister is a doctor. *He works* at County General Hospital.
Correct	My sister is a doctor. *She* works at County General Hospital.
Incorrect	Carolyn went to see *his* boyfriend.
Correct	Carolyn went to see *her* boyfriend.

Also, notice that English has different forms for subject and object pronouns (see pp. 321–325).

Two types of words often cause errors in pronoun agreement: indefinite pronouns and collective nouns.

Indefinite Pronouns

An **indefinite pronoun** does not refer to a specific person, place, thing, or idea. Indefinite pronouns often take singular verbs.

Indefinite Pronouns

Always singular

another	everybody	no one
anybody	everyone	nothing
anyone	everything	one (of)
anything	much	somebody
each (of)	neither (of)	someone
either (of)	nobody	something

Always plural

both	many
few	several

May be singular or plural

all	none
any	some
most	

When you see or write a sentence that has an indefinite pronoun, choose the word that goes with this pronoun carefully.

Incorrect

The priests assembled in the hall. Each had *their* own seat.

Almost no one likes to hear a recording of *their* voice.

Correct

The priests assembled in the hall. Each had *his* own seat.
[The singular pronoun *his* matches the singular pronoun *each*.]

Almost no one likes to hear a recording of *his or her* voice.

[The singular pronouns *his or her* match the singular pronoun *no one*.]

In some cases, indefinite nouns are plural. (Check the chart on p. 315 to see which ones are always plural.)

Incorrect

Several professional athletes admit that *he or she* has used performance-enhancing drugs.

Correct

Several professional athletes admit that *they* have used performance-enhancing drugs.

> **PRACTICE 1**

Underline the indefinite pronoun, and circle the correct pronoun or group of words in parentheses.

1 Anyone who goes to a seminar thinking that (he or she/they) can ignore high-pressure sales tactics for a free gift is probably mistaken. 2 Each of these types of sales representatives has perfected (his or her/their) sales pitch to guarantee some success. 3 Few people can resist the promise of a free gift in exchange for a small amount of (his or her/their) time. 4 The pitch begins in a friendly and comfortable setting, usually with refreshments, where nobody would feel that (he or she/they) might get taken advantage of. 5 Everyone at the seminar is assigned (his or her/their) own personal "consultant" to find out which product—such as real estate, insurance, financial investments— would best suit (his or her/their) needs. 6 After the gentle informational stage, one of the salespeople will begin (his or her/their) heavy sales pitch. 7 One widespread tactic used by salespeople is to make everybody think the product will never again be available to (him or her/them). 8 Some also use harassment techniques: (he or she/they) make anybody who does not agree to a purchase feel bad about (himself or herself/themselves). 9 Many salespeople will use the common practice of calling on the "big guns": (He or she brings/They bring) in a supervisor to make the customer feel guilty for wasting the sales representative's time. 10 Many of these "free gift" seminars are not really free: (It/They) often take more time than promised, and (it/they) can bring on stress and frustration.

Collective Nouns

A **collective noun** names a group that acts as a single unit.

Common Collective Nouns

audience	company	group
class	crowd	jury
college	family	society
committee	government	team

Collective nouns are often singular, so when you use a pronoun to refer to a collective noun, it too must usually be singular.

Incorrect

The class was assigned *their* first paper on Monday.

The team won *their* first victory in ten years.

Correct

The class was assigned *its* first paper on Monday.

[The class as a whole was assigned the paper, so the meaning is singular, and the singular pronoun *its* is used.]

The team won *its* first victory in ten years.

[The team, acting as one, had a victory, so the singular pronoun *its* is used.]

If the people in a group are acting separately, however, the noun is plural and should be used with a plural pronoun.

The audience shifted in *their* seats.

[The people shifted at different times in different seats. They were not acting as one.]

Because the plural pronoun may sound awkward in this case, many writers add a plural noun:

The audience members shifted in their seats.

> **PRACTICE 2**
>
> Circle the antecedent, and fill in the correct pronoun (*its* or *their*) in each of the following sentences.
>
> Example: Last week, the [school] presented ___*its*___ annual faculty talent show.

1. The crowd that was waiting outside the auditorium shouted _____ approval when the doors opened early.

2. The audience hurried to _____ seats in anticipation of the fun event.

3. The show began when the faculty wearing _____ academic gowns danced down the aisles.

4. Arriving on the stage, the group formed a circle and sang _____ favorite song.

5. The library staff read several of _____ poems that had been published in the newspaper.

6. Next, the chorus began _____ song, and the audience applauded loudly.

7. To everyone's amusement, the faculty juggling troupe put on _____ famous dish-dropping act.

8. The show stopped temporarily while the clean-up crew did _____ job and swept up the broken dishes.

9. Because there was so little time, the band played only _____ most popular tune.

10. The faculty ended the performance by dressing in _____ favorite old clothes and telling jokes.

Check Pronoun Reference

A pronoun should refer to only one noun, and it should be clear what that noun is.

Confusing

I put the shirt in the drawer, even though *it* was dirty.
[Was the shirt or the drawer dirty?]

If you cannot find your doctor's office, *they* can help.
[Who are *they*?]

An hour before the turkey was to be done, *it* broke.
[What broke?]

Clear

I put the dirty shirt in the drawer.

If you cannot find your doctor's office, *the information desk* can help.

An hour before the turkey was to be done, *the oven* broke.

 Language note: In writing formal papers, do not use *you* to mean *people*.

Incorrect
When working in a doctor's office, you need to wash your hands frequently.

Correct
People who work in a doctor's office need to wash **their** hands frequently.

> **PRACTICE 3**

Edit each sentence to eliminate problems with pronoun reference. Some sentences may be revised in more than one way.

Example: **When we were young, our babysitter gave my sister Jan and me a**
                                Jan's
book that became one of her favorites.
                            ∧

1. The babysitter, Jan, and I were fascinated by *Twenty Thousand Leagues under the Sea*, and she is now studying marine biology.

2. I know little about the ocean except for what it says in occasional magazine articles.

3. I enjoy visiting the aquarium and have taken a biology class, but it did not focus on ocean life as much as I would have liked.

4. I did learn that it covers about 71 percent of the earth's surface.

5. Both space and the ocean are largely unexplored, and it contains a huge proportion of all life on Earth.

6. They say that the ocean might contain as many as a million undiscovered species.

7. Jan says that they have found some odd creatures in the ocean.

8. In Indonesia, they have found an octopus that uses camouflage and "walks" across the ocean floor on two legs.

9. According to marine biologists who made the discovery, it looks like a piece of seaweed bouncing along the sand.

10. Scientists say that it might help them develop better robot arms.

Tip For more on subjects, verbs, and other sentence parts, see Chapter 11.

A pronoun should replace the subject of a sentence, not repeat it.

Pronoun repeats subject

The doctor, *she* told me to take one aspirin a day.

The plane, *it* arrived on time despite the fog.

Correct

The doctor told me to take one aspirin a day.

The plane arrived on time despite the fog.

 Language note: In some languages, such as Spanish, it is correct to repeat a noun with a pronoun. In English, however, a pronoun *replaces* a noun: Do not use both.

PRACTICE 4

Correct repetitious pronoun references in the following sentences.

Example: Many objects that we use today ~~they~~ were invented by the Chinese.

1. Fireworks they were originally used by the Chinese to scare enemies in war.

2. The wheelbarrow, also invented in China, it was called the "wooden ox."

3. People who use paper fans to cool off they should thank the Chinese for this invention.

4. The Chinese they were the first to make kites, which were used both as toys and in wartime to fly messages over enemy lines.

5. A counting device called the *abacus* it was used for counting and led to the development of the calculator.

6. Many people, they do not know that spaghetti was first made in China, not Italy.

7. The oldest piece of paper in the world it was discovered in China.

8. In fact, paper money it was invented in China.

9. Chinese merchants they were using paper money by 900 C.E.

10. Matches were also invented in China when a woman she wanted an easier way to start fires for cooking.

Use the Right Pronoun Case

There are three pronoun cases: subject, object, and possessive. Subject pronouns act as the subject of a verb, object pronouns act as the object of a verb or preposition, and possessive pronouns show ownership.

Subject pronoun	*She* entered the race.
	Dan got nervous when *he* heard the news.
Object pronoun	Shane gave *her* the keys.
	Marla went to the store with *them*.
Possessive pronoun	*My* feet hurt.
	The puppies are now *yours*.

Tip For more on pronoun case, see pages 175–177.

Choosing between subject and object case can be especially difficult in:

- sentences with more than one subject or object,
- sentences that make a comparison, and
- sentences that use *who* or *whom*.

Pronouns in Sentences with More Than One Subject or Object

When a subject or an object has more than one part, it is called **compound**. The parts are joined by *and* or *or*.

Compound subject	Travis and *I* play soccer.
	[The two subjects are *Travis* and *I*.]
Compound object	Becky made the candles for the boys and *me*.
	[The two objects are *boys* and *me*.]

To decide what type of pronoun is correct in compound subjects or objects, use the following chart.

Personal Pronouns

	Subject		**Object**		**Possessive**	
	Singular	Plural	Singular	Plural	Singular	Plural
First person	I	we	me	us	my/mine	our/ours
Second person	you	you	you	you	your/yours	your/yours
Third person	he/she/it	they	him/her/it	them	his/her/hers/its	their/theirs

Tip When you are writing about yourself and someone else, always put yourself after everyone else. *My friends and I went to the movies,* not *I and my friends went to the movies.*

Incorrect

Harold and *me* like to go to the races.

The boss gave the hardest job to Rico and *I.*

I sent the e-mail to Ellen and *she.*

Correct

Harold and *I* like to go to the races.
[Think: *I* like to go to the races.]

The boss gave the hardest job to Rico and *me.*
[Think: The boss gave the hardest job to *me.*]

I sent the e-mail to Ellen and *her.*
[Think: I sent the e-mail to *her.*]

Many people make the mistake of writing *between you and I.* It should be *between you and me.*

The girl sat between you and ~~I~~ ^me^.

> **PRACTICE 5**

Circle the correct pronoun in each of the following sentences.

Example: When I was eight, my parents got a surprise for my sister Lara and (I/me).

1. When Dad got home from work, Mom and (he/him) left for the mall, but my sister Lara and I did not get to go with them.

2. (Her/She) and I had begged for a pet for months.

3. Our parents were tired of our pleas and got (we/us) a hamster at the mall pet store.

4. I was happy even though (we/us) had hoped for a puppy.

5. My aunt arrived with an old aquarium that she gave to my sister and (I/me).

6. We set it up for our hamster and called Dominic, my best friend, to tell (he/him) about our new pet.

7. Several days later, something happened that surprised (we/us).

8. Lara ran into the room crying and told (I/me) that little pink things had

   gotten into the aquarium.

9. I ran to look at (they/them) and counted eight baby hamsters.

10. Between you and (I/me), I think my parents were sorry they did not get us

    a puppy.

PRACTICE 6

Edit each sentence using the correct pronoun case. Two sentences are correct;
write **C** next to them.

Example: **Because Calico Jack was a famed pirate of the Caribbean, him and**
                     he
                the crew of his ship *Vanity* were greatly feared and respected.

1. On a trip to the Bahamas, he and a woman named Anne Bonny fell in
   love.

2. Because women were considered bad luck on a ship, Anne disguised
   herself as a man and kept the secret between she and Calico Jack.

3. No one guessed that Calico Jack's new first mate was a woman, and her
   and the other pirates became friends.

4. With Calico Jack and she in command, the *Vanity* raided Spanish ships
   throughout the Caribbean.

5. On one ship, her and Calico Jack discovered Mary Read, another female
   sailor disguised as a man.

6. Her and Mary became good friends.

7. When Calico Jack learned of their friendship, him and Anne decided to let
   Mary sail on the *Vanity*.

8. Soon, she and Anne became known as two of the most dangerous pirates
   in the Caribbean.

9. Anne and Mary were skilled pirates and fierce fighters, but the British
   Navy finally captured they and their pirate crew in 1720.

10. The two women were sentenced to hang, but because they were
    pregnant, them and their babies were spared.

Pronouns Used in Comparisons

A **comparison** describes similarities and differences between two things. It often includes the word *than* or *as*.

> Terrence is happier *than* Elena.

> Terrence is as happy *as* Carla.

Pronouns have specific meanings in comparisons, so be sure to use the right ones. To do so, mentally add the words that are missing.

Subject (of "I like video games")

Ann likes video games more than *I*.

[This sentence means "Ann likes video games more than I like them." You can tell by adding the missing words to the end: *more than **I like video games**.*]

Object (of "she likes me")

Ann likes video games more than *me*.

[This sentence means "Ann likes video games more than she likes me." You can tell by adding the missing words to the end: *more than **she likes** me.*]

Incorrect

Bettina is taller than *me*.

I wish I could sing as well as *her*.

Our neighbors are quieter than *us*.

Correct

Bettina is taller than *I*.
[Think: Bettina is taller than *I* am.]

I wish I could sing as well as *she*.
[Think: I wish I could sing as well as *she* sings.]

Our neighbors are quieter than *we*.
[Think: Our neighbors are quieter than *we* are.]

In each of the following sentences, decide what words could be added to the end of each comparison. Speak the sentences, including the added words, aloud.

> Dave drives as fast as I.

> No one can make a better lasagna than we.

> We decided that Alicia was a better candidate than he.

PRACTICE 7

Edit each sentence using the correct pronoun case. One sentence is correct; write **C** next to it.

Example: **When MTV's Video Music Awards are on every year, nobody gets more excited than me.**

1. There are many awards shows, but none are as fun and unpredictable as them.

2. My friends watch the show with me even though they don't like music as much as me.

3. My boyfriend enjoys watching it too, although I know much more than him about pop music.

4. My boyfriend sometimes jokes that he is jealous and says that I like MTV more than he.

5. The performances on the VMA show are always great; there is nothing I like better than they.

6. Because the VMA show is live, there are often unplanned stunts, and some people are more interested in they than the music.

7. For example, when Taylor Swift won Best Female Video award in 2009, nobody was more surprised than she at what happened.

8. Kanye West interrupted Swift during her acceptance speech because he thought another singer deserved the award more than her.

9. I have never seen a singer as embarrassed as her after that.

10. When the audience booed him, however, West realized that other people did not feel the same as him.

Who *versus* Whom

Who is always a subject; use it if the pronoun performs an action. *Whom* is always an object; use it if the pronoun does not perform any action.

Who = subject   Dennis is the neighbor *who* helped us build the deck.
[*Who* (*Dennis*) is the subject.]

Whom = object   Carol is the woman *whom* I met at school.
[You can turn the sentence around: *I met whom* (*Carol*) *at school.*
Whom (*Carol*) is the object of the verb *met*.]

In most cases, for sentences in which the pronoun is followed by a verb, use *who*. When the pronoun is followed by a noun or pronoun, use *whom*.

> The man (who/whom) called 911 was unusually calm.
> [The pronoun is followed by the verb *called*. Use *who*.]

> The woman (who/whom) I drove to the train was from Turkey.
> [The pronoun is followed by another pronoun: *I*. Use *whom*.]

Whoever is a subject pronoun; *whomever* is an object pronoun.

> **PRACTICE 8**
>
> In each sentence, circle the correct word, *who* or *whom*.
>
> **Example: Mary Frith was a thief (who/whom) lived in the 1600s.**
>
> 1. She joined a gang of thieves (who/whom) were known as cutpurses.
>
> 2. People (who/whom) had money and jewelry carried the items in purses tied around their waists.
>
> 3. Mary and her gang would cut the purse strings, steal the purses, and find someone to (who/whom) they could sell the goods.
>
> 4. Mary, (who/whom) was not one to pass up a chance to make money, opened her own shop to sell the "used" goods.
>
> 5. She often sold items back to the people from (who/whom) she had stolen them.

Edit Pronouns in Everyday Life

Complete the editing reviews as instructed, referring to the chart on page 329.

> **EDITING PARAGRAPHS 1**
>
> Correct pronoun errors in the following e-mail. Three sentences are correct; write **C** next to them. The first sentence has been edited for you.
>
> Thursday, 2/6/15, 12:09 p.m.
> FROM: Thomas Hamson
> TO: Juan Alvarez
> CC: Alicia Newcombe, Allegra Conti
> SUBJECT: New color printer

1 On January 20, you asked Allegra Conti and ~~I~~ *me* to look into purchasing a new color printer for our department. 2 This e-mail ~~it~~ presents our findings and recommendations.

3 Two printers will meet our needs: the FX 235 and the AE 100. 4 It says that both handle 8½″ × 11″, 8½″ × 14″, and A4 size paper. 5 They are also able to print labels, photographs, and overhead transparencies. 6 It, however, has several capabilities that are not found in the AE 100. 7 The FX 235 offers more flexibility for employees whom have unique needs. 8 For example, if Allegra wants to print something more quickly than me, the FX model offers a low-quality setting that prints documents at a higher speed. 9 Although the two printers are similarly priced, replacement ink cartridges for the FX 235 are 35 percent cheaper than cartridges for the AE 100. 10 It also has a better warranty.

11 We read several reviews of both printers, and every reviewer recommends the FX as their top choice in our price range. 12 Additionally, the IT Department agrees that their favorite is the FX 235. 13 Today, I will bring you brochures for both printers. 14 Allegra and me will answer any additional questions you might have. 15 Please let us know when the company has made their decision.

EDITING PARAGRAPHS 2

Correct pronoun errors in the following passage. Three sentences are correct; write **C** next to them. The first sentence has been edited for you.

1 The Internet is continually changing to meet the needs of the people ~~whom~~ *who* use it. 2 They originally thought it would be used primarily for business and research. 3 However, the Internet has become a place where people share his or her thoughts and opinions.

4 In the past ten years, for example, Web logs (blogs) have become an Internet craze. 5 Blogs, they began as online diaries where people could regularly post their thoughts and links to favorite Web sites for friends and family. 6 Today, many previously unknown bloggers are writing for huge audiences across the world. 7 They cover every topic imaginable, including

politics, current events, sports, music, and technology. 8 Anyone using the Internet can start their own blog. 9 When a lot of people blog about a particular political or social controversy, it is called a blogstorm.

10 More recently, another type of Web site—the wiki—has become popular among people whom like to share information. 11 People can post information to a wiki or edit information that has already been posted. 12 For a class project, my partner and me evaluated an online encyclopedia's article about a wildlife refuge near our college. 13 Because the site is a wiki, her and me were able to edit outdated facts and add new information.

Write and Edit Your Own Work

ASSIGNMENT 1   **Write**

Write about a time when you worked with others to get something done. Be sure to use several pronouns. When you are done, use the chart on page 329 to check the pronouns, and correct any mistakes that you find.

ASSIGNMENT 2   **Edit**

Using the chart on page 329, edit pronoun errors in a paper that you are writing for this course or another course or in a piece of writing from your work or everyday life.

Chapter Review

1. A pronoun must _____ (match) its antecedent (the noun or pronoun to which it refers) in number and in gender.

2. An _____ does not refer to a specific person, place, or thing. What are three examples of this kind of pronoun? _____

3. A _____ names a group that acts as a single unit. What are two examples? _____

4. If a pronoun repeats the subject of a sentence rather than replacing it, the pronoun should be _____ .

5. _____ pronouns serve as the subject of the verb. Give an example: _____

   _____. _____ pronouns receive the action of a verb or are part of a

   prepositional phrase. Give an example: _____

6. _____ pronouns show ownership. Give an example: _____

7. When a subject or an object has more than one part, it is described

   as _____.

8. Use *who* when the pronoun is followed by a _____. Use *whom* when the

   pronoun is followed by a _____.

Finding and Fixing Pronoun Problems

↓

Edit for correct pronoun usage by checking three things.

Make sure that each pronoun agrees with the noun or pronoun to which it refers (see p. 314).	Make sure that the pronoun reference is clear, not confusing or repetitious (see p. 318).	Make sure that you have used the right pronoun case: subject, object, or possessive (see p. 321).
↓		↓
Check pronouns that refer to indefinite pronouns.		Check compound subjects and objects.
↓		↓
Check pronouns that refer to collective nouns.		Check comparisons.
		↓
		Check *who* and *whom*.

REFLECTING ON THE JOURNEY

Skills Learned

Now that you've completed the chapter, look again at this paragraph.

> In March, a major corporation made their decision to relocate to a new production facility in our town. The mayor, who we elected just last year, gave his approval to the project. He knew they would help the town's economy. A construction company was chosen to build the factory, and workers broke ground in late May. Me and my dad have been offered jobs in the new factory. It's a great opportunity, since the company would offer great benefits to both he and I. For example, each company employee can have their families covered under the medical insurance program for a cheap rate. Also, the president of the company likes to get to know the employees. In fact, the president hisself interviewed my dad and me.

Using what you've learned in this chapter, edit this paragraph for problems in pronoun use. Then answer the questions below.

1. Are you confident that you have identified the mistakes?

2. Are you confident that you have corrected the mistakes?

3. What questions do you have about using pronouns correctly?

18

Adjective and Adverb Problems

READING ROADMAP

Learning Objectives

Chapter Goal: Find and correct sentences with adjective and adverb problems.

Tools to Achieve the Goal

- Adjective vs. Adverbs (p. 334)
- Reference chart: comparative and superlative forms (p. 335)
- Reference chart: forms of *good*, *well*, and *badly* (p. 338)
- Review chart: editing for correct usage of adjectives and adverbs (p. 343)

Key Terms

Skim Chapter 18 before you begin reading. Can you find each of these words in **bold** type? Put a check mark next to each word once you have located it in the chapter.

____ adjective   ____ comparative
____ adverb   ____ superlative

Highlight or circle any of these words that you already know.

Before You Read

Before you begin reading this chapter, study the following paragraph and complete the chart on page 334. At the end of the chapter, you will examine the paragraph again and reflect on what you have learned.

> Martin City Juvenile Boot Camp teaches respect and discipline to teenagers who behave bad. Some parents worry that sending a teen to camp will cause them to behave even worser. But Martin City teaches life skills and offers a pleasanter environment than military boot camps. Student can choose a specifically program at Martin City. In the basketball program, for example, students spend weeks learning how to become more good at the game, and at the end of the camp, the bestest players compete in a tournament with professional players. In another program, creative teens work to write a novel or screenplay. This camp is difficulter than it sounds; when they aren't writing, teens must do some difficult workouts and challenges. In the end, the students who complete the program have learned some importantly skills, and they can handle their emotions good. When Martin City graduates return home, they don't get into trouble as muchly as they did before.

This paragraph has problems with adjectives and adverbs. Put a check mark by the statement that best describes you.

Skill Statement	
I understand what the mistakes are, and I know how to fix them.	
I understand what the mistakes are, but I am not sure how to fix them.	
I think I understand what the mistakes are.	
I don't understand what the mistakes are.	

LaunchPadSolo

Visit **LaunchPad Solo for Readers and Writers > Adjectives and Adverbs** for more practice with finding and fixing common errors.

This chapter explains how to find and fix common errors with adjectives and adverbs. For a review of these parts of speech, see pages 188–190.

Adjectives describe nouns and pronouns. They add information about what kind, which one, or how many.

Maria is **tired**.

Maria works **two** shifts and takes **three** classes.

Maria babysits for her **younger** sister.

Adverbs describe verbs, adjectives, or other adverbs. They add information about how, how much, when, where, or why. Adverbs often end with -ly.

Stephan **accidentally** banged his toe on the table.

He was **extremely** late for work.

His toe became swollen **very** quickly.

Choose between Adjectives and Adverbs

Many adverbs are formed by adding -ly to the end of an adjective.

Adjective	Adverb
The *fresh* vegetables glistened in the sun.	The house was *freshly* painted.
She is an *honest* person.	She answered the question *honestly*.

Incorrect

I was *real* pleased about the news.

We saw an *extreme* funny show last night.

We had a *peacefully* view of the lake.

Tip Note that nouns can be used as adjectives—for example, **City** *traffic is terrible.*

Correct

I was *really* pleased about the news.

[An adverb, *really,* describes the verb *pleased.*]

We saw an *extremely* funny show last night.

[An adverb, *extremely,* describes the adjective *funny.*]

We had a *peaceful* view of the lake.

[An adjective, *peaceful,* describes the noun *view.*]

 Language note: The *-ed* and *-ing* forms of adjectives are sometimes confused. Common examples include *bored/boring, confused/confusing, excited/exciting,* and *interested/interesting.*

Incorrect   Janelle is *interesting* in ghosts and ghost stories.

Correct   Janelle is *interested* in ghosts and ghost stories.

Correct   Janelle finds ghosts and ghost stories *interesting.*

Often, the *-ed* form describes a person's reaction, while the *-ing* form describes the thing being reacted to.

PRACTICE 1

In each sentence, underline the word that is being described, and then circle the correct adjective or adverb in parentheses.

Example: In the 1970s, Richard O'Brien, (poor/poorly) and unemployed, wrote a musical about a mad scientist from outer space.

1. His play *The Rocky Horror Show* opened in London in 1973, and audiences were (wild/wildly) enthusiastic.

2. Filmmakers decided that it would make a (successful/successfully) movie.

3. Just before the movie *The Rocky Horror Show* was to be released in 1975, the play opened in New York, and the reviews were (poor/poorly).

4. Because critics complained (constant/constantly) about the play, the movie did not make much money at first.

5. The producer persuaded a theater in Greenwich Village to show the (unusual/unusually) film nightly at midnight.

6. Then, something strange (slow/slowly) began to happen.

7. (Serious/Seriously) fans attended the movie every night and began dressing like the characters.

8. Soon the audience was (loud/loudly) shouting the lines, and watching the audience became entertaining in itself.

9. People covered their heads with newspapers during rainy scenes and danced (happy/happily) in the aisles during the theme song.

10. The movie is almost forty years old, but (devoted/devotedly) fans still attend midnight showings at theaters across the country.

Adjectives and Adverbs in Comparisons

To compare two persons, places, things, or ideas, use the **comparative** form of adjectives or adverbs. This form often includes *than*.

> Trina runs *faster* than I do.
>
> Davio dances *more gracefully* than Harper does.

To compare three or more persons, places, things, or ideas, use the **superlative** form of adjectives or adverbs.

> Trina runs the *fastest* of all our friends.
>
> Davio is the *most graceful* of all the ballroom dancers.

Use either an ending (*-er* or *-est*) or an extra word (*more* or *most*) to form a comparative or superlative—not both at once.

> Some say that Dale Earnhardt was the most greatest NASCAR driver ever.

Language note: Some languages, such as Spanish, always use words meaning *more* or *most* in comparisons, even when there is already the equivalent of an *-er* or *-est* ending on an adjective or adverb. In English, use either an *-er* or *-est* ending or *more* or *most*.

Comparative and Superlative Forms

Adverbs and adjectives of one syllable: Add *-er* to form the comparative and *-est* to form the superlative.

> **Example** Miguel is the *tallest* boy in the class.

Tip Think of a syllable as a "beat": the word *ad-jec-tive* has three beats, or syllables.

Adjective or Adverb	Comparative	Superlative
tall	taller	tallest
fast	faster	fastest

Adjectives ending in -y: Follow the same rule as for one-syllable words, but change the *-y* to *-i* before adding *-er* or *-est*.

> **Example** That is the *silliest* joke I have ever heard.

Tip For more on changing a final *-y* to *-i* when adding endings, and on other spelling changes involving endings, see Chapter 25.

Adjective or Adverb	Comparative	Superlative
happy	happier	happiest
silly	sillier	silliest

Adverbs and adjectives of more than one syllable: Add *more* to make the comparative and *most* to make the superlative.

> **Example** Last night's debate was the *most intelligent* one I have ever seen.

Adjective or adverb	Comparative	Superlative
graceful	more graceful	most graceful
gracefully	more gracefully	most gracefully
intelligent	more intelligent	most intelligent
intelligently	more intelligently	most intelligently

PRACTICE 2

In the blank next to each word, write the comparative form of the adjective or adverb.

Examples: tall   _____*taller*_____

beautiful   _____*more beautiful*_____

1. smart   _____

2. strong   _____

3. quietly   _____

4. joyful   _____

5. brief _____

6. wealthy _____

7. patiently _____

8. funny _____

9. thankful _____

10. normal _____

PRACTICE 3

In the blank next to each word, write the superlative form of the adjective or adverb.

Examples: tall _____*tallest*_____

grateful ___*most grateful*___

1. rich _____

2. glossy _____

3. proud _____

4. skillfully _____

5. sensible _____

6. cheap _____

7. bitter _____

8. hairy _____

9. impatiently _____

10. skinny _____

PRACTICE 4

In each sentence, fill in the blank with the correct form of the adjective or adverb in parentheses.

Example: Some of the ___*most interesting*___ **(interesting) inventions were accidental.**

1. Ruth Wakefield, manager of the Toll House Inn, was baking butter cookies and wanted them to taste _____ (sweet) than other cookies.

2. She was out of baker's chocolate, so she cut a chocolate candy bar into the _____ (small) pieces possible.

3. She was certain that she would have the _____ (tasty) chocolate cookies she had ever eaten.

4. The chocolate was supposed to melt and make the cookies _____ _____ (delicious) than regular butter cookies.

5. When she took the cookies out of the oven, she was the _____ _____ (surprised) person in the inn.

6. The chocolate had not melted, and the cookies looked _____ (strange) than she had expected.

7. She served them anyway, and her guests were the first to sample what became the _____ (popular) cookie in America.

8. She published her recipe, and everyone thought it made the _____ _____ (wonderful) cookie ever baked.

9. The chocolate-bar company responded _____ (generously) than she had hoped, offering her a lifetime supply of free chocolate if she allowed her recipe to be published on the chocolate bars' wrappers.

10. Today, Ruth Wakefield's Toll House chocolate chip cookies are the _____ (favorite) cookies in the United States.

PRACTICE 5

Find and correct problems with comparative and superlative forms in the following paragraph. One sentence is correct; write **C** next to it.

1 Each year, people attempting to break the land speed record head to the salt flats of the western United States to see who can move the most swiftest. 2 In previous decades, events to determine which of the year's new vehicles were the speedyest were usually held at the Bonneville Salt Flats in Utah. 3 More recently, the impressivest land speed records are being set in Nevada's Black Rock Desert, which is more larger than Bonneville. 4 In the fall of 1997, a jet-propelled car at Black Rock moved more rapider than the previous record holder and earned the new world record. 5 Even more remarkabler than the record was that this vehicle, called *ThrustSSC*, was the first land vehicle to travel fastest than the speed of sound. 6 *ThrustSSC*

achieved the higher speed ever recorded on land: 760 miles per hour. 7 The *ThrustSSC* team said the most excitingest moment was when the car broke the sound barrier and they heard the sonic boom. 8 This supersonic vehicle, which is basically a rocket with wheels on it, now has the distinction of being the fastest car on the planet.

Good, Well, Bad, and *Badly*

Good, well, bad, and *badly* do not follow the regular rules for forming comparatives and superlatives.

Forms of *Good, Well, Bad,* and *Badly*

Adjective	Comparative	Superlative
good	better	best
bad	worse	worst
Adverb	**Comparative**	**Superlative**
well	better	best
badly	worse	worst

People often get confused about whether to use *good* or *well*. *Good* is an adjective, so use it to describe a noun or pronoun. *Well* is an adverb, so use it to describe a verb or an adjective.

| **Adjective** | Mike is a *good* person. |
| | [The adjective *good* describes the noun *person*.] |

| **Adverb** | He works *well* with others. |
| | [The adverb *well* describes the verb *works*.] |

Well can also be an adjective to describe someone's health.

| **Incorrect** | Louisa is not feeling *good* today, so she might not run well. |
| **Correct** | Louisa is not feeling *well* today, so she might not run well. |

PRACTICE 6

In each of the following sentences, underline the word that *good* or *well* modifies, and then circle the correct word in parentheses.

Example: **For some people, the fields of hair care, cosmetology, and wellness are (good/well) career choices.**

1. Ideally, a person choosing to work with people on their appearance should be a (good/well) listener.

2. The ability to communicate (good/well) can be the difference between being a successful and an unsuccessful beauty consultant.

3. Another important characteristic for beauty-care workers is to be (good/well) in creative areas such as art and graphic design.

4. People with artistic talent and a strong sense of visual style usually do (good/well) in the beauty industry.

5. One thing that beauty professionals love about their work is that they get to make their clients feel (good/well) about themselves.

6. Another benefit of working in the beauty industry, especially hair care, is that it is always necessary, whether the economy is performing (good/well) or badly.

7. If you do a (good/well) job, your clients will stick with you no matter what.

8. Customers will also tip (good/well) for satisfactory customer service.

9. A (good/well) way to learn about the industry is to talk to professionals who enjoy what they do.

10. You should also be certain to enroll in a school that will prepare you (good/well) for the career of your choice.

PRACTICE 7

In each of the following sentences, underline the word that is being described. Then, circle the correct comparative or superlative form of *good* or *bad* in parentheses.

Example: **When combined with regular exercise, a healthful diet is one of the (better/best) ways to stay fit.**

1. Many people think that a salad is a (better/best) choice than a burger.

2. However, a salad that is loaded with high-fat cheese, bacon, and dressing could be (worse/worst) than a sensible turkey burger.

3. What is the (better/best) beverage to drink in the morning?

4. Orange juice is (better/best) than coffee, but eating an orange is the healthiest choice.

5. The (better/best) choice is plain water; your body loses fluid while you sleep and needs to be rehydrated in the morning.

6. What is the (worse/worst) type of breakfast food?

7. Doughnuts are much (worse/worst) than some kinds of cereal.

8. A fiber-rich food that contains B vitamins is among the (better/best) breakfast foods.

9. Bran flakes are good, but oatmeal is even (better/best).

10. Add some toasted pumpkin seeds and honey, and you will have the (better/best) breakfast for your health.

Edit Adjectives and Adverbs in Everyday Life

Complete the editing reviews as instructed, referring to the chart on page 343.

EDITING PARAGRAPHS 1

Edit the adjectives and adverbs in the following paragraph. Two sentences are correct; write **C** next to them. The first sentence has been edited for you.

1 College tuition costs are ~~more~~ higher than ever before. 2 At Merriweather College, financial aid advisers are available to help students understand the different types of financial aid available. 3 The commonest types of aid include scholarships, loans, and military aid. 4 Scholarships exist for students who perform good in academics or athletics. 5 Scholarships are also available for students specializing in fields such as agriculture or nursing. 6 For many students, government loans are gooder than private loans. 7 Government loans do not require credit checks, and they usual offer the lowest interest rates. 8 The popularest loans are the Stafford and the Perkins. 9 Finally, students can enroll in Reserve Officers Training Corps (ROTC) for funds, and veterans can also obtain well tuition benefits. 10 Students with

questions should contact the financial aid department, and a meeting with an adviser will be set up quick.

EDITING PARAGRAPHS 2

Edit the adjectives and adverbs in the following business letter. Two sentences are correct; write **C** next to them. The first sentence has been edited for you.

Mr. David Jones
Cooperative Canning Company
235 Paxton Boulevard
Philadelphia, PA 19104

Dear Mr. Jones:

1 Thank you for interviewing me on Thursday and giving me such a ~~thoroughly~~ *thorough* tour of your factory. 2 Your production line was one of the efficientest I have seen in my years in the industry. 3 I was particular impressed with the quality-control system. 4 As I said when we met, I am real interested in the position of production manager. 5 I have fifteen years' experience in similar positions and a degree in mechanical engineering. 6 My education and experience would help me operate your good system even gooder. 7 I would also enjoy the challenge of developing more newer methods for increasing production and improving plant safety.

8 If you have questions or would like to interview me again, you can reach me at (123) 555-1234. 9 I hope you consider me a well candidate for your management team. 10 I am available to begin immediate.

Sincerely,

Ty Manfred

Write and Edit Your Own Work

ASSIGNMENT 1   Write

Describe a city park such as the one in the photo on the next page. Use as many adjectives and adverbs as you can. When you are done, use the chart on page 343 to check the adjectives and adverbs. Correct any mistakes that you find.

SONGQUAN DENG/SHUTTERSTOCK

ASSIGNMENT 2   **Edit**

Using the chart on page 343, edit adjectives and adverbs in a paper that you are writing for this course or another course or in a piece of writing from your work or everyday life.

Chapter Review

1. _____ describe nouns, and _____ describe verbs, adjectives, or other adverbs.

2. Adverbs often end in _____.

3. The comparative form of an adjective or adverb is used to compare how many people, places, or things? _____ It is formed by adding an _____ ending or the word _____ .

4. The superlative form of an adjective or adverb is used to compare how many people, places, or things? _____ It is formed by adding an _____ ending or the word _____ .

5. What four words do not follow the regular rules for forming comparatives and

   superlatives? _____

6. *Good* is an (adjective/adverb) and *well* is an (adjective/adverb).

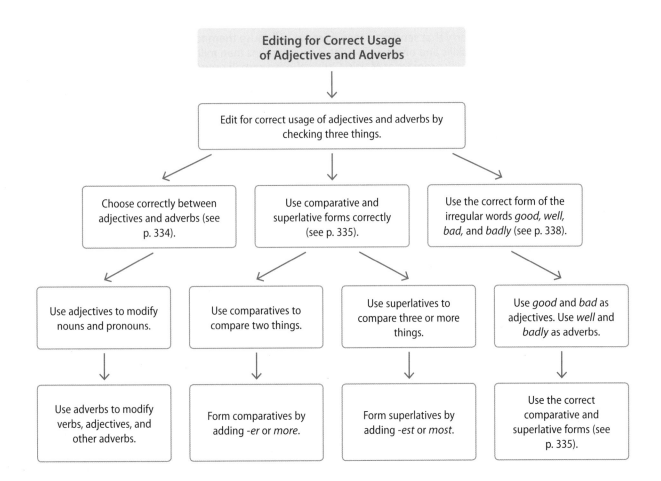

REFLECTING ON THE JOURNEY

Skills Learned

Now that you've completed the chapter, look again at this paragraph.

Martin City Juvenile Boot Camp teaches respect and discipline to teenagers who behave bad. Some parents worry that sending a teen to camp will cause them to behave even worser. But Martin City teaches life skills and offers a pleasanter environment than military boot camps. Student can choose a specifically program at Martin City. In the basketball program, for example, students spend weeks learning how to become more good at the game, and at the end of the camp, the bestest players compete in a tournament with professional players. In another program, creative teens work to write a novel or screenplay. This camp is difficulter than it sounds; when they aren't writing, teens must do some difficult workouts and challenges. In the end, the students who complete the program have learned some importantly skills, and they can handle their emotions good. When Martin City graduates return home, they don't get into trouble as muchly as they did before.

Using what you've learned in this chapter, edit this paragraph for mistakes in adjectives and adverbs. Then answer the questions below.

1. Are you confident that you have identified the mistakes?

2. Are you confident that you have corrected the mistakes?

3. What questions do you have about adjectives and adverbs?

19

Misplaced and Dangling Modifiers

READING ROADMAP

Learning Objectives

Chapter Goal: Find and correct sentences with confusing modifiers.

Tools to Achieve the Goal

- Understanding misplaced modifiers (p. 346)
- Understanding dangling modifiers (p. 349)
- Review chart: editing for misplaced and dangling modifiers (p. 353)

Key Terms

Skim Chapter 19 before you begin reading. Can you find each of these words in **bold** type? Put a check mark next to each word once you have located it in the chapter.

____ modifier ____ dangling modifier
____ misplaced
modifier

Highlight or circle any of these words that you already know.

Before You Read

Before you begin reading this chapter, study the following paragraph and complete the chart. At the end of the chapter, you will examine the paragraph again and reflect on what you have learned.

> Hoping to make their streets safer, new crime-fighting programs are being tried by some communities. Community policing links police departments with local community groups, which is one of these new programs. Identifying problems that are most important to the community, goals are set. Working together, the goals are easier to meet. Actively involved with the people in their precincts, the program requires a strong commitment. Often, officers set up programs within neighborhoods. For example, patrolling on foot rather than in cars, a sense of security and community is created.

This paragraph has problems with misplaced and dangling modifiers. Put a check mark by the statement that best describes you.

Skill Statement	
I understand what the mistakes are, and I know how to fix them.	
I understand what the mistakes are, but I am not sure how to fix them.	
I think I understand what the mistakes are.	
I don't understand what the mistakes are.	

Understand What Misplaced Modifiers Are

Modifiers are words or word groups that describe other words in a sentence.

The man *who came in late* is Marlee's father.
[The words *who came in late* modify *man*.]

Unless the modifier is near the words it describes, the sentence can be confusing or funny. A **misplaced modifier** is placed incorrectly in the sentence and ends up describing the wrong word or words.

LaunchPadSolo

Visit **LaunchPad Solo for Readers and Writers > Modifier Placement** for more practice with fixing misplaced modifiers.

Misplaced   Risa saw Sanjay's cat *standing on a ladder*.

[Was Sanjay's cat standing on a ladder? No, Risa was standing on a ladder, so the modifier must come right before or right after her name.]

Correct   *Standing on a ladder,* Risa saw Sanjay's cat.

Four types of modifiers are often misplaced:

- **Modifiers such as *only, almost, hardly, nearly,* and *just***

      only
  I ~~only~~ drove thirty miles on my vacation.

                  nearly
  Carla ~~nearly~~ needed ten cans of peaches.

- **Modifiers that start with *-ing* verbs**

  Using a soft cloth,
  Taylor polished the car hood. ~~using a soft cloth.~~

  Opening the closet,
  Candice found her daughter's hamster. ~~opening the closet.~~

- **Modifiers that are prepositional phrases**

                        to the taxi
  Catherine was carrying the luggage for her sister. ~~to the taxi.~~

                  from the dry cleaner
  I found the bill in the drawer. ~~from the dry cleaner.~~

- **Modifiers that are clauses starting with *who, whose, that,* or *which***

                  who play with children
  Babysitters are the most popular. ~~who play with children.~~

                      that was torn
  I returned the shirt to the store. ~~that was torn.~~

Language note: People whose native language is not English often confuse the word pairs *almost/most* and *too/very*.

Almost = nearly
Most = the largest share of

Incorrect	Almost students had problems with that question.
Correct	Most students had problems with that question.
Incorrect	We are most there.
Correct	We are almost there.

Too = more than desired
Very = extremely

Incorrect	The weather today is too beautiful.
Correct	The weather today is very beautiful.
Incorrect	This food is too delicious.
Correct	This food is very delicious.

Find and Correct Misplaced Modifiers

PRACTICE 1

Find and correct misplaced modifiers in the following sentences. One sentence
is correct; write **C** next to it.

Even though it was thought to be unsinkable, the
Example: The SS *Titanic* sank on April 15, 1912, even though it
         ^
was thought to be unsinkable on its maiden voyage.

1. It nearly was impossible to see distant icebergs on the night the ship

   sank, because there was no moon and the seas were calm.

2. Wireless operators on board the *Titanic* ignored warning messages

   about dangerous icebergs being sent by other ships in the region.

3. At 11:40 p.m., an iceberg was spotted by a ship's officer sticking
                                  ^
   out of the water.

4. The helmsman frantically changed the direction of the ship trying

   to avoid a crash.

5. The people on board the ship could only see the tip of the iceberg.
                                  ^
6. There was a massive amount of ice under the surface of the water that
   ^
   ripped a gaping hole in the ship's hull.

7. Almost all the women and children in first and second class made it to the

   safety of the lifeboats.

8. Many third-class passengers on board the *Titanic*, because they had
   ∧
   trouble making their way to the upper decks, were not able to reach the
   lifeboats in time.

9. The ship sank after the spotting of the iceberg in just a few hours.
   ∧

10. Rescuers almost saved all the people in the lifeboats, but some of the
    ∧
    passengers died from exposure to the cold.

PRACTICE 2

Rewrite each of the following sentences, adding a modifying word or phrase according to the directions in parentheses.

, which happens to almost everyone,

Example: Having a flat tire is not a pleasant experience. (Add *which
                                                          ∧
***happens to almost everyone* to make the sentence mean that most people
have had this experience.)**

1. The first step is finding your spare tire, jack, and tire iron. (Add *after you*
   ∧
   have pulled over to a safe place to make the sentence mean that first you
   pull over.)

2. Car manufacturers place the spare tire underneath the floor mat of the
   ∧
   trunk. (Add *usually* to make the sentence mean that the spare tire is
   typically located there.)

3. Once you find it, remove the spare tire and make sure that it is not flat
   ∧
   also. (Add *carefully* to make the sentence mean that you should remove
   the spare tire with caution.)

4. Next, make sure that your vehicle is in "park" and that the emergency
   brake is set. (Add *which should be resting on level pavement if possible*
   to make the sentence mean that, for safety's sake, you want to avoid
   changing your tire on a hill.)

5. Loosen each of the wheel lugs with the tire iron. (Add *which tend to be*
   ∧
   quite tight to make the sentence mean that the lugs are hard to turn.)

6. Once the lugs are loose, move the jack into place. (Add *underneath your*
   ∧
   car to make the sentence mean that the jack goes in that location.)

7. Start to raise the jack until it contacts the car's frame and the tire begins
   to lift from the ground. (Add *cautiously* to make the sentence mean that
   you move the jack carefully.)

8. When the tire is no longer touching the ground, remove the wheel lugs. (Add *using the tire iron again* to make the sentence say how you take out the lugs.)

9. Take off the flat tire, and then, push the spare tire into place. (Add *lining the spare tire up with the wheel studs* to make the sentence mean that the spare tire has to be in position before being pushed on.)

10. Screw the wheel lugs back on until they are snug, and then tighten them with the tire iron. (Add *finally* to make the sentence mean that the last step is screwing on the lugs again.)

Understand What Dangling Modifiers Are

A **dangling modifier** "dangles" because the word or words that it is supposed to describe are not in the sentence. A dangling modifier is usually at the beginning of the sentence and seems to modify the noun after it, but it really does not.

Dangling	*Looking under the dresser,* a dust ball went up my nose.
	[Was the dust ball looking under the dresser? No.]
Correct	*Looking under the dresser,* I inhaled a dust ball.
	[The correction adds the word being modified right after the opening modifier.]
Correct	While I was *looking under the dresser,* a dust ball went up my nose.
	[The correction adds the word being modified to the opening modifier itself.]

Find and Correct Dangling Modifiers

Add the word being modified right after the modifying words, or make it part of the modifying words.

Dangling	Eating at Jimmy's Restaurant, the pizza had a bug on it.
Correct	Eating at Jimmy's Restaurant, I found a bug on my pizza.
Dangling	Buying stereo equipment online, shipping can cost more than the equipment.
	[*Buying stereo equipment online* does not modify *shipping.*]
Correct	When buying stereo equipment online, you may find that the shipping costs more than the equipment.
	[By adding *when* to the modifying words *buying stereo equipment online* and changing the second part of the sentence to *you may find that,* the correction makes the modifying words describe the right word: *you.*]

PRACTICE 3

Find and correct dangling modifiers in the following sentences. Three sentences are correct; write **C** next to each of them. It may be necessary to add new words or ideas to some sentences.

I found

Example: Getting ready to audition for the talent show, the backstage area was noisy.
                                                                        ^

1. Practicing my song, my costume made a ripping sound.

2. Terrified that something was wrong, the audition was about to start.

3. With fear closing my throat, I tried to find where the costume had torn.

4. With two of my friends helping me, the tiny dressing room was crowded.

5. Checking the whole costume, it was hard to see in the dimly lit dressing room.

6. Sensing my panic, the costume was checked again to reassure me.

7. Worried, the ripping sound still echoed in my head.

8. Trying to focus on my song, my costume still bothered me.

9. Pulling myself together, I went onstage.

10. Beginning to sing my song, the people in the audience laughed as they noticed the hole in my dress.

PRACTICE 4

Combine the sentence pairs, turning one sentence into a modifying word group.

Deciding

Example: I decided to get a dog. I went to the Humane Shelter.
                   ^

1. I looked at the large dogs. I chose a German Shepherd.

2. He barked loudly. He seemed to be saying hello.

3. The volunteer grinned. She knew this was the dog for me.

4. I filled out the paperwork. I was eager to take my new friend home.

5. We walked out to my car. The dog seemed as excited as I was.

6. I drove home slowly. I kept stealing glances at him.

7. I saw the dog put his head out of the window. I named him Breezy.

8. We got out of the car at the same time. We raced to the front door.

9. I unlocked the door. I nearly tripped over Breezy as he ran inside.

10. I laughed at him as he climbed up on the couch. I knew that I had made the right decision.

Edit Misplaced and Dangling Modifiers in Everyday Life

Complete the editing reviews as instructed, referring to the chart on page 353.

> **EDITING PARAGRAPHS 1**

Edit the modifiers in the following recruitment section of a police department Web site. Three sentences are correct; write **C** next to them. The first sentence has been edited for you.

1 The Chesterfield County Police Department only exists ^only^ to enforce laws, preserve order, and improve the quality of life within our community. 2 We strive to protect the safety, rights, and property of every person within the county. 3 We work, while holding ourselves to the highest professional and ethical standards, in partnership with our community.

4 Earning praise from state law enforcement agencies, our community agrees that our department's work is professional, reliable, and helpful. 5 We have nearly received a five-star approval rating by our citizens every year for the last ten years.

6 In the past year, Chesterfield County has witnessed tremendous growth. 7 The population almost grew to 150,000. 8 We need to ensure that our police department is fully staffed   for this reason.

9 Qualified candidates are encouraged to submit their applications looking for a career in law enforcement. 10 The starting pay for a Chesterfield Police Officer is $39,102, but new hires who have a college degree in criminal justice will receive a higher salary. 11 Applicants without a high school diploma, when they pass their high school equivalency test,   may apply for a job as patrol officer. 12 Applications may be submitted either online or in persons   for new recruits.

EDITING PARAGRAPHS 2

Edit the modifiers in the following passage. Two sentences are correct; write **C** next to them. The first sentence has been edited for you.

1 Free credit report scams ~~nearly~~ ^nearly^ are everywhere. 2 An ad might give the impression that a certain Web site gives free credit report information on television. 3 Sent directly to your inbox, companies make convincing arguments that your credit score is doomed unless you act fast. 4 The most frustrating thing is that these credit report sites claim to be free.

5 In reality, the federal government has only authorized one site, AnnualCreditReport.com, to provide people with a free credit report each year. 6 The other sites all almost charge a fee to get the "free" report. 7 The unauthorized sites also lure in unsuspecting customers requiring a minimum subscription to their monthly reports.

8 Understanding that many ads are misleading, fraud claims are being investigated by the government. 9 Caused by past credit history, a person cannot adjust a low score just by visiting a Web site. 10 The best things you can do to improve your credit score are paying your bills on time and getting out of debt.

Write and Edit Your Own Work

ASSIGNMENT 1   **Write**

Write about a busy day, using as many modifying word groups as you can. When you are done, use the chart on page 353 to check for misplaced and dangling modifiers. Correct any mistakes that you find.

ASSIGNMENT 2   **Edit**

Using the chart on page 353, edit modifiers in a paper you are writing for this course or another course or in a piece of writing from your work or everyday life.

Chapter Review

1. _____ are words or word groups that describe other words in a sentence.

2. A _____ describes the wrong word or words.

3. Modifiers need to be placed _____ the words they describe.

4. When there is a _____, the word or words that are supposed to be modified are not in the sentence.

5. When you find a dangling modifier, add the word being modified _____ the opening modifier, or add the word being modified _____ _____.

Editing for Misplaced and Dangling Modifiers

A misplaced modifier modifies the wrong sentence element because it is incorrectly placed (see p. 346).

A dangling modifier is an opening word group that modifies an element that is not in the sentence (see p. 349).

Check the modifiers *only, almost, hardly, nearly,* and *just.*

Check opening modifiers, especially phrases and clauses.

Check prepositional phrases.

Check phrases beginning with *-ing* verb forms.

Check clauses beginning with *who, whose, that,* or *which.*

Edit to make sure the sentence element to be modified is in the sentence and is as close as possible to the modifier.

REFLECTING ON THE JOURNEY

Skills Learned

Now that you've completed the chapter, look again at this paragraph.

Hoping to make their streets safer, new crime-fighting programs are being tried by some communities. Community policing links police departments with local community groups, which is one of these new programs. Identifying problems that are most important to the community, goals are set. Working together, the goals are easier to meet. Actively involved with the people in their precincts, the program requires a strong commitment. Often, officers set up programs within neighborhoods. For example, patrolling on foot rather than in cars, a sense of security and community is created.

Using what you've learned in this chapter, edit this paragraph for misplaced and dangling modifiers. Then answer the questions below.

1. Are you confident that you have identified the mistakes?

2. Are you confident that you have corrected the mistakes?

3. What questions do you have about misplaced and dangling modifiers?

20

Illogical Shifts

READING ROADMAP

Learning Objectives

Chapter Goal: Find and correct sentences with confusing shifts in tense and person.

Tools to Achieve the Goal
- Understanding consistent tense (p. 356)
- Understanding consistent person (p. 358)
- Review chart: editing for consistent tense and person (p. 362)

Key Terms

Skim Chapter 20 before you begin reading. Can you find each of these words in **bold** type? Put a check mark next to each word once you have located it in the chapter.

____ tense   ____ second person
____ consistent tense   ____ third person
____ first person   ____ consistent person

Highlight or circle any of these words that you already know.

Before You Read

Before you begin reading this chapter, study the following paragraph and complete the chart. At the end of the chapter, you will examine the paragraph again and reflect on what you have learned.

> As people answer phones, review e-mail messages, and respond to text messages, you become overwhelmed. Many people answer messages while on vacation and worked extra hours on their days off. Even worse, overuse of technology may lower people intelligence quotient (IQ) and damaged their relationships. So it makes sense for people to monitor their use of technology so that you don't have problems in your thinking or your social life.

This paragraph has problems with illogical shifts. Put a check mark by the statement that best describes you.

Skill Statement	
I understand what the mistakes are, and I know how to fix them.	
I understand what the mistakes are, but I am not sure how to fix them.	
I think I understand what the mistakes are.	
I don't understand what the mistakes are.	

Understand Consistent Tense

Tense is the time when an action takes place (past, present, or future). **Consistent tense** means that all verbs in a sentence that describe actions happening at the same time are in the same tense: all in the present, all in the past, or all in the future.

Inconsistent	As soon as the man *climbed* onto the life raft, the shark *leaps* from the water.
	[Both actions (the man's climbing and the shark's leaping) happened at the same time, but *climbed* is in the past tense, and *leaps* is in the present tense.]
Consistent, present tense	As soon as the man *climbs* onto the life raft, the shark *leaps* from the water.
	[The actions and verb tenses are both in the present.]
Consistent, past tense	As soon as the man *climbed* onto the life raft, the shark *leaped* from the water.
	[The actions and verb tenses are both in the past.]

Find and Correct Inconsistent Tenses

Replace the inconsistent verb with a form that is consistent.

Tip To do this chapter, you need to know what subjects and verbs are. For a review, see Chapter 11.

Inconsistent

June *pulled* out of the driveway just as the salesperson *arrives*.
[*Pulled* is in the past tense, but *arrives* is in the present tense.]

Good service *pleases* customers and *was* good for business.
[*Pleases* is in the present tense, but *was* is in the past tense.]

Consistent

Jane *pulled* out of the driveway just as the salesperson *arrived*.
[Both verbs are in the past tense.]

Good service *pleases* customers and *is* good for business.
[Both verbs are in the present tense.]

A common error is not using a *-d* in *used to* and *supposed to*.

Incorrect	I *use to* love peanut butter, but now I hate it.
	[The verb *use* should be in the past tense: *used*.]
Correct	I *used to* love peanut butter, but now I hate it.
Incorrect	John *was suppose to* be here an hour ago.
	[The verb *suppose* should be in the past tense: *supposed*.]
Correct	John *was supposed to* be here an hour ago.

PRACTICE 1

In each of the following sentences, circle the correct verb tense.

1 Although he wanted to be an artist, Rube Goldberg (begins/began) his career as an engineer. 2 After six months, he left his job and (gets/got) a position as an office assistant at a newspaper. 3 In his free time, he drew cartoons and (submits/submitted) them to one of the newspaper's editors. 4 He continued submitting cartoons until the editor finally (agrees/agreed) to publish them. 5 Goldberg quickly gained fame as a sports cartoonist, but a different type of cartoon (becomes/became) his most famous creation. 6 In 1914, he sketched a funny-looking professor and (names/named) him Professor Lucifer Gorgonzola Butts. 7 Goldberg (begins/began) drawing comic strips that featured the professor's crazy inventions. 8 In one strip, for example, Goldberg (draws/drew) an automatic stamp licker consisting of a tiny robot, a bucket of ants, and an anteater. 9 Today, people use the term *Rube Goldberg* to describe any process that (is/was) unnecessarily complicated. 10 Goldberg died in 1970, but fans today still (enjoy/enjoyed) his funny drawings.

PRACTICE 2

In the following paragraph, correct any unnecessary shifts in verb tense. Three sentences are correct; write **C** next to them.

1 The first time I tried skydiving, I was terrified. 2 Even though I knew I was going to be jumping with an instructor, I got more and more nervous as the plane climb to ten thousand feet. 3 The side door was open so that I could see the fields far below me. 4 I think, "Why am I doing this?" 5 When my instructor gave the sign to jump, we leap out together and fell for what seemed like forever. 6 Then, the instructor activates my parachute, and I get pulled up suddenly. 7 After the parachute opened, I begin a graceful and relaxing landing. 8 That was the best part of all.

Understand Consistent Person

Tip For more on pronouns, see pages 175–184 and Chapter 17.

Person is the point of view a writer uses: **first person** (the pronouns *I* or *we*), **second person** (the pronoun *you*), or **third person** (the pronouns *he, she, it,* or *they*). To find out which pronouns go with what person, see the table on page 321.

Consistent person means that the nouns and pronouns stay consistent.

Inconsistent person	When *a customer* comes into the office, *you* cannot tell where the reception area is.
	[The sentence begins with a third-person noun (*a customer*) but shifts to the second person (with the pronoun *you*).]
Consistent person	When *a customer* comes into the office, *he or she* cannot tell where the reception area is.
	[The sentence stays with the third person.]
Consistent person, plural	When *customers* come into the office, *they* cannot tell where the reception area is.
	[The sentence stays with the third person.]

Find and Correct Inconsistent Person

Inconsistent

Every *student* must learn how to manage *your* own time.
[The sentence shifts from third to second person.]

I like to go to crafts fairs because *you* can get good ideas for projects.
[The sentence shifts from first to second person.]

Consistent

Every *student* must learn how to manage *his or her* time.
[The sentence stays in the third person. **Note:** This sentence could also be fixed by making the subject and the pronoun referring to it plural: *Students must learn to manage their own time.*]

I like to go to crafts fairs because *I* can get good ideas for projects.
[The sentence stays in the first person.]

PRACTICE 3

In the following sentences, correct any illogical shifts in person. There may be more than one way to correct some sentences.

Example: Drivers can follow some simple tips to help improve *their* your gas mileage.

1. Whether a person has a new car or an old one, you can still take some steps to save gas.

2. For example, I combine my errands so that you do not have to make a lot of separate trips.

3. A driver should also make sure that their trunk is empty because extra weight causes the car to use more gas.

4. Drivers can save fuel by taking the roof rack off your cars.

5. People should not drive aggressively or fast if you want to improve gas mileage.

6. I have been told to keep your engine tuned.

7. I know that keeping the tires inflated improves your gas mileage.

8. Every driver should read their owner's manual.

9. It tells drivers about correct tire inflation and gasoline quality so that your cars will be cheaper to run.

10. I also learned that changing the air filter regularly can increase your gas mileage by 10 percent or more.

Edit Illogical Shifts in Everyday Life

Complete the editing reviews as instructed, referring to the chart on page 362.

EDITING PARAGRAPHS 1

Edit illogical shifts in the following paragraph, which is similar to one you might find in an anthropology textbook. Two sentences are correct; write **C** next to them. The first sentence has been edited for you.

1 Around ten thousand years ago, early humans ~~learn~~ *learned* how to keep animals and grow crops. 2 Before then, all people were hunter-gatherers, and you survived on wild animals and plants. 3 The men used simple tools to hunt, while the women gather wild fruits, vegetables, honey, and birds' eggs. 4 Although hunter-gatherers moved about in search of food, the area you covered was relatively small. 5 Hunter-gatherer societies typically consisted

of about twenty to fifty people, and tasks are shared by all. 6 In fact, sharing was critical to survival. 7 According to archaeologists, people treat each other equally in hunter-gatherer societies. 8 Today, less than 0.1 percent of the world's population lives in a hunter-gatherer society. 9 When agriculture spread throughout the world, the hunter-gatherer way of life mostly ends. 10 Anthropologists know of a few groups that can still be considered hunter-gatherer societies, but you cannot find many people who are untouched by agriculture and industry.

EDITING PARAGRAPHS 2

Edit illogical shifts in the following paragraph. Outside of the first sentence, which has been marked for you, two sentences are correct; write **C** next to them.

C

1 In a typical marketing exchange, companies sell products, services, or ideas to buyers. 2 For example, an advertising agency might design and sold a logo to a start-up corporation. 3 Automobile manufacturers build cars, and then you sell them to customers. 4 Until the 1980s, many companies were satisfied with these one-time sales, and you did not focus on long-term customer relationships. 5 Today, however, marketing departments want to create repeat customers. 6 Automakers want to sell current customers your next car as well. 7 The ad agency might help the start-up organization place ads on radio and television. 8 When companies and buyers form long-term partnerships, you both benefit.

Write and Edit Your Own Work

ASSIGNMENT 1 **Write**

Look at the photo on the next page. Write about a situation in which you or someone else tries (or tried) to multitask. When you are finished, check the verbs for consistency of tense, and the nouns and pronouns for consistency of person. Use the chart on page 364 as a guide, and correct any mistakes that you find.

© STEVE PREZANT/CORBIS

ASSIGNMENT 2   **Edit**

Using the chart on page 362, edit illogical shifts in a paper that you are writing for this course or another course or in a piece of writing from your work or everyday life.

Chapter Review

1. _____ means that all verbs in a sentence that describe actions happening at the same time are in the same tense.

2. To fix sentences that are inconsistent in tense, replace inconsistent _____ with forms that are consistent.

3. _____ means that the point of view of a piece of writing does not shift without reason.

4. To fix sentences that are inconsistent in person, replace inconsistent _____ so that they are consistent with the nouns they refer to.

Editing for Consistent Tense and Person

↓

Make sure that you have been consistent with verb tenses: Use all past-tense verbs for past-tense actions, and so on (see p. 356).

↓

Make sure that you have been consistent in points of view: Avoid shifts from first to second person, and so on (see p. 358).

↓

Look especially for sentences that use *I* and *you* instead of the correct *I* and *I* (see p. 358).

REFLECTING ON THE JOURNEY

Skills Learned

Now that you've completed the chapter, look again at this paragraph.

> As people answer phones, review e-mail messages, and respond to text messages, you become overwhelmed. Many people answer messages while on vacation and worked extra hours on their days off. Even worse, overuse of technology may lower people intelligence quotient (IQ) and damaged their relationships. So it makes sense for people to monitor their use of technology so that you don't have problems in your thinking or your social life.

Using what you've learned in this chapter, edit this paragraph for illogical shifts. Then answer the questions below.

1. Are you confident that you have identified the mistakes?

2. Are you confident that you have corrected the mistakes?

3. What questions do you have about illogical shifts?

21

Choppy Sentences

READING ROADMAP

Learning Objectives

Chapter Goal: Use coordination and subordination to combine short, choppy sentences.

Tools to Achieve the Goal

- Using coordinating conjunctions (p. 364)
- Using semicolons (p. 367)
- Using subordination (p. 369)
- Review chart: combining choppy sentences (p. 376)

Key Terms

Skim Chapter 21 before you begin reading. Can you find each of these words in **bold** type? Put a check mark next to each word once you have located it in the chapter.

____ coordination
____ coordinating
    conjunction
____ semicolon

____ conjunctive
    adverb
____ subordination

Highlight or circle any of these words that you already know.

Before You Read

Before you begin reading, study the following paragraph and complete the chart. At the end of the chapter, you will examine the paragraph again and reflect on what you have learned.

> I am a good mechanic. My friends bring their cars to me. My best friend's car broke down. She had it towed to my house. I made the repairs. She gave me a giftcard for Best Buy. I am happy to help out when I can. Fixing cars is easy for me.

This paragraph is choppy. Put a check mark by the statement that best describes you.

Skill Statement	
I understand what the problem is, and I know how to fix it.	
I understand what the problem is, but I am not sure how to fix it.	
I think I understand what the problem is.	
I don't understand what the problem is.	

If all your sentences are short, they will seem choppy and hard to read. There are two common ways to combine two short sentences into one longer one: coordination and subordination.

Use Coordination to Join Sentences

LaunchPadSolo

Visit **LaunchPad Solo for Readers and Writers > Coordination and Subordination** for more practice with joining sentences.

In **coordination**, two sentences with closely related ideas are joined into a single sentence, either with a comma and a coordinating conjunction or with a semicolon.

Two sentences, unrelated ideas	It was hot today. My neighbor called to ask me to stay with her baby.
	[These sentences should not be combined because the ideas are not related.]
Two sentences, related ideas	Today, my son got an iPad and a new computer. He is using them right now.
Combined through coordination	Today, my son got an iPad and a new computer, *and* he is using them right now.
	[The sentences are joined with a comma and the coordinating conjunction *and*.]
Combined through coordination	Today, my son got an iPad and a new computer; he is using them right now.
	[The sentences are joined with a semicolon.]

Using Coordinating Conjunctions

One way to join independent clauses (complete sentences) is by using a comma and a **coordinating conjunction**. You can remember the coordinating conjunctions by thinking of *fanboys:* **f**or, **a**nd, **n**or, **b**ut, **o**r, **y**et, **s**o. Do not choose just any conjunction; choose the one that makes the most sense.

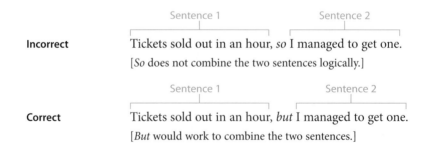

Incorrect   Tickets sold out in an hour, *so* I managed to get one.

[*So* does not combine the two sentences logically.]

Correct   Tickets sold out in an hour, *but* I managed to get one.

[*But* would work to combine the two sentences.]

Here are the meanings of the coordinating conjunctions and more examples of their use:

| Sentence 1 | + | Coordinating conjunction | + | Sentence 2 |

I bought a new car

, and

[*and* = joins two ideas]

I am excited about it.

It took me a long time to make the decision

, but

[*but* = a contrast]

I finally did.

I bought a gas/electric hybrid

, for

[*for* = a reason or cause]

I want to save money on gas.

The car is not expensive

, nor

[*nor* = a negative]

it is fancy.

Either my friends will think the car is great

, or

[*or* = alternative]

they will question my decision.

My friend Lisa is worried about the environment

, so

[*so* = a result]

she will be happy about my news.

My friend Dan does not like hybrids

, yet

[*yet* = a contrast]

how can he argue with saving money and reducing pollution?

Tip To do this chapter, you need to know how compound and complex sentences work. For a review, see Chapter 12.

Two sentences	Joined through coordination
Texting is a great way to stay in touch with friends. It is fun.	Texting is a great way to stay in touch with friends, *and* it is fun.
I wanted to go swimming after work. The pool was closed.	I wanted to go swimming after work, *but* the pool was closed.
You can drive to work with me. You can wait for the bus.	You can drive to work with me, *or* you can wait for the bus.

PRACTICE 1

In each of the following sentences, fill in the blank with an appropriate coordinating conjunction. There may be more than one correct answer for some sentences.

Example: Most workers receive only two to three weeks of vacation a year, ___so___ they choose their vacation destinations carefully.

1. Las Vegas is one of the hottest vacation spots in America, _____ it is

   not just because of the warm, sunny weather.

2. Las Vegas is famous for its casinos, _____ there is more to the city than many people think.

3. You can browse in the many shops, _____ you can relax in a cool swimming pool.

4. Hotel workers will treat you well, _____ they want you to spend your money in their restaurants and gaming areas.

5. You can take a tour to the Hoover Dam, _____ you might prefer to tour the Grand Canyon by helicopter.

6. Good meals are not hard to find, _____ do they have to be expensive.

7. Prime rib buffets start at around $7, _____ they are usually delicious.

8. Casinos compete fiercely for business, _____ they offer free attractions.

9. The MGM Grand Hotel has a lion's den, _____ the Bellagio presents a beautiful fountain show every fifteen minutes in the evenings.

10. Many tourists who visit Las Vegas do not like gambling, _____ they can have a wonderful time there.

PRACTICE 2

Combine each pair of sentences into a single sentence by using a comma and a coordinating conjunction. In some cases, there may be more than one correct answer.

Example: Instructors want students to be creative/ *, but when* When it comes to excuses, they prefer honesty.

1. Teachers hear a variety of interesting excuses. Some are more creative than others.

2. In the past, students claimed that the dog ate their homework. Students now say that the computer ate their file.

3. The due date for a major term paper approaches. Distant relatives die in surprising numbers.

4. The dearly departed grandmother remains one of the most frequently heard excuses. What instructor would be so cruel as to question a student's loss?

5. A noble excuse always sounds good. A student might claim that he had to shovel snow from an elderly neighbor's driveway.

6. Excuses involving animals can hit a soft spot in some instructors' hearts. Caring for a sick puppy would make an excellent excuse.

7. It is always best to be honest about a missed deadline. Students get caught more often than one would think.

8. One student claimed that she was at a funeral. Her professor, who happened to be watching a televised baseball game, saw the student catch a fly ball in the stands.

9. The professor did not accept the funeral excuse. He did not allow the student to make up the missed quiz.

10. As long as there are term papers due, there will be excuses. Many instructors will doubt them.

Using Semicolons

Another method of combining related sentences is to use a **semicolon (;)** between them. Occasional semicolons are fine, but do not overuse them.

Sentence 1	;	Sentence 2
My favorite hobby is bike riding	;	it is the best way to see the country.
It is faster than running but slower than driving	;	that is the prefect speed for me.

A semicolon alone does not tell readers much about how the two ideas are related. Use a **conjunctive adverb** after the semicolon to give more information about the relationship. Put a comma after the conjunctive adverb.

Equal idea + Conjunctive adverb + Equal idea

; afterward,
; also,
; as a result,

Equal idea	+	Conjunctive adverb	+	Equal idea
		; besides,		
		; consequently,		
		; frequently,		
		; however,		
		; in addition,		
		; in fact,		
		; instead,		
		; still,		
		; then,		
		; therefore,		
I ride my bike a lot		; as a result,		I am in good enough shape for a long-distance ride.
My boyfriend wants me to go on a bike tour with him		; however,		I would find that stressful.
I ride my bike to relax		; therefore,		I suggested that he take a friend on the tour.

PRACTICE 3

Join each pair of sentences by using a semicolon alone.

Example: Some foods are not meant to be eaten by themselves, *; macaroni* **Macaroni would be no fun without cheese.**

1. Homemade chocolate chip cookies are delicious. They even better with a glass of cold milk.

2. A hamburger by itself seems incomplete. It needs a pile of fries to be truly satisfying.

3. Fries have another natural partner. Most people like to eat them with ketchup.

4. Apple pie is just apple pie. Add a scoop of vanilla ice cream, and you have an American tradition.

5. A peanut butter sandwich is boring. A little jelly adds some excitement.

PRACTICE 4

Combine each pair of sentences by using a semicolon and a conjunctive adverb. In some cases, there may be more than one correct answer.

Example: Few people manage to survive being lost at sea for more than a
few weeks; however, Steven Callahan is one of those lucky few.

1. In January 1982, Steven Callahan set sail from the Canary Islands in a small homemade boat. The boat sank six days into his journey across the Atlantic.

2. Callahan was an experienced sailor. He was prepared for emergency situations.

3. Alone on a five-foot inflatable raft, he knew his chances for survival were slim. He was determined to live.

4. Callahan had just three pounds of food, eight pints of water, and a makeshift spear. He had a device that changes seawater into drinking water.

5. With his spear, Callahan was able to catch food. He lost a significant amount of weight.

6. Callahan suffered serious sunburn. He had to fight off sharks.

7. Several ships passed Callahan. Nobody on board saw him.

8. His raft sprang a leak thirty-three days before he was rescued. He did not give up hope.

9. For a total of seventy-six days, he drifted alone. Three fishermen found him.

10. Callahan had a tremendous will to live. He never gave up and lived to tell his tale.

Use Subordination to Join Sentences

Like coordination, **subordination** is a way to combine short, choppy sentences with related ideas into a longer sentence. With subordination, you put a dependent word (such as *after, although, because,* or *when*) in front of one of the sentences. The resulting sentence will have one complete sentence and one dependent clause, which is no longer a complete sentence.

Before you join two sentences, make sure they have closely related ideas.

Two sentences, unrelated ideas	I was hospitalized after a car accident. I had a pizza for lunch.
	[These two sentences should not be combined because the ideas are not related.]
Two sentences, related ideas	I was hospitalized after a car accident. My friends showed me how supportive they could be.
Joined through subordination	*When* I was hospitalized after a car accident, my friends showed me how supportive they could be.
	[The dependent word *when* logically combines the two sentences. The underlined word group is a dependent clause, and the second word group is a complete sentence.]

Tip The word *subordinate* means "lower in rank" or "secondary." In the workplace, for example, you are subordinate to your boss. In the army, a private is subordinate to an officer.

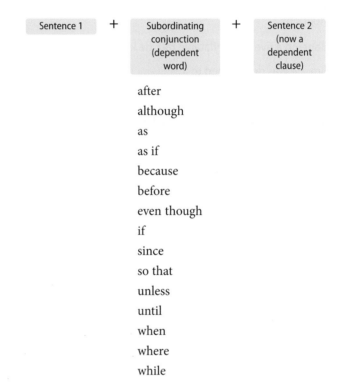

Sentence 1 + Subordinating conjunction (dependent word) + Sentence 2 (now a dependent clause)

after

although

as

as if

because

before

even though

if

since

so that

unless

until

when

where

while

Choose the conjunction that makes the most sense with the two sentences.

Sentence 1

Incorrect   The ducklings are cute (*after, because, before, so that*)

Dependent clause

they misbehave.

[None of these words expresses a logical link between the two sentences.]

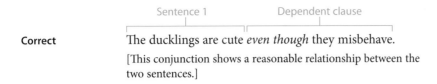

Correct   The ducklings are cute *even though* they misbehave.

[This conjunction shows a reasonable relationship between the two sentences.]

When the *complete sentence* is before the dependent clause, do not use a comma. However, when the *dependent clause* is before the complete sentence, put a comma after it.

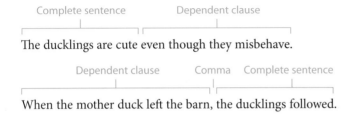

The ducklings are cute even though they misbehave.

When the mother duck left the barn, the ducklings followed.

> **Tip** When you join sentences with subordination, watch out for misplaced and dangling modifiers. See Chapter 19.

Two sentences	Joined through subordination
I raked the entire yard. I was tired.	*After* I raked the entire yard, I was tired.
You must drive with an adult. You have your driver's license.	You must drive with an adult *even though* you have your driver's license.
Patti works overtime. She will make an extra $200 this week.	*If* Patti works overtime, she will make an extra $200 this week.

PRACTICE 5

In the following sentences, fill in the blank with an appropriate subordinating conjunction. In some cases, there may be more than one correct choice.

Example: ___*Although*___ **most people vacation with family or friends, some people prefer traveling alone.**

1. _____ you travel with a group, you must make compromises.

2. For instance, you will not be able to try that inviting Thai restaurant _____ everyone else in the group enjoys Thai food.

3. _____ you can split up for certain activities, it is silly to spend too much time apart on a group vacation.

4. You might also have to endure crankiness _____ travel can make people tired and irritable.

5. _____ you return from a family vacation, you might be more stressed out than you were before you left.

6. _____ you travel alone, you make your own plans and go at your own pace.

7. You can plan your activities _____ the entire vacation suits your own preferences.

8. _____ you spot an interesting shop, you do not have to ask anyone's permission to stop in and browse.

9. Vacationing alone also provides valuable private time _____ you are not distracted by others.

10. _____ family vacations make nice memories, everyone ought to vacation alone every now and then.

PRACTICE 6

Combine each pair of sentences into a single sentence by using an appropriate subordinating conjunction either at the beginning of the first sentence or between the two sentences. In some cases, there may be more than one correct answer.

Example: *Since the* ~~The~~ Toy Industry Association's annual toy fair began in 1903. ~~It~~ *, it* has given toy makers a chance to exhibit their newest products.

1. Hundreds of toy manufacturers from all over the world come to the toy fair in New York City each February. They hope to generate sales.

2. Buyers attend the toy fair to learn about the latest products. They can carry new toys in their stores.

3. Members of the press write about the year's new toys. They attend Toy Fair.

4. Toy Fair visitors are encouraged to touch and try out the toys. A representative explains how it works and why kids will love it.

5. Children are the ones most interested in toys. Only people over age eighteen are allowed to enter Toy Fair.

6. Companies want to attract Toy Fair visitors to their booths. They set up elaborate displays.

7. Marketing reps at one company set up a stage with dancing robots. They could show off their latest inventions.

8. There are more than 100,000 new toys at Toy Fair each year. Only one toy can be chosen "toy of the year."

9. The winning toy is announced. A large crowd gathers to see it for themselves.

10. Toy industry workers must have fun jobs. They do actually have to work at Toy Fair.

Edit for Choppy Sentences in Everyday Life

Complete the editing reviews as instructed, referring to the chart on page 000.

EDITING PARAGRAPHS 1

In the following letter, join the underlined sentences through coordination and subordination.

Ms. Clara Martinez, Director
Personnel Office
Heart's Home Health
22 Juniper Drive
Greenfield, NM 87401

Dear Ms. Martinez:

1 Please consider my application for the Certified Nursing Assistant position advertised in the *Daily Sun* last week. 2 I am currently enrolled in the nursing program at Greenfield College. 3 This job would help me further develop skills in my field while letting me offer my services to your clients. 4 My adviser, Dr. Wes Arrowsmith, praised your organization and encouraged me to apply.

5 In May 2015, I became certified as a nurse's aide through Greenfield College, with 60 hours of work experience at Pine Manor Retirement Home. 6 In my course work and practice, I learned to assist patients with basic

hygiene procedures and meals. 7 I monitored patients' vital signs and reported to the nurse on duty. 8 I worked with these patients for over two months. 9 I understood the true value of health-care work. 10 In addition to my experience and education, my personality also makes me a strong candidate for the position. 11 I bring a smile and a positive attitude to my nursing assistant duties. 12 My cheerful nature makes me a strong team member. 13 Finally, I am fluent in Navajo, English, and Spanish. 14 I would be able to speak with all of your clients and assist staff with translation if needed.

15 My background and qualifications meet your agency's needs. 16 Please contact me anytime at (505) 555-2322. 17 I am very interested in joining the team at Heart's Home Health. 18 I hope to hear from you. 19 Thank you for your time.

Sincerely,

Florence Redhouse

EDITING PARAGRAPHS 2

Join the underlined sentences through coordination and subordination.

1 What did you do to prevent diabetes today? 2 Did your breakfast consist of coffee and a doughnut? 3 Did you skip breakfast altogether? 4 You do not maintain healthy eating habits. 5 You may be headed the way of 8.2 million Americans who have diabetes. 6 This number may seem high. 7 It is actually low compared to the 41 million Americans who have prediabetes, a condition that puts people at risk for developing diabetes in the future. 8 Sadly, many of the hundreds of thousands of diabetes-related deaths each year could be prevented through diet and exercise.

9 The death rate for people with diabetes is twice as high as for those without the disease. 10 Diabetics have two to four times the risk of dying of heart disease or having a stroke. 11 They are fifteen to forty times more likely to have a limb amputated. 12 Yet, with careful management, diabetes can usually be kept under control. 13 People can use the categories of the American Diabetes Association's Diabetes Food Pyramid to select foods by calorie and sugar content. 14 They can plan meals according to their needs and preferences.

15 Healthy lifestyles need to be supported through our mass media.
16 The media have a strong influence in our lives. 17 Advertising should promote a healthy diet instead of sugary, caffeinated sodas and greasy, salty fast foods. 18 Advertising has also promoted the idea that Americans can lose weight without work. 19 The message should be that exercise and a sensible diet are required—and worthwhile.

Write and Edit Your Own Work

ASSIGNMENT 1   Write

What have you done—or what would you like to do—to stay or get healthy? Describe the steps that you have taken or plan to take. When you are done, see if you can join any of the sentences using coordination and subordination. Use the chart on page 000 as a guide.

ASSIGNMENT 2   Edit

Referring to the chart on page 000, use coordination and subordination to join choppy sentences in a paper that you are writing for this course or another course or in a piece of writing from your work or everyday life.

Chapter Review

1. _____ combines two short, related sentences into a longer one.

2. The coordinating conjunctions are _____ .

3. A _____ is a punctuation mark that can join two sentences through coordination.

4. Use a _____ after a semicolon to give more information about the two sentences joined by the semicolon. List four conjunctive adverbs:

   _____

5. _____ are dependent words that join two related sentences. List four subordinating conjunctions: _____

   _____

6. When a dependent clause begins a sentence, use a _____ to separate it from the rest of the sentence.

Combining Choppy Sentences

Coordination joins two sentences with related ideas. There are two ways to join sentences through coordination.

Subordination joins two sentences with related ideas by adding a dependent word (such as *although, because, unless,* or *when*) in front of the sentence with the less important idea. That sentence is now a dependent clause (see p. 369).

1. Use a comma and a coordinating conjunction (see p. 364). The coordinating conjunctions are *for, and, nor, but, or, yet,* and *so* (see p. 365).

2. Use a semicolon (;) or a semicolon and a conjunctive adverb followed by a comma (see p. 367). Some conjunctive adverbs are *also, however, in fact, instead, still, then,* and *therefore* (see pp. 367–368).

If the complete sentence comes before the dependent clause, do not use a comma.

If the dependent clause comes before the complete sentence, add a comma after the dependent clause.

REFLECTING ON THE JOURNEY

Skills Learned

Now that you've completed the chapter, look again at this paragraph.

> I am a good mechanic. My friends bring their cars to me. My best friend's car broke down. She had it towed to my house. I made the repairs. She gave me a giftcard for Best Buy. I am happy to help out when I can. Fixing cars is easy for me.

Using what you've learned in this chapter, revise this paragraph and answer the questions that follow.

1.   Are you confident that you have identified the problem?

2.   Are you confident that you have improved the paragraph?

3.   What questions do you have about coordination and subordination?

22

Parallelism

Learning Objectives

Chapter Goal: Use parallel structures to balance ideas in pairs, lists, and comparisons.

Tools to Achieve the Goal

- Parallelism in pairs and lists (p. 378)
- Parallelism in comparisons (p. 380)
- Parallelism with certain paired words (p. 381)
- Review chart: editing for parallelism (p. 385)

READING ROADMAP

Key Term

Skim Chapter 22 before you begin reading. Can you find this word in **bold** type? Put a check mark next to the word once you have located it in the chapter.

_____ parallelism

Before You Read

Before you begin reading this chapter, study the following paragraph and complete the chart. At the end of the chapter, you will examine the paragraph again and reflect on what you have learned.

> In most divorce cases involving an abusive spouse, visitation rights should be granted only if steps can be taken to protect the safety of both the children and for keeping the abused spouse safe. A judge can make visitation safe by limiting the length of the visits and to not allow overnight stays. Visits should be supervised by a trained, court-appointed individual or an agency could do it. Children should be sheltered from tension, conflict, and not seeing potential violence between parents as much as possible. Unsupervised visits should be allowed only after the abuser has completed a counseling program and he has been maintaining nonviolent relationships for a certain period of time.

This paragraph has problems with parallel structure. Put a check mark by the statement that best describes you.

Skill Statement	
I understand what the mistakes are, and I know how to fix them.	
I understand what the mistakes are, but I am not sure how to fix them.	
I think I understand what the mistakes are.	
I don't understand what the mistakes are.	

Understand What Parallelism Is

(🅐) LaunchPadSolo

Visit **LaunchPad Solo for Readers and Writers > Parallelism** for more practice with parallelism.

Parallelism in writing means that similar parts of a sentence have the same structure: nouns are with nouns, verbs with verbs, and phrases with phrases.

Read the following sentences, emphasizing the underlined parts. Can you hear the problems with parallelism? Can you hear how the corrections help?

Not parallel	Caitlin likes <u>history</u> more than <u>studying math</u>.
	[*History* is a noun, but *studying math* is a phrase.]
Parallel	Caitlin likes <u>history</u> more than <u>math</u>.
Not parallel	The performers <u>sang</u>, <u>danced</u>, and <u>were doing</u> magic tricks.
	[*Were doing* is not in the same form as the other verbs.]
Parallel	The performers <u>sang</u>, <u>danced</u>, and <u>did</u> magic tricks.
Not parallel	I would rather go <u>to my daughter's soccer game</u> than <u>sitting in the town meeting</u>.
	[*To my daughter's soccer game* and *sitting in the town meeting* are both phrases, but they have different forms.]
Parallel	I would rather go <u>to my daughter's soccer game</u> than <u>to the town meeting</u>.

Use Parallel Structure

Parallelism in Pairs and Lists

When two or more items in a series are joined by *and* or *or*, use the same form for each item.

Not parallel	The state fair featured a <u>rodeo</u> and <u>having a pie-eating contest</u>.
	[*Rodeo,* the first of the pair of items, is a noun, so the second item should also be a noun. *Having a pie-eating contest* is more than just a noun, so the pair is not parallel.]
Parallel	The state fair featured a <u>rodeo</u> and a <u>pie-eating contest</u>.
	[*Rodeo* and *pie-eating contest* are both nouns, so they are parallel.]
Not parallel	The neighborhood group picked up trash <u>from deserted property</u>, <u>from parking lots</u>, and <u>they cleaned up the riverbank</u>.
	[The first two underlined items in the list have the same structure (*from . . .*), but the third is different (*they cleaned . . .*).]

Parallel The neighborhood group picked up trash <u>from deserted property</u>, <u>from parking lots</u>, and <u>from the riverbank</u>.

[All items in the list now have the same *from . . .* structure.]

PRACTICE 1

In each sentence, underline the parts of the sentence that should be parallel. Then, edit the sentence to make it parallel.

Example: In 1964, two crew members and five tourists <u>boarded</u> the
                          sailed
SS *Minnow* and <u>were sailing</u> from Hawaii for a three-hour tour.
                    ^

1. On the television comedy *Gilligan's Island,* the title character was sweet, silly and he was clumsy.

2. The Skipper liked Gilligan and was tolerating his clumsiness most of the time.

3. The passengers included a friendly farm girl named Mary Ann and there was a science teacher called Professor.

4. Mary Ann gardened and was a cook.

5. Also on board was Ginger, an actress who liked singing and to perform plays for the castaways.

6. The millionaire Howells continually bragged about their money, education, and owning numerous vacation homes.

7. The seven castaways faced storms, wild animals, and they were attacked by natives of the island.

8. The professor designed inventions to help them escape or making living conditions more comfortable.

9. For three years they tried to escape the island, and for three years they were failing.

10. The show was canceled after three seasons, but reruns have kept *Gilligan's Island* in our homes and it is in our hearts since 1967.

Parallelism in Comparisons

Comparisons often use the words *than* or *as*. To be parallel, the items on either side of the comparison word(s) need to have the same structure. In the examples that follow, the comparison word(s) are circled.

Not parallel	Learning how to play the drums is as hard as the guitar.
Parallel	Learning how to play the drums is as hard as learning how to play the guitar.
Not parallel	Swimming is easier on your joints than a run.
Parallel	Swimming is easier on your joints than running.
Or	A swim is easier on your joints than a run.

To make the parts of a sentence parallel, you may need to add or drop a word or two.

Not parallel	A weekend trip can sometimes be as restful as going on a long vacation.
Parallel, word added	**Taking** a weekend trip can sometimes be as restful as going on a long vacation.
Not parallel	Each month, my bill for day care is more than to pay my rent bill.
Parallel, words dropped	Each month, my bill for day care is more than my rent bill.

PRACTICE 2

In each sentence, circle the comparison words, and underline the parts of the sentence that should be parallel. Then, edit the sentence to make it parallel.

Example: Giving homemade gifts is often better than to buy gifts. *(buying)*

1. To make a gift yourself takes more time than buying one.

2. More thought goes into creating a homemade gift than to buy something at a store.

3. Most people appreciate homemade cookies more than getting a new sweater.

4. They think that making cookies or a loaf of bread is more thoughtful than to buy towels or a tie.

5. Making homemade gifts is generally not as expensive as the purchase of commercial gifts.

6. Homemade gifts send a message that thoughtfulness is better than spending money on an expensive gift.

7. Knitting a scarf will make a better impression than to buy an expensive one.

8. To receive a pretty tin filled with homemade fudge means more to most people than getting an expensive watch or piece of crystal.

9. Of course, sometimes finding a rare book or an antique vase is better than to make a pot holder.

10. Still, most people like a homemade gift more than opening a store-bought one.

Parallelism with Certain Paired Words

When a sentence uses certain paired words, the items joined by these words must be parallel. Here are common ones:

both . . . and	neither . . . nor	rather . . . than
either . . . or	not only . . . but also	

Not parallel	Tasha *both* cuts hair *and* she gives pedicures.
Parallel	Tasha *both* cuts hair *and* gives pedicures.
Not parallel	We would *rather* stay home *than* going dancing.
Parallel	We would *rather* stay home *than* go dancing.

> **PRACTICE 3**
>
> In each sentence, circle the paired words, and underline the parts of the sentence that should be parallel. Then, edit the sentence to make it parallel. You may need to change one of the paired elements to make the sentence parallel.
>
> Example: For our spring break, we wanted either to go camping or
>   to
>   ~~we~~ could go on a cruise.

1. I would rather take a camping trip than to take a cruise.

2. A cruise is not only expensive but also it is crowded with people.

3. My husband and I are neither gamblers nor do we like to sunbathe.

4. Yet, a cruise has both entertaining shows and has top-rated food.

5. Nevertheless, we would rather go to a national park than be partying on a cruise.

6. In the end, however, we decided that staying at home would be both fun and we could relax.

7. As an added bonus, staying at home would not only cost less but also it would be less stressful.

8. We can either relax at our apartment's pool or shopping downtown would be fun.

9. My husband said that he would much rather relax at home than going on a stressful vacation.

10. I think that our plan sounds not only fun but also I think that it is smart.

For each item, add the second part of the word pair, and complete the sentence.

Example: **Having a new kitten in the house is both fun** _____*and exhausting*_____.

1. Our new kitten, Tiger, is not only curious _____.

2. He would rather shred the sofa _____.

3. During the day, we must either lock him in the bedroom _____

   _____.

4. Trying to reason with Tiger is neither effective _____.

5. Still, having Tiger as my new friend is both a joy _____.

Edit for Parallelism in Everyday Life

Complete the editing reviews as instructed, referring to the chart on page 385.

Fix problems with parallelism in the following paragraph, which is similar to one that you might find in a criminal-justice textbook. The first sentence has been marked for you. Aside from this sentence, one other sentence is correct; write **C** next to it.

C
1 Since the 1970s, law enforcement's approach to domestic-violence calls has changed. 2 In the past, police often would neither make arrests nor would they record detailed information on the incident. 3 Resolving a domestic-abuse call commonly involved "cooling off" the abuser by walking him around the block or to talk to him privately. 4 In the late 1970s, however, approaches to partner abuse changed because of research findings and pressure from victims' advocates was increased. 5 Police agencies began to develop policies and programs for dealing with domestic incidents. 6 Today, police who respond to domestic-violence reports usually follow not only formal department guidelines but also there are statewide policies. 7 In some states, the criminal-justice system attempts to protect abuse survivors by pursuing cases even if the alleged victim does not show up in court or is not wanting to press charges. 8 Despite increased training and developing clearer policies, police officers often face unclear situations. 9 For example, when they arrive on the scene, officers may find that the allegedly abusive spouse is absent or discovering that the partner who made the call says that nothing happened. 10 Most officers today would rather record every detail of a domestic incident than risking being charged with failing to enforce domestic-violence laws.

EDITING PARAGRAPHS 2

Fix problems with parallelism in the following memo. The first sentence has been marked for you. Aside from this sentence, two other sentences are correct; write **C** next to them.

Date: August 14, 2015
To: All Employees
From: Glenda Benally, field administrative specialist, Technical Services
Subject: Minutes of employee meeting, August 7, 2015

C
1 Last week, Rhonda Schaeffer, personnel director from the main office, spoke to us about our new domestic-violence policy. 2 Our company is committed to raising awareness of spousal abuse and to provide help for employees who are victims of domestic violence. 3 Rhonda defined domestic violence as abusive behavior between two people in an intimate relationship; it may include physical violence, economic control, emotional intimidation, or verbally abusing someone.

4 Under the new program, Southwestern Oil and Gas will provide free counseling and referrals through the confidential Employee Assistance Program. 5 The company will also offer leave necessary for obtaining medical treatment, attending counseling sessions, or legal assistance. 6 Rhonda also outlined several procedures for the safety and protecting employees in the workplace. 7 She suggested documenting any threatening e-mail or voice-mail messages. 8 Employees who have a restraining order against a partner should keep a copy on hand at work and another copy should be given to the security office.

9 Finally, if you know that a coworker is experiencing domestic violence, please consider asking if he or she would like to talk or you might suggest our counseling resources.

Write and Edit Your Own Work

ASSIGNMENT 1   **Write**

Look at the picture below. The man is getting ready to give a toast to the bride and groom. In his speech, he will talk about his relationship to the bride and groom and his memories of them. He will also express his wishes for them. In a paragraph, write the man's speech. When you are done, check your sentences for parallelism, correcting any mistakes that you find. Use the chart on page 385 as a guide.

© 2/OCEAN/CORBIS

ASSIGNMENT 2   **Edit**

Using the chart below, edit for parallelism a paper you are writing for this course or another course or a piece of writing from your work or everyday life.

Chapter Review

1. _____ in writing means that similar parts of a sentence are balanced by having the same structure.

2. In what three situations do problems with parallelism most often occur? _____

   _____

3. List three paired words that occur in sentences that might not be parallel:

   _____

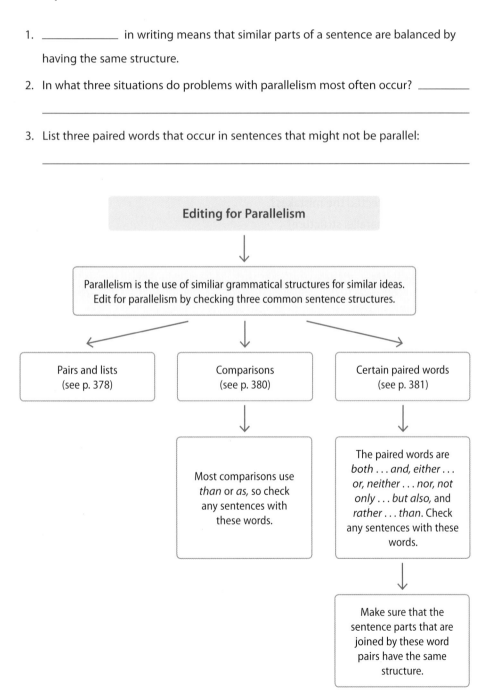

Editing for Parallelism

↓

Parallelism is the use of similiar grammatical structures for similar ideas. Edit for parallelism by checking three common sentence structures.

| Pairs and lists (see p. 378) | Comparisons (see p. 380) | Certain paired words (see p. 381) |

Most comparisons use *than* or *as,* so check any sentences with these words.

The paired words are *both . . . and, either . . . or, neither . . . nor, not only . . . but also,* and *rather . . . than.* Check any sentences with these words.

↓

Make sure that the sentence parts that are joined by these word pairs have the same structure.

REFLECTING ON THE JOURNEY

Skills Learned

Now that you've completed the chapter, look again at this paragraph.

> In most divorce cases involving an abusive spouse, visitation rights should be granted only if steps can be taken to protect the safety of both the children and for keeping the abused spouse safe. A judge can make visitation safe by limiting the length of the visits and to not allow overnight stays. Visits should be supervised by a trained, court-appointed individual or an agency could do it. Children should be sheltered from tension, conflict, and not seeing potential violence between parents as much as possible. Unsupervised visits should be allowed only after the abuser has completed a counseling program and he has been maintaining nonviolent relationships for a certain period of time.

Using what you've learned in this chapter, edit this paragraph for problems in parallel structure. Then answer the questions that follow.

1. Are you confident that you have identified the mistakes?

2. Are you confident that you have corrected the mistakes?

3. What questions do you have about parallel structure?

Part 5

Editing Words in Sentences

23

Word Choice

Learning Objectives

Chapter Goal: Choose the right words for sentences.

Tools to Achieve the Goal

- Dictionary entry (p. 390)
- Thesaurus entry (p. 391)
- Reference chart: vague words (p. 392)
- Example of slang (p. 393)
- Reference chart: common wordy expressions (p. 395)
- Reference chart: common clichés (p. 397)
- Review chart: editing for word choice (p. 400)

READING ROADMAP

Key Terms

Skim Chapter 23 before you begin reading. Can you find these words in **bold** type? Put a check mark next to each word once you have located it in the chapter.

_____ vague words _____ clichés
_____ slang

Highlight or circle any of these words that you already know.

Before You Read

Study the following paragraph and complete the chart on page 390. At the end of the chapter, you will examine the paragraph again and reflect on what you have learned.

> The tradition of the Olympic torch relay is really cool. The ancient Greeks used fire in their religious ceremonies and stuff, so it makes sense that they always had a flame burning in front of major temples. In Olympia, where the ancient games took place, the people lit extra flames during the games due to the fact that it was a pretty important event. The torch relay, though, is a modern thing. Several months before the start of the games, relay runners carry the torch from Olympia to the host city for the games that year. The host countries usually pick famous dudes to carry the torch, because it's a big deal for the country. The fact of the matter is that most of us are into the whole Olympic spirit, and we love watching the torch get to the games.

This paragraph has problems with word choice. Put a check mark by the statement that best describes you.

Skill Statement	
I understand what the problems are, and I know how to fix them.	
I understand what the problems are, but I am not sure how to fix them.	
I think I understand what the problems are.	
I don't understand what the problems are.	

Understand the Importance of Choosing Words Carefully

When you talk with others, you show what you mean by the look on your face, your tone of voice, and your gestures. In writing, however, you have only the words on the page to make your point, so you must choose them carefully.

Two important tools will help you find the best words for your meaning: a dictionary and a thesaurus.

Dictionary

You need a dictionary, whether in traditional book form or in an electronic format. For not much money, you can get a good one that has all kinds of useful information about words: spelling, division of words into syllables, pronunciation, parts of speech, other forms of words, definitions, and examples of use.

The following is a part of a dictionary entry:

Tip For online help with words, visit Merriam-Webster Online at **www.m-w.com**. You can use this site's dictionary and thesaurus features to look up words.

Spelling and end-of-line division   Pronunciation   Definition   Example   Parts of speech   Other forms

con • crete (kon'-krēt, kong'-krēt, kon-krēt', kong-kreēt'), *adj., n., v.* **-cret • ed, -cret • ing,** *adj.* **1.** constituting an actual thing or instance; real; perceptible; substantial: *concrete proof.* **2.** pertaining to or concerned with realities or actual instances rather than abstractions; particular as opposed to general: *concrete proposals.* **3.** referring to an actual substance or thing, as opposed to an abstract quality: The words *cat, water,* and *teacher* are concrete, whereas the words *truth, excellence,* and *adulthood* are abstract. . . .

—*Random House Webster's College Dictionary*

PRACTICE 1

Look up the following terms from this chapter in a dictionary. Then, in the blank following each word, write a brief definition.

1. synonym _____

2. vague _____

3. concrete _____

   _____

4. slang _____

5. wordy _____

6. cliché _____

Thesaurus

A thesaurus gives synonyms (words that have the same meaning) for the words you look up. Like dictionaries, thesauruses come in inexpensive and even electronic editions. Use a thesaurus when you cannot find the right word for what you mean. Be careful, however, to choose a word that has the meaning you intend. If you are not sure how a word should be used, look it up in the dictionary.

Concrete, *adj.* 1. Particular, specific, single, certain, special, unique, sole, peculiar, individual, separate, isolated, distinct, exact, precise, direct, strict, minute; definite, plain, evident, obvious; pointed, emphasized; restrictive, limiting, limited, well-defined, clear-cut, fixed, finite; determining, conclusive, decided.

—J. I. Rodale, *The Synonym Finder*

 Language note: Make sure to use the right kinds of words in sentences: Use a noun for a person, place, or thing. Use an adjective when you want to describe a noun.

Incorrect	Everyone in the world wants happy.
	[*Happy* is an adjective, but a noun is needed in this case.]
	Smoking is not health.
	[*Health* is a noun, but an adjective is needed in this case.]
Correct	Everyone in the world wants **happiness**.
	Smoking is not **healthful**.

Avoid Four Common Word-Choice Problems

Four common problems with word choice—vague words, slang, wordy language, and clichés—can make it difficult for readers to understand you.

Vague Words

Your words need to create a clear picture for your readers. **Vague words** are too general to make an impression. The following are some common vague words.

Vague Words

a lot	dumb	old	very
amazing	good	pretty	whatever
awesome	great	sad	young
bad	happy	small	
beautiful	nice	terrible	
big	OK (okay)	thing	

When you see one of these words or another general word in your writing, try to replace it with a concrete, or more specific, word. A concrete word names something that can be seen, heard, felt, tasted, or smelled.

Vague	The cookies were good.
Concrete	The cookies were warm, chewy, and sweet and had a rich, buttery taste.

The first version is too general. The second version creates a clear, strong impression.

PRACTICE 2

In the following sentences, cross out any vague words. Then, edit each sentence by replacing the vague words with concrete ones. You may invent any details you like.

Springfield State College   sensible   that will have lifelong benefits.
Example: **My school is a good choice for me.**
              ^   ^   ^

1. It offers a lot of programs and whatever.

2. The teachers are OK.

3. My academic adviser is really nice.

4. The campus is pretty.

5. My commute is great.

6. The awesome dining hall has many various foods.

7. The tuition is very low, so the school is a good value.

8. They have a really good career center with amazing counselors to help you find a great job.

9. The class schedules are very flexible, which is good.

10. This school makes me very happy.

Slang

Slang, informal language, and the abbreviations of text messaging should be used only in casual situations. Avoid them when you write for college classes or at work.

Slang

I *wanna hang out* with you this weekend.

Dude, time to leave.

Sasha showed off her *bling* at the party.

This cell phone is *busted.*

Edited

I *would like to spend time* with you this weekend.

Joe [or whoever], it is time to leave.

Sasha showed off her *jewelry* at the party.

This cell phone is *broken.*

Imagine that you are a human resources officer who must hire someone for a customer-service position. The person you hire must communicate clearly and professionally. Read the following e-mail from a candidate for the job. What impression does it give you of the writer?

Dude,
I got the 411 on this gig from the local rag. I'm the man for the job, no doubt. Customer service is my game—I've been doin' it for five years. Drop me a line or you'll lose out big-time.

Later,
Bart Bederman

PRACTICE 3

In the following sentences, cross out any slang words. Then, edit the sentences by replacing the slang with language appropriate for a formal audience and purpose. Imagine that you are writing to your landlord.

concern

Example: **I have a beef about the condition of my apartment.**
⌃

1. I am bummed about the kitchen.

2. I am creeped out by the mouse that lives under the refrigerator.

3. The previous tenant trashed the dishwasher, and the rinse cycle does not work.

4. The inside of the refrigerator is covered in gross green and black stains.

5. It would be cool if you could correct these problems.

6. I am also not down with the bathroom.

7. The mildew stains in the shower really freak me out.

8. I would give you mad props if you would fix the leaky faucets.

9. I hope it does not tick you off that I would like these problems taken care of as soon as possible.

10. I would be psyched if you could stop by and talk to me about these issues.

Wordy Language

Wordy language contains unnecessary words. Sometimes, people think that using big words or writing long sentences will make them sound smart and important. However, using too many words in a piece of writing can make the point weaker or harder to find.

Wordy	*A great number of* students complained about the long registration lines.
Edited	*Many* students complained about the long registration lines.
Wordy	*Due to the fact that* we arrived late to the meeting, we missed the first speaker.
Edited	*Because* we arrived late to the meeting, we missed the first speaker.
Wordy	We cannot buy a car *at this point in time.*
Edited	We cannot buy a car *now.*

Sometimes, sentences are wordy because some words in them repeat others, as in the italicized parts of the first sentence below.

Repetitive   Our dog is *hyper* and *overactive.*

Edited   Our dog is hyper.

Common Wordy Expressions

Wordy	Edited
As a result of	Because
Due to the fact that	Because
In spite of the fact that	Although
It is my opinion that	I think (or just make the point)
In the event that	If
The fact of the matter is that	(Just state the point.)
A great number of	Many
At that time	Then
In this day and age	Now, Nowadays
At this point in time	Now
In this paper I will show that . . .	(Just make the point; do not announce it.)

PRACTICE 4

In the following sentences, cross out the wordy or repetitive language. Then, edit each sentence to make it more concise. Some sentences may contain more than one wordy phrase.

Example: **In this day and age,** one of the most popular and commonly
watched types of television shows is the reality show.
Today,

1. A great number of people are of the opinion that some reality shows do well because they allow the watchers to feel good about their own lives.

2. They let us see that movie stars who are aging and housewives who are wealthy are not perfect.

3. It is my opinion that people watching the show temporarily forget about their own mundane problems for a little while.

4. Other reality shows are exciting competitions to see who can be the contestant who is the most successful.

5. The main concentration of the show is usually focused on a specific topic such as health, business, cooking, or singing.

6. Due to the fact that they are competitive, these reality shows allow watchers to root for or cheer on their favorite contestants.

7. In spite of the fact that they can be entertaining, some reality shows are just plain cruel.

8. It is an unfortunate actuality that they focus on people who have problems such as hoarding, drug addiction, or bad parenting skills.

9. In these shows, a great number of subjects are not cured at the end of the episode.

10. The fact of the matter is that reality shows can be funny, exciting, or depressing, but they all usually let you forget about your own life for a little while.

Clichés

Clichés are phrases that have been used so often that people no longer pay attention to them. To make your point clearly and to get your readers' attention, replace clichés with fresh, specific language.

Clichés

June *works like a dog.*

This dinner roll is *as hard as a rock.*

Edited

June works at least sixty hours every week.

This dinner roll would make a good baseball.

PRACTICE 5

In the following sentences, cross out the clichés. Then, edit each sentence by replacing the clichés with fresh language that precisely expresses your meaning.

Example: For every person who has his or her dream job, there are a dozen other people who are ~~green with envy.~~
envious

1. Are you stuck in a rut in your current job?

2. Perhaps you work like a dog but dislike what you do.

3. You might think that dream jobs are few and far between.

Common Clichés

as big as a house	no way on earth
better late than never	110 percent
break the ice	playing with fire
the corporate ladder	raining cats and dogs
crystal clear	spoiled brat
a drop in the bucket	spoiled rotten
easier said than done	starting from scratch
as hard as a rock	sweating blood (or bullets)
hell on earth	24 / 7
last but not least	work like a dog
as light as a feather	worked his or her way up the ladder

Tip Search online for lists of common clichés to avoid.

4. Finding your dream job, however, can be as easy as pie if you take the right approach.

5. Find a skill that you enjoy using and that is near and dear to your heart.

6. Maybe you can write songs that tug at the heartstrings.

7. Maybe your investigative skills leave no stone unturned.

8. Seek education and experience so that you can be the best that you can be.

9. Changing jobs may seem like playing with fire.

10. You might have to start from scratch, but getting your dream job is worth that effort.

A final note: Language that favors one gender over another or that assumes that only one gender performs a certain role is called *sexist*. Avoid such language.

Sexist

A doctor should politely answer *his* patients' questions.
[Not all doctors are male.]

Revised

A doctor should politely answer *his or her* patients' questions.

Doctors should politely answer *their* patients' questions.

[The first revision changes *his* to *his or her* to avoid sexism. The second revision changes the subject to a plural noun (*Doctors*) so that a genderless pronoun (*their*) can be used.]

Tip See Chapter 17 for more advice on using pronouns.

Edit for Word Choice in Everyday Life

Complete the editing reviews as instructed, referring to the chart on page 400.

EDITING PARAGRAPHS 1

Edit the following paragraph, a student's response to an essay-exam question, for word choice. Two sentences are correct; write **C** next to them. The first sentence has been edited for you.

1 In the past few years, carbohydrates have ~~gotten a lot of flak from~~ the *been criticized by* media. 2 Popular diets made us believe that carbohydrates were really bad. 3 Some people decided that there was no way on earth they would ever eat pasta again. 4 Lately, however, a great number of dieters have changed their minds. 5 Carbohydrates are starting to be recognized as an important part of a healthy diet because they are the main source of energy for humans. 6 Current research demonstrates that while too many carbohydrates can be bad news, eliminating them completely is not wise. 7 The fact of the matter is that people should include healthy carbohydrates such as fruits, vegetables, and whole grains in their daily diets. 8 The overall key to good nutrition is eating balanced meals. 9 It is my opinion that people can eat many types of foods as long as they do so in moderation. 10 Maintaining a proper diet is easier said than done, but being fit as a fiddle is worth the work.

EDITING PARAGRAPHS 2

Edit the following business memo for word choice. One sentence is correct; write **C** next to it. The first sentence has been edited for you.

DATE: February 27, 2015
TO: All employees
FROM: Jason Connors
SUBJECT: Overtime pay

1 It has come to my attention that some employees are ~~wigging out~~ *upset* about a lack of overtime hours. 2 Although I have covered this information in

previous memos, I will attempt to do so again. 3 I hope this memo will make it crystal clear how overtime hours are assigned.

4 Each month, two to five employees are asked to pull one all-nighter. 5 I rotate the names so that no one will become too beat. 6 If an employee cannot work overtime at that point in time, I move to the next name on the list, and that employee must wait until the rotation reaches his or her name again. 7 It is my opinion that this is an effective technique; it has worked great for some time.

8 I work like crazy to make sure that each employee has a chance to earn overtime at least twice a year. 9 I hope that we all agree about the fact that this policy is okay. 10 Please speak with me in the event that you have any further questions about overtime.

Write and Edit Your Own Work

ASSIGNMENT 1   **Write**

Write about a time when you had to choose your words carefully—for example, when having a tough conversation with a friend or coworker, when explaining something difficult to a child, or when breaking up an argument. When you are done, edit your writing for vague words, slang, wordiness, and clichés, referring to the chart on page 400.

ASSIGNMENT 2   **Edit**

Using the chart on the next page, edit for word choice a paper that you are writing for this course or another course or a piece of writing from your work or everyday life.

Chapter Review

1. What two tools will help you choose the best words for your meaning?

   _____

2. When you see a _____ word in your writing, replace it with a concrete, or more specific, word.

3. _____ should be used only in informal and casual situations.

4. _____ language uses words when they are not necessary.

5. _____ are phrases used so often that people no longer pay attention to them.

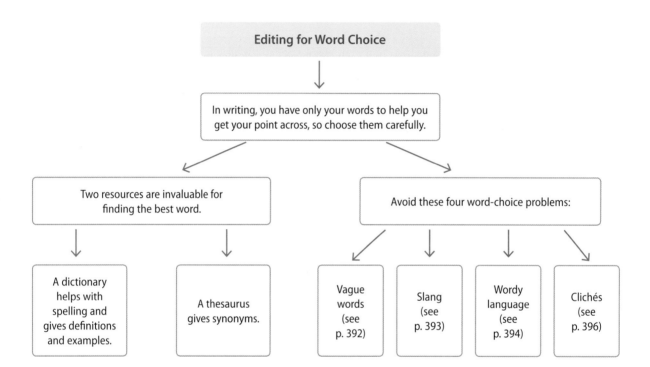

REFLECTING ON THE JOURNEY

Skills Learned

Now that you've completed the chapter, look again at this paragraph.

> The tradition of the Olympic torch relay is really cool. The ancient Greeks used fire in their religious ceremonies and stuff, so it makes sense that they always had a flame burning in front of major temples. In Olympia, where the ancient games took place, the people lit extra flames during the games due to the fact that it was a pretty important event. The torch relay, though, is a modern thing. Several months before the start of the games, relay runners carry the torch from Olympia to the host city for the games that year. The host countries usually pick famous dudes to carry the torch, because it's a big deal for the country. The fact of the matter is that most of us are into the whole Olympic spirit, and we love watching the torch get to the games.

Using what you've learned in this chapter, edit this paragraph for word choice. Then answer the questions below.

1. Are you confident that you have identified the problems?

2. Are you confident that you have corrected the problems?

3. What questions do you have about word choice?

24

Commonly Confused Words

READING ROADMAP

Learning Objectives

Chapter Goal: Choose correctly between commonly confused words.

Tools to Achieve the Goal
- Editing strategies (p. 403)
- Reference list of commonly confused words (pp. 403-411)

Key Terms

Skim Chapter 24 before you begin reading. Can you find these words in **bold** type? Put a check mark next to each word once you have located it in the chapter.

_____ proofread   _____ soundalike words
_____ dictionary

Highlight or circle any of these words that you already know.

Before You Read

Before you begin reading this chapter, study the following paragraph and complete the chart. At the end of the chapter, you will examine the paragraph again and reflect on what you have learned.

> I hope that you are ready to take this test. Please follow this advise carefully. Your sure to do well if you do. As you look threw the questions, keep in mine that there is only one right answer to each. Take the time to read every question before answering it. It's easy to miss an word here and there. In the passed, students have rushed through the test and regretted it. You are allowed the full class hour to complete the test. Use that time well, and you cannot loose. I no you will do well.

This paragraph has problems with commonly confused words. Put a check mark by the statement that best describes you.

Skill Statement	
I understand what the mistakes are, and I know how to fix them.	
I understand what the mistakes are, but I am not sure how to fix them.	
I think I understand what the mistakes are.	
I don't understand what the mistakes are.	

Understand Strategies for Editing Soundalike Words

Certain words in English are confusing because they sound alike and may have similar meanings. In writing, words that sound alike may be spelled differently, and readers rely on the spelling to understand what you mean. Edit your writing carefully to make sure that you have used the correct words.

1. **Proofread carefully.** Use the techniques discussed on pages 416–417.
2. **Use a dictionary** to look up words and check their meanings.
3. **Find and correct mistakes** that you make with the twenty-seven sets of commonly confused words discussed in this chapter.
4. **Develop a personal list of soundalike words that confuse you.** Before you turn in any piece of writing, consult your personal list to make sure that you have used the correct words.

Use Commonly Confused Words Correctly

Study the different meanings and spellings of the following twenty-seven sets of commonly confused words. Complete the sentence after each set of words, filling in each blank with the correct word.

A/AN/AND

> **a:** a word used before a word that begins with a consonant sound (article)
>
>> *A* large brown bear pawed the tent.
>
> **an:** a word used before a word that begins with a vowel sound (article)
>
>> *An* egg on toast is delicious for breakfast.
>
> **and:** a word used to join two words (conjunction)
>
>> Patrice *and* Dylan dated for three months.
>
>> In my favorite children's poem, *an* owl *and* a pussy-cat floated in *a* boat.

You will find _____ job if you have _____ impressive résumé _____ good personal skills.

Tip The vowels in the alphabet are *a, e, i, o, u,* and sometimes *y*. All other letters are consonants.

ACCEPT/EXCEPT

> **accept:** to agree to receive or admit (verb)
>
>> Please *accept* my sincere apology.
>
> **except:** but, other than (preposition)
>
>> I like all the songs on this CD *except* the last one.
>
>> The store will *accept* all credit cards *except* the one that I am carrying.

I cannot _____ the fact that I can use my card at every store _____

my favorite ones.

ADVICE/ADVISE

advice: opinion (noun)

> Can you give me some *advice* about which course to take?

advise: to give an opinion (verb)

> A park ranger *advised* us not to approach wild animals.

> Grandma *advised* us girls to wear dresses to the concert; her *advice* is sweet but old-fashioned.

You might think that my _____ is wrong, but I _____ you to listen

to me.

Tip To understand this chapter, you will need to know what nouns, verbs, adjectives, adverbs, and prepositions are. For a review, see Chapter 10.

AFFECT/EFFECT

affect: to make an impact on, to change something (verb)

> The rising gas prices will *affect* our vacation plans.

effect: a result (noun)

> The drought will have an *effect* on the citrus crop.

> The new retirement policy will *affect* all future employees, but it will have no *effect* on current employees.

The realistic special _____ in the war film deeply _____ the

audience.

ARE/OUR

are: exist (a form of the verb *be*)

> Those yellow roses *are* beautiful.

our: a word used to show ownership (adjective)

> Have you seen *our* new car?

> *Are* you interested in seeing *our* vacation pictures?

_____ new cats _____ shredding our furniture.

BY/BUY

by: next to, before (preposition)

> My trusty dog walks *by* my side.

> I must finish my essay *by* Tuesday.

buy: to purchase (verb)

I need to *buy* a new washing machine.

By the time I was eighteen, I was living on my own and saving to *buy* a new car.

We are required to _____ our textbooks _____ the second day of class.

CONSCIENCE/CONSCIOUS

conscience: a personal sense of right and wrong (noun)

Tiffany's *conscience* made her turn in the wallet she found.

conscious: awake, aware (adjective)

I became *conscious* of a steadily increasing rattle in my car.

We cannot sell this product in good *conscience* since we are quite *conscious* that it is addictive.

The detectives were _____ of the fact that the suspect's _____

was bothering her.

Tip Remember that one of the words is *con-science;* the other is not.

FINE/FIND

fine: of high quality (adjective); feeling well (adverb); a penalty for breaking a law (noun)

Charles and Marilyn received a set of *fine* china as a wedding gift.

Mandy had only three hours of sleep, but she feels *fine.*

If you park in the faculty parking lot, expect a $10 *fine.*

find: to locate, to discover (verb)

I need to *find* my car keys.

Did you *find* the book interesting?

I *find* that my grandmother's *fine* wood furniture looks great in my house.

Ahmand did not _____ the rented DVD until yesterday, so he had to pay a

_____ when he returned it.

ITS/IT'S

its: a word used to show ownership (possesive pronoun)

The jury has reached *its* verdict.

it's: a contraction of the words *it* (pronoun) and *is* (verb)

Did you know that *it's* snowing outside?

It's clear that the dog has injured *its* paw.

_____ difficult to forecast the track of a hurricane because of _____

unpredictable nature.

Tip If you are not sure whether to use *its* or *it's* in a sentence, try substituting *it is.* If the sentence does not make sense with *it is,* use *its.*

KNEW/NEW/KNOW/NO

knew: understood, recognized (past tense of the verb *know*)

I *knew* you would get the job.

new: unused, recent, or just introduced (adjective)

I think Jill has a *new* boyfriend.

know: to understand, to have knowledge of (verb)

Do you *know* how to operate this DVD player?

no: a word used to form a negative (adverb or adjective)

We have *no* more eggs.

I *know* that *no* job is too hard for this *new* employee.

I _____ that _____ faculty members would receive _____ computers

this year. Didn't you _____ that?

LOOSE/LOSE

loose: baggy, relaxed, not fixed in place (adjective)

The handle on this frying pan is *loose*.

lose: to misplace, to give up possession of (verb); to be defeated (verb)

I *lose* my mittens every winter.

Are we going to *lose* the game?

You will *lose* your trousers if your belt is too *loose*.

If your pet lizard gets _____ from its cage, you might _____ it forever.

MIND/MINE

mind: to object to (verb); the thinking or feeling part of the brain (noun)

Do you *mind* if I change the TV channel?

I wanted to be a rock star, but I have changed my *mind*.

mine: belonging to me (pronoun); a source of ore and minerals (noun)

I am afraid that the ringing cell phone is *mine*.

We visited an abandoned silver *mine* in Colorado.

The boss does not *mind* if I hire a friend of *mine* to clean our offices.

Enrique has made up his *mind* to move to Alaska and take over his grandfather's gold *mine*.

Do you _____ if I take that pen back from you? It is _____ .

OF/HAVE

of: coming from, caused by, part of a group, made from (preposition)

One *of* the puppies is already weaned.

have: to possess (verb; also used as a helping verb)

> We *have* two dogwood trees in our backyard.

> You could *have* bought that computer for a lower price across town.

> Three *of* our best basketball players *have* quit the team.

We should _____ asked one _____ the security guards for directions.

Tip Do not use *of* after *could, would, should,* or *might.* Use *have* after those words.

PASSED/PAST

passed: went by, went ahead (past tense of the verb *pass*)

> We *passed* several slow-moving cars on the country road.

past: time that has gone by (noun); earlier (adjective); gone by, over, just beyond (preposition)

> My grandparents often talked about the *past*.

> Jim has been an engineer for the *past* six years.

> We accidentally drove right *past* our exit.

> As we drove *past* the historic settlement, we felt that we had *passed* into a different era—the *past*.

The speeding car _____ us on the right and then zoomed _____ a

parked police car. It was the third speeder that we had seen in the _____

week. Drivers did not speed as much in the _____.

PEACE/PIECE

peace: a lack of disagreement, calm (noun)

> The *peace* was disrupted when the cat attacked the dog.

piece: a part of something larger (noun)

> All I had for breakfast was a *piece* of toast.

> After that *piece* of chocolate fudge cake, I felt completely at *peace*.

Two signatures on a single _____ of paper began a new era of _____

between the two lands.

PRINCIPAL/PRINCIPLE

principal: main (adjective); the head of a school or leader in an organization (noun)

> The *principal* cause of the fire is still unknown.

> Nobody likes to be summoned to the *principal's* office.

> The request must be approved by a *principal* in the regional office.

principle: a standard of beliefs or behaviors (noun)

> Her decision was based on strong moral *principles*.

We are seeking someone with high *principles* to be the next *principal.*

The _____ reason for the building's collapse is a simple _____ of physics.

QUIET/QUITE/QUIT

quiet: soft in sound, not noisy (adjective)

The children, for once, were *quiet.*

quite: completely, very (adverb)

It is *quite* foggy outside.

quit: to stop (verb)

Kenneth finally *quit* the band.

After the birds *quit* singing, the forest grew *quiet* and *quite* eerie.

The mayor is _____ right; even if she _____ her job, her critics will not be _____ .

RIGHT/WRITE

right: correct (adjective); in a direction opposite from left (noun)

The *right* job is not easy to find.

His office is two doors down the hall on the *right.*

write: to put words on paper (verb)

You must *write* your name and address clearly.

Now is the *right* time to *write* your résumé.

Do you see the blue box to the _____ of your name? That is the _____ place to _____ your job preference.

SET/SIT

set: a collection of something (noun); to place an object somewhere (verb)

What am I going to do with my old *set* of encyclopedias?

Please *set* those groceries on the counter.

sit: to be supported by a chair or other surface (verb)

I wish those children would *sit* down and be quiet.

Set down that broom. Will you *sit* down and choose a *set* of dishes for Felicia's wedding gift?

If we _____ the television on the top shelf, we can _____ on the sofa and see the screen clearly. We also need a _____ of good speakers.

SUPPOSE/SUPPOSED

suppose: to imagine or assume to be true (verb)

I *suppose* you are right.

Do you *suppose* that Jared has a girlfriend?

supposed: intended (past tense and past participle of the verb *suppose*)

We *supposed* that you had simply forgotten Chad's birthday.

I am *supposed* to leave by 6:00 p.m.

Suppose you lost your job. Who is *supposed* to pay your bills?

I do not think that we are _____ to leave those candles burning.

_____ they catch something on fire?

THAN/THEN

than: a word used to compare two or more things or persons (preposition)

Cooper is a stronger bicyclist *than* Mitchell is.

He likes apples more *than* peaches.

then: at a certain time, next in time (adverb)

First, I was late to class; *then,* my cell phone rang during the lecture.

Back *then,* I was happier *than* I am now.

If you score higher _____ 90 percent on your exam, you are _____ ready

to move on to the next course.

THEIR/THERE/THEY'RE

their: a word used to show ownership (possessive pronoun)

My grandparents have sold *their* boat.

there: a word indicating existence (pronoun) or location (adverb)

There are four new kittens over *there.*

they're: a contraction of the words *they* (pronoun) and *are* (verb)

They're good friends of mine.

There is proof that *they're* stealing from *their* neighbors.

We stopped by _____ house, but apparently _____ no longer living

_____ .

Tip If you are not sure whether to use *their* or *they're,* substitute *they are.* If the sentence does not make sense, use *their.*

THOUGH/THROUGH/THREW

though: however, nevertheless, in spite of (conjunction)

I bought the computer *though* it seemed overpriced.

through: finished with (adjective); from one side to the other (preposition)

After you are *through* with the computer, may I use it?

The tornado passed *through* the north side of town.

threw: hurled, tossed (past tense of the verb *throw*)

Elena *threw* her worn-out socks into the trash can.

Though Zak *threw* well in his last baseball game, he said he was *through* with baseball.

_____ Shawn is usually calm, he _____ his alarm clock against the wall when he realized that it did not go off. He had slept _____ his eight o'clock class.

TO/TOO/TWO

to: a word indicating a direction or movement (preposition); part of the infinitive form of a verb

We are driving *to* Denver tomorrow.

I tried *to* ride my bicycle up that hill.

too: also, more than enough, very (adverb)

I like chocolate *too*.

Our steaks were cooked *too* much.

That storm came *too* close to us.

two: the number between one and three (adjective)

Marcia gets *two* weeks of vacation a year.

We are simply *too* tired *to* drive for *two* more hours.

If we wait even _____ more minutes for Gail, we will arrive at the dock

_____ late _____ catch the early ferry.

USE/USED

use: to employ or put into service (verb)

Are you going to *use* that computer?

used: past tense of the verb *use*. *Used to* can indicate a past fact or state, or it can mean "familiar with."

Mother *used* a butter knife as a screwdriver.

Marcus *used to* play baseball for a minor league team.

I am not *used to* traveling in small airplanes.

You can *use* my truck if you are *used to* driving a standard transmission.

I _____ hem my pants with duct tape because it is easy to _____ ;

however, I have grown _____ repairing my clothes with a needle and thread.

WHO'S/WHOSE

who's: a contraction of the words *who is* or *who has* (pronoun and verb)

May I tell her *who's* calling?

Who's been eating my cereal?

whose: a word showing ownership (possessive pronoun)

I do not know *whose* music I like best.

Whose car is parked in my flower bed? *Who's* responsible for this crime?

I do not know _____ supposed to work this shift, but we can check to see

_____ name is on the schedule.

> **Tip** If you are not sure whether to use *whose* or *who's,* substitute *who is*. If the sentence does not make sense, use *whose*.

YOUR/YOU'RE

your: a word showing ownership (possessive pronoun)

Is this *your* dog?

you're: a contraction of the words *you* (pronoun) and *are* (verb)

I hope *you're* coming to Deb's party tonight.

You're bringing *your* girlfriend to the company picnic, aren't you?

I think _____ right; _____ bingo card is a winner.

> **Tip** If you are not sure whether to use *your* or *you're,* substitute *you are*. If the sentence does not make sense, use *your*.

Edit Commonly Confused Words in Everyday Life

EDITING PARAGRAPHS 1

Edit misused words in the following excerpt from a career-center brochure. Each sentence has one error; the first sentence has been edited for you.

1 Is a career in criminal justice ~~write~~ *right* for you? 2 The first thing to understand is that there are three principle levels of law enforcement: local, state, and federal. 3 Local officers enforce state and local laws within there city or county. 4 State law enforcement agents include state police, who's duties are chiefly investigative, and state troopers, who enforce state laws on highways. 5 In most cases, a person needs an associate's degree too work as either a local or state police officer. 6 Federal law enforcement agents include Secret Service agents an FBI agents. 7 Federal jobs can take longer to get then state and local jobs, and they usually require a bachelor's degree. 8 Most law enforcement jobs have great pay, good benefits, and excellent job security, but these careers our not for everyone. 9 All officers must perform difficult tasks, and they constantly see people at they're worst. 10 However, if your

self-motivated and want to make a difference in people's lives, a career in law enforcement may be for you.

EDITING PARAGRAPHS 2

Edit misused words in the following essay. Two sentences are correct; write **C** next to them. The first sentence has been edited for you.

1 Mars in the springtime is not the most pleasant place ~~too~~ ^{to} be. 2 Daytime temperatures may be 68 degrees Fahrenheit, but nighttime temperatures are much lower then on Earth, sometimes dropping to 130 degrees below zero. 3 The fun does not stop their, however.

4 On Earth, you probably except dust balls as part of life. 5 You might fine them under your desk or behind your computer monitor. 6 Believe it or not, dust balls also blow across the surface of Mars; there, however, they are as large as clouds. 7 Springtime on Earth usually brings some extra wind, but you might not no that it does the same thing on Mars. 8 During the spring, dust clouds known as dirt devils have been seen blowing they're way across Mars in several directions. 9 NASA's rover *Spirit* not only spotted them but took pictures of them two. 10 Experts at NASA went threw the pictures and created a twelve-minute black-and-white film.

11 Watching a dust devil on film would certainly be much better then experiencing one in person. 12 These are not little dust storms like the ones that blow across are prairies and deserts. 13 Instead, dirt devils that have past measurement equipment have been recorded as being several miles high and hundreds of feet wide. 14 Brown sand an dust whip around at speeds of seventy miles per hour or more, and, as if that is not enough, some of these dust devils may also be full of miniature lightning bolts. 15 These dust storms are so powerful that they can be seen even from an orbiting spacecraft. 16 Scientists think the storms effect the surface of Mars, carving ridges into the planet.

17 When it comes to dust devils, stick to the ones under you're bed. 18 Unless you have not cleaned in a few decades, the dust you find there will be easier to clean up and not quiet so scary!

Write and Edit Your Own Work

ASSIGNMENT 1   **Write**

Write a paragraph explaining the features and rules of your college's library. When you are done, edit your writing, looking especially for commonly confused words.

MIKE BOOTH/ALAMY

ASSIGNMENT 2   **Edit**

Using this chapter as a guide, edit commonly confused words in a paper you are writing for this course or another course or in a piece of writing from your work or everyday life.

Chapter Review

1. What are four strategies that you can use to avoid confusing words that sound alike or have similar meanings? _____

_____

_____

_____

2. What are the top five commonly confused words on your list?

_____

REFLECTING ON THE JOURNEY

Skills Learned

Now that you've completed the chapter, look again at this paragraph.

> I hope that you are ready to take this test. Please follow this advise carefully. Your sure to do well if you do. As you look threw the questions, keep in mine that there is only one right answer to each. Take the time to read every question before answering it. It's easy to miss an word here and there. In the passed, students have rushed through the test and regretted it. You are allowed the full class hour to complete the test. Use that time well, and you cannot loose. I no you will do well.

Using what you've learned in this chapter, edit this paragraph for commonly confused words. Then answer the questions below.

1. Are you confident that you have identified the mistakes?

2. Are you confident that you have corrected the mistakes?

3. What questions do you have about commonly confused words?

25

Spelling

READING ROADMAP

Learning Objectives

Chapter Goal: Correct misspelled words in writing.

Tools to Achieve the Goal

- List of ten troublemakers (p. 417)
- List of seven spelling rules (pp. 418-424)
- Reference list of commonly misspelled words (p. 424)

Key Terms

Skim Chapter 25 before you begin reading. Can you find these words in **bold** type? Put a check mark next to each word once you have located it in the chapter.

_____ dictionary	_____ spell checker
_____ spelling list	_____ proofreading techniques

Highlight or circle any of these words that you already know.

Before You Read

Before you begin reading this chapter, study the following paragraph and complete the chart. At the end of the chapter, you will examine the paragraph again and reflect on what you have learned.

> My Uncle Brian got exsited when he saw a sale advertizing the digital camera he wanted. The camera was 30 percent off the reguler price, and if he used his store credit card, he could recieve an extra 10 percent off. He rushed to the store, but he found it packed with noisy shopers. My uncle fought his way to the front of the store agressively, and he purchased the camera. Now, the camra is his favorit toy.

This paragraph has problems with spelling. Put a check mark by the statement that best describes you.

Skill Statement	
I understand what the mistakes are, and I know how to fix them.	
I understand what the mistakes are, but I am not sure how to fix them.	
I think I understand what the mistakes are.	
I don't understand what the mistakes are.	

Understand the Importance of Spelling Correctly

Some smart people are poor spellers. Unfortunately, spelling errors are easy to see. If you are serious about improving your spelling, you need to use a dictionary and make a list of words that you often misspell. When in doubt about spelling, always look up the word.

A **dictionary** contains the correct spellings of words, along with information on how they are pronounced, what they mean, and where they came from. The following are two popular Web sites with online dictionaries:

- Merriam-Webster Online at **www.merriam-webster.com**. If you are not sure how to spell a word, type how you think the word is spelled into the Search box, and suggestions will appear.

- Your Dictionary at **www.yourdictionary.com**. This site has dictionaries for business, computer science, law, medicine, and other fields.

Keeping a **spelling list** of words that you often misspell will help you edit your papers and learn how to write the words correctly. From this list, identify your personal spelling "demons"—the five to ten words that you misspell most frequently. Write these words, spelled correctly, on an index card, and keep the card with you so that you can look at it whenever you write.

Practice Spelling Correctly

Do not try to correct your grammar, improve your message, and check your spelling at the same time. Instead, do separate steps for each. Remember to check the dictionary whenever you are unsure about the spelling of a word and to add all the spelling mistakes you find to your personal spelling list.

Most word-processing programs have a **spell checker** that finds and highlights a word that may be misspelled and that suggests other spellings. However, a spell checker ignores anything it recognizes as a word, so it will not help you find commonly confused words such as those discussed in Chapter 24. For example, a spell checker would not highlight any of the problems in the following sentences:

I am not *aloud* to do that.
[Correct: I am not *allowed* to do that.]

He took my *advise*.
[Correct: He took my *advice*.]

Did you feel the *affects*?
[Correct: Did you feel the *effects*?]

Use some of the following **proofreading techniques** to focus on the spelling of one word at a time.

- Put a piece of paper or a ruler under the line that you are reading.
- Proofread your paper backward, one word at a time.

- Exchange papers with a partner for proofreading, identifying only possible misspellings. The writer of the paper should be responsible for checking the words that you have identified and correcting any that are actually misspelled.

After you proofread each word in your paper, look at your personal spelling list and your list of demon words one more time. If you used any of these words in your paper, go back and check their spelling again.

You can practice correct spelling by playing spelling games online. Type "online spelling bees" into a search engine to find good sites.

> **PRACTICE 1**
>
> Take the last paper that you wrote—or one that you are working on now—and find and correct any spelling errors. Use any of the tools and techniques discussed in this chapter. How many spelling mistakes did you find? Were you surprised? How was the experience different from what you normally do to edit for spelling?

Follow These Steps to Better Spelling

Remember Ten Troublemakers

Writing teachers have identified the ten words in the following list as the words that students most commonly misspell.

Incorrect	Correct
alot	**a** lot
arguement	arg**um**ent
definate, defenite	defi**n**ite
develo**pe**	develop
lite	lig**ht**
necesary, nesesary	ne**c**essary
reci**ev**e	rec**ei**ve
seperate	sep**a**rate
surpri**z**e, sup**r**ise	su**r**prise
until**l**	unti**l**

Defeat Your Personal Spelling Demons

Try some of the following techniques to defeat your spelling demons:

- Create an explanation or saying that will help you remember the correct spelling. For example, "*surprise* is no *prize*" may remind you to spell *surprise* with an *s,* not a *z.*

Tip Think of syllables as the number of "beats" that a word has. The word *syllable* has three beats (*syl-la-ble*).

- Say each separate part (syllable) of the word out loud so that you do not miss any letters (*dis-ap-point-ment, Feb-ru-ar-y, prob-a-bly*). You can also say each letter of the word out loud.
- Write the word correctly ten times.
- Write a paragraph in which you use the word at least three times.
- Ask a partner to give you a spelling test.

Learn about Commonly Confused Words

Look back at Chapter 24, which discusses twenty-seven sets of words that are commonly confused because they sound alike. If you can remember the differences between the words in each set, you will avoid many spelling mistakes.

Learn Seven Spelling Rules

The following seven rules can help you avoid or correct many spelling errors. Quickly review vowels and consonants before you read the rules:

Vowels: a e i o u

Consonants: b c d f g h j k l m n p q r s t v w x z

The letter *y* can be either a vowel (when it sounds like the *y* in *fly* or *hungry*) or a consonant (when it sounds like the *y* in *yellow*).

Rule 1
I before *e*
Except after *c*.
Or when sounded like *a*
As in *neighbor* or *weigh*.

piece (*i* before *e*)

receive (except after *c*)

eight (sounds like *a*)

Exceptions: either, neighter, foreign, height, seize, society, their, weird

> **PRACTICE 2**
>
> In the spaces provided, write more examples of words that follow Rule 1. Do not use words that have already been covered.
>
> 1. _____
>
> 2. _____

3. _____

4. _____

5. _____

6. _____

Rule 2

When a word ends in *e*, drop the final *e* when adding an ending that begins with a vowel.

hop**e** + ing = hoping

imagin**e** + ation = imagination

When a word ends in *e*, keep the final *e* when adding an ending that begins with a consonant.

achiev**e** + ment = achievement

definit**e** + ly = definitely

Exceptions: argument, awful, truly (and others)

| PRACTICE 3 |

For each item, circle the first letter in the ending, and decide whether it is a consonant or a vowel. Then, add the ending to the word, and write the new word in the space.

1. fame + ous = _____

2. confuse + ing = _____

3. care + ful = _____

4. use + able = _____

5. nice + ly = _____

Rule 3

When adding an ending to a word that ends in *y*, change the *y* to *i* when a consonant comes before the *y*.

lonel**y** + est = loneliest

hap**py** + er = happier

apolog**y** + ize = apologize

likel**y** + hood = likelihood

Do not change the *y* when a vowel comes before the *y*.

> boy + ish = boyish
>
> pay + ment = payment
>
> survey + or = surveyor
>
> buy + er = buyer

Exceptions

1. When adding *-ing* to a word ending in *y*, always keep the *y*, even if a consonant comes before it: study + ing = studying.
2. Other exceptions include *daily*, *said*, and *paid*.

PRACTICE 4

For each item, circle the letter before the *y*, and decide whether it is a vowel or a consonant. Then, add the ending to the word, and write the new word in the space provided.

1. say + ing = _____

2. gray + er = _____

3. easy + ly = _____

4. healthy + er = _____

5. beauty + ful = _____

Rule 4

When adding an ending that starts with a vowel to a one-syllable word, double the final consonant only if the word ends with a consonant-vowel-consonant.

> trap + ed = trapped
>
> drip + ing = dripping
>
> fat + er = fatter
>
> fit + er = fitter

Do not double the final consonant if the word ends with some other combination.

Vowel-vowel-consonant	Vowel-consonant-consonant
clean + est = cleanest	slick + er = slicker
poor + er = poorer	teach + er = teacher
clear + ed = cleared	last + ed = lasted

Rule 5

When adding an ending that starts with a vowel to a word of two or more syllables, double the final consonant only if the word ends with a consonant-vowel-consonant and the stress is on the last syllable.

ad**mit** + ing = admit**t**ing

cont**rol** + er = control**l**er

oc**cur** + ence = occur**r**ence

pre**fer** + ed = prefer**r**ed

com**mit** + ed = commit**t**ed

Do not double the final consonant in other cases.

problem + atic = problematic

understand + ing = understanding

offer + ed = offered

PRACTICE 5

For each item, circle the last three letters in the main word, and decide whether they fit the consonant-vowel-consonant pattern. In words with more than one syllable, underline the stressed syllable. Then, add the ending to each word, and write the new word in the space provided.

1. clap + ing = _____

2. thunder + ing = _____

3. drop + ed = _____

4. appear + ance = _____

5. talent + ed = _____

Rule 6

To change a verb form to the third-person singular (*he, she, it*), add -*s* to the base form of most regular verbs.

walk + s = walk**s** (She **walks**.)

jump + s = jump**s** (He **jumps**.)

arrive + s = arrive**s** (The train **arrives**.)

Add -*es* to most verbs that end in *s, sh, ch,* or *x*.

push + es = push**es** (She **pushes**.)

fix + es = fix**es** (He **fixes**.)

miss + es = miss**es** (The man **misses** the train.)

PRACTICE 6

For each base verb, circle the last two letters, and decide which of the Rule 6 patterns applies. Add *-s* or *-es* and write the new verb form in the space provided.

Example: **purr** _____*purrs*_____

1. stir _____

2. race _____

3. floss _____

4. catch _____

5. wax _____

Rule 7
To form the plural of most regular nouns, including nouns that end in *o* preceded by a vowel, add *-s*.

book + s = book**s**

college + s = college**s**

rad**io** + s = radio**s**

ster**eo** + s = stereo**s**

Add *-es* to nouns that end in *s*, *sh*, *ch*, or *x*, and nouns that end in *o* preceded by a consonant.

cla**ss** + es = class**es**

ben**ch** + es = bench**es**

pota**to** + es = potato**es**

he**ro** + es = hero**es**

Certain nouns form the plural irregularly, meaning that there are no rules to follow. The easiest way to learn irregular plurals is to use them and say them aloud to yourself. Here are some common examples:

Singular	Plural	Singular	Plural
child	children	ox	oxen
foot	feet	person	people
goose	geese	tooth	teeth
man	men	woman	women
mouse	mice		

Other irregular plurals follow certain patterns.

Nouns ending in -y. Usually, to make these nouns plural, you change the *y* to *ie* and add *-s*.

city + s = cit**ies**
lady + s = lad**ies**

However, when a vowel (*a, e, i, o,* or *u*) comes before the *y,* just add a final *-s*.

boy + s = boy**s**
day + s = day**s**

Nouns ending in -f or -fe. Usually, to make these nouns plural, you change the *f* to *v* and add *-es* or *-s*.

life + s = li**ves**
shelf + es = shel**ves**
thief + es = thie**ves**

Exceptions: *cliffs, beliefs, roofs.*

Hyphenated nouns: Sometimes, two or three words are joined with hyphens (-) to form a single noun. Usually, the *-s* is added to the first word.

attorney-at-law + s = attorney**s**-at-law
commander-in-chief + s = commander**s**-in-chief
runner-up + s = runner**s**-up

> **PRACTICE 7**
>
> For each noun, circle the last two letters, and decide which of the Rule 7 patterns the word fits. Add *-s* or *-es* and write the plural noun in the space provided.
>
> 1. phone   _____
>
> 2. glass   _____
>
> 3. echo   _____
>
> 4. patio   _____
>
> 5. ruby   _____
>
> 6. key   _____
>
> 7. box   _____

8. wife   _____

9. ash   _____

10. sister-in-law _____

Check a Spelling List

The following is a list of one hundred commonly misspelled words. Check this list as you proofread your writing.

One Hundred Commonly Misspelled Words

absence	convenient	height	receive
achieve	cruelty	humorous	recognize
across	daughter	illegal	recommend
aisle	definite	immediately	restaurant
a lot	describe	independent	rhythm
already	dictionary	interest	roommate
analyze	different	jewelry	schedule
answer	disappoint	judgment	scissors
appetite	dollar	knowledge	secretary
argument	eighth	license	separate
athlete	embarrass	lightning	sincerely
awful	environment	loneliness	sophomore
basically	especially	marriage	succeed
beautiful	exaggerate	meant	successful
beginning	excellent	muscle	surprise
believe	exercise	necessary	truly
business	fascinate	ninety	until
calendar	February	noticeable	usually
career	finally	occasion	vacuum
category	foreign	occurrence	valuable
chief	friend	perform	vegetable
column	government	physically	weight
coming	grief	prejudice	weird
commitment	guidance	probably	writing
conscious	harass	psychology	written

In the following paragraph, fill in each blank with the correct spelling of the base word plus the ending in parentheses. You may want to refer to Rules 2–5 on pages 419–421.

1 Located near San Antonio, Texas, the Wild Animal Orphanage is one of the _____ (big + est) wildlife refuges in the country. 2 Since it _____ (open + ed) in 1983, the orphanage has cared for thousands of _____ (abandon + ed) exotic animals such as lions, tigers, bears, monkeys, and birds. 3 Most of these _____ (neglect + ed) animals are consequences of the exotic pet trade. 4 People can _____ (easy + ly) purchase wild animals from flea markets, classified ads, or Web sites. 5 However, few people have the space or the knowledge _____ (need + ed) to properly care for exotic animals, many of which end up _____ (live + ing) unhappy lives. 6 _____ (Unfortunate + ly), others are killed when breeders cannot find homes for them. 7 Tarzan, a lion cub, spent the first eighteen months of his life _____ (unhappy + ly) confined to a three-foot-by-four-foot cage in Cancun, Mexico. 8 He had only one toy for _____ (amuse + ment), a coconut shell. 9 Rescuers brought him to the Wild Animal Orphanage, and Tarzan is now _____ (run + ing) and _____ (play + ing) with other lions. 10 The orphanage offers public tours, _____ (educate + ing) people and _____ (discourage + ing) them from _____ (purchase + ing) animals meant to remain in the wild.

Find and correct any spelling mistakes in the following paragraph. You will find ten misspelled words. Three sentences are correct; write **C** next to them. You may want to refer to Rules 1–7 on pages 418–424 or the list of commonly misspelled words on page 424.

1 When I stopped by my freind Vanessa's cubicle at work, I noticed a small vase of beautiful flowers and two boxs of chocolates sitting on her desk. 2 "Who sent you flowers?" I asked her. 3 "I did," she admited. 4 Vanessa thought they helped make her cubicle a better environment for studing some

documents for a report she was writing. 5 "I beleive they help me while I'm thinking and writeing," she said. 6 At first, I thought Vanessa was jokeing. 7 Still, I bought some pink roses for my own desk. 8 I was aware of their lovely pink buds and delicate scent as I worked. 9 Even my accounting tasks seemed easyer than usual. 10 Fresh flowers in my work area definitly led to an improvment in my mood and concentration.

Edit Spelling Errors in Everyday Life

EDITING PARAGRAPHS 1

Edit spelling errors in the following paragraph, which is like one that you might find in an international-relations textbook. One sentence is correct; write **C** next to it. The first sentence has been edited for you.

1 The Channel Tunnel, or Chunnel, is the rail tunnel ~~connectting~~ *connecting* England and France. 2 Requireing ten individual contractors and thousands of workers, it was a challengeing project. 3 To complete this huge construction, a partnership had to be formed between two countrys with different languages, goverments, and sets of laws and safety codes. 4 England was definitly the more difficult country of the two. 5 For yeares, it had viewed itself as a seperate country from the rest of Europe. 6 It wanted to remain distinct, and this new connection to Europe made many English people uncomfortable. 7 Nevertheless, others saw the Chunnel as one of the best wayes to truely bring together the two countries. 8 Financeing the project was another one of the bigest obstacles. 9 The Chunnel cost billions of dollares, averaging $5 million each day of construction. 10 Ultimately, it cost seven hundred times more to develope than the Golden Gate Bridge in San Francisco, California.

EDITING PARAGRAPHS 2

Edit spelling errors in the following cover letter for a job application. Two sentences are correct; write **C** next to them. The first sentence has been edited for you.

Maya Collins

M & R Shipping

42 Park Forest Highway

Baton Rouge, LA 70816

Dear Ms. Collins:

1 I am ~~writeing~~ *writing* in response to your classified ad in the *Baton Rouge Advocate*. 2 The advertisment stated that you are looking for an office secratary for your shipping business. 3 I beleive I am the perfect person for the job. 4 I am both skiled and experienced in this kind of work. 5 I have worked at the front desk of three local business, where I grieted customers, answered phone calls, processed invoices, and managed the ordering of office supplys. 6 I am currently attendding Pearson Community College part-time, and my shedule meshs well with the hours you mentioned.

7 My résumé is enclosed with this letter. 8 If nesessary, I can start work immediately. 9 I look forward to hearing from you.

10 Sincerly,

Gina Thomasson

Write and Edit Your Own Work

ASSIGNMENT 1   Write

Write about an old trend that you see coming back (like muscle cars or a certain hairstyle or fashion). Do you like the trend or not? Why? When you are done, read each word carefully, looking for spelling errors.

ASSIGNMENT 2   Edit

Using the rules and strategies from this chapter, edit spelling errors in a paper that you are writing for this course or another course or in a piece of writing from your work or everyday life.

Chapter Review

1. To improve your spelling, you need to have a _____ and
   _____.

2. What are two proofreading techniques? _____

3. What are the five steps to better spelling?

   _____

   _____

   _____

   _____

   _____

4. For each of the seven spelling rules in this chapter, write one word that shows how
   each rule works.

   RULE 1: _____ ; RULE 2: _____ ;

   RULE 3: _____ ; RULE 4: _____ ;

   RULE 5: _____ ; RULE 6: _____ ;

   RULE 7: _____.

REFLECTING ON THE JOURNEY

Skills Learned

Now that you've completed the chapter, look again at this paragraph.

> My Uncle Brian got exsited when he saw a sale advertizing the digital camera he wanted. The camera was 30 percent off the reguler price, and if he used his store credit card, he could recieve an extra 10 percent off. He rushed to the store, but he found it packed with noisy shopers. My uncle fought his way to the front of the store agressively, and he purchased the camera. Now, the camra is his favorit toy.

Using what you've learned in this chapter, edit this paragraph for spelling mistakes. Then answer the questions below.

1. Are you confident that you have identified the mistakes?

2. Are you confident that you have corrected the mistakes?

3. What questions do you have about spelling?

Editing for Punctuation and Mechanics

26

Commas

READING ROADMAP

Learning Objectives

Chapter Goal: Use commas correctly in writing sentences.

Tools to Achieve the Goal

- Commas between items in a series (p. 432)
- Commas in compound sentences (p. 434)
- Commas after introductory words (p. 435)
- Commas around appositives and interrupters (p. 436)
- Commas around adjective clauses (p. 438)
- Other uses for commas (p. 440)

Key Terms

Skim Chapter 26 before you begin reading. Can you find these words in **bold** type? Put a check mark next to each word once you have located it in the chapter.

____ comma	____ interrupter
____ compound sentence	____ adjective clause
____ appositive	____ quotation marks

Highlight or circle any of these words that you already know.

Before you begin reading this chapter, study the following paragraph and complete the chart. At the end of the chapter, you will examine the paragraph again and reflect on what you have learned.

> Santiago Calatrava a Spanish architect has designed a special apartment building for the city of Malmö Sweden. The building is made of nine stacked cubes and each of the cubes is slightly turned. There is full ninety-degree twist between the top, and the bottom. Calatrava's building has won several awards. "There was a wish to get something exceptional" he told the media. He added "I also wanted to deliver something technically unique." The people, who choose to live in one of the apartments, will certainly have great views. However monthly rent payments are as high as $3,700 so the experience is only for those who can afford it.

This paragraph has problems with commas. Put a check mark by the statement that best describes you.

Skill Statement	
I understand what the mistakes are, and I know how to fix them.	
I understand what the mistakes are, but I am not sure how to fix them.	
I think I understand what the mistakes are.	
I don't understand what the mistakes are.	

Understand What Commas Do

LaunchPadSolo

Visit **LaunchPad Solo for Readers and Writers** > **Commas** for more practice using commas correctly.

A **comma (,)** is a punctuation mark that separates words and word groups to help readers understand a sentence. Read the following sentences, pausing when there is a comma. How does the use of commas change the meaning?

No comma	When **you** call Alicia I will leave the house.
One comma	When **you** call Alicia, I will leave the house.
Two commas	When **you** call, Alicia, I will leave the house.

Use Commas Correctly

Commas between Items in a Series

Use commas to separate three or more items in a series. The last item usually has *and* or *or* before it, and this joining word should be preceded by a comma.

item	,	item	,	item	, *and/or*	item

I put away my winter *sweaters, scarves, gloves, and hats.*

The candidates *walked to the stage, stood behind their microphones, and began yelling at each other.*

Some writers leave out the comma before the final item in a series, but doing so can lead to confusion or misreading. In college writing, it is best to include this comma.

Incorrect

I bought bread milk and bananas.

Dan will cook I will clean and Dara will do the laundry.

Tara likes to bike, and run.

Correct

I bought bread, milk, and bananas.

Dan will cook, I will clean, and Dara will do the laundry.

Tara likes to bike and run.

[No comma is necessary because there are only two items.]

> **PRACTICE 1**
>
> In the following sentences, underline the items in the series. Then, add commas where they are needed. One sentence is correct; write **C** next to it.
>
> **Example: At the moment, I am typing on my computer, listening to music, and talking on the phone; doing more than one thing is called multitasking.**
>
> 1. Multitasking is easier than ever thanks to gadgets such as cell phones laptop computers and portable music players.
>
> 2. At one time, I could just sit in my easy chair put my feet on the coffee table and do nothing.
>
> 3. Sometimes, I miss the simpler days of record players black-and-white televisions and hula hoops.
>
> 4. People today feel the need to do two things or even three things at once.
>
> 5. Earlier today, I ate lunch watched the news and read a book at the same time.

6. Then, I walked the dog listened to the baseball game on my portable radio and called my sister on my cell phone.

7. Tonight, I will clean the house cook dinner and watch the children.

8. I get nervous when I see someone driving talking and applying makeup at the same time.

9. I try to avoid using my cell phone while driving eating or seeing a movie.

10. Do you believe that multitasking is useful simply annoying or downright dangerous?

Commas in Compound Sentences

Tip The words *and, but, for, nor, or, so,* and *yet* are called coordinating conjunctions (see Chapter 12).

A **compound sentence** contains two sentences joined by one of these words: *and, but, for, nor, or, so, yet.* Use a comma before the joining word to separate the two clauses.

Sentence 1	,	and, but, for, nor, or, so, yet	sentence 2

The toddler knocked over the oatmeal bowl, *and* then she rubbed the mess into her hair.

I love my criminal justice course, *but* the tests are difficult.

You will not be at the meeting, *so* I will tell you what we decide.

 Language note: Remember that a comma alone cannot connect two sentences in English. This creates an error known as a comma splice (see Chapter 14). A comma is *not* needed if a coordinating conjunction joins two sentence elements that are *not* complete sentences.

Incorrect

Jess is good with numbers and she is a hard worker.

Manuel hates to swim yet he wants to live by the water.

I meant to go, but could not.

Correct

Tip For a review of compound sentences, see Chapter 12.

Jess is good with numbers, and she is a hard worker.

Manuel hates to swim, yet he wants to live by the water.

I meant to go but could not.

[This sentence is not a compound, so a comma should not be used. *I meant to go* is a sentence, but *could not* is not a sentence.]

PRACTICE 2

Edit the following compound sentences by adding commas where they are needed. One sentence is correct; write **C** next to it.

Example: **Companies today realize the importance of diversity‚ but prejudice still exists in the workplace.**

1. Many professions used to be dominated by men and the majority of those men were white.

2. Some workplaces still look like this but most do not.

3. Workplace diversity is now common yet discrimination still occurs.

4. Researchers recently conducted a survey of 623 American workers and the results revealed some alarming statistics.

5. Some respondents had been victims of prejudice over the previous year or they had overheard others making intolerant statements.

6. Nearly 30 percent of respondents said that they had overheard statements of racial prejudice at their workplace, and 20 percent said that coworkers had made fun of others because of their sexual orientation.

7. Age discrimination is another problem for 20 percent of respondents reported prejudice against older workers.

8. The survey did not report on the characteristics of the respondents nor did it give details about the people expressing the prejudice.

9. The American workforce is more diverse than ever before and it will become even more diverse in the future.

10. This trend is a positive one but steps need to be taken to eliminate prejudice in the workplace.

Commas after Introductory Words

Putting a comma after introductory words lets your readers know when the main part of the sentence is starting.

Introductory word or word group	,	main part of sentence.

Introductory word	*Luckily‚* they got out of the burning building.
Introductory phrase	*Until now‚* I had never seen a ten-pound frog.
Introductory clause	*As I explained‚* Jacob eats only red jelly beans.

Tip Introductory clauses start with dependent words (subordinating conjunctions). For a review of these types of clauses, see Chapter 10.

PRACTICE 3

In each of the following sentences, underline any introductory word or word group. Then, add commas after introductory word groups where they are needed. Two sentences are correct; write **C** next to them.

Example: <u>As many people know</u>‚ stepping on a rusty nail can cause tetanus, a potentially deadly infection.

1. Yesterday I accidentally stepped on a nail.

2. Although the nail was not rusty I decided to call the hospital.

3. According to my doctor a shiny nail is just as likely to cause tetanus as a rusty one.

4. Though some people are unaware of it rust itself does not cause tetanus.

5. Apparently, tetanus is caused by bacteria that live in dust, soil, and human and animal waste.

6. Once the bacteria get deep enough inside a wound they begin growing as long as oxygen is not present.

7. Producing poisons that attack muscles all over the body, these bacteria kill an estimated fifty to one hundred people every year.

8. Fortunately nearly all children receive the tetanus vaccine.

9. However the vaccine's effects wear off after ten years.

10. Because of this the doctor recommended that I come in for a tetanus shot.

Commas around Appositives and Interrupters

Tip For more on nouns, see Chapter 10.

An **appositive**, a phrase that renames a noun, comes directly before or after the noun.

| Noun | ‚ | appositive | ‚ | rest of sentence. |

Claire‚ *my best friend*‚ sees every movie starring Johnny Depp.
[*My best friend* renames *Claire*.]

You should go to Maxwell's‚ *the new store that opened downtown*.
[*The new store that opened downtown* renames *Maxwell's*.]

An **interrupter** is a word or word group that interrupts a sentence yet does not affect the meaning of the sentence.

| Main part of sentence | , | interrupter not essential to meaning | , | rest of sentence. |

The baby, *as you know,* screams the moment I put her to bed.

Mitch hit his tenth home run of the season, *if you can believe it.*

Putting commas around appositives and interrupters tells readers that these words are not essential to the meaning of a sentence. If an appositive or interrupter is in the middle of a sentence, put a comma before and after it.

Your pants, *by the way,* are ripped.

If an appositive or interrupter comes at the beginning or end of a sentence, separate it from the rest of the sentence with one comma.

By the way, your pants are ripped.

Your pants are ripped, *by the way.*

Sometimes, appositives and interrupters are essential to the meaning of a sentence. When a sentence would not have the same meaning without the appositive, the appositive *should not* be set off with commas.

| Noun | interrupter essential to meaning | rest of sentence. |

The former seamstress *Rosa Parks* became one of the nation's greatest civil rights figures.

[The sentence *The former seamstress became one of the nation's greatest civil rights figures* does not have the same meaning.]

Incorrect

The actor, Marlon Brando, was secretive.

Lila the best singer in my high school class is starring in a play.

He wore a clown suit to work believe it or not.

Correct

The actor Marlon Brando was secretive.

Lila, the best singer in my high school class, is starring in a play.

He wore a clown suit to work, believe it or not.

> **PRACTICE 4**
>
> Underline any appositives and interrupters in the following sentences. Then, use commas to set them off as needed. One sentence is correct; write **C** next to it.
>
> **Example: One of my favorite local shops is Melville's, a used book store.**

1. The owner a nice lady is Francine Smythe.

2. I suppose she named the bookstore after her favorite writer Herman Melville.

3. I have not however found any of Melville's books in her store.

4. Mrs. Smythe in any case is happy to order any book that she does not have in stock.

5. Melville's books, always excellent bargains, have given me great pleasure.

6. I once found a rare book on collecting antique glassware my favorite hobby.

7. My favorite part of the shop the basement is dimly lit and particularly quiet.

8. A bare lightbulb the only source of light hangs from a long cord.

9. The dim light is bad for my eyes of course but it gives the basement a cozy feel.

10. Melville's is closing next month sadly because a chain bookstore around the corner has taken away much of its business.

Commas around Adjective Clauses

An **adjective clause** is a group of words that

- often begins with *who, which,* or *that*
- has a subject and verb
- describes the noun right before it in a sentence

If an adjective clause can be taken out of a sentence without completely changing the meaning, put commas around the clause.

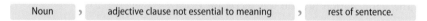

| Noun | , | adjective clause not essential to meaning | , | rest of sentence. |

The governor, *who is finishing his first term in office,* will probably not be reelected.

Devane's, *which is the best bakery in the city,* is opening two more stores.

If an adjective clause is essential to the meaning of a sentence, do not put commas around it. You can tell whether a clause is essential by taking it out and seeing if the meaning of the sentence changes significantly.

| Noun | adjective clause essential to meaning | rest of sentence. |

Homeowners *who put their trash out too early* will be fined.

The jobs *that open up first* will be the first ones we fill.

Tip For more on adjectives, see Chapter 18.

Use *who* to refer to a person; *which* to refer to places or things (but not to people); and *that* to refer to people, places, or things.

Incorrect

I like chess *which I learned to play as a child.*

The house, *that you like,* is up for sale.

Clive *who lives next door* grew a one-hundred-pound pumpkin.

Correct

I like chess, *which I learned to play as a child.*

The house *that you like* is up for sale.

Clive, *who lives next door,* grew a one-hundred-pound pumpkin.

PRACTICE 5

In the following sentences, underline the adjective clauses. Then, add commas where they are needed. Remember that if an adjective clause is essential to the meaning of a sentence, you should not use commas. Four sentences are correct; write **C** next to them.

Example: **Chicago's newest sushi restaurant, which I read about in a magazine, offers some unusual dishes.**

1. The restaurant's dishes which look like sushi are made of paper.

2. The restaurant's chef who is interested in technology makes images of sushi dishes on an ink-jet printer.

3. He prints the images on paper that people can eat.

4. The edible paper which tastes much like sushi is flavored with food-based inks.

5. Soybeans and cornstarch which are the main ingredients of the paper are also found in many other foods.

6. Customers can even eat the menu which they break up into a bowl of soup.

7. The chef sometimes seasons the menu which changes daily to taste like a main course.

8. He may season the menu to taste like the steak that is being served that day.

9. People who can afford the restaurant's high prices keep the place busy.

10. The chef has lately been testing scientific tools to see if he can make a meal that floats in the air.

Other Uses for Commas

COMMAS WITH QUOTATION MARKS

Quotation marks (" ") are used to show that you are repeating exactly what some-one said or wrote. Generally, use commas to set off the words inside quotation marks from the rest of the sentence. Notice the position of the commas in the fol-lowing dialogue:

"Pardon me," said a stranger who stopped me on the street.

"Can you tell me," he asked, "where Newland Bank is?"

I replied, "Yes, you are standing right in front of it."

Tip For more on quotation marks, see Chapter 28.

PRACTICE 6

In each of the following sentences, add or move commas as needed. Two sentences are correct; write **C** next to them.

Example: **"Thank you for coming in to interview at Parts Plus," Mr. Marcus said to me as he shook my hand.**

1. "Please sit down and make yourself comfortable" he added.

2. "Thank you very much", I responded.

3. Mr. Marcus sat down as he said "Now tell me how you heard about our company."

4. "I'm one of your customers," I replied.

5. "I think it's great" said Mr. Marcus, "to hear that you are familiar with us and that you are interested in working here."

6. I, said "I was actually wondering if I could get a refund for this distributor cap."

7. Mr. Marcus cleared his throat and murmured, "Excuse me," as he walked out of the room.

8. "Please forgive me", he said when he returned "for mistaking you for another appointment."

9. "No problem," I replied "as long as you can tell me where the returns desk is."

10. "Of course" Mr. Marcus said with a laugh.

COMMAS IN ADDRESSES

Use commas to separate the parts of an address included in a sentence. However, do not use a comma before a zip code.

> My address is 421 Elm Street, Burgettstown, PA 15021.

If a sentence continues after the address, put a comma after the address. Also, when you include a city and a state in the middle of a sentence, use commas before and after the state name. If the state name is at the end of a sentence, put a period after it.

> We moved from Nashville, Tennessee, to Boulder, Colorado.

COMMAS IN DATES

Separate the day from the year with a comma. If you give only the month and year, do not separate them with a comma.

> The coupon expires on May 31, 2012.
> I have a doctor's appointment in December 2012.

If a sentence continues after a date that includes the day, put a comma after the date.

> My grandmother was born on October 31, 1935, not far from where she lives now.

PRACTICE 7

In each of the following sentences, add, move, or delete commas as needed. Two sentences are correct; write **C** next to them.

Example: It was on November 10, 2012, that we finally moved to San Francisco.

1. Michiko came here from Osaka Japan when she was four years old.

2. Were you living at 849 Livermore Avenue, Memphis, Tennessee 38104, last year?

3. I had my car's brakes fixed in July, 2014 and in January, 2015.

4. I will never forget March 18, 2008 because it was the day we met.

5. The snowstorm hit St. Paul Minnesota on February 3, 2005.

6. Since April 16 2014 the house at 2187 Court Place Tucson Arizona 85701 has had nobody living in it.

7. Leaving your job before June 2 2017, caused you to lose your health benefits.

8. Los Angeles, California, was my home until I moved here in December 2007.

9. I was driving to Houston, Texas on May 4, 2015 to see my parents.

10. They visited Camden Maine in September 1996 and have not been back since then.

COMMAS WITH NAMES

When a sentence "speaks" to someone by name, use a comma (or commas) to separate the name from the rest of the sentence.

Maria, could you please come here?

Luckily, Stan, the tickets have not sold out.

You can sit here, Phuong.

PRACTICE 8

In each of the following sentences, add commas as needed. One sentence is correct; write **C** next to it.

Example: "Nicole, it is time for the family portrait to be taken."

1. "Because I am on a limited time schedule Nicole please get everyone in place."

2. "Get the twins Marius and Marcus into their jackets."

3. "Joseph we need you to be in the back because you are the tallest."

4. "Since there are so many of you Nicole some will need to sit down."

5. "Nicole, I think we are ready for the first shot."

COMMAS WITH *YES* OR *NO*

Put commas around the word *yes* or *no* in response to a question or comment.

Yes, I understand.

I decided, no, I would not have any more soda.

PRACTICE 9

In each of the following sentences, add commas as needed.

Example: "Yes, I'd like to speak with someone about a problem with my computer."

1. "No I did not purchase my computer within the last year."

2. "I realize yes that the warranty expires after a year."

3. "Yes I still need help with this problem."

4. "Unfortunately no I am not willing to pay for this service."

5. "Yes I am willing to chat for free online instead of on the phone."

Edit Commas in Everyday Life

EDITING PARAGRAPHS 1

Add commas as needed in the following paragraph, which is like one that you might find in a history textbook. One sentence is correct; write **C** next to it. The first sentence has been edited for you.

1 Alice Hamilton, who earned a medical degree at the University of Michigan in the late 1800s, was a pioneer in the field of occupational health and safety. 2 After studying bacteriology in Europe Hamilton led the U.S. movement to clean up dangerous workplaces. 3 She focused especially on industries that used toxic materials and employed poor immigrants. 4 In her quest to make the workplace safer she visited factories interviewed workers and studied medical records. 5 "No young doctor" she wrote "can hope for work as exciting and rewarding." 6 Hamilton, an expert on industrial toxins became the first-ever woman faculty member at Harvard University in 1916. 7 Although she retired from teaching in 1935 Hamilton never ended her commitment to civil rights, political activism and America's poorest workers. 8 She died on September 22, 1970 at the age of 101.

EDITING PARAGRAPHS 2

Add or delete commas as needed in the following memo. One sentence is correct; write **C** next to it. The first sentence has been edited for you.

DATE: August 27, 2015
TO: Kendra Landry
FROM: Benjamin Cooper
SUBJECT: Promotion

1 For the past five years, you have been one of our most valued employees. 2 You have stocked shelves filled orders processed invoices and trained interns effectively. 3 You have been on time every day and you rarely use your sick days. 4 Your supervisor Cameron Lawson praises your performance often. 5 He told me that you are the best floor manager in the company, and recommended you for a promotion. 6 Because you are such a hard worker I am happy to promote you from floor manager to division manager. 7 Your new position which begins next week will pay an additional $4 per hour. 8 This raise will be effective on Monday September 14 2015. 9 You will also be granted an extra week of vacation time annually. 10 Congratulations Kendra and thank you again for your excellent service to our company.

Write and Edit Your Own Work

OLEKSANDR BEREZKO/SHUTTERSTOCK

ASSIGNMENT 1   **Write**

An accident has smashed your smart phone (see photo at left). Write a letter to the phone company to explain what happened and to request a new phone. When you are done, read your writing carefully, checking that you have used commas correctly.

ASSIGNMENT 2   **Edit**

Using this chapter as a guide, edit for comma usage a paper that you are writing for this course or another course or a piece of writing from your work or everyday life.

Chapter Review

1. A comma (,) is a punctuation mark that _____ words and word groups to help readers understand a sentence.

2. Use commas
   - To separate three or more items in a _____.
   - To separate two _____ joined by *and, but, for, nor, or, so,* or *yet.*
   - _____ introductory words.
   - Around _____ (which rename a noun) and _____ (which interrupt a sentence).
   - Around _____ (which often begin with *who, which,* or *that;* have a subject and verb; and describe the noun right before them in a sentence).

3. What are two other uses of commas? _____

   _____

REFLECTING ON THE JOURNEY

Skills Learned

Now that you've completed the chapter, look again at this paragraph.

> Santiago Calatrava a Spanish architect has designed a special apartment building for the city of Malmö Sweden. The building is made of nine stacked cubes and each of the cubes is slightly turned. There is full ninety-degree twist between the top, and the bottom. Calatrava's building has won several awards. "There was a wish to get something exceptional" he told the media. He added "I also wanted to deliver something technically unique." The people, who choose to live in one of the apartments, will certainly have great views. However monthly rent payments are as high as $3,700 so the experience is only for those who can afford it.

Using what you've learned in this chapter, edit this paragraph for spelling mistakes. Then answer the questions below.

1. Are you confident that you have identified the mistakes?
2. Are you confident that you have corrected the mistakes?
3. What questions do you have about commas?

27

Apostrophes

Learning Objectives

Chapter Goal: Use apostrophes correctly in writing.

Tools to Achieve the Goal

- Apostrophes to show ownership (p. 447)
- Reference list of possessive pronouns (p. 448)
- Apostrophes in contractions (p. 449)
- Reference list of common contractions (p. 450)
- Apostrophes with letters, numbers, and time (p. 451)

READING ROADMAP

Key Terms

Skim Chapter 27 before you begin reading. Can you find these words in **bold** type? Put a check mark next to each word once you have located it in the chapter.

____ apostrophe   ____ contraction

Highlight or circle any of these words that you already know.

Before You Read

Before you begin reading this chapter, study the following paragraph and complete the chart. At the end of the chapter, you will examine the paragraph again and reflect on what you have learned.

> You need to take Professor Smiths class. In the course, youll be given four tests and ten quizzes. The point's from those exams will be one-half of your overall grade. But he allows you to take two make-up exam's during the course. Do'nt bother asking for any other makeups, because he wont allow it. The other part of your grade come's from easy things: attendance, homework, and class participation. Now, all students papers must be submitted on time to get full credit, so watch the calendar carefully. One more thing: he is picky about honesty. If you turn in others work as your's, he will automatically give you an F.

This paragraph has problems with apostrophes. Put a check mark by the statement that best describes you.

Skill Statement	
I understand what the mistakes are, and I know how to fix them.	
I understand what the mistakes are, but I am not sure how to fix them.	
I think I understand what the mistakes are.	
I don't understand what the mistakes are.	

Understand What Apostrophes Do

An **apostrophe (')** is a punctuation mark that

LaunchPadSolo

Visit **LaunchPad Solo for Readers and Writers > Apostrophes** for more practice using apostrophes correctly.

- shows ownership: *Susan's* shoes, *Alex's* coat

OR

- shows that a letter (or letters) has been left out of two words that have been joined: *I + am = I'm; that + is = that's; they + are = they're.* The joined words are called *contractions.*

Although an apostrophe looks like a comma (,), it has a different purpose, and it is written higher on the line than a comma is.

apostrophe'   comma,

Use Apostrophes Correctly

Apostrophes to Show Ownership

- **Add -'s to a singular noun to show ownership even if the noun already ends in -s.**

    The president's speech was shown on every television station.

    The suspect's abandoned car was found in the woods.

    Travis's strangest excuse for missing work was that his pet lobster died.

- **If a noun is plural (meaning *more than one*) and ends in -s, just add an apostrophe to show ownership. If it is plural but does not end in -s, add -'s.**

    Why would someone steal the campers' socks?

    [There is more than one camper.]

    The salesclerk told me where the girls' shoe department was.

    Men's hairstyles are getting shorter.

    Tip For more on nouns, see Chapter 10.

- **The placement of an apostrophe makes a difference in meaning.**

    My brother's ten dogs went to a kennel over the holiday.

    [One brother has ten dogs.]

    My brothers' ten dogs went to a kennel over the holiday.

    [Two or more brothers together have ten dogs.]

- **Do not use an apostrophe to form the plural of a noun.**

  The fan's were silent as the pitcher wound up for the throw.

  Horse's lock their legs so that they can sleep standing up.

- **Do not use an apostrophe with a possessive pronoun. These pronouns already show ownership (possession).**

  My motorcycle is faster than your's.

  That shopping cart is our's.

ITS OR *IT'S*

The most common error with apostrophes and pronouns is confusing *its* (a possessive pronoun) with *it's* (a contraction meaning "it is"). Whenever you write *it's*, test to see if it is correct by reading it aloud as *it is*.

> **PRACTICE 1**
>
> Rewrite each of the following phrases to show ownership by using an apostrophe.
>
> Example: **the baseball cards of my brothers** *my brothers' baseball cards*
>
> 1. the motorcycle of my uncle _____
>
> 2. the essays of the students _____
>
> 3. the value of the necklace _____
>
> 4. the smile of James _____
>
> 5. the friendship of my sisters _____

Tip For more on pronouns, see Chapters 10 and 17.

Possessive Pronouns

my	his	its	their
mine	her	our	theirs
your	hers	ours	whose
yours			

PRACTICE 2

Edit the following sentences by adding -'s or an apostrophe alone to show ownership and by crossing out any incorrect use of an apostrophe or -'s.

Example: Our galaxy is the Milky Way, and astronomer͟s have made an interesting discovery about one of this galaxy'͟s stars.

1. What happen͟s when a galaxy loses one of it͟'s star͟'s?

2. Recently, one of the Milky Ways stars was observed flying out of the galaxy.

3. This observation was astronomers first discovery of a star escaping from a galaxy.

4. The stars high speed, 1.5 million miles per hour, is fast enough for it to escape the Milky Ways' gravity.

5. It is currently about 196,000 light-year͟'s from the galaxys center.

6. The suns distance from the center of the galaxy is about 30,000 light-years, which make͟'s us fairly far out, too.

7. The stars official name is a long combination of letters and numbers, but some scientist͟'s call it the Outcast.

8. According to some astronomers͟', the star almost got sucked into the black hole at the center of the Milky Way.

9. This near miss could have increased the Outcasts speed.

10. The star might not have been our͟'s to begin with; perhaps it was just passing through the Milky Way.

Apostrophes in Contractions

A **contraction** is formed by joining two words and leaving out one or more of the letters.

Wilma'͟s always the loudest person in the room.
[*Wilma is* always the loudest person in the room.]

I'͟ll babysit so that you can go to the mechanic.
[*I will* babysit so that you can go to the mechanic.]

When writing a contraction, put an apostrophe where the letter or letters have been left out, not between the two words.

He does'͟n͟'t understand the risks of smoking.

Common Contractions

aren't = are not	she'll = she will
can't = cannot	she's = she is, she has
couldn't = could not	there's = there is
didn't = did not	they'd = they would, they had
don't = do not	they'll = they will
he'd = he would, he had	they're = they are
he'll = he will	they've = they have
he's = he is, he has	who'd = who would, who had
I'd = I would, I had	who'll = who will
I'll = I will	who's = who is, who has
I'm = I am	won't = will not
I've = I have	wouldn't = would not
isn't = is not	you'd = you would, you had
it's = it is, it has	you'll = you will
let's = let us	you're = you are
she'd = she would, she had	you've = you have

 Language note: Contractions including a *be* verb (like *am, are,* or *is*) cannot be followed by the base form of a verb or another helping verb (like *can, does,* or *has*).

Incorrect	I'm try to study.	He's can come.
Correct	**I'm trying** to study.	**He can** come.

Avoid contractions in formal papers for college. Some instructors believe that contractions are too informal for college writing.

PRACTICE 3

Write the following words as contractions, putting an apostrophe where the letter or letters have been left out.

Example: **you + have = _____*you've*_____**

1. there + is = _____

2. would + not = _____

3. it + is = _____

4. can + not = _____

5. you + will = _____

6. she + is = _____

7. I + am = _____

8. they + are = _____

PRACTICE 4

Edit the following sentences by adding apostrophes where needed and crossing out misplaced apostrophes.

Example: **There's a cute toddler next to me at the bus stop.**

1. The little girl is dancing around the sidewalk, and shes certainly enjoying herself.

2. Ive got a lot of admiration for a mother who lets her daughter express herself so freely.

3. When they take a seat next to me on the bus, I think that wer'e going to have a great time together.

4. I quickly discover that Im wrong about that.

5. I ca'nt hear my own thoughts because the girl is singing so loudly.

6. Soon, I feel a sharp pain in my leg and realize that shes kicking me as hard as she can.

7. Then, theres a hand reaching across my book, and the girls tearing a page out of it.

8. I expect her mother to stop this behavior, but she does'nt; in fact, she completely ignores it.

9. Im' a mother myself, so I hope you wont think that I dislike all children.

10. What I do dislike are parents who think its okay to let their children run wild.

Apostrophes with Letters, Numbers, and Time

- **Use an apostrophe or -'s when time nouns are treated as if they own something.**

   We took two weeks' vacation last year.
   This year's car models use less gas than last year's.

Note: Some people and publications choose to use 's to indicate plurals with numbers (The store was out of size 8's). Other people and publications omit the apostrophe in these cases (The store was out of size 8s). Ask your teacher which style he or she prefers, and make sure you are consistent within your paper.

PRACTICE 5

Edit the following sentences by adding apostrophes where needed and crossing out misplaced apostrophes.

Example: **When I graduated from high school, I had saved enough money for three months' rent.**

1. I got a secretarial job that paid well, and I lived on my own for a few year's.

2. I was laid off with just two weeks pay.

3. After a few month's, I moved back in with my parents.

4. They convinced me that I could earn a respectable salary with a medical assistants degree.

5. I got all As and Bs in my first semester back at school, and I have never been happier.

Edit Apostrophes in Everyday Life

EDITING PARAGRAPHS 1

Edit the following paragraph from an employee handbook, adding or deleting apostrophes as needed. Two sentences are correct; write **C** next to them. The first sentence has been edited for you.

1 This addition to the employee handbook further describes the company's safety code. 2 Its this business' goal to have all employees stay safe and injury-free while on the job. 3 Last years inspection earned us all 4s and 5s (out of 5) on our safety scores. 4 This year weve set a goal to make all 5s. 5 Recently, a number of people have had questions about safety procedures in different parts of the plant. 6 To address those employee's questions, we created these simplified guidelines. 7 First, hard hats must be worn at all time's by employees working on the main floor. 8 Second, safety goggles are always required in the sanding and packing areas. 9 Third, anyone loading truck's must wear a brace and steel-toed shoes or boots. 10 Finally, everyone in the warehouse needs

an hours worth of basic safety instruction each month. 11 We will be placing

additional reminders around the plant, so be sure to watch for your's. 12 We'll

also have a general safety meeting as next years inspection time approaches.

EDITING PARAGRAPHS 2

Edit the following brief article, adding or deleting apostrophes as needed.
Besides the first sentence, which has been marked for you, four sentences are
correct; write **C** next to them.

C

1 When it comes to insects, small is indeed mighty. 2 Despite their tiny

size, insects manage to build some of natures most fascinating and complex

homes. 3 Using materials from their own bodies or from their surrounding

environment, they build their homes anywhere from high up in trees to deep

underground.

4 For example, termites tall, complicated towers are the insect worlds

equivalent to todays modern skyscrapers. 5 Considering the size of the

construction workers, these towers are amazingly tall. 6 Some reach heights of

fifteen feet or more, have twenty-inch-thick wall's, and are as hard as concrete.

7 Some termite homes have been around for more than fifty year's and

contain millions of occupants.

8 Inside these unique and complex towers are four main sections.

9 Fungus gardens and food storage rooms are on the upper levels, and living

areas are closer to the ground. 10 The towers shapes vary, depending on

the specific environment where they are built. 11 Towers in rain forest's, for

example, are shaped like umbrellas to direct water away from the nest. 12 In

the desert, the towers have long, thin tops and chimneys that cool down the

nest for it's inhabitants.

13 A towers internal chambers and tunnels are complicated. 14 Nevertheless,

termite's are able to make their way from one place to another in complete

darkness. 15 They like to stay at home, leaving their' amazing towers only to

eat and mate. 16 Why, then, are several termite's crawling on my floor?

Write and Edit Your Own Work

> **ASSIGNMENT 1**   **Write**
>
> Write about a party or other event that you attended recently, describing what people wore, said, or did. Make sure to use contractions in your descriptions (for example, *my friend's shoes, it's fun*). When you are done, read your writing carefully, checking that you have used apostrophes correctly.

> **ASSIGNMENT 2**   **Edit**
>
> Using this chapter as a guide, edit for apostrophe usage a paper that you are writing for this course or another course or a piece of writing from your work or everyday life.

Chapter Review

1. An apostrophe (') is a punctuation mark that shows _____ or shows that a letter (or letters) have been left out of words that have been _____.

2. To show ownership, adds _____ to a singular noun, even if the noun already ends in -*s*. For a plural noun, add an _____ alone if the noun ends in -*s;* add _____ if the noun does not end in -*s*.

3. Do not use an apostrophe with a _____ pronoun.

4. Do not confuse *its* and *it's*. *Its* shows _____ ; *it's* is a _____ meaning "it is."

5. A _____ is formed by joining two words and leaving out one or more of the letters. Use an apostrophe to show where _____ _____ .

6. Use -'*s* to make letters _____ .

7. Use an apostrophe or -'*s* when _____ are treated as if they own something.

REFLECTING ON THE JOURNEY

Skills Learned

Now that you've completed the chapter, look again at this paragraph.

> You need to take Professor Smiths class. In the course, youll be given four tests and ten quizzes. The point's from those exams will be one-half of your overall grade. But he allows you to take two make-up exam's during the course. Do'nt bother asking for any other makeups, because he wont allow it. The other part of your grade come's from easy things: attendance, homework, and class participation. Now, all students papers must be submitted on time to get full credit, so watch the calendar carefully. One more thing: he is picky about honesty. If you turn in others work as your's, he will automatically give you an F.

Using what you've learned in this chapter, edit this paragraph for incorrect and missing apostrophes. Then answer the questions below.

1. Are you confident that you have identified the mistakes?

2. Are you confident that you have corrected the mistakes?

3. What questions do you have about apostrophes?

28

Quotation Marks

READING ROADMAP

Learning Objectives

Chapter Goal: Use quotation marks correctly.

Tools to Achieve the Goal

- Quotation marks for direct quotations (p. 457)
- Quotation marks for certain titles (p. 460)

Key Terms

Skim Chapter 28 before you begin reading. Can you find these words in **bold** type? Put a check mark next to each word once you have located it in the chapter.

____ quotation marks	____ direct quotations
____ indirect quotations	____ single quotation marks

Highlight or circle any of these words that you already know.

Before You Read

Before you begin reading this chapter, study the following paragraph and complete the chart. At the end of the chapter, you will examine the paragraph again and reflect on what you have learned.

> I have been struggling with my research paper. I approached my professor, and I asked her How do I find the sources I need for this paper? My professor was very encouraging. She said "Most students struggle the first time that they write a research paper, and your problems are normal." She also said that "I just need to make a plan and follow it." Next, she showed me how to look up articles on our library's database. I found a great article in "The New York Times." I think I am ready to start writing my paper now.

This paragraph has problems with quotation marks. Put a check mark by the statement that best describes you.

Skill Statement	
I understand what the mistakes are, and I know how to fix them.	
I understand what the mistakes are, but I am not sure how to fix them.	
I think I understand what the mistakes are.	
I don't understand what the mistakes are.	

Understand What Quotation Marks Do

Quotation marks (" ") are used around **direct quotations**: someone's speech or writing repeated exactly, word for word.

    Direct quotation   Ellis said, "I'll finish the work by Tuesday."

Quotation marks are not used around **indirect quotations**: restatements of what someone said or wrote, not word for word.

    Indirect quotation   Ellis said that he would finish the work by Tuesday.

Use Quotation Marks Correctly

Quotation Marks for Direct Quotations

When you write a direct quotation, use quotation marks around the quoted words. These marks tell readers that the words used are exactly what was said or written.

1. "Did you hear about Carmela's date?" Rob asked me.
2. "No," I replied. "What happened?"
3. "According to Carmela," Rob said, "the guy showed up at her house in a black mask and cape."
4. I said, "You're joking, right?"
5. "No," Rob answered. "Apparently, the date thought his costume was romantic and mysterious."

Quoted words are usually combined with words that identify who is speaking, such as *Rob asked me* in the first example. The identifying words can come after the quoted words (example 1), before them (example 4), or in the middle (examples 2, 3, and 5). Here are some guidelines for capitalization and punctuation:

- Capitalize the first letter in a complete sentence that is being quoted, even if it comes after some identifying words (example 4).

- Do not capitalize the first letter in a quotation if it is not the first word in a complete sentence (*the* in example 3).

- If it is a complete sentence and its source is clear, you can let a quotation stand on its own, without any identifying words (example 5, second sentence).

- Attach identifying words to a quotation; these identifying words cannot be a sentence on their own.

- Use commas to separate any identifying words from quoted words in the same sentence.

- Always put quotation marks after commas and periods. Put quotation marks after question marks and exclamation points if they are part of the quoted sentence.

Quotation mark   Quotation mark
            | |
I said, "You're joking, right?"
            | |
     Comma   Question mark

Tip For more on commas with quotation marks, see page 440. For more on capitalization, see Chapter 30.

If a question mark or exclamation point is part of your own sentence, put it after the quotation mark.

                              Quotation mark
                                     |
What comedian said, "I have had a perfectly wonderful evening, but
                                     |
                                  Comma

Quotation mark
        |
this wasn't it"?
        |
Question mark

SETTING OFF A QUOTATION WITHIN ANOTHER QUOTATION

Sometimes, you may directly quote someone who quotes what someone else said or wrote. Put **single quotation marks (' ')** around the quotation within a quotation so that readers understand who said what.

The owner's manual said, "When the check-engine light comes on, see a mechanic immediately."

                                          Quotation within a quotation
                                                       |
The owner told her mechanic, "The owner's manual said 'see a mechanic immediately' when the check-engine light comes on, and the light is now on constantly."

No Quotation Marks for Indirect Quotations

When you report what someone said or wrote but do not use the person's exact words, you are writing an indirect quotation. Do not use quotation marks for indirect quotations. Indirect quotations often begin with the word *that*.

Indirect quotation

The man asked me how to get to the store.

Martino told me that he loves me.

Carla said that she won the lottery.

Direct quotation

The man asked me, "How do I get to the store?"

"I love you," Martino whispered in my ear.

"I won the lottery!" Carla said.

PRACTICE 1

For each of the following sentences, circle **I** if it is an indirect quotation or **D** if it is a direct quotation. In the blanks, write direct quotations as indirect and indirect quotations as direct.

Example: I /D "I would rather send an e-mail than use the phone," said Johan.

Rewrite: *Johan said that he would rather send an e-mail than use the phone.*

1. I / D Dana noted that phoning is more personal than e-mailing.

    Rewrite: _____

2. I / D Johan said, "I agree, but e-mail allows me to keep records of my conversations."

    Rewrite: _____

    _____

3. I / D Dana answered, "I don't see the point in keeping a record of asking someone to dinner."

    Rewrite: _____

    _____

4. I / D Johan responded that their date last week was a perfect example.

    Rewrite: _____

5. I / D Dana said, "I don't see your point."

    Rewrite: _____

6. I / D Johan asked, "Do you remember how late I was for dinner?"

    Rewrite: _____

7. I / D Dana said that she certainly remembered.

    Rewrite: _____

8. I / D Johan answered, "If we had arranged dinner by e-mail, I would have had the exact time in writing and wouldn't have been late."

    Rewrite: _____

    _____

    _____

    _____

    _____

PRACTICE 2

Edit the following sentences by adding quotation marks and commas where needed.

Example: "**Mr. Rivera will now answer questions from the audience,**" said **Dr. Sandler.**

1. Robert exclaimed I cannot believe that you quit a fantastic job as president of a huge advertising agency.

2. That was not a question said Mr. Rivera but I will respond to it anyway.

3. Mr. Rivera continued I loved my job, but it left me with hardly any time to see my family.

4. So you gave up a great job just to be with your family? asked Mary Alice.

5. I consider myself lucky Mr. Rivera responded.

6. My wife wanted to keep her job he said, and she's able to support our family.

7. Mr. Rivera admitted I never pictured myself in this position, but now that I am, I can't imagine otherwise.

8. About a year ago said Gerry you were quoted in a newspaper as saying There's nothing in the world like having a satisfying job.

9. Mr. Rivera laughed and then said I was exactly right, Gerry, and the most satisfying job I've ever had is the one I have now, being a stay-at-home dad.

10. Genine said With your permission, I'd like to quote you in our student newspaper as saying The most satisfying job I've ever had is the one I have now, being a stay-at-home dad.

Quotation Marks for Certain Titles

When referring to a short work such as a magazine or newspaper article, a chapter in a book, a short story, an essay, a song, or a poem, put quotation marks around the title of the work.

Newspaper article	"City Disaster Plan Revised"
Short story	"The Swimmer"
Essay	"A Brother's Murder"

Usually, titles of longer works—such as novels, books, magazines, newspapers, movies, television programs, and CDs—are italicized. The titles of sacred books such as the Bible and the Qu'ran are neither underlined, italicized, nor surrounded by quotation marks.

Book	*The House on Mango Street*
Newspaper	*Washington Post*
	[Do not underline, italicize, or capitalize the word *the* before the name of a newspaper or magazine, even if it is part of the title: **I saw that in the *New York Times*.** However, do capitalize and italicize *The* when it is the first word in titles of books, movies, and other sources.]

Note: When you write a paper for class, do not put quotation marks around the paper's title.

PRACTICE 3

Edit the following sentences by adding quotation marks around titles as needed. Underline any book, magazine, newspaper, or movie titles.

Example: My doctor is also a writer, and his latest short story is titled "The Near-Dead."

1. He told me that his idea for that title came from James Joyce's short story The Dead, which was part of Joyce's book Dubliners.

2. I told my doctor that I love Joyce's works and once wrote an essay called The Dead Live On.

3. One of my band's most popular songs is The Day of the Living Dead, which we wrote to honor our favorite old movie, The Night of the Living Dead.

4. We also have a song called You Never Die, based on a poem I wrote titled Forever.

5. My doctor told me that our songs inspired him to write a story that he will call The Death of Death, which he plans to submit to his favorite Web site.

Edit Quotation Marks in Everyday Life

EDITING PARAGRAPHS 1

Add or delete quotation marks as needed in the following paragraph, which is similar to one that you might find in a history textbook. Commas may also need to be added. Besides the first sentence, which has been marked for you, one other sentence is correct; write **C** next to it.

C
1 You may know Orville and Wilbur Wright for their famous accomplishment: inventing and flying the world's first airplane. 2 Did you know, however, that they "began their careers repairing bicycles?" 3 As the newly invented bicycle began to sweep the nation, the brothers opened a repair shop because "they wanted to make sure people kept their new mode of transportation in good shape." 4 However, they later admitted that "working with bicycles kept them satisfied for only a short time." 5 As Wilbur wrote in a letter to a friend, The boys of the Wright family are all lacking in determination and push. 6 In search of a new hobby, Wilbur wrote a letter to the Smithsonian Institution and said that "he needed some information." 7 I have some pet theories as to the proper construction of a flying machine, he wrote. 8 I wish to avail myself of all that is already known and then, if possible, add my knowledge to help the future worker who will attain final success. 9 He reassured the experts at the Smithsonian that "he and his brother were serious," not just simply curious. 10 "I am an enthusiast, but not a crank", he added. 11 Even so, the brothers likely had no idea that they were close to achieving fame in aviation.

EDITING PARAGRAPHS 2

Edit the following work e-mail, adding or deleting quotation marks as needed. Commas may also need to be added. Three sentences are correct; write **C** next to them. The first sentence has been edited for you.

Mr. Cooperman:

1 This afternoon, I asked freelance reporter Elaine Bosco to write next month's feature article, tentatively titled ʻWhere's the Beef? Corpus Christi's Best Steakhouses."2 As a reminder of Elaine's excellent work, I am attaching a copy

of her article on Texas diners, 830 Miles of Chicken Fried Steak. 3 She said that "she would be glad to take on another project." 4 In fact, she said, My schedule just opened up, so the timing is perfect. 5 I gave her the details and asked her if she could finish the article within two weeks. 6 She said that "the deadline wouldn't be a problem for her."

7 Elaine recently finished several articles for "Texas Monthly" online magazine, and I am concerned that it might hire her full-time. 8 If possible, I'd like to keep her working for us. 9 Jenna Melton, who worked with Elaine on the diner article, told me, Elaine is a talented food writer, and we should hire her as a staff writer if a position opens up. 10 In the meantime, I told Elaine that we will consider giving her more regular assignments.

Best,

Tina Lopez

Write and Edit Your Own Work

ASSIGNMENT 1   **Write**

Look at the photo below. Following the example on page 457, write a dialogue between these two people, adding quotation marks around their exact words. Make sure that it is clear who is saying what. When you are done, read your writing carefully, checking that you have used quotation marks and other punctuation carefully.

IMAGE SOURCE VIA AP IMAGES

| ASSIGNMENT 2 | **Edit** |

Using this chapter as a guide, edit quotation marks in a paper that you are writing for this course or another course or in a piece of writing from your work or everyday life.

Chapter Review

1. Quotation marks are used around _____: someone's speech or writing repeated exactly, word for word.

2. An _____ is a restatement of what someone said or wrote, not word for word.

3. Put _____ around a quotation within a quotation.

4. Put quotation marks around the titles of short works such as (give four examples)

   _____.

5. For longer works such as magazines, books, newspapers, and so on, either

   _____ or _____the titles.

REFLECTING ON THE JOURNEY

Skills Learned

Now that you've completed the chapter, look again at this paragraph.

   I have been struggling with my research paper. I approached my professor, and I asked her How do I find the sources I need for this paper? My professor was very encouraging. She said "Most students struggle the first time that they write a research paper, and your problems are normal." She also said that "I just need to make a plan and follow it." Next, she showed me how to look up articles on our library's database. I found a great article in "The New York Times." I think I am ready to start writing my paper now.

Using what you've learned in this chapter, edit this paragraph for mistakes in quotation marks. Then answer the questions below.

1. Are you confident that you have identified the mistakes?

2. Are you confident that you have corrected the mistakes?

3. What questions do you have about quotation marks?

Other Punctuation Marks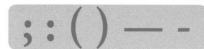

29

READING ROADMAP

Learning Objectives

Chapter Goal: Use punctuation marks correctly.

Tools to Achieve the Goal

- Reference list of punctuation marks (p. 466)
- Use semicolons (p. 466)
- Use colons (p. 467)
- Use parentheses (p. 469)
- Use dashes (p. 470)
- Use hyphens (p. 471)

Key Terms

Skim Chapter 29 before you begin reading. Can you find these words in **bold** type? Put a check mark next to each word once you have located it in the chapter.

_____ semicolon	_____ dash
_____ colon	_____ hyphen
_____ parentheses	

Highlight or circle any of these words that you already know.

Before You Read

Study the following paragraph and complete the chart. At the end of the chapter, you will examine the paragraph again and reflect on what you have learned.

> Service learning provides excellent opportunities for college students. First while students are helping others, they are gaining something even more valuable; experience. For example: a student in the medical field who works at a free clinic provides much needed assistance, but he also learns practical skills that relate to his major. These skills include: dealing with people who are afraid, who don't know the language, or who are in pain which can be a scary situation. In the end, students have as much to gain from service learning as the organizations they work for maybe even more.

This paragraph has problems with punctuation. Put a check mark by the statement that best describes you.

Skill Statement	
I understand what the mistakes are, and I know how to fix them.	
I understand what the mistakes are, but I am not sure how to fix them.	
I think I understand what the mistakes are.	
I don't understand what the mistakes are.	

465

Understand What Punctuation Does

Punctuation helps readers understand your writing. If you use punctuation incorrectly, you send readers a confusing message — or, even worse, a wrong one. This chapter covers five punctuation marks that people sometimes use incorrectly.

Five common punctuation marks		
Name	**Symbol**	**Purpose**
Semicolon	;	Joins two complete sentences (independent clauses)
		Separates items in a list that already has commas within individual items
Colon	:	Introduces a list after an independent clause
		Announces an explanation or examples
Parentheses	( )	Set off extra information that is not essential to the meaning of the sentence
Dash	—	Sets off words for emphasis
Hyphen	-	Joins two or more words that together form a single description
		Indicates that a word at the end of a line of type continues on the next line

Use Punctuation Correctly

Semicolon   ;

SEMICOLONS TO JOIN TWO CLOSELY RELATED SENTENCES

Use a semicolon to join two closely related sentences and make them into one sentence.

Tip To do this chapter, you need to know what a complete sentence is. For a review, see Chapters 11 and 12.

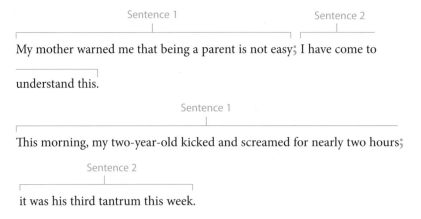

Sentence 1   Sentence 2

My mother warned me that being a parent is not easy; I have come to understand this.

Sentence 1

This morning, my two-year-old kicked and screamed for nearly two hours;

Sentence 2

it was his third tantrum this week.

SEMICOLONS WHEN ITEMS IN A LIST CONTAIN COMMAS

Use semicolons to separate items in a list that themselves contain commas. Otherwise, it is difficult for readers to tell where one item ends and another begins.

> We drove through Pittsburgh, Pennsylvania; Columbus, Ohio; and Indianapolis, Indiana.

PRACTICE 1

Edit the following sentences by adding semicolons where needed and deleting or revising any punctuation that is incorrectly used.

Example: I have a difficult decision to make before I graduate in May; I have been offered three jobs that I am interested in taking.

1. The jobs are in Miami, Florida, Atlanta, Georgia, and Boston, Massachusetts.

2. The Miami job is at a nonprofit organization, it doesn't pay very well, but I would be able to live at my mother's house for free.

3. The Atlanta job offers a great benefits package: health insurance, which I really need, dental insurance, which is a good bonus, and a 401(k) savings plan, which I understand is very important.

   Tip For more on using semicolons to join sentences, see Chapter 21.

4. The Boston job is at a prestigious hospital, the pay is good, but I have never been that far north.

5. Overall; I think I am leaning toward the high-paying Boston job, it is probably time for a new adventure.

Colon　:

COLONS BEFORE LISTS

Use a colon to introduce a list after a complete sentence.

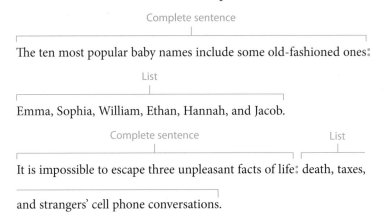

Complete sentence

The ten most popular baby names include some old-fashioned ones:

List

Emma, Sophia, William, Ethan, Hannah, and Jacob.

Complete sentence　　　　　　　　List

It is impossible to escape three unpleasant facts of life: death, taxes,

and strangers' cell phone conversations.

COLONS BEFORE EXPLANATIONS OR EXAMPLES

Use a colon after a complete sentence that introduces an explanation or example. If the explanation or example is also a complete sentence, capitalize the first letter after the colon.

The refrigerator is empty: Our new roommate loves to eat.

The roommate ate everything except for one item: a ketchup packet.

Note: A colon must follow a complete sentence. A common error is to place a colon after a phrase that includes *such as* or *for example*.

Incorrect	Shara likes winter sports, such as: skiing, ice hockey, and snowshoeing.
	Hector has annoying habits, for example: talking loudly, singing with the radio, and interrupting others.
Correct	Shara likes winter sports: skiing, ice hockey, and snowshoeing.
	OR
	Shara likes winter sports, such as skiing, ice hockey, and snowshoeing.
	Hector has annoying habits: talking loudly, singing with the radio, and interrupting others.

COLONS IN BUSINESS CORRESPONDENCE AND BEFORE SUBTITLES

Use a colon after a greeting in a business letter and after the headings at the beginning of a memorandum. (Memos are used to share information within many businesses.)

Dear Ms. Ramirez:

To: All employees

From: Mira Cole

Colons are also used between the main title and subtitle of publications.

The book that Doug read is called *Technicolor: Race, Technology, and Everyday Life.*

PRACTICE 2

Edit the following sentences by adding colons where needed and deleting or revising any punctuation that is incorrectly used. You may need to capitalize some letters.

Example: **My three-year-old daughter, Courtney, has one problem⁒ that makes traveling with her difficult⁚she is allergic to peanuts.**

1. Because of her allergy, my wife and I always bring three things when we go on vacation with Courtney, medication, Courtney's medical information, and our doctor's emergency number.

2. We have to ask several questions about food, for example: whether restaurant meals contain peanuts or whether a host's sandwiches contain peanut butter.

3. On our last vacation, a waitress made a serious mistake she was not aware that the restaurant used peanut oil in a dish that we ordered.

4. When Courtney started showing signs of an allergic reaction, we needed to follow the doctor's instructions, we had to administer emergency medication to her.

5. Luckily, Courtney responded immediately, and her next words made us all laugh "Peanuts are not a friend."

Parentheses   ( )

Use parentheses to set off information that is not essential to the meaning of a sentence. Do not overuse parentheses. When you do use them, they should be in pairs.

My favorite dessert (and also the most difficult one to make) is cherry strudel.

The twins have stopped arguing (at least for now) about who should get the car on Saturday.

PRACTICE 3

Edit the following sentences by adding parentheses where needed and deleting any that are incorrectly used.

Example: **In this age of casual dress ⁽at least for most people⁾ there are still times when ⁽I feel most comfortable⁾ wearing a suit.**

1. Last year, I needed a new suit, but the suits that I liked at stores were just too expensive some outrageously expensive.

2. I had heard about an excellent tailor who made custom suits that were fairly affordable about $300, on average.

3. This tailor, Mr. Shephard, measured me and had me try on several suits at least six to see what would work the best (given my height and body type.)

4. Together, we chose a gray suit with thin stripes called "chalk stripes" that looked really good on me.

5. Mr. Shephard was able to adjust (the suit) quickly in about a week, and it looks great on me.

Dash —

Use dashes as you use parentheses: to set off additional information, particularly information that you want to emphasize.

> The test—worth 30 percent of your final grade—will have forty questions.
>
> Over the holiday, the police officers gave huge tickets—some as much as $300—to speeders.

A dash can also indicate a pause, much as a comma does but somewhat more forcefully.

> I want to go on vacation—alone.

To make a dash, type two hyphens together, and your word processing program will automatically convert them to a dash. Alternatively, you can insert a dash as a symbol. Do not leave any extra spaces around a dash.

> **PRACTICE 4**
>
> Edit the following sentences by adding dashes where needed and deleting any that are incorrectly used.
>
> **Example: People who live in cool, dry climates get more exercise than others at least that is what one study found.**

1. This study matched the percentage of people in an area—who meet the exercise recommendations of the Centers for Disease Control and Prevention—with weather reports from all over the United States.

2. The recommendations are thirty minutes of moderate physical activity five to seven days a week or twenty minutes of energetic physical activity three to seven days a week; the exercise can be done anywhere indoors or outdoors.

3. Several states with cool climates Montana, Utah, Wisconsin, New Hampshire, and Vermont had the highest percentages—of people who met the exercise requirements.

4. The areas with the lowest percentages—of people meeting the exercise requirements Hawaii, North Carolina, Mississippi, and Puerto Rico all have hot and humid weather.

5. These unsurprising results few people like to exercise in hot, humid weather make me wonder why anyone even bothered to do this study.

Hyphen -

HYPHENS TO JOIN WORDS THAT FORM A SINGLE DESCRIPTION

Use a hyphen to join words that together form a single description of a person, place, thing, or idea.

The fourteen-year-old actor went to school while making the movie.

The senator flew to Africa on a fact-finding mission.

When will the company file its year-end report?

HYPHENS TO DIVIDE A WORD AT THE END OF A LINE

Use a hyphen to divide a word when part of the word must continue on the next line. Most word processing programs do this automatically, but if you are writing by hand, you need to insert hyphens yourself.

At the recycling station, you will be asked to separate newspapers from aluminum cans and glass.

If you are not sure where to break a word, look it up in a dictionary. The word's main entry will show you where you can break the word: *dic-tio-nary*. If you still are not sure that you are putting the hyphen in the right place, do not break the word; write it all on the next line.

> **PRACTICE 5**
>
> Edit the following sentences by adding hyphens where needed and deleting any that are incorrectly used. One sentence is correct; write **C** next to it.
>
> Example: **In 2011, ninety-eight-year-old Nancy Wake died in London.**
>   ^   ^   ^
>
> 1. During World War II, Wake had been a thirty one year old agent for the British military.
>
> 2. Wake's Nazi killing stories were legendary among British and American-forces.

3. Because she was not a gun wielding man, German-soldiers rarely suspected her.

4. Nicknamed "White Mouse" by the Germans, the well trained Wake always avoided capture.

5. A best-selling biography about Wake was published in 2001.

Edit Other Punctuation in Everyday Life

EDITING PARAGRAPHS 1

Edit the following memo by adding or deleting punctuation as needed. One sentence is correct; write **C** next to it. The first sentence has been edited for you.

To: All employees
From: Todd Grayson, Personnel Department
Re: Office picnic

1 I would like to remind you all about this Friday's company picnic (our first at) Shelton Community Park. 2 Please plan to arrive at the park by 10:30 Friday morning, latecomers may not get the best parking. 3 We need each person to bring some food to share, snacks, desserts, side dishes, casseroles, and salads. 4 Drinks will be brought by Jim Terrino, activity coordinator, Sally Bursal, head of administration, and Rita Perez, director of personnel. 5 Our tables will be set up by the east gate, and my nineteen year old son, Rob, will be directing you to the correct parking area. 6 Please remember to bring folding chairs, tables will be provided by the park. 7 Anyone who cannot attend and I hope there will not be anyone on this list should let me know by the end of the day tomorrow. 8 I am looking forward to seeing you at this event.

EDITING PARAGRAPHS 2

Edit the following essay by adding or deleting punctuation as needed. Three sentences are correct; write **C** next to them. The first sentence has been edited for you. You may need to capitalize some letters.

1 Many people would complain if they had to spend an entire day at the mall; if it was the Mall of America, however, the story would be different.

2 Located in the Twin Cities suburb of Bloomington, Minnesota, this mall has something for everyone. 3 The number and variety of places in this mall are staggering: more than five hundred stores, fifty restaurants, fourteen movie theaters with multiple screens, several concession areas, and great sound, eight nightclubs, a casino, a concert hall, and a bowling alley.

4 The Mall of America is also home to Nickelodeon Universe the nation's largest indoor theme park, featuring thirty rides. 5 A four story Lego Imagination Center shows what can be made with thousands of plastic bricks. 6 If your kids like ocean creatures, there is something they have to see the Sea Life Minnesota Aquarium, where children can touch real stingrays.

7 If these offerings do not sound like enough fun; keep exploring. 8 Flight simulators give you a chance to feel what it would be like to fly. 9 The NASCAR Motor Speedway offers fast paced excitement for racing fans.

10 A popular attraction is the large collection of sets, costumes, and props from the *Star Trek* television series and films. 11 This one of a kind exhibit is fun for the whole family even those who have never seen the show. 12 Be sure not to take any personal photographs of the displays it's one of the rules of the exhibit.

13 My mother a tough woman to please loves the Mall of America, and that says a lot. 14 Where else can you: shop, eat, see a movie, ride a Ferris wheel, pet a stingray, and have an auto race all in the same building?

Write and Edit Your Own Work

ASSIGNMENT 1   Write

Imagine that you are selling something—for example, your car or another possession or a real or an imaginary product. Write an advertisement for the item, including details about the item's features and benefits. If you can, invent a headline for the ad to get potential buyers' attention. When you are done, read your writing carefully, checking especially for punctuation errors.

ASSIGNMENT 2   Edit

Using this chapter as a guide, edit punctuation errors in a paper that you are writing for this course or another course or in a piece of writing from your work or everyday life.

Chapter Review

1. Use a semicolon to _____ and make them into one sentence and to _____ .

2. A colon can be used after a complete sentence that introduces a _____ or an _____ . A colon can also be used after a _____ in a business letter, after the _____ at the beginning of a memorandum, and between the main title and _____ of publications.

3. Use parentheses to set off _____ _____ .

4. _____ also set off additional information, particularly information that you want to emphasize.

5. Use a hyphen to join words that together _____ and to _____ a word at the end of a line.

REFLECTING ON THE JOURNEY

Skills Learned

Now that you've completed the chapter, look again at this paragraph.

Service learning provides excellent opportunities for college students. First while students are helping others, they are gaining something even more valuable; experience. For example: a student in the medical field who works at a free clinic provides much needed assistance, but he also learns practical skills that relate to his major. These skills include: dealing with people who are afraid, who don't know the language, or who are in pain which can be a scary situation. In the end, students have as much to gain from service learning as the organizations they work for maybe even more.

Using what you've learned in this chapter, edit this paragraph for missing or incorrect puncutation. Then answer the questions below.

1. Are you confident that you have identified the mistakes?

2. Are you confident that you have corrected the mistakes?

3. What questions do you have about punctuation?

30

Capitalization

READING ROADMAP

Learning Objectives

Chapter Goal: Use capital letters correctly.

Tools to Achieve the Goal

- Capitalization of sentences (p. 476)
- Capitalization of names (p. 477)
- Capitalization of titles (p. 480)

Before You Read

Before you begin reading this chapter, study the following paragraph and complete the chart. At the end of the chapter, you will examine the paragraph again and reflect on what you have learned.

> In the 1970s, richard O'Brien wrote a musical about a mad scientist from outer space. His play, which was called *the rocky horror picture show*, opened in London in 1973 to wildly enthusiastic audiences. Filmmakers decided it would make a good movie. Before it was released on film, the play opened in new York, and the reviews weren't really good. As a result, the movie didn't make much money. Then a Producer asked a theater in greenwich village to show the film every night at midnight. some fans attended every night and dressed like the characters. Soon the film was considered a classic, and today people still attend midnight showings. Two years ago i attended a midnight showing in chicago, and i can't wait to go again.

This paragraph has problems with missing or incorrect capital letters. Put a check mark by the statement that best describes you.

Skill Statement	
I understand what the mistakes are, and I know how to fix them.	
I understand what the mistakes are, but I am not sure how to fix them.	
I think I understand what the mistakes are.	
I don't understand what the mistakes are.	

LaunchPadSolo

Visit **LaunchPad Solo for Readers and Writers > Capitalization** for more practice with capitalization.

Understand Capitalization

Capital letters are generally bigger than lowercase letters, and they may have a different form.

Capital letters	A, B, C, D, E, F, G, H, I, J, K, L, M, N, O, P, Q, R, S, T, U, V, W, X, Y, Z
Lowercase letters	a, b, c, d, e, f, g, h, i, j, k, l, m, n, o, p, q, r, s, t, u, v, w, x, y, z

Capitalize (use capital letters for) the first letter of

- every new sentence
- names of specific people, places, dates, and things
- important words in titles

Use Capitalization Correctly

Capitalization of Sentences

Tip To do this chapter, you need to know what a sentence is. For a review, see Chapter 11.

Capitalize the first letter of each new sentence, including the first word in a direct quotation.

> The police officer broke up our noisy party.
>
> He said, "Do you realize how loud your music is?"

PRACTICE 1

Edit the following paragraph, changing lowercase letters to capital letters as needed. One sentence is correct; write **C** next to it.

1 Mark Twain is well known for the books that he wrote, but when he was alive, he was almost as famous for his clever sayings. 2 for instance, Twain once said, "a banker is a fellow who lends you his umbrella when the sun is shining and wants it back the minute it begins to rain." 3 he also made people laugh when he stated, "get your facts first, and then you can change them as much as you please." 4 Along with Twain's humor came a touch of bitterness, as when he said, "always do right. This will gratify some people and astonish the rest." 5 People liked it best when Twain passed on comical advice, such as, "be respectful to your superiors, if you have any."

Capitalization of Names of Specific People, Places, Dates, and Things

Capitalize the first letter in names of specific people, places, dates, and things (also known as proper nouns). Do not capitalize general words such as *college* as opposed to the specific name: *Witley College*.

PEOPLE

Capitalize the first letter in names of specific people and in titles used with names of specific people.

Specific	Not specific
Patty Wise	my friend
Dr. Jackson	the physician
President Barack H. Obama	the president
Professor Arroyo	your professor
Aunt Marla, Mother	my aunt, my mother

The name of a family member is capitalized when the family member is being addressed directly or when the family title is replacing a first name.

> Sit down here, Sister.
>
> I wish Mother would see a doctor.

In other cases, do not capitalize.

> My sister came to the party.
>
> I am glad that my mother is seeing a doctor.

PLACES

Capitalize the first letter in names of specific buildings, streets, cities, states, regions, and countries.

Specific	Not specific
the Seagram Building	that building
Elm Street	our street
Jacksonville, Florida	my town
Wisconsin	this state
the South	the southern part of the country
Chinatown	my neighborhood
Pakistan	her birthplace

Do not capitalize directions in a sentence: *Drive north for three miles.*

DATES

Capitalize the first letter in the names of days, months, and holidays. Do not capitalize the names of the seasons (winter, spring, summer, fall).

Specific	Not specific
Friday	today
July	summer
Martin Luther King Jr. Day	my birthday

ORGANIZATIONS, COMPANIES, AND SPECIFIC GROUPS

Specific	Not specific
Doctors Without Borders	the charity
Starbucks	the coffee shop
Wilco	his favorite band

LANGUAGES, NATIONALITIES, AND RELIGIONS

Specific	Not specific
English, Spanish, Chinese	my first language
Christianity, Islam	her religion

The names of languages should be capitalized even if you are not referring to a specific course: *I am studying economics and French.*

 Language note: Some languages, such as Spanish, French, and Italian, do not capitalize days, months, and languages. In English, such words must be capitalized.

Incorrect	I study Russian every monday, wednesday, and friday from january through may.
Correct	I study Russian every **Monday, Wednesday,** and **Friday** from **January** through **May.**

COURSES

Specific	Not specific
English 100	a writing course
Psychology 100	the introductory psychology course

COMMERCIAL PRODUCTS

Specific	Not specific
Nikes	sneakers
Tylenol	pain reliever

PRACTICE 2

Edit the following sentences by adding capitalization as needed or removing capitalization where it is inappropriate.

Example: Going to los angeles valley college gives me the chance to learn near one of the Country's most exciting cities.

1. My favorite classes at College are Sociology, biology, and french.

2. On tuesdays and thursdays, I have a great class on shakespeare's Plays.

3. That Class is taught by professor John Sortensen, who happens to be my Uncle.

4. I decided to go to this College in the first place because uncle john recommended it.

5. On weekends, I can catch the Train into los angeles at the north hollywood station, which is not far from where I live.

6. Before it closed, I used to go to the carole and barry kaye museum, which displayed miniatures.

7. The Museum had a miniature Courtroom showing the o.j. simpson Trial and tiny Palaces furnished with chandeliers the size of rice.

8. I also like to visit the los angeles county museum of art, the craft and folk art museum, and an Automotive Museum that has some famous cars.

9. The City's Restaurants are another reason to visit often, and so far I have tried mexican, japanese, thai, italian, indian, argentinian, and, of course, chinese Food.

10. My Uncle was right about the city's great Cultural Attractions, but I have also made sure to see disneyland and two theme parks: universal studios and six flags magic mountain.

Capitalization of Titles

Tip For advice on punctuating titles, see Chapter 28. For a list of common prepositions, see Chapter 10.

Capitalize the first word and all other important words in titles of books, movies, television programs, magazines, newspapers, articles, stories, songs, papers, poems, and so on. Words that do not need to be capitalized (unless they are the first or last word) include *the, a,* and *an;* the conjunctions *and, but, for, nor, or, so,* and *yet;* and prepositions.

> *American Idol* is Marion's favorite television show.
>
> Did you read the article titled "Humans Should Travel to Mars"?
>
> We read *The Awakening,* a novel by Kate Chopin.

PRACTICE 3

Edit the following paragraph by capitalizing titles as needed.

1 "I married your mother because I wanted children," said Groucho Marx in the movie *horse feathers*. "Imagine my disappointment when you arrived." 2 One of the best-known comedians of all time, Marx got his first big break in show business costarring with his brothers in a 1924 Broadway comedy called *i'll say she is*. 3 As a team, the Marx Brothers followed up with more Broadway hits, including *animal crackers*. 4 They went on to make fifteen movies together, including *a night at the opera* and *a night in casablanca*. 5 In their movie *duck soup,* Groucho Marx said to another character, "I got a good mind to join a club and beat you over the head with it." 6 After a successful movie career, Marx appeared in several radio shows, the most famous of which was the quiz show *you bet your life*. 7 Later, he brought *you bet your life* to TV. 8 Marx also wrote several books, including his autobiography *groucho and me,* which was published in 1959.

Edit for Capitalization in Everyday Life

EDITING PARAGRAPHS 1

Following is part of an instructor's handout for a history course. Edit it by capitalizing words as needed or by deleting unnecessary capital letters. The first sentence has been marked **C**, for correct, for you.

C
1 This first unit of American History 101 will focus on the civil rights movement. 2 We will explore this movement from the Civil War until Current times. 3 Six of the eight weeks devoted to this unit will concentrate on the

1960s, when struggles for Civil Rights made daily headlines across the Nation. 4 we will learn about leaders such as Martin Luther King Jr., Rosa Parks, Malcolm X, and jesse jackson. 5 We will also examine the history of the Ku Klux Klan, the development of the National association for the advancement of Colored People, and the passage of the Civil Rights act of 1964. 6 As we work through the material, you will be given reading assignments from your textbook, *the American promise*. 7 A final exam covering the course material will be given on december 15 in howard hall. 8 Tutoring in this unit will be available through my Teaching assistants, Ms. Chambers and Mr. Carlin. 9 If you have any questions, please see me after class or during my Office Hours.

EDITING PARAGRAPHS 2

Following is an advertisement for a job at a health-care company. Edit it by capitalizing words as needed or by deleting unnecessary capital letters. The first sentence has been edited for you. One sentence is correct; write **C** next to it.

1 At bridges health-care partners, we are leaders in rehabilitative and
long-term care. 2 We are currently hiring a billing and collection coordinator for our tampa, florida, location. 3 our office is in a modern downtown building near many restaurants and shopping areas. 4 The candidate we are seeking should have a two-year degree in Accounting and good Communication skills. 5 Three years of experience in Health-care billing is preferred. 6 We offer a competitive salary and generous benefits. 7 Please submit your cover letter and résumé by monday, september 24, to Carlo hawkins, bridges health-care partners, 5200 city walk gardens, tampa, fl 33607.

Write and Edit Your Own Work

ASSIGNMENT 1   Write

Choose one of the following people: Maya Angelou, Robert Griffin III, Steve Jobs, Jennifer Lawrence, Lionel Messi, Kate Middleton, or Neil Patrick Harris. Search for biographical information about that person online: birthplace, family, education, and achievements. Write a brief biographical paragraph, paying attention to capital letters. When you are done, read your writing carefully, checking especially for capitalization errors.

ASSIGNMENT 2   Edit

Using this chapter as a guide, edit capitalization errors in a paper that you are writing for this course or another course or in a piece of writing from your work or everyday life.

Chapter Review

1. Capitalize the _____ of each new sentence.

2. Capitalize the first letter in names of specific _____ , _____ , _____ , and _____ .

3. Capitalize the first letters of first and last words and all other _____ in titles.

REFLECTING ON THE JOURNEY

Skills Learned

Now that you've completed the chapter, look again at this paragraph.

> In the 1970s, richard O'Brien wrote a musical about a mad scientist from outer space. His play, which was called *the rocky horror picture show*, opened in London in 1973 to wildly enthusiastic audiences. Filmmakers decided it would make a good movie. Before it was released on film, the play opened in new York, and the reviews weren't really good. As a result, the movie didn't make much money. Then a Producer asked a theater in greenwich village to show the film every night at midnight. some fans attended every night and dressed like the characters. Soon the film was considered a classic, and today people still attend midnight showings. Two years ago i attended a midnight showing in chicago, and i can't wait to go again.

Using what you've learned in this chapter, edit this paragraph for problems with capital letters. Then answer the questions below.

1. Are you confident that you have identified the mistakes?

2. Are you confident that you have corrected the mistakes?

3. What questions do you have about punctuation?

Part 7

ESL Concerns

31

Subjects

Academic, or formal, English is the English that you are expected to use in college and in most work situations, especially in writing. If you are not used to using formal English or if English is not your native language, the chapters in this part will help you avoid the most common problems with key sentence parts.

Note: In Chapters 31–33, we use the word *English* to refer to formal English.

Include a Subject in Every Sentence

Every sentence in English must have a subject and a verb. The most basic sentence pattern is **SUBJECT-VERB (S-V)**.

	S V
Example	The <u>dog</u> <u>ate</u>.

To find the subject in a sentence, ask, Who or what is doing the main action of the sentence? In the previous example, the answer is *dog*.

The complete subject includes all the words that make up the subject.

Examples   <u>Great Smoky Mountains National Park</u> <u>is</u> famous for its beauty.

              <u>The old apple tree</u> <u>produced</u> a lot of fruit.

In some sentences, the subject is the pronoun *it*.

Incorrect   <u>Is</u> cold today.
              [The sentence has no subject.]

Correct   <u>**It**</u> <u>is</u> cold today.

Visit **LaunchPad Solo for Readers and Writers** > **Sentence Structure** for more practice with subjects in sentences.

Tip For more on basic English sentence patterns, see Chapter 11.

Tip In this chapter, subjects are underlined, and verbs are double-underlined.

Tip For more on pronouns, see Chapter 10.

Incorrect	The soccer game was canceled. Will be played next week.

[The second sentence has no subject.]

Correct	The soccer game was canceled. **It** will be played next week.

Remember, pronouns are used to replace nouns or pronouns, not to repeat them.

Incorrect	The driver **he** hit another car.

[*Driver* is the subject noun, and *he* just repeats it.]

Correct	The driver hit another car.

PRACTICE 1

Underline the complete subject in each sentence. If there is no subject, add one and underline it. If a pronoun repeats the subject, delete it.

Most people like

Example: ~~Like~~ a good ghost story.
          ^

1. Recently, a professor he found similarities between modern and ancient ghost stories.

2. Ghost stories from ancient Greece and Rome describe white, black, or gray spirits.

3. Modern ghost stories also have spirits of these colors.

4. Is common for ancient and modern ghosts to bring news.

5. Sometimes may bring a warning.

6. Animals they always see spirits that humans cannot.

7. In the scariest stories, ghosts they want revenge.

8. Good stories of the present and past have frightening details.

9. Bring life to the tales.

10. For example, a severed hand may open a door.

More Than One Subject

Some sentences can have more than one subject. Consider these three cases:

1. Subjects joined by *and* or *or*.

Examples	Taxes **and** tests are not on anyone's list of fun things to do.
	Tatiana **or** Bill will wash the car.

2. Sentences that are really two sentences joined with the words *and, but, for, or, so, nor,* or *yet*.

Tip For more on how to join sentences with these words, see Chapters 12 and 21.

Examples   Kim <u>went</u> to English class, **and** Dan <u>went</u> to math.

Kim <u>went</u> to English class, **but** she <u>was</u> late.

3. Sentences joined by dependent words, such as *after, before, if, since, unless, until,* and *while*.

Tip For a more complete list of dependent words, see page 224.

Examples   Dan <u>went</u> to math class **before** he <u>ate</u> lunch.

Dan <u>did</u> his homework **after** he <u>ate</u>.

Important: The subject of a sentence can never be in a prepositional phrase. For more information, see page 203.

> **PRACTICE 2**
>
> Underline all the subjects in the sentences below.
>
> **Example: <u>Bill</u> and <u>Jane</u> are my neighbors, and <u>they</u> have a toddler.**

1. He is a boy, and his name is David.

2. David is two years old, and he is just starting to talk.

3. Whenever Bill and Jane go out, I babysit for him.

4. David and I walk to the park, eat ice cream, or play games.

5. David loves to ask questions, and he enjoys going down the slide.

6. When David sees me, he always smiles.

7. On Saturdays, after he takes his morning nap, I often take him for a walk.

8. In some ways, David and I are like brothers.

9. If I ever have a child, I want him to be just like David.

10. David and I will be friends even after I have children of my own.

Chapter Review

1. How can you find the subject in a sentence? _____

_____

2. Does every sentence need a subject? _____

3. Can a sentence have more than one subject? _____

32

Verbs

Understand Verbs

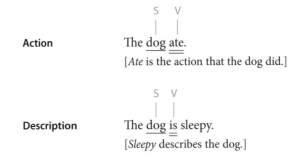

Visit **LaunchPad Solo for Readers and Writers > Verbs** for more practice with verbs.

Every sentence in English must have a subject and a verb. The most basic sentence pattern is **SUBJECT-VERB (S-V)**.

A **verb** can show action, or it can be used to describe a condition or state of being.

Tip For more on English sentence patterns, see Chapters 11 and 12.

Tip In this chapter, subjects are underlined, and verbs are double-underlined.

	S V
Action	The <u>dog</u> <u><u>ate</u></u>. [*Ate* is the action that the dog did.]
Description	The <u>dog</u> <u><u>is</u></u> sleepy. [*Sleepy* describes the dog.]

Tip For more on the kinds of English verbs (action, linking, and helping), see Chapter 10. For more on irregular verb forms, see Chapter 16.

English verbs, like verbs in most other languages, have different tenses to show when something happened: in the past, present, or future.

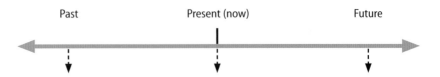

Past   Present (now)   Future

Chapter 16 presents information about common errors with verb tense, and it includes detailed explanations, practices, and reference charts. This chapter reviews some verb trouble spots for students whose first language is not English.

Use *Be* to Show Age, Emotion, or Physical Condition

The irregular verb *be* is used very often in English. The simple present and past forms of *be* are:

	Singular		Plural	
First person	I	am/was	we	are/were
Second person	you	are/were	you	are/were
Third person	he/she/it	is/was	they	are/were

Be (not *have*) is used to show age, emotion, or physical condition.

- Use *be* to express **age**.

Incorrect	I *have* twenty-two years.
Correct	I *am* twenty-two.
Correct	I *am* twenty-two years old.

- Use *be* to express **emotion**.

Incorrect	Dara *has* sad.
Correct	Dara *is* sad.

- Use *be* to express a **physical condition**.

Incorrect	They *have* sick.
Correct	They *are* sick.

Every sentence must include a verb, even when the verb is just linking the subject to the description word.

Incorrect	Chelsea quiet.
	Tagen sorry.
	Sylvia forty-two.
Correct	Chelsea *is* quiet.
	Tagen *is* sorry.
	Sylvia *is* forty-two.

PRACTICE 1

Fill in the blank with the correct verb.

Example: We ___*are*___ excited about the party next weekend.

1. The party _____ a surprise for a friend.

2. All the guests _____ twenty-one or older.

3. I _____ twenty-two.

4. The party _____ in a renovated warehouse.

5. Keegan and Nick _____ sad that they will be out of town.

Form Negatives Correctly

To form a negative statement, use one of the following words, often with a helping verb:

never	nobody	no one	nowhere
no	none	not	

Common Helping Verbs

Forms of *be*	Forms of *have*	Forms of *do*	Other
be	have	do	can/could
am	has	does	may/might/must
are	had	did	shall/should
been			will/would
being			
is			
was			
were			

Notice in the example sentences that the word *not* comes after any helping verb.

Statement   The <u>bird</u> <u>could talk</u>.

Negative   The <u>bird</u> <u>~~no~~ could talk</u>.
        _{not}

Statement	My boss yells at us.
	does not
Negative	My boss ~~no~~ yell~~s~~ at us.
	^

Statement	The store sells peppers.
	no
Negative	The store not sells peppers.
	does not sell ^
Negative	The store ~~no has~~ peppers.
	^
	[Note that the helping verb must be used with *not*.]

Do not use double negatives.

Incorrect	Paolo not owns *no* car.
Correct	Paolo *does not* own a car.
Correct	Paolo owns *no* car.

When forming a negative in the simple past tense, use the past tense of the helping verb *do* and the base form of the verb.

did	+	*not*	+	base verb	=	negative simple past tense

Statement	Gina *called* the police.
Negative	Gina *did not call* the police.

Statement	The customer *paid* for her order.
Negative	The customer *did not pay* for her order.

Tip For more on regular and irregular verbs in the simple past tense, see page 276.

PRACTICE 2

Rewrite the statements to make them negative statements.

not
Example: Manny's computer is working well.
^

1. It starts up quickly.

2. Manny thinks it is as fast as ever.

3. He is satisfied with the applications.

4. Manny has money for a new computer.

5. He saves money every month.

6. His former job paid overtime regularly.

7. Tuition rose last semester.

8. Manny made enough to cover the increase.

9. He decided what to do about the computer.

10. He will buy a new one.

Form Questions Correctly

To turn a statement into a question, put the helping verb *before* the subject.

| Statement | Chris *will go* with Tim. |
| Question | *Will* Chris go with Tim? |

If the only verb in the statement is a form of *be,* put it *before* the subject.

| Statement | Trayla *is* sick today. |
| Question | *Is* Trayla sick today? |

If there is no helping verb or form of *be* in the statement, add a form of *do,* and put it *before* the subject. For a singular verb, drop the final *-s* or *-es.* For a plural verb, keep the verb the same.

Statement	The pizza place delivers.
Question	*Does* the pizza place deliver?
	[The verb *delivers* is singular (to match the singular subject *pizza place*), so the final *-s* is dropped to make the question. The singular form of *do* (*does*) is added before the subject.]

Statement	The children play in the park.
Question	*Do* the children play in the park?
	[The verb *play* is plural (to match the plural subject *children*), so the verb *play* stays the same.]

PRACTICE 3

Rewrite the statements to make them into questions.

Example: **Duane sings in a band.** *Does Duane sing in a band?*

1. The band is popular.

   _____

2. It plays every weekend.

   _____

3. The band has made a CD.

   _____

4. The band has contacted a local radio station.

   _____

5. The station has agreed to play the band's CD.

   _____

Form the Present-Progressive Tense Correctly

The present progressive is used to describe an action or a condition that is happening now. Following are some common errors in forming the present progressive.

- **Forgetting to add -*ing* to the verb**

  Incorrect

  I am type now.

  She/he is not work now.

  Correct

  I am typ**ing** now.

  She/he is not work**ing** now.

- **Forgetting to include a form of *be* (*am/is/are*)**

  Incorrect

  He typing now.

  They typing now.

  Correct

  He **is** typing now.

  They **are** typing now.

- **Forgetting to use a form of *be* (*am/is/are*) to start questions**

Incorrect	They <u>typing</u> now?
Correct	<u>**Are**</u> they <u>typing</u> now?

PRACTICE 4

Rewrite the following sentences as indicated.

1. Dan is mowing the grass.

   Make the sentence a question: _____

   _____

2. It was freezing this morning.

   Make the sentence a negative statement: _____

   _____

3. You are wearing a new dress.

   Make the sentence a question: _____

   _____

4. They are driving to the park.

   Make the sentence a negative statement: _____

   _____

5. Chad was working when you saw him.

   Make the sentence into a question: _____

   _____

Use Modal Auxiliaries/Helping Verbs Correctly

Tip For more on helping verbs, see Chapter 10.

Tip The past participle of regular verbs ends in *-d* or *-ed*. For past-participle forms of irregular verbs, see Chapter 16.

If you have taken an English-as-a-second-language (ESL) course, you might recognize the term **modal auxiliary**, a type of helping verb that expresses a writer's view about an action. As shown in the following chart, these helping verbs join with a main (base) verb to make a complete verb.

HELPING VERB (MODAL AUXILIARY)

<table>
<tr>
<td>

General formulas for all modal auxiliaries (More helping verbs are shown on pp. 495–498.)

</td>
<td>

STATEMENTS

Present:	Subject	+	Helping verb	+	Base verb
	Dumbo		can		fly.

Past: Forms vary (see below).

NEGATIVES

Present:	Subject	+	Helping verb + *not*	+	Base verb
	Dumbo		cannot		fly.

Past: Forms vary (see below).

QUESTIONS

Present:	Helping verb	+	Subject	+	Base verb
	Can		Dumbo		fly?

Past: Forms vary (see below).

</td>
</tr>
<tr>
<td>

Can (**could** in past tense)

Can means *ability*.

</td>
<td>

STATEMENTS

Present: Beth **can** work fast.

Past: Beth **could** work fast.

NEGATIVES

Present: Beth **can**not work fast.

Past: Beth **could** not work fast.

QUESTIONS

Present: **Can** Beth work fast?

Past: **Could** Beth work fast? ➔

</td>
</tr>
</table>

HELPING VERB (MODAL AUXILIARY)

Could	
Could means *possibility*. It can also be the past tense of *can*.	**STATEMENTS** **Present:** Beth **could** work fast if she had better tools. **Past:** Beth **could** have worked fast if she had better tools.
	NEGATIVES *Can* is used for present negatives. (See above.) **Past:** Beth **could** not have worked fast.
	QUESTIONS **Present: Could** Beth work fast? **Past: Could** Beth have worked fast?
May *May* means *permission*. For past-tense forms, see *might*.	**STATEMENTS** **Present:** You **may** borrow my car.
	NEGATIVES **Present:** You **may** not borrow my car.
	QUESTIONS **Present: May** I borrow your car?
Might *Might* means *possibility*. It can also be the past tense of *may*.	**STATEMENTS** **Present (with *be*):** Lou **might** be asleep. **Past (with *have* + past participle of *be*):** Lou **might** have been asleep. **Future:** Lou **might** sleep.
	NEGATIVES **Present (with *be*):** Lou **might** not be asleep. **Past (with *have* + past participle of *be*):** Lou **might** not have been asleep. **Future:** Lou **might** not sleep.
	QUESTIONS In questions, *might* is very formal and rarely used.

HELPING VERB (MODAL AUXILIARY)	
Must *Must* means *necessary*.	**STATEMENTS** **Present:** We **must** try. **Past (with *have* + past participle of base verb):** We **must** have tried.
	NEGATIVES **Present:** We **must** not try. **Past (with *have* + past participle of base verb):** We **must** not have tried.
	QUESTIONS **Present: Must** we try? Past-tense questions with *must* are unusual.
Should *Should* means *duty* or *expectation*.	**STATEMENTS** **Present:** They **should** call. **Past (with *have* + past participle of base verb):** They **should** have called.
	NEGATIVES **Present:** They **should** not call. **Past (with *have* + past participle of base verb):** They **should** not have called.
	QUESTIONS **Present: Should** they call? **Past (with *have* + past participle of base verb): Should** they have called?
Will *Will* means *intend to* (future). For past-tense forms, see *would*.	**STATEMENTS** **Future:** I **will** succeed.
	NEGATIVES **Future:** I **will** not succeed.
	QUESTIONS **Future: Will** I succeed? →

Note: Two other modal auxiliary verbs communicate a sense of duty or intention: **shall** and **ought to**:

Shall we go now?

We **ought to** send a thank-you note to our host.

HELPING VERB (MODAL AUXILIARY)	
Would	STATEMENTS
Would means *prefer*. It also is used to start a future request. It can also be the past tense of *will*.	**Present:** I would like to travel.
	Past (with *have* + past participle of base verb): I **would** have traveled if I had the money.
	NEGATIVES
	Present: I **would** not like to travel.
	Past (with *have* + past participle of base verb): I **would** not have traveled if it hadn't been for you.
	QUESTIONS
	Present: Would you like to travel?
	(*or* to start a request) **Would** you help me . . .?
	Past (with *have* + past participle of base verb): **Would** you have traveled with me if I had asked you?

Following are some common errors in using modal auxiliaries.

- **Using more than one helping verb**

Incorrect	They **will can** help.
Correct	They **will** help. (future intention)
Correct	They **can** help. (are able to)

- **Using *to* between the helping verb and the main (base) verb**

Incorrect	Emilio **might to** come with us.
Correct	Emilio **might** come with us.

- **Using *must* instead of *had to* in the past**

Incorrect	She **must** work yesterday.
Correct	She **had to** work yesterday.

- **Forgetting to change *can* to *could* in the past negative**

Incorrect	Last night, I **can**not sleep.
Correct	Last night, I **could** not sleep.

- Forgetting to use *have* with *could/should/would* in the past tense

Incorrect	Tara **should** called last night.
Correct	Tara **should have** called last night.

- Using *will* instead of *would* to express a preference in the present tense

Incorrect	I **will** like to travel.
Correct	I **would** like to travel.

PRACTICE 5

Fill in modal auxiliaries (helping verbs) in the sentences below.

Example: **When Carlos walked into the department store, a salesclerk asked, "__May__ I help you?"**

1. "Hi," said Carlos. "I _____ like to buy a gift for my girlfriend."

2. "Okay," said the clerk. "We have lots of nice things here. _____ you be more specific?"

3. Carlos shuffled his feet and said, "I know I _____ have thought of something before I got here, but I was hoping you might have some suggestions."

4. "Certainly," said the salesclerk, leading him to a large glass case. "She _____ like jewelry."

5. "Hmm," said Carlos. "Jewelry would be nice, but I _____ afford to spend over $50."

6. "That _____ be a problem," said the clerk. "We have some earrings for under $50."

7. "Really?" asked Carlos, obviously pleased. "_____ you show them to me?"

8. "Absolutely!" said the clerk. "What about these? She _____ like pearls. They're so delicate."

9. "Perfect!" exclaimed Carlos. "I _____ take them!"

10. "Excellent," said the clerk. "How _____ you like to pay?"

PRACTICE 6

Rewrite the following sentences as indicated.

1. You can tell me the secret.

   Make the sentence a question: _____

2. We might go to dinner on Friday.

   Make the sentence a negative statement: _____

   _____

3. They should leave the house before us.

   Make the sentence a question: _____

4. They could make breakfast.

   Make the sentence a negative statement: _____

   _____

5. Cathy would like to go sailing with us.

   Make the sentence into a question: _____

   _____

PRACTICE 7

Fill in the blanks with the correct verbs, adding helping verbs as needed. Refer to the verb charts if you need help.

Example: How many planets ___*are*___ (be) in our solar system?

1 For decades, the answer was "nine," but that _____ (change), at least according to scientists. 2 Since its discovery in 1930, Pluto _____ (be) considered a planet. 3 However, the discovery of an ice ball larger than Pluto made scientists wonder whether we _____ (continue) to label Pluto as a planet. 4 At a 2006 meeting of the International Astronomical Union, astronomers _____ (vote) to relabel Pluto as a "dwarf planet," decreasing the number of full-sized planets to eight. 5 The astronomers determined that to be a full-sized planet, an object _____ (pass) three tests. 6 First, it _____ (be) big enough to be shaped into a ball by the forces of gravity. 7 Second, it _____ (orbit) the sun. 8 Third, it _____ (knock)

other objects out of the path of its orbit. 9 To be labeled a dwarf planet,

an object simply _____ (be) round. 10 However, since people

_____ (consider) Pluto a planet for nearly eighty years, many

_____ (continue) to do so.

Use Gerunds and Infinitives Correctly

A **gerund** is a verb form that ends in *-ing* and acts as a noun. An **infinitive** is a verb form that is preceded by the word *to*. Gerunds and infinitives cannot be the main verbs in sentences; each sentence must have another word that is the main verb.

Tip For other problems with verbs, see Chapter 16.

Gerund	Mika <u>loves</u> **swimming**.
	[*Loves* is the main verb, and *swimming* is a gerund.]
Infinitive	Mika <u>loves</u> **to run**.
	[*Loves* is the main verb, and *to run* is an infinitive.]

How do you decide whether to use a gerund or an infinitive? The decision often depends on the main verb in a sentence. Some verbs can be followed by either a gerund or an infinitive.

Tip To improve your ability to write and speak standard English, read magazines and your local newspaper, and listen to television and radio news programs. Also, read magazines and newspaper articles aloud; this will help your pronunciation.

Verbs That May Be Followed by Either a Gerund or an Infinitive

begin	hate	remember	stop
continue	like	start	try
forget	love		

Sometimes, using an infinitive or a gerund after one of these verbs results in the same meaning.

Gerund	Joan <u>likes</u> **playing** the piano.
Infinitive	Joan <u>likes</u> **to play** the piano.

Other times, however, the meaning changes depending on whether you use an infinitive or a gerund.

Gerund	Carla stopped **helping** me.
	[This sentence means that Carla no longer helps me.]
Infinitive	Carla stopped **to help** me.
	[This sentence means that Carla stopped what she was doing and helped me.]

Verbs That May Be Followed by an Infinitive

agree	decide	need	refuse
ask	expect	offer	want
beg	fail	plan	
choose	hope	pretend	
claim	manage	promise	

Example	Aunt Sally wants **to help**.
Example	Cal hopes **to become** a millionaire.

Verbs That May Be Followed by a Gerund

admit	discuss	keep	risk
avoid	enjoy	miss	suggest
consider	finish	practice	
deny	imagine	quit	

Example	The politician risked **losing** her supporters.
Example	Sophia considered **quitting** her job.

Do not use the base form of the verb when you need a gerund or an infinitive.

Incorrect	*Skate* is my favorite activity.
	[*Skate* is not a noun. It is the base form of the verb and cannot function as the subject of the sentence. Use the gerund *skating*.]
Correct	Skating is my favorite activity.

Incorrect	My <u>goal</u> <u>is</u> *graduate* from college.
	[*Graduate* is the base form of the verb. Use the infinitive form *to graduate*.]
Correct	My <u>goal</u> <u>is</u> *to graduate* from college.

Incorrect	I <u>need</u> *pass* test.
	[The main verb *need* shows the action of the subject *I*. Use the infinitive form *to pass*.]
Correct	I <u>need</u> *to pass* the test.

PRACTICE 8

Read the following paragraphs, and fill in the blanks with either a gerund or an infinitive as appropriate.

Example: Have you ever wanted ___to start___ **(start) your own business?**

1 Every day, people imagine _____ (work) for themselves.
2 They might hate _____ (feel) as if their efforts are making profits for someone else. 3 If you are one of these people, stop _____ (dream) and start _____ (make) your dream come true.

4 Try _____ (picture) yourself as the boss; are you self-motivated? 5 Will you enjoy _____ (develop) your own projects and _____ (ensure) that they are done correctly? 6 Will you manage _____ (stay) organized and meet deadlines without someone else watching over you? 7 Are you certain you will like _____ (be) independent, having no one to praise or blame but yourself? 8 If you answered "yes" to all the above, you are ready for the greatest adventure of your career.

9 To avoid _____ (go) into this process blindly, you must create a business plan. 10 For example, you should determine what you want _____ (do), what skills you possess, and how you might market your services.

Include Prepositions after Verbs When Needed

Tip For more on prepositions, see Chapter 10.

Many verbs consist of a verb plus a preposition (or an adverb). The meaning of these combinations is not usually the meaning that the verb and the preposition would each have on its own. Often, the meaning of the verb changes completely depending on which preposition is used with it.

You <u>must</u> **take out** the trash.   [*take out* = bring to a different location]

You <u>must</u> **take in** the exciting sights of New York City.   [*take in* = observe]

Here are some other common combinations.

Common verb/preposition combinations

call in	You can *call in* your order.
call off (cancel)	They *called off* the party.
call on (choose)	A teacher might *call on* you in class.
drop in (visit)	Jane might *drop in* tonight.
drop off (leave behind)	I need to *drop off* my son at school.
drop out (quit)	Carlos wants to *drop out* of school.
fight for (defend)	U.S. soldiers *fight for* democracy.
fill in (refill)	Please *fill in* the holes in the ground.
fill out (complete)	Please *fill out* this application form.
fill up (make something full)	Don't *fill up* the tank all the way.
find out (discover)	Did you *find out* her name?
give up (forfeit; stop)	Don't *give up* your place in line.
go over (review)	Please *go over* your answers.
grow up (mature)	Children *grow up* to become adults.
hand in (submit)	You may *hand in* your homework now.
lock up (secure)	Don't forget to *lock up* the house.
look up (check)	I *looked up* the word in the dictionary.
pick out (choose)	Sandy *picked out* a dress.
pick up (take or collect)	When do you *pick up* the keys?
put off (postpone)	I often *put off* chores.
sign in (sign one's name)	I have to *sign in* at work.
sign up (register for)	I want to *sign up* for the contest.
think about (consider)	She likes to *think about* the weekend.
turn in (submit)	Please *turn in* your exams.

PRACTICE 9

Edit the following sentences to make sure that the correct prepositions are used.

Example: **Because fighting HIV/AIDS is important, we cannot give out** *up* **without a fight.**

1. Organizations such as the Centers for Disease Control are fighting over an HIV/AIDS epidemic in the rural United States.

2. Many people put by testing because they have limited incomes and limited access to testing centers.

3. However, finding off their HIV status is the first step toward life-saving treatment for those who are infected.

4. Because people may not want their testing made public, some clinics allow patients to fill test forms anonymously.

5. Signing over for testing shows courage and responsibility.

Chapter Review

1. What are three main uses of the verb *be*? _____
   _____

2. Does every sentence need a verb? _____

3. In a negative sentence, should the word *not* come before or after the helping verb?
   _____

4. In a question, should the helping verb come before or after the subject? _____
   _____

5. What is the present-progressive tense used to show? _____
   _____

6. Write a sentence with a gerund in it. _____

7. Write a sentence with an infinitive in it. _____

33

Nouns and Articles

Articles announce a **noun**. To use the correct article, you need to know whether the noun being announced is count or noncount.

Count and Noncount Nouns

LaunchPadSolo

Visit **LaunchPad Solo for Readers and Writers > Articles and Nouns** for more practice with nouns and articles.

Count nouns name things that can be counted, and count nouns can be made plural, usually by adding *-s* or *-es*. **Noncount nouns** name things that cannot be counted, and they are usually singular. They cannot be made plural.

Count/single	I got a **ticket** for the concert.
Count/plural	I got the **tickets** for the concert.
Noncount	The **music** will be great.
	[You would not say, *The musics will be great.*]

Tip For a review of nouns, see Chapter 10.

Here are some count and noncount nouns. This is just a brief list; all nouns in English are either count or noncount.

Count	Noncount	Noncount
apple/apples	beauty	love
chair/chairs	flour	money
computer/computers	furniture	music
dollar/dollars	grass	postage
lab/labs	grief	poverty
letter/letters	happiness	rain
smile/smiles	health	wealth

Articles

English uses only three **articles**—*a, an,* and *the*—to announce a noun. The same articles are used for both masculine and feminine nouns.

In general, the article *the* is used for specific count and noncount nouns.

the president of the United States   *the* final exam in biology

The articles *a* and *an* are used with nonspecific count nouns. To choose whether to use *a* or *an*, listen to the sound of the word that comes immediately after it. The article *an* is used before a vowel sound (*a, e, i, o,* and *u*) or a silent *h*.

an egg   *an* honor

The article *a* is used before a consonant, and with words that start with vowels but sound like consonants, such as *union,* which starts with a "yoo" sound.

a book   *a* university

If an adjective comes before a nonspecific count noun, follow the rules above to choose *a* or *an* depending on the word immediately following the article.

an egg   *a* **fried** egg

an ancestor   *a* **European** ancestor

a manager   *an* **assistant** manager

Use the following chart to determine when to use *a, an, the,* or no article. Note that the word *some* might be used for both plural nonspecific count nouns and nonspecific noncount nouns (see examples in chart).

Articles with Count and Noncount Nouns

Singular		
Count nouns		**Article used**
Specific	→	*the* I want to read **the book** on taxes that you recommended. [The sentence refers to one particular book: the one that was recommended.] I cannot stay in **the sun** very long. [There is only one sun.]
Nonspecific	→	*a or an* I want to read **a book** on taxes. [It could be any book on taxes.] I usually sit under **an umbrella** at the beach. [Any umbrella will provide shade.] ▶

Articles with Count and Noncount Nouns

Plural		
Count nouns		**Article used**
Specific	→	*the* I enjoyed **the books** that we read. [The sentence refers to a particular group of books: the ones that we read.]
Nonspecific	→	*some* or no article She found **some books**. [I don't know which books she found.] I usually **enjoy books**. [The sentence refers to books in general.]

Singular		
Noncount nouns		**Article used**
Specific	→	*the* I put away **the food** that we bought. [The sentence refers to particular food: the food that we bought.]
Nonspecific	→	*some* or no article Give **some food** to the neighbors. [The sentence refers to an indefinite quantity of food.] There **is food** all over the kitchen. [The reader does not know what food is all over the kitchen.]

PRACTICE 1

Fill in the correct article (*a, an,* or *the*) in each of the following sentences. If no article is needed, write "no article."

Example: **When my dog Smitty died last year, I was overcome with**
_____*no article*_____ **grief.**

1. My parents bought him when I was _____ infant.

2. They thought that it would be good for me to have _____ pet.

3. Because of Smitty, I have always loved _____ animals.

4. He was my best friend, and all _____ other children in the neighborhood loved him, too.

5. One time, he saved my cousin from drowning in _____ pond on our property.

6. We treated him like _____ king that day.

7. My mom baked him _____ dog-food cake.

8. _____ cake smelled horrible to us, but Smitty ate it all up.

9. He seemed to have _____ stomachache afterward.

10. Now, I smile when I think of _____ good times that we had.

PRACTICE 2

Edit the following paragraphs, adding, revising, or deleting articles as necessary.

Motherhood

Example: ~~The~~ motherhood is both rewarding and difficult.
          ∧

1 In 2005, national study about motherhood was released. 2 The mothers from the variety of ages, ethnicities, and economic backgrounds were surveyed. 3 As it turns out, mothers from around the country have many of same attitudes and concerns.

4 Of mothers surveyed, most stated that they are happy in their role. 5 Most mothers believe that their role is the important one. 6 Also, most feel the tremendous love for their children. 7 They admit they had never experienced the love so intensely before they had children.

8 That is only part of a story, however. 9 These women also had few concerns. 10 About half of women surveyed said they did not feel appreciated by the others. 11 In fact, some felt less valued as mothers than they did before they had the children. 12 Also, more than half felt that society should do more for the mothers, children, and families.

13 Biggest concerns of the mothers surveyed were education and safety. 14 The lower an income of the mother, the more she was concerned about education.

Chapter Review

1. _____ nouns can be made plural, and _____ nouns cannot be made plural.

2. What three articles are used in English? _____

3. The articles _____ and _____ are used for nonspecific nouns, and the article _____ is used for specific nouns.

Editing Review Test 1
The Four Most Serious Errors (Chapters 13–16)

Directions: Each of the underlined word groups contains one or more errors. As you locate and identify each error, write its item number on one of the lines below to indicate whether the error is a fragment, run-on or comma splice, verb-tense error, or subject-verb agreement error. Then, edit the underlined word groups to correct the errors.

2 fragments _____   2 verb-tense errors _____

2 run-ons or comma splices _____   4 subject-verb agreement errors _____

1 Each day, millions of people go online to check the weather, local news, and national headlines. 2 If you live in Alaska, however, you might also log on to see if the Augustine volcano are likely to erupt. 3 Alaska's Augustine volcano is not a quiet one it rumbles, belches, and blows smoke often. 4 Alaskans are familiar with volcanoes since the state has more than one hundred; forty are classified as active. 5 Since Augustine is active, it has its own Web site. 6 Scientists kept it updated so that people know what to expect. 7 Spitting out dust sometimes. 8 When it does, people need to wear masks and keep their windows closed because the dust can hurt their lungs. 9 If Augustine start to erupt, everyone have to evacuate.

10 Augustine has not had a large eruption since 1986. 11 Multiple cameras keep a close eye on it satellites in space also observe it carefully. 12 Any changes are immediately post to the Web site. 13 Though a Web cam offers up-to-the-minute images for anyone who visits the Internet site. 14 Of all volcanoes, this volcano are definitely under the watchful eyes of many.

Editing Review Test 2

The Four Most Serious Errors (Chapters 13–16)

Directions: Each of the underlined word groups contains one or more errors. As you locate and identify each error, write its item number on one of the lines below to indicate whether the error is a fragment, run-on or comma splice, verb-tense error, or subject-verb agreement error. Then, edit the underlined word groups to correct the errors.

2 fragments _____   2 verb-tense errors _____

3 run-ons or comma splices _____   3 subject-verb agreement errors _____

    1 Emergency medical technicians and paramedics provides life-saving care to people in all communities. 2 Neither of these jobs are easy both are exciting. 3 The field of emergency medical services (EMS) have a long history. 4 During wars, wounded soldiers have always need medical care on or near the battlefield. 5 Over time, emergency care becomed more sophisticated. 6 In the United States in the 1960s. 7 The modern era of EMS was born. 8 Medical professionals knew that time was a major factor in an emergency, they began to realize that on-the-scene care helped save lives. 9 Paramedics today are specially trained and licensed these professionals are usually the first to provide treatment for an accident victim or medical patient. 10 Rushing to the scene of falls, car accidents, or heart attacks. 11 The care that is given in those first minutes of an emergency can mean the difference between life and death.

Editing Review Test 3

The Four Most Serious Errors (Chapters 13–16)
Other Errors and Sentence Style (Chapters 17–22)

3

Directions: Each of the underlined word groups contains one or more errors. As you locate and identify each error, write its item number on the appropriate line below. Then, edit the underlined word groups to correct the errors.

1 fragment _____	1 pronoun error _____
1 run-on or comma splice _____	1 adjective error _____
1 misplaced/dangling modifier _____	1 adverb error _____
1 illogical shift _____	1 coordination error _____
1 verb-tense error _____	1 subordination error _____
1 subject-verb agreement error _____	1 parallelism error _____

 1 Since exercise builds stronger bones and bigger muscles. 2 Some recently studies have shown, however, that it might also make a person smarter. 3 In fact, some experts have gone so far as to call exercise "food for the brain." 4 Almost any kind of exercise carries blood to the brain in turn, the blood brings oxygen and nutrients with it. 5 Studies have shown that exercise builds new brain cells in the same part of the brain use for memory and learning.

 6 One group of scientists were so sure of exercise's benefits that they conducted a special experiment on sixth graders. 7 They divided 214 students into three groups, or they gave each group a different amount of exercise. 8 They careful monitored the amount and type of each group's exercises. 9 The one that exercised the most do the best on tests. 10 The more active the exercise was, the more they affected the scores. 11 For example, children who engaged in basketball, soccer, and swimming performed the highest.

 12 With less than thirty minutes of exercise a day, scientists worry about today's young people. 13 Too many students spend their days watching television, working on the computer, or they play video games. 14 Because the children are entertained, their muscles, health, and brains may be paying the price for it.

Editing Review Test 4

4

The Four Most Serious Errors (Chapters 13–16)
Other Errors and Sentence Style (Chapters 17–22)

Directions: Each of the underlined word groups contains one or more errors. As you locate and identify each error, write its item number on the appropriate line below. Then, edit the underlined word groups to correct the errors.

1 fragment _____   1 run-on or comma splice _____

1 verb-tense error _____   1 subject-verb agreement error _____

1 pronoun error _____   1 adjective error _____

1 adverb error _____   1 misplaced/dangling modifier _____

1 illogical shift _____   1 parallelism error _____

1 coordination error _____   1 subordination error _____

1 When Barbara Morgan reminds a student to reach for their dreams, she knows what she is talking about. 2 In 2007, Morgan, a teacher and an astronaut, traveled to the International Space Station (ISS) aboard the space shuttle *Endeavor*. 3 Lasting for thirteen days, Morgan rose to the challenge of this important journey.

4 The *Endeavor*'s mission were to take supplies and equipment to the ISS. 5 As part of the mission, Morgan took ten million seeds with her. 6 She brought the seeds back and distribute them to schools around the world so you could plant them. 7 She used a voice and video connection to speak with students in the United States and Canada she wanted to stay in contact. 8 She and other astronauts demonstrated living in a weightless environment, using shampoo in space, and they crawled into a sleeping bag.

9 Morgan eventual appeared at Walt Disney World though she wanted to share what she learned on her adventure. 10 A plaque with her name was added to Disney's Wall of Honor, or she joined such importantly names as John F. Kennedy, Charles Lindbergh, and Carl Sagan. 11 Reminding people in the audience to reach for their dreams as she did.

Editing Review Test 5

The Four Most Serious Errors (Chapters 13–16)
Other Errors and Sentence Style (Chapters 17–22)
Words in Sentences (Chapters 23–25)

5

Directions: Each of the underlined word groups contains one or more errors. As you locate and identify each error, write its item number on the appropriate line below. Then, edit the underlined word groups to correct the errors.

2 fragments _____	2 subject-verb agreement errors _____
2 coordination errors _____	1 misplaced/dangling modifier _____
1 subordination error _____	1 illogical shift _____
1 adverb error _____	1 parallelism error _____
1 word-choice error _____	1 commonly confused word _____
1 spelling error _____	

1 As the country slow became more connected by power lines, the image of the windmill faded from America. 2 Even though rural communities had depended on wind power to generate electricity for decades, it seemed as if power plants would make windmills obsolete. 3 All of that have changed in recent years. 4 Windmills are returning to the United States, or they are known now as wind turbines.

5 When wind blows across the blades located on the top of a turbine's tower, it spun a shaft. 6 The shaft is connected to a generator, yet this connection makes electricity for people's homes and farms. 7 In schools too, such as the one in Spirit Lake, Iowa. 8 The school raise dough by selling the extra electricity back to the power company.

9 Some people beleive that turbines are an important energy source, since others think that they are a nuisance. 10 They state that turbines make noise, ruin the view, and hurting birds that fly into the blades. 11 Despite this, wind turbines are gaining acceptance in this country. 12 Home to one of the largest wind farms in the world, the 4,500 turbines are scattered across Altamont Pass in northern California. 13 The government has created a new wind power bill. 14 So that a bill provides grants, low-interest loans, and tax credits for any home owners who install there own windmills.

Editing Review Test 6

6

The Four Most Serious Errors (Chapters 13–16)
Other Errors and Sentence Style (Chapters 17–22)
Words in Sentences (Chapters 23–25)

Directions: Each of the underlined word groups contains one or more errors. As you locate and identify each error, write its item number on the appropriate line below. Then, edit the underlined word groups to correct the errors.

1 fragment _____   2 commonly confused words _____

2 word-choice errors _____   1 run-on or comma splice _____

1 verb-tense error _____   1 subject-verb agreement error _____

1 pronoun error _____   1 adjective error _____

1 adverb error _____   1 misplaced/dangling modifier _____

1 illogical shift _____   1 parallelism error _____

1 coordination error _____   1 subordination error _____

2 spelling errors _____

1 Young children have lost something important: eight to twelve hours of playtime per week in the last two decades. 2 According to a number of studies, children have less free time in their schedules to relax and play, yet some experts think that this problem is bad. 3 Causing a situation as serious as obesity.

4 Why are children loosing all of this important time? 5 One reason is that parents tend to shedule too many activities for their kids, leaving little time for relaxing. 6 Another reason is that young people are spending an increasing number of hours participating in sports and taking nonacademic classes. 7 All of these activities cuts into the availabel hours of a day. 8 Schools no longer provide regular breaks administrators at a number of schools now have shorten or even eliminated recesses. 9 An overall increase in the amount of your daily homework is lousy too.

10 Until these other activities may be important, less playtime effects children in a number of ways. 11 They say that too little play can lead to obesity, anxiety, attention-deficit disorder, and depression, although most research is needed. 12 In the meantime, psychologists say that an adequate amount of playtime allows children to stay healthy, learn good, and they can develop properly.

Editing Review Test 7

The Four Most Serious Errors (Chapters 13–16)
Other Errors and Sentence Style (Chapters 17–22)
Words in Sentences (Chapters 23–25)
Punctuation and Mechanics (Chapters 26–30)

7

Directions: Each of the underlined word groups contains one or more errors. As you locate and identify each error, write its item number on the appropriate line below. Then, edit the underlined word groups to correct the errors.

1 fragment _____   1 word-choice error _____

1 spelling error _____   2 comma errors _____

2 apostrophe errors _____   1 quotation-mark error _____

1 semicolon error _____   1 capitalization error _____

1 The many unknown consequences of global warming frighten people a lot. 2 During a recent conference about these consequences presenters raised a new topic of concern. 3 Experts testified that half the worlds population could face a lack of clean water by the year 2080.

4 One of the professors from the university of Singapore stated that global warming has been shown to interfere with water-flow patterns; increasing the risk of floods, droughts, and violent storms. 5 These serious conditions reduce the amount of available drinking water on the planet. 6 Floods, drought, changing rainfall patterns, and rising temperatures are signs of our misdeeds to nature," stated this expert.

7 Looking even further ahead the professor predicted that by 2050 as many as two billion people will be without easy access to clean water. 8 Up to 3.2 billion thirty years later. 9 The most vulnerable area of the world would be Asia. 10 Without doubt, we need to consider a failing water supply when we think about the futures problems.

Editing Review Test 8

8

The Four Most Serious Errors (Chapters 13–16)
Other Errors and Sentence Style (Chapters 17–22)
Words in Sentences (Chapters 23–25)
Punctuation and Mechanics (Chapters 26–30)

Directions: Each of the underlined word groups contains one or more errors. As you locate and identify each error, write its item number on the appropriate line below. Then, edit the underlined word groups to correct the errors.

1 fragment _____   1 word-choice error _____

1 spelling error _____   2 comma errors _____

2 apostrophe errors _____   1 hyphen error _____

1 parenthesis error _____   1 capitalization error _____

1 For years, police departments and insurence companies have been telling drivers that it is dangerous to text-message on a cell phone while driving. 2 Now, the American Medical association has announced that it agrees with that statement. 3 It is supporting the current movement for legal ban's on text-messaging while driving.

4 While only a handful of states have laws in place regarding text-messaging. 5 The reasons behind these laws are pretty clear. 6 A recent study demonstrated that text-messaging while driving causes a 400 percent increase in time spent with eyes not on the road (where they need to be. 7 Simply talking on a cell phone is dangerous and has been shown to cause accidents. 8 Text-messaging is, even more, life threatening. 9 With new laws in place police would have the right to pull over any drivers whom they spot text-messaging while behind the wheel.

10 Although cell phones' are a modern high tech gadget that people have come to depend on, they also have the potential to be deadly. 11 Cell phone owners may want the latest in technology, but they also need to practice careful driving.

Appendix: Succeeding on Tests

Adam Moss
DeVry South Florida

This appendix will help you prepare for any testing situation, increasing your confidence and your chances of success.

Understand Testing Myths and Facts

Here are some common myths about tests.

Myth: Test makers pick obscure topics for reading passages to confuse you.

Fact: Test makers often avoid common topics because they do not want students who are familiar with those topics to have an unfair advantage.

Myth: Test answers often have hidden patterns, and if you can just figure out these patterns, you will get a good score.

Fact: Test answers rarely follow a pattern, and if they do, the pattern is often hard to figure out, and you will waste time trying. The best strategy is good preparation.

Myth: Some people are just good at taking tests, but I am not one of them.

Fact: Students who are good at tests are usually those who have learned to manage their anxiety and to be "test wise": They know what to find out about the test, they know how to study, and they know how to read and answer test questions. In other words, they are informed about and prepared for tests. You, too, can be a good test-taker if you learn the strategies that are discussed in the pages that follow.

Understand What to Do Before and During Tests

Before the Test

To do well on a test, take the time to gather information that will help you study effectively.

ASK QUESTIONS

Although your instructors will not give you the test questions in advance, most will give you general information that will help you prepare. Ask a few key questions, and write down the answers.

- What subjects are on the test or what chapters are covered? If the test has more than one part, do I have to take all the parts or just some?

- What kinds of questions appear on the test? (Question types include multiple choice, true-or-false, matching, short answer, and essay. Many tests combine several types of questions.)

- How much time do I have for the entire test? How much time do I have for each section? Are there breaks between sections?

- What should I review? The text? Handouts? Lecture notes? Something else?

- Is the test paper-and-pencil or computerized? (If it will be paper-and-pencil, practice that format. If it will be computerized, practice that. In some cases, your teacher may be able to provide or refer you to sample tests on paper or on a computer. See also the suggestions in the next section.)

- What materials am I required or allowed to bring? Do I need pens, pencils, or both? Can I use notes or the textbook? Am I allowed to use a calculator? Do I need to bring an ID? Am I required to provide my own scratch paper?

- What score do I need to pass? If I do not pass, am I allowed to retake the test?

- For multiple-choice tests, will I be penalized for guessing answers?

STUDY EFFECTIVELY

Once you have collected information about the test that you are about to take, write out a plan of what you need to study and follow it. The following tips will also help you study effectively.

- Choose a good place to study. Find a straight-backed chair and table in the dining room or kitchen and study there, or study in the library or another quiet place with similar conditions. Be careful about studying in bed or on a sofa; you may fall asleep or lose concentration.

- Use test-specific study materials like "prep" books, software, and Web sites if they are available. These materials often include old, real test questions and usually have full practice tests. Be sure to get an up-to-date book to ensure that any recent changes to the test are covered. Also, your instructor may have practice tests. Note that this textbook has sample tests at the end of each writing and grammar chapter and part.

- Make up and answer your own test questions. Try to think like your instructor or the test writer.

- Take a test-preparation class if one is available. Many schools offer free or reduced-cost classes to students who are preparing for entrance or exit tests.

- If your test is going to be timed, try to do a sample test within a time limit. Use the timer function on your cell phone or watch so that it will alert you when time is up.

- Use all the study aids that are available to you: chapter reviews, summaries, or highlighted terms in your textbook; handouts from your instructor; study guides; and so on. Also, many schools have writing centers that offer tutoring or study-skills worksheets. Check out your school's resources. Your tuition pays for these services, so you should take advantage of them.

- Learn what study strategies work best for you. Some students find that copying over their notes is effective because they are doing something active (writing) as they review the material. Other students find that reading their notes aloud helps them to remember the ideas. Still others find that drawing or mapping out a concept helps them remember it.

- Study with other students in your class. By forming a study group, you can share each other's notes and ideas.

- Don't give up! The key to studying well is often to study until you are "sick" of the material. Whatever pain you feel in studying hard will be offset by the happiness of doing well on the test.

REDUCE TEST ANXIETY

Everyone gets test anxiety. The trick is to manage your nerves instead of letting them control you. Turn your nervousness into positive energy, which can sharpen your concentration. Also, the following tips can help.

- Study! Study! Study! No test-taking strategies or anxiety-reducing techniques can help if you do not know the material. Think about a job you do well. Why don't you get nervous when you do it, even under pressure? The answer is that you know how to do it. Similarly, if you have studied well, you will be more relaxed as you approach a test.

- Eat a light meal before the test; overeating can make you uncomfortable or sleepy. Consider including protein, which can help your brain work better. Do not consume too much caffeine or sugar, however. Be especially wary of soft drinks, because many contain both. Take a bottle of water with you if you are allowed to. Sipping water as you work will help you stay hydrated, especially during long testing periods.

- If possible, take the test at a time that is good for you. For example, if you are a "morning person," take the test early in the day. With computerized testing, more and more schools offer flexible test schedules or individual appointments. If you can choose your testing time, do not take the test after a long day of work or if you are very tired.

- Get to the test early. Arriving late is stress inducing, and you might miss valuable pre-test instructions. If you arrive too late, you may not be allowed to take the test at all.

- Resist the urge to discuss the test with others before you begin. Anxiety can be contagious, and others who are less prepared can make you needlessly nervous.

- Breathe deeply, in through your nose and out through your mouth. When you get nervous, your breathing becomes rapid and shallow. By controlling your breathing, you can reduce your nervousness.

- Think positive thoughts. Do not think about how terrible it will be if poor test scores keep you from getting accepted into school, advancing to the next class, or getting a new job. Instead, remind yourself of how much you know and how well prepared you are. Harness your energy and believe in yourself.

During the Test

As the test begins, it is important to listen to the directions that your instructor or test monitor gives. Resist the temptation to start flipping through the test as soon as you get it; if you are not paying attention, you might miss important instructions that are not included in the written directions.

Also, it is important to monitor your time. Many test takers lose track of time and then complain, "I didn't have time to finish." Do not let that happen to you. After you have listened to the directions, survey the whole test, unless you are told not to do so. This way, you will know how many parts the test has, what kinds of questions are asked, and, in some cases, how many points each part or question is worth. Then, make a time budget.

Look at one student's time budget.

	Minutes (55 total)
Part 1: 10 multiple-choice questions (2 points each)	5
Part 2: 10 fill-ins (3 points each)	10
Part 3: 2 paragraphs to edit (10 points each)	15
Part 4: 1 paragraph to write (30 points)	20
Final check of work	5

Here is a good strategy for taking this test:

1. In Parts 1 and 2, do items that you know the answers to; do not spend time on items that you cannot answer immediately. (However, if you are not penalized for guessing, you may want to fill in answers; you can always change them later.)

2. Move on to Part 3, making all the edits you can and leaving at least twenty minutes for Part 4.

3. Write the paragraph for Part 4. Reread it to fix any problems that you see.

4. Go back and try to answer questions from Parts 1 and 2 that you were unsure of.

5. If you have time, do a final check of your work.

Do not work too slowly or too quickly. Spending too much time on questions can lead to "overthinking" and a loss of attention. You have only so much energy, so use it wisely. However, rushing is as big a problem as overthinking. Test designers sometimes make the first choice in a multiple-choice question appear correct, while the truly correct answer is presented later. This approach trips up students who do not take the time to read each question and answer carefully.

Understand How to Answer Different Types of Test Questions

The general strategies just described will help you on any test. However, it is equally important to develop strategies to attack specific types of questions. Following are some ways to approach typical kinds of questions.

Multiple-Choice Questions

- Read the directions carefully. Most tests allow only one answer choice per question, but some tests allow multiple responses.

- For each question, try to come up with an answer before looking at the answer choices.

- Be sure to read all answer choices. Answer A may seem correct, but B, C, or D may be a better answer. Multiple-choice questions often ask you to choose the "best" answer.

- Use the process of elimination, ruling out those answers that you know are incorrect first. Your odds of guessing correctly will increase with every answer eliminated.

- Stick with your first choice unless you are sure that it is wrong. Your initial thinking will often be correct.

- If there is no penalty for guessing, try to answer even those questions for which you are unsure of the answer. If there is a penalty, make an educated guess, a guess based on having narrowed the choices to one or two.

- Many students fear "all of the above" and "none of the above" questions, but you can actually use them to your advantage. If you know that any single answer is correct, you can eliminate "none of the above"; likewise, if you know that any single answer is incorrect, you can eliminate "all of the above." If you know that more than one answer is correct, you can safely choose "all of the above."

- Be sure to interpret questions correctly. A question that asks "Which of the following is not true?" is actually asking "Which of the following is false?" Consider the following example.

  Which of the following instruments does not belong in an orchestra?
  a. tympani drum
  b. cello
  c. electric guitar
  d. oboe

  The question is asking which instrument is *not* in an orchestra, but students who do not read carefully may miss the word *not* and choose incorrectly. The correct answer is C.

- Pay attention when there are two similar but opposite answers. The following example question is based on a reading passage not shown here.

  Which of the following is true based on the passage you have read?
  a. Drug abusers who enter treatment under legal pressure are as likely to benefit from it as those who enter treatment voluntarily.
  b. Drug abusers who enter treatment under legal pressure are less likely to benefit from it than are those who enter treatment voluntarily.
  c. Drug abusers who have committed crimes should be treated only in high-security facilities.
  d. Drug abusers can overcome their addictions more easily if they get treatment in isolated facilities.

  Answer options A and B say the opposite things, so one of them must be eliminated as incorrect. In this case, A happens to be the correct answer.

- Usually, you can eliminate two answers that say the same thing in different words. If one is true, the other must be too. You cannot choose both of them, unless the test allows you to select more than one answer.

  Upton Sinclair's novel *The Jungle* was famous for its stark view of what?
  a. unsafe and filthy working conditions in the American meat-packing industry
  b. the situation of poor and jobless Americans during the Great Depression
  c. the events of the last days of the Vietnam War
  d. working-class Americans and their plight during the Depression era

  Answers B and D can clearly be eliminated because they contain the same idea. If one were to be correct, the other would automatically be correct as well. Eliminate these two choices. The correct answer is A.

- Keep in mind that longer and more detailed answers are often the correct ones. Test makers may put less time and effort into creating the wrong answer choices. See the example below.

    One role of hemoglobin in the bloodstream is to

    a. fight disease.

    b. bind to oxygen molecules and carry them to cells.

    c. help form blood clots.

    d. carry proteins to cells.

  Answer choice B is the longest and most detailed answer, and it is the correct choice. Be sure, however, to read every answer option because the longest one is not always correct.

- Be aware of absolute statements that include words like *all, always, every, everyone, never, none,* and *only.* They are rarely the correct answer. The following example question is based on a reading passage not shown here.

    Which of the following statements is true based on the reading passage?

    a. Catheter-based infections are less treatable than other hospital infections.

    b. Methicillin-resistant *Staphylococcus aureus* is always more serious than regular *Staphylococcus aureus.*

    c. Methicillin-resistant *Staphylococcus aureus* is treatable, but fewer antibiotics work against it than against other staph infections.

    d. Hand-washing plays a small role in preventing the spread of staph infections.

  B contains the word *always,* suggesting that there are no exceptions. This is not true; therefore, B can be eliminated. C happens to be the correct answer.

True-or-False Questions

- You have a 50 percent chance of guessing correctly, so it is usually wise to guess on true-or-false questions when you are unsure of the correct answer.

- There are usually more true answers than false answers on a test. Start with the presumption that an item is true, and then look for information that may make it false.

- If any part of a question is false, the whole question is false. Students tend to focus on just the true section. Even though most of the statement below is correct, the mistake in the third name, which should read "*Santa Maria,*" is enough to make the whole statement false.

    True or false? In 1492, Christopher Columbus reached the New World with three ships: the *Niña,* the *Pinta,* and the *Santa Dominga.*

- Be aware that statements with absolute words like *all, always, never,* and *none* are usually false (see p. 525).

- However, "possibility" words like *most, often, probably, some, sometimes,* and *usually* often indicate true answers. Since penguins do not always live in cold climates, and the word *usually* allows for these exceptions, the following statement is true.

> True or false? Penguins usually live in cold climates.

- Beware of cause-and-effect statements that may seem true at first but that show a false cause. In the following example, it is true that a koala is both a marsupial and eats eucalyptus leaves, but it is not a marsupial *because* it eats eucalyptus leaves.

> True or false? A koala bear is a marsupial because it eats eucalyptus leaves.

Reading Comprehension Questions

These questions are usually based on a paragraph (or paragraphs) that you have to read. Follow these tips for success:

- Read all the questions before reading the passage. This will help you pay attention to important points as you read.

- Understand that you must "read for speed." Reading passages are the number one time killer on tests. If you take too long to read, you will use up much of your time.

- On a related point, try to absorb whatever you can, and do not stop on any one word or idea. Chances are that the questions will not require a perfect understanding of the word(s) that you find difficult.

- Take a "leap of faith" when answering reading comprehension questions. Sometimes, students will agonize over a question even if they are fairly sure that they know the right answer. In this case, take an educated guess and move on.

Essay Questions and Timed Writing Assignments

Many students think essay questions are harder than other types of questions, but they actually offer a little more flexibility because there is not just one limited answer. There are, however, certain standards you need to follow. These are described in the following sections.

UNDERSTAND THE ESSAY RUBRIC

Most standardized or departmental essay tests have their own answer scales, called *rubrics*. Rubrics show the elements that graders rate in an essay answer or timed writing, and they often present the maximum number of points for each element.

Rubrics are often available from a college's testing center, writing center, or learning lab. Also, instructors may include scoring rubrics as part of a course syllabus.

Regardless of the particular rubric used, every essay test is graded based on similar fundamentals, described in the following chart.

Typical Rubric for an Essay Exam Answer
(what elements it may be graded on)

Element	Criteria for Evaluation	Score / Comments
Relevance	The essay should address the question completely and thoroughly. If there is more than one part to the question, the answer should address all parts.	Total points possible: [will vary] This essay's score:
Organization	The essay should follow standard essay structure, with the following items: —an introduction with a clear and definite thesis statement —body paragraphs, each of which starts with a topic sentence and supports the thesis —a conclusion If a paragraph, as opposed to an essay, is called for, the paragraph should include a topic sentence followed by enough supporting sentences to back up the main point.	Total points possible: [will vary] This essay's score:
Support	The body paragraphs contain sufficient, detailed examples to support the thesis statement.	Total points possible: [will vary] This essay's score:
Coherence	The essay sticks to the thesis, with all support related to it. There are no detours. The writer uses transitions to move the reader smoothly from one idea to the next.	Total points possible: [will vary] This essay's score:
Conciseness	The essay does not repeat the same points.	Total points possible: [will vary] This essay's score:
Sentence structure	The sentences are varied in length and structure; they are not all short and choppy.	Total points possible: [will vary] This essay's score:
Sentence grammar	The essay should not have any of the following: —fragments —run-ons or comma splices —errors in subject-verb agreement —errors in verb tense	Total points possible: [will vary] This essay's score:
Consistency	The essay should use consistent point of view and verb tense.	Total points possible: [will vary] This essay's score: ▶

Typical Rubric for an Essay Exam Answer (what elements it may be graded on)

Element	Criteria for Evaluation	Score / Comments
Word choice	The essay should use the right words for the intended meaning and demonstrate an understanding of formal, academic English, especially avoiding slang.	Total points possible: [will vary] This essay's score:
Punctuation	The essay should use commas, periods, semicolons, question marks, and other punctuation correctly.	Total points possible: [will vary] This essay's score:
Spelling	Most words should be spelled correctly.	Total points possible: [will vary] This essay's score:
Legibility	The essay should be readable. (If it is handwritten, the cross-outs should be neat.)	Total points possible: [will vary] This essay's score:
Total score:		

UNDERSTAND THE QUESTION

Every writing test comes with a topic or set of topics from which you must choose one. Read the topic(s) and directions and make sure that you understand whether a single paragraph or a whole essay is required. Is there a minimum or maximum length for the paragraph or essay? How many words should it be? How much time do you have, and does that include "prewriting" time?

Then, read the question or topic carefully, looking for **key words** that tell you

- what subject to write on,

- how to write about it, and

- how many parts your answer should have.

When the directions include the key words from the chart on the next page, circle them.

FOLLOW KEY WRITING STEPS USING STANDARD ESSAY STRUCTURE

Once you understand the question or topic, plan your answer, using prewriting to get ideas and at least three major support points. (See Chapter 4.)

As you begin to write, bear in mind that your test essay, just like other essays that you write, should have the parts shown in the chart on the left in the margin.

Follow this process to complete the essay:

1. Try to write a scratch outline based on your prewriting. This should include your thesis statement and at least three support points. The outline does not have to be in complete sentences.

Introduction
Include a thesis sentence stating your main point.

↓

Supporting paragraph 1
with topic sentence

↓

Supporting paragraph 2
with topic sentence

↓

Supporting paragraph 3
with topic sentence

↓

Conclusion

Common Key Words in Essay Exam Questions

Key word	What it means
Analyze	Break into parts (classify) and discuss.
Define	State the meaning and give examples.
Describe the **stages of**	List and explain steps in a process.
Discuss the **causes of**	List and explain the causes.
Discuss the **effects/results of**	List and explain the effects.
Discuss the **concept of**	Define and give examples.
Discuss the **differences between**	Contrast and give examples.
Discuss the **similarities between**	Compare and give examples.
Discuss the **meaning of**	Define and give examples.
Explain the **term**	Define and give examples.
Follow/trace the **development of**	Give the history.
Follow/trace the **process of**	Explain the sequence of steps or stages in a process.
Identify	Define and give examples.
Should	Argue for or against something.
Summarize	Give a brief overview of something.

Tip When considering the length of your answer, be especially careful with paragraphs. Some test graders penalize short paragraphs, even if they are well written.

2. Write an introduction, concluding with your thesis statement.

3. Write your body paragraphs. Each paragraph should begin with a topic sentence based on the support points that you wrote for step 1. You should include at least three minor supporting details in each body paragraph.

4. Finish with a short concluding paragraph. It should refer back to your main point and make an observation.

5. If you have time, revise and proofread your essay, looking for any grammar errors and other issues from the rubric on pages 527–528. Usually, it is acceptable to make corrections by crossing out words and neatly writing the correction above.

SAMPLE STUDENT ESSAYS

The following three sample essays were written in response to one exam topic. After each sample is an analysis of the essay.

Here is the topic to which the three writers were responding:

Topic: As we mature, our hobbies and interests are likely to change. In an essay of no more than five hundred words, describe how your interests have changed as you have gotten older.

Tip Ask if you will be penalized for using contractions in writing for tests. Some graders do not care, but others might mark you down for this.

1. Low-level essay

I had many hobbies over the years. I use to play T-ball but I moved on to playing real Baseball. I played baseball for more than ten years finaly I became a pitcher for my High School varsity squad. The one hobby that I can think of that I use to have that I don't do anymore is riding bicycles. My friends and I cruised all over our neighborhood on our bicycles looking for trouble to get into all the time and once even running from the cops, who caught my friend Jimmy, who was the leader of our so called gang. When I got in high school, though I got another hobby which took all my time and money, my car was my new love. I got it when I was 17 and I put everything I had into it and I loved it almost as much as my girlfriend Kate. As you can see, by my senior year, my only hobbies were playing baseball for my school team and taking care of my sweet car.

Analysis: This response likely will not pass. It is a single paragraph, which is unacceptable given that the question requires an essay. It begins with a general thesis and has no real conclusion. The essay offers examples of hobbies but gives no supporting details about them, and it fails to clearly show the changes in interests over the years. The writer strays from the topic when discussing his gang and follows no pattern of organization. In addition, the writing lacks varied sentence structure and contains few transition words. There are a number of grammar and spelling errors, and the language is too informal for an essay.

2. Mid-level essay

Everybody has some kind of hobby, whether it is playing piano, or skiing. People's hobbies change sometimes over the years as they change too. This is certainly true for me. I have had many hobbies over the years, and they have certainly changed.

As a child, I played T-ball, and I eventually moved on to playing real baseball. I played baseball for more than ten years; finally, I became a pitcher for my High School varsity squad, and I played during my junior and senior years. I am looking forward to pitching in the college ranks.

The one favorite hobby I used to have that I don't have anymore is riding bicycles. My friends and I cruised all over our neighborhood on our bicycles looking for trouble to get into all the time and once even running from the cops, who caught my friend Jimmy, who was the leader of our so called gang. I eventually outgrew this hobby, as it was replaced by a new more exciting vehicle.

When I got in high school, though I got another hobby which took all my time and money, my car was my new love. It is a Nissan 300 ZX, and it is black with a black interior. It had 160 rims and a sweet body kit. I got it when I was 17 and I put everything I had into it and I loved it almost as much as my girlfriend Kate.

As you can see, by my senior year, my only hobbies were playing baseball for my school team and taking care of my car. I once spent all my time riding my bicycle with my friends but I guess I've outgrown that. The one hobby that has lasted throughout my life is my love for baseball. I will probably play that until I am an old man.

Analysis: This essay is better, showing a clearly identifiable introduction, body, and conclusion. A thesis statement addresses the topic, but it could be more specific. The body paragraphs are generally cohesive, and the essay shows chronological (time order) development. However, the writing still strays from the topic in a few areas and could use several more transitions to help readers move smoothly from one paragraph to the next. This essay has fewer grammar and punctuation errors than the previous one, but the language is still too informal in spots. The essay's biggest problem remains a lack of supporting details about the hobbies and the changes in them over the years.

3. High-level essay

Everybody has some kind of hobby, whether it is a craft, a musical instrument, or a sport. While some hobbies last a lifetime, many fade or appear at different times during our lives. Some people play sports as youngsters that they cannot play later in life, and some people adopt new hobbies as adults that they would never have enjoyed as a young person. This is certainly true for me. I have had many hobbies over the years, and as I have gotten older, they have changed. As I have grown, I have lost my interest in riding bicycles, gained a love for cars, and undergone some changes in the way I play baseball, the one hobby I have always enjoyed.

My earliest hobby was one that I outgrew sometime during junior high school: riding bicycles with my friends. As a child, my bicycle was my only real means of independence. My friends and I rode all over our neighborhood, looking for trouble to get into and even tangling with the police on one occasion. As I got older and my friends began to get cars, this hobby faded and a new one emerged, featuring a new type of vehicle.

Working on my car is my new interest, and it is a hobby that grew from my love for my bicycle. The car is a Nissan 300 ZX, and it is black with a black interior, sixteen-inch rims, and a beautiful body kit. I got it when I was seventeen, and for the past two years, I have put all of my time and money into it. My high school friends joked that I loved it almost as much as my girlfriend, Kate. It offers me the same sense of freedom as the bicycle, and I feel the same pride in keeping it in perfect shape.

My one love that has remained throughout my life is baseball, but even that hobby has undergone some changes as I have matured. As a young child, I played T-ball and quickly grew to love it. I eventually moved on to playing real baseball and played second base and shortstop in Little League for more than ten years. After years of hard work, I became a pitcher for my high school varsity squad, and I pitched in the starting rotation for both my junior and senior years. I am looking forward to pitching in college and beginning a new stage in my baseball "career."

My hobbies have changed as I've matured, but in many ways, they have stayed the same. My first hobby, riding my bicycle, grew into my love for my car, and in many ways, the change from two wheels to four wheels reflects my growing maturity. My one lifetime hobby, baseball, has evolved as well, as I've lost the "T" and changed positions. One day, I may play another position or even another sport. However, like my love for speed, my love for competition will always define my hobbies.

Analysis: This essay is clear, effective, and well supported. All the essential elements are present, and the thesis is specific, clearly setting up the rest of the essay. The writer has described his hobbies in a clear chronological order, and he uses transitions effectively. The introduction and conclusion are reflective, and descriptions of the hobbies are detailed, using more varied and exciting language and sentence structure than the previous examples. The writing stays on topic throughout and answers the essay question thoughtfully and thoroughly.

Use *Real Skills* to Succeed on Standardized Tests

Many standardized, departmental, and state exams test for the same basic skills, whether through multiple-choice questions, essay questions, or other items. Following is a list of typical skills tested and where you can get help in *Real Skills*.

Skill	Chapter in *Real Skills*
Writing and Essay Questions	
Using thesis statements and topic sentences (main ideas)	4, 6, 7, 8, 9
Using adequate and relevant support	4–9
Arranging ideas in a logical order	4, 6, 7, 8, 9
Writing unified sentences and paragraphs	5
Using effective transitions	5
Choosing appropriate words	23
Avoiding confused or misused words	24
Taking a position on an issue (typical in essay exams)	6, 7, 8
Reading	
Understanding readings	1, 6, 7, 8
Understanding purpose and audience	2
Identifying thesis statements and topic sentences (main ideas)	4, 6, 7, 8, 9
Identifying adequate and relevant support	4–9
Grammar and Mechanics	
Using modifiers correctly	19
Using coordination and subordination correctly	21
Understanding parallel structure	22
Avoiding fragments	13
Avoiding run-ons and comma splices	14
Using standard verb forms and tenses	16
Avoiding inappropriate shifts in verb tense	20
Making subjects and verbs agree	15
Making pronouns and antecedents agree	17

Skill	**Chapter in *Real Skills***
Avoiding pronoun shifts in person	20
Maintaining clear pronoun references	17
Using proper case forms of pronouns	17
Using adjectives and adverbs correctly	18
Using standard spelling	25
Using standard punctuation	26–29
Using standard capitalization	30

Acknowledgments

Adams, Mary. "From Embarrassing Stories to Favorite Memories." Used with permission.

Alfakeeh, Alieh. "What Girls Are For." Used with permission.

Brown, Arnold. "Relationships, Community, and Identity in the New Virtual Society." *Futurist*, Mar/Apr 2011, Vol. 45 Issue 2. 29–34.

Brown, Rashad. "When I Grow Up . . ." Used with permission.

Bustin, Andrew Dillon. "Airports Are for Watching People." Used with permission.

Cisneros, Sandra. "Only Daughter." Copyright © 1990 by Sandra Cisneros. First published in *GLAMOU*R, November 1990. By permission of Susan Bergholz Literary Services, New York, NY and Lamy, NM. All rights reserved.

Cleveland, Delia. "Champagne Taste, Beer Budget." Originally appeared in *Essence Magazine*, March 2001. Adapted from an essay published in *Starting with "I"* (Persea Books, 1997).

CNN iReport, "Brick and Mortar vs. Online Shopping." March 10, 2009.

Deam, Jenny. From "E-Books vs. Print: What Parents Need to Know." Published in *SCHOLASTIC PARENT & CHILD*, February 2013. Copyright © 2013 by Scholastic, Inc. Reproduced by permission.

Dray, Stephanie. "Five Kinds of Friends Everyone Should Have." *Associated Content/Yahoo! Voices*, 8/17/2007.

Federal Trade Commission. Excerpt from "Building a Better Credit Report."

Felts, Tony. "English as an Official Language: The Injustice of One Language." Used with permission.

Fouch, Kristy. "Servers." Used with permission.

Friedman, Ron. "When to Schedule Your Most Important Work." *Harvard Business Review Blogs*, June 26, 2014. One-time permission to reproduce granted by Harvard Business Publishing.

Haygood, Wil. "Underground Dads." *New York Times Magazine*. 11/30/97, Vol. 147 Issue 50992. 156.

Ivey, Sheena. "English as an Official Language: One Language for One Nation." *The Vanguard*.

Main, Douglas. "Who Are the Millennials?" livescience.com, July 9, 2013. Reprinted by permission.

McGill, Natalie. "Caffeine: Don't Let Your Pick-me-up Drag You Down." Reprinted with permission from *The Nation's Health*, American Public Health Association, 44.1 (2014): 36.

Mevs, Christina. "How My Community College Experience Has Changed My Life." Lone Star College Scholarship Essay published February 4, 2010.

Montgomery, Marvin. "Types of Sales People." Smart Business Blog, from *Smart Business Online*, June 13, 2011.

Nutrition MD. Excerpt from "Eating Healthy," from "How Does My Diet Affect My Health?"

Pajazetovic, Sabina. "My Mother, My Hero." www.teenlink.com.

Phelps, Faye. "The Bachelor Life." Used with permission.

Planas, Roque. "Chicano: What Does The Word Mean And Where Does It Come From?" *Huffington Post* posted October 21, 2012.

Pollan, Michael. "Vegetarians and Human Culture." From *THE OMNIVORE'S DILEMMA: A NATURAL HISTORY OF FOUR MEALS* by Michael Pollan, copyright © 2006 by Michael Pollan. Used by permission of Penguin Press, an imprint of Penguin Publishing Group, a division of Penguin Random House LLC.

Rippel, Kendal. "We Need Sleep," from Health Blog #2- "Five letter word." *The Quill, the Newspaper of Carroll Community College*. October 7, 2012.

Rock, Spencer. "Mask-ulinity: The Price of Becoming a Man." *The Current*, November 25, 2013.

Sanders, Russell Scott. "The Paradise Of Bombs" from "The Men We Carry in Our Minds," by Scott Russell Sanders. Copyright © 1987 by Scott Russell Sanders Reprinted by permission of Beacon Press, Boston.

Sellers, James. "His and Hers." Used with permission.

Simon-Valdez, Jonathan. "Impossible, Difficult, Done." Used with permission.

SOBE® LIFEWATER® B-ENERGY Strawberry Apricot drink.™ © South Beach Beverage Company, Inc. Used with permission.

Tan, Amy. "Fish Cheeks." © 1987 by Amy Tan. First appeared in *Seventeen Magazine*. Reprinted by permission of the author and the Sandra Dijkstra Literary Agency.

Tasey, Sydney. "Sex vs. Gender." *The Centurion*. Bucks County Community College. April 29, 2014.

Weiten, Wayne and Margaret Lloyd. "What Makes Us Happy." *Psychology Applied to Modern Life: Adjustment in the 21st Century* by WEITEN. Reproduced with permission of Wadsworth in the format Republish in a book via Copyright Clearance Center.

Womenshealth.gov. "A 911 Call Saved My Life."

Woodrell, Lauren. "Cheating." Used with permission.

Vasquez, Yolanda Castaneda. "Classroom Culture, Past and Present." Used with permission.

Index

Easy Reference: Selected Lists and Charts